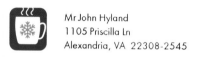

Mr John Hyland
1105 Priscilla Ln
Alexandria, VA 22308-2545

MW00380744

THE ZIMMERMANN
TELEGRAM

THE ZIMMERMANN
TELEGRAM

Intelligence, Diplomacy, and
America's Entry into World War I

THOMAS BOGHARDT

Naval Institute Press
Annapolis, Maryland

This book has been brought to publication with the
generous assistance of Marguerite and Gerry Lenfest.

Naval Institute Press
291 Wood Road
Annapolis, MD 21402

Library of Congress Cataloging-in-Publication Data
Boghardt, Thomas.
  The Zimmermann telegram : intelligence, diplomacy, and America's entry into
World War I / Thomas Boghardt.
    pages cm
  Includes bibliographical references and index.
  ISBN 978-1-61251-148-1 (hardcover : alk. paper) — ISBN 978-1-61251-147-4
(e-book) 1. World War, 1914-1918—Diplomatic history. 2. Mexico—Foreign
relations—Germany. 3. Germany—Foreign relations—Mexico. 4. World War,
1914-1918—United States. 5. Zimmermann, Arthur, 1864-1940. I. Title.
  D619.3.B64 2012
  940.3'112—dc23
                                                          2012026570

⊗ This paper meets the requirements of ANSI/NISO z39.48-1992
(Permanence of Paper).
Printed in the United States of America.

20 19 18 17 16 15 14 13 12   9 8 7 6 5 4 3 2 1
First printing

To
Lori, Adam, and Jacob

Contents

Illustrations

Acknowledgments

Writing *The Zimmermann Telegram: Intelligence, Diplomacy, and America's Entry into World War I* has been a journey, and I wish to express my gratitude to the people and organizations that helped me bring it to a successful conclusion. A generous scholarship from the Fritz-Thyssen-Stiftung enabled me to launch my project on the Zimmermann telegram and conduct extensive archival research in Europe and the United States. Special thanks are due to board member Frank Suder for his support during this important stage. A visiting fellowship from Georgetown University's BMW Center for German and European Studies allowed me to assess my research in the setting of a superb academic institution. Discussions with the university's scholarly community provided valuable historical insight and intellectual stimulation. I am particularly grateful to Georgetown University professor Roger Chickering for his advice during the early stages of my work and for sharing his expertise on imperial Germany and World War I.

Working for several years as the historian for the International Spy Museum in Washington, D.C., was a richly rewarding experience and helped me gain a deeper understanding of the world of intelligence. I would like to thank Executive Director E. Peter Earnest as well as the museum's educational staff and advisory board for sharing so many aspects of the "secret world." The U.S. Army Center of Military History provided me with an outstanding intellectual environment in which to complete this book. I wish to thank my fellow historians at the center for the numerous productive discussions on issues pertaining to World War I and American, German, and British military history.

Archives, libraries, and research institutes are the lifeblood of historians, and *The Zimmermann Telegram* could not have been completed without the resources of a number of such institutions and the assistance of their dedicated and expert staff. Over several years, Peter Grupp and Sabine Schafferdt of the German foreign office archives in Berlin patiently answered my numerous queries and pointed me toward important documents. The late John E. Taylor identified material pertaining to the Zimmermann telegram in the National Archives and Records Administration (NARA) in College Park, Maryland, and NARA's Mitchell Yockelson provided a number of helpful suggestions. The University of Cambridge's Churchill College, which holds the papers of Admiral Sir William Reginald Hall, Britain's wartime director of naval intelligence, permitted me to use and cite from Hall's autobiography. I also must thank the staff of the German military archives in Freiburg, the Hoover Institution at Stanford University, the National Archives in London, and the Library of Congress in Washington, D.C., who assisted in my review of their primary source collections.

While completing this project, I have had the privilege of meeting and exchanging ideas with many exceptional historians, and it is my pleasure to express my gratitude to them for their suggestions and assistance. Nicholas Hiley of the University of Kent allowed me to tap into his unrivaled knowledge of Britain's early intelligence community, and intelligence historian Phil Tomaselli alerted me to important records in the National Archives in London about British intelligence operations in Mexico. Markus Pöhlmann of the Militärgeschichtliches Forschungsamt in Potsdam generously shared with me records pertaining to German military cryptanalysis during World War I, and Johannes Hürter of the University of Mainz provided me with valuable information on Arthur Zimmermann's career in the German foreign office. Christoph Jahr of the University of Heidelberg helped me obtain copies of files from the German foreign office archives in Berlin, and Jennifer Wilcox of the National Cryptologic Museum at Ft. George G. Meade, Maryland, helped me navigate the terminology of cryptology. I also would like to thank the following scholars for their help and feedback on the telegram, intelligence history, and World War I: Holger Afflerbach, University of Leeds; Lisa M. Budreau, National World War I Museum, Kansas City; Silvia Daniel, University of Bonn; Cord Eberspächer, director of the Confucius Institute, Düsseldorf; John F. Fox, historian at the Federal Bureau of Investigation; Julia Hauser, University of Göttingen; Christoph Mauch, University of Munich; Klaus-Jürgen Müller, University of Hamburg; David S. Painter, Georgetown University; Bernard Porter, Newcastle University; and Gerhard Wiechmann, Oldenburg University.

I was fortunate to be able to consult many insightful studies on various aspects of the Zimmermann telegram, and I would like to thank a number of people for discussing their findings with me: Joachim von zur Gathen, Bonn-Aachen Center for Information Technology; intelligence historian David Kahn;

the late Friedrich Katz, University of Chicago; Martin Nassua, University of the Federal Armed Forces, Hamburg; and David Paull Nickles, historian at the U.S. Department of State. I also wish to express my gratitude to the late Peter Freeman, historian of Britain's Government Communications Headquarters. Our dialogue allowed me to develop a deeper comprehension of British cryptanalysis during World War I. Peter's premature death was a severe loss to the community of intelligence historians.

The Naval Institute Press did a superb job in turning the manuscript into a book. I would like to express my gratitude to managing editor Susan Corrado, publicist Judy A. Heise, marketing manager Claire Noble, graphic designer Maryam Rostamian, director Rick Russell, and my copy editor, Robin O. Surratt.

Last but certainly not least, I would like to thank my family for their practical and emotional support while I was working on this book. My wife, Lori, patiently endured many hours of book writing instead of conversation and carefully reviewed the draft manuscript. My mother, Christiane Ebeling, helped me decipher dozens of documents in near-illegible old German *Sütterlin* handwriting. My children, Adam and Jacob, reminded me daily that there is indeed a world beyond libraries, archives, and history conferences.

INTRODUCTION

By the winter of 1916–1917, World War I had reached a deadlock. The Allies commanded greater resources and fielded more soldiers than the Central Powers, but German armies had advanced deep into France and Russia and tenaciously held on to their conquered territories. Hoping to break the military stalemate on the western front, the Allies sought to bring the neutral United States into the war. A golden opportunity to force U.S. intervention seemed at hand when British naval intelligence in January 1917 intercepted and decrypted a secret telegram detailing a German alliance proposal to Mexico. In the message, Berlin's foreign secretary, Arthur Zimmermann, offered his country's support to Mexico for reconquering "the lost territory in Texas, New Mexico, and Arizona" in exchange for a Mexican attack on the United States should the Americans enter the war on the side of the Allies. The German foreign secretary also exhorted the Mexican leadership to approach Japan, with a view toward breaking Tokyo away from its alliance with Great Britain. The director of British naval intelligence, Captain William Reginald Hall, handed a copy of the telegram to the U.S. embassy in London in the hope that it would trigger America's entry into the war. Apparently, he succeeded. On April 2, 1917, President Woodrow Wilson asked Congress for a declaration of war, citing the Zimmermann telegram as one reason for intervention. The lawmakers consented, and on April 6, the United States formally entered World War I.

The telegram's disclosure occurred at a critical moment in the conflict. For the first three years of the war, the United States had refrained from overtly supporting either group of belligerents across the Atlantic. Despite President Wilson's exhortation to Americans to remain "impartial in thought, as well as

1

action," political, cultural, and economic ties lent U.S. neutrality a distinctly pro-Allied flavor.[1] From the German perspective, the growing volume of arms sales by American companies to the Allied nations was especially troubling. The policies devised in Berlin did little, however, to reverse the United States' pro-Allied tilt. German submarines roaming the North Atlantic, threatening American lives and goods, proved a particular source of irritation to Washington. In February 1917, U.S.-German relations took a drastic turn for the worse when the German leadership launched unrestricted submarine warfare, making any ship traveling in the northern Atlantic subject to a potentially deadly attack. In response, Wilson formally broke diplomatic relations with Berlin, and Germany and the United States entered a kind of twilight zone, with American intervention being a distinct possibility, if not yet a foregone conclusion. It was during this tense moment between peace and war, as Americans hotly debated the pros and cons of intervention, that news of the secret telegram reached the United States.

Few historians would argue that the telegram alone pushed the United States into World War I, but most would agree that it constituted one of the factors that helped bring the country into the conflict. Indeed, several American and British decision makers involved in handling the telegram at the time regarded its disclosure as tilting the scales decisively in favor of American intervention. Secretary of State Robert Lansing wrote in his memoirs, "From the time that the telegram was published . . . the United States' entry into the war was assured."[2] Likewise, Hall stated in his autobiography that in the wake of the telegram's publication, "[W]ar was inevitable."[3] President Wilson, a man given neither to careless remarks nor to hyperbole, cited the telegram as a reason for his decision to abandon neutrality. In his war address to Congress, Wilson referred to the scheme laid out in the telegram as "eloquent evidence" of Germany's intention "to stir up enemies against us at our very doors."[4]

Because of its influential role in the war, the telegram has attracted the attention of journalists and historians alike. Many authors have looked at the telegram in the context of American intervention, others have examined the efforts of British naval intelligence to intercept and decrypt it, and a few have explored the German rationale behind it. Until recently, only one book, *The Zimmermann Telegram* by Barbara Tuchman, has sought to examine this subject by addressing developments in Germany, Britain, and the United States roughly in equal parts. Although the present study agrees with Tuchman's implicit argument that the entire story of the telegram is indeed greater than its parts, it questions many of her conclusions.

The primary flaw in Tuchman's work lies in the author's limited access to and use of government records. First published in 1958, her account draws on a number of U.S. State Department files, but she did not have access to U.S. and British intelligence records. Instead, she relied for the most part on contemporary published accounts, memoirs, and a few translated works. Her limited usage of pertinent intelligence records detracts greatly from her book. "[L]acking classified sources and also suffering from lack of cryptologic insight," as a historian of the National Security Agency noted, the author bought into some of the deliberate disinformation planted by Hall.[5] Barred from examining the relevant U.S. and British intelligence sources, Tuchman can hardly be blamed for succumbing to Hall's yarns; she was far from the only author caught up in the old spymaster's web of lies. As a result of her limited use of primary sources, however, her book is plagued by "errors, inaccuracies and obsolete theses."[6] Tuchman's work was further undermined by the omission of German-language materials, including archival records, memoirs, and secondary sources. By not taking into account the detailed German foreign office records on the telegram that were available at the time of her writing, Tuchman misread the political decision-making process in imperial Germany and the basic motivations of individual German officials.

Primary sources, if available, should form the basis of any serious study in the fields of political, military, and intelligence history. In this respect, the declassification of virtually all relevant government records for the World War I period provides the opportunity to finally tell the full story of the Zimmermann telegram, from its origins in Germany to its publication in the United States and its impact and perception in subsequent decades. The present study represents an endeavor to deliver the first comprehensive account of the telegram, based in equal measure on key contemporary sources from Germany, Britain, and the United States.

Despite nearly a century of journalistic and historical research on the Zimmermann telegram, many new documents were discovered in preparation for this book. Several collections of official records proved particularly valuable. The files of the German foreign office (Auswärtiges Amt) illuminated the thinking and actions of Berlin's diplomats on the eve of U.S. intervention. Of special importance is the hitherto overlooked personnel file of one of Zimmermann's subordinates, Hans Arthur von Kemnitz, the official who first suggested the Mexican-Japanese alliance proposal and produced the original draft of the telegram. His multivolume file includes, inter alia, the only known firsthand account of the German foreign office conference at which the proposal was conceived and sanctioned.

For the chapters dealing with cryptanalysis, and the British decision to disclose the telegram, Hall's autobiography remains a key source, but here his account is juxtaposed with British and U.S. intelligence and diplomatic records as well as with the memoirs of the British and American officials intimately involved in the exposure of the German alliance scheme. The findings of recent pathbreaking research on the cryptanalytic work of British naval intelligence during World War I further helped to set the record straight on Hall's operations.

On the American side, the records of the State Department's Bureau of Secret Intelligence shed much light on the cooperation between U.S. and British intelligence agencies during the war, especially on their joint handling of Zimmermann's diplomatic initiative. American nongovernmental sources yielded a wealth of information as well. This study is the first to examine a comprehensive set of historical newspaper articles and op-eds in order to gauge American public opinion on the telegram. Moreover, the book draws on a large number of contemporary publications and memoirs in addition to unpublished personal papers scattered among archives and university libraries around the world, many of which are exploited here for the first time.

Neither the discovery of new documents nor the careful reexamination of already known records necessarily leads to reassessments of a particular historical event, but in the case of the Zimmermann telegram, it does require new thinking in several respects. Regarding the rationale behind Zimmermann's alliance proposal, this study concludes that it was neither the result of a carefully crafted, long-term German strategy to project power into the Western Hemisphere nor one "of history's classic stupidities."[7] Rather, the telegram was the product of a particular historic situation in wartime Germany, when developments in the realms of domestic politics and foreign policy converged. Arthur Zimmermann had conducted intelligence operations for the German foreign office since the early twentieth century, and with the outbreak of war, he became Berlin's point man for a global covert program designed to stir up trouble against the Allies in Europe, Africa, and Asia. When the Mexican-Japanese alliance scheme was proposed to him by Kemnitz in January 1917, Zimmermann's previous routine handling of covert activities biased him in favor of the scheme. Another policy strand woven into the telegram was Germany's intermittent pursuit of a separate peace with Japan, starting in 1915. In early 1917, Japan's strained relationship with the United States led German diplomats to believe that Tokyo might be amenable to resuming peace negotiations via Mexico. The military's growing influence over German policy making provided a further impetus to the Mexican-Japanese alliance scheme. In the wake of the declaration of unrestricted submarine warfare, the German supreme army command considered U.S. intervention highly likely and expected diplomatic initiatives from the Wilhelmstrasse—shorthand for the foreign office because of its location on this narrow street in Berlin—to counterbalance the United States' joining the Allies. Zimmermann could not ignore the military's demands. The text of the telegram reflects this multitude of policies and agendas, which contradicted each other at times, and has posed significant interpretational challenges for historians.

Furthermore, the book places interception, decryption, and disclosure to the U.S. government of the telegram firmly in the context of Captain Hall's management of Room 40 and Anglo-American intelligence cooperation throughout the war. Beginning with his tour of duty as director of the Admiralty's intelligence division in late 1914, Hall went beyond his original mandate—the collection of information—by repeatedly using the intelligence gathered by his agency to conduct covert actions in Europe and overseas. Time and again, he sidestepped his superiors in the government in these endeavors; they often learned of Hall's operations only after the fact.

Long before the telegram incident, Hall had found American diplomats and intelligence personnel to be willing partners in the execution of his schemes. Beginning in 1915, the State Department's diplomats and agents collaborated closely with the British secret services in an effort to compromise German diplomacy and to bring the United States into the war. Taking advantage of the Americans' pro-Allied stance, Hall carefully developed relationships with intelligence personnel at the U.S. embassy in London and confidentially involved the Americans in many of his plots. On several occasions during the period of U.S. neutrality, he traded classified information with his American contacts without first clearing these actions with his government. In early 1917, he shared knowledge of the telegram with his contact at the U.S. embassy before receiving authorization from the Foreign Office to do so. In retrospect, Hall's modus operandi proved to be a mixed blessing for Britain. On the one hand, British naval intelligence scored a number of scoops under his leadership. On the other hand, Hall's independence, obsessive secrecy, and habitual disregard for the chain of command contributed to the emergence of an intelligence community in Britain that came close to being a state within a state, and for political reasons turned against an elected British government during the inter-war years.

As for the impact of the Zimmermann telegram in the United States, this study examines reactions to it on three levels: the Wilson administration, Congress, and the public. After Germany's declaration of unrestricted submarine warfare, virtually all members of Wilson's cabinet advocated war, with the notable exception of the president himself. As a consequence of the telegram, Wilson abandoned all hope of reaching a negotiated settlement with Germany and aligned his thinking more closely with his pro-war cabinet. At the same time, however, the telegram exacerbated divisions in Congress and the public over the question of joining the Allies. A heated debate in the Senate on March 1 pitted interventionists, who touted the telegram as a *casus belli*, against non-interventionists, who questioned the administration's motives behind the document's disclosure and suspected British involvement. Similar frictions emerged in the public debate. While many interventionists demanded a declaration of war in response to the German scheme, non-interventionists either ignored it or made light of it. Overall, this study concludes, the telegram failed to persuade Americans of the wisdom of intervention.

The Zimmermann Telegram approaches its subject conceptually through three thematic lenses. The first is geographical balance. The book contends that Zimmermann's plot gained traction as a historically significant event through the interplay of German politics, British intelligence, and American intervention, hence equal weight is given to all three areas. Because the scheme had no discernible effect on Japan and Mexico, the actions and reactions of representatives of Tokyo and Mexico City are referenced merely when necessary for understanding events.

The second lens is intelligence, defined as "secret, state activity to understand or influence foreign entities."[8] This book treats intelligence as a key element of the entire story, not only in terms of interception and decryption. The emergence of powerful intelligence organizations and techniques in Germany, Britain, and the United States created a new factor in governmental decision making and directly affected responses to the telegram. From the earliest days of the war, the Germans had employed covert action to instigate insurrections against the Allies, and the telegram fit neatly into this policy. On the other side of the North Sea, interception and decryption of the telegram by British naval intelligence ensured the scheme's failure while significantly strengthening Hall's position along Whitehall, the London road lined with British governmental institutions. Furthermore, the close collaboration of and trusting relationship between British and U.S. intelligence personnel not only resulted in the timely publication of Zimmermann's proposal in the American press, but also prevented the American public and the German foreign office from learning by which means the Wilson administration had obtained it. Covert action, espionage, and cryptanalysis all played into the telegram affair, making it one of the great intelligence stories of World War I.

The third lens is the telegram's historical effect and long-term consequences, what the Germans call *Wirkungsgeschichte*. The repercussions of Zimmermann's alliance proposal profoundly affected perceptions, organizations, and individuals on both sides of the Atlantic for many years after the war, yet a systematic study of the scheme's consequences has been conspicuously absent. In an effort to fill this gap, *The Zimmermann Telegram* traces the ripples of the telegram through the twentieth century and beyond in Germany, Britain, and the United States.

Chapter One

THE ZIMMERMANN
TELEGRAM IN HISTORY

The so-called Zimmermann telegram has intrigued contemporaries and historians ever since it made headlines in the United States on March 1, 1917. The widespread coverage the telegram received at the time of its public release may partially account for the fact that the historiography of the telegram has been chiefly, though not exclusively, an American affair. Another reason may be that the telegram is inextricably linked to U.S. intervention in World War I. For Great Britain and Germany, U.S. intervention marked merely one more turning point in their years-long struggle, but for the United States it was a watershed event that transformed the country from a satellite in the international system to one of its central players. Any historian researching the American entry into World War I is bound to stumble across news of the telegram.

Members of the Wilson administration were, not surprisingly, the first to frame the debate surrounding the telegram. As early as March 4, Secretary of State Robert Lansing claimed in a memorandum that the telegram's disclosure had "created a profound sensation throughout the country."[1] With this assertion, the administration's foremost champion of intervention laid the foundation for the persistent notion that Zimmermann's telegram had rallied a hesitant public for war. By inference, this argument bolstered and vindicated Lansing's own interventionist agenda.

President Woodrow Wilson, in his war address to Congress on April 2, 1917, put forth another enduring theme of the telegram's historiography. First he accused Berlin of having infiltrated "our unsuspecting communities and even our offices of government with spies and set[ting] criminal intrigues everywhere afoot against our national unity of counsel." He then concluded, "That [the German government] means to stir up enemies against us at our very doors, the intercepted Zimmermann note to the German Minister at Mexico City is eloquent evidence." With these words, Wilson insinuated that the overture to Mexico by the German foreign secretary, Arthur Zimmermann, constituted merely one instance in a series of German plots in the Western Hemisphere. It was a far-fetched allegation, to be sure, but a potent one nevertheless. Whenever members of the Wilson administration (and wartime authors supporting them) mentioned the Zimmermann telegram, they typically did so by describing it as a subplot in a broader German scheme directed against the entire hemisphere.[2]

Members of the Wilson administration continued to argue along the same lines during the postwar period. In his memoirs, published in 1935, Lansing referred to the telegram as an event that "caused the greatest excitement throughout the country and aroused the people against the German government even more, I believe, than the announced policy of submarine ruthlessness."[3] In 1921 Wilson's former personal secretary Joseph Tumulty cited the telegram as evidence that "German intrigue was busy in Mexico."[4] Yale University history professor Charles Seymour, who headed the Austro-Hungarian division of the U.S. peace commission to Paris in 1919, asserted that "nothing could have brought the . . . unfriendliness of Germany closer to the American public."[5]

The Wilsonian interpretation of the telegram was tied closely to a popular belief in the righteousness of U.S. intervention, but when the fog of war had cleared, many Americans took account of the sacrifices made in joining the Allies yet could not see commensurate benefits. Americans suffered more than 100,000 casualties in making "the world safe for democracy," as Wilson had postulated, but the postwar world that emerged looked uncertain and menacing, especially in view of the global economic depression and the rise of totalitarianism in Europe. Moreover, many Americans saw the Treaty of Versailles between the Allies and Germany as unnecessarily vindictive. In fact, the United States did not sign it, and U.S. relations with Britain and France deteriorated when the two nations balked at paying their U.S. war debts. Consequently, many Americans began to question the wisdom of having gone to war in 1917 and advocated a policy of isolationism going forward.

This widespread sentiment among Americans found practical expression in several neutrality acts passed by Congress in the 1930s that sought to keep the United States out of overseas conflicts. In the same spirit, on the occasion of the twentieth anniversary of the U.S. entry into World War I, Congress honored those members who had voted against the war in 1917. The many revisionist publications at the time generally deplored U.S. participation in the war, deemphasizing German aggression as a reason for intervention and instead stressing domestic factors or Allied policies, such as commercial interests or British propaganda, as the cause of it.[6]

The telegram fit neatly into the revisionists' agenda as details about the interception and decryption of Zimmermann's alliance proposal emerged. In 1920 Johann Heinrich von Bernstorff, Germany's wartime ambassador to Washington, informed the public in his memoirs that "a certain Englishman" had told him that British intelligence had intercepted and forwarded the telegram to the U.S. government.[7] Six years later, the journalist Burton J. Hendrick's biography of Walter Hines Page, the wartime U.S. ambassador to London, lent additional weight to Bernstorff's recollections. In response to revelations about Britain's involvement in the telegram, American revisionists denounced the efforts by Captain William Reginald Hall, director of British naval intelligence, as a Machiavellian propaganda stunt to pull the United States into the war against the nation's better interests. By the same token, they typically disparaged American interventionists as naive British stooges, warmongers, or selfish profiteers while crediting Germany's overtures to Mexico as a legitimate effort in preparation for U.S. belligerence.

An early product of revisionism, John Kenneth Turner's *Shall It Be Again* (1922) delivers a powerful indictment of what the author considers the Wilson administration's imperialist policies. So sympathetic to Germany was Turner that even the exiled kaiser cited him favorably in his memoirs. With regard to the telegram, *Shall It Be Again* exculpates Zimmermann by pointing to his alliance proposal's contingency on the United States joining the Allies. Moreover, Turner argues, Germany "would have been physically incapable of invading America even had she possessed no other enemies."[8]

As the postwar world moved further and further away from the new global politics and ideals envisioned by Wilson, revisionism continued to blossom, and along with it revisionist interpretations of the telegram. The journalist C. Hartley Grattan wrote mockingly in *Why We Fought* (1929) that the telegram "was made available by the British out of the kindness of their heart" and argues that "[i]n the hands of the pro-war group, this cable became very useful propaganda. It will be observed that everything that Zimmermann proposed was contingent upon the failure of the German effort to keep the United States out of the war." Like many other revisionist authors, Grattan ignores Zimmermann's subsequent message of February 5, 1917, instructing the German envoy in Mexico, Heinrich von Eckardt, to begin negotiations with the Mexican president, Venustiano Carranza, even before the United States entered the war. Instead, he considered the telegram "a legitimate effort to obtain an ally in case of war with the United States" and compares Zimmermann's offer to the promises of territory made by the Allies to Italy (at the expense of Austria), with a view toward inducing Italian intervention on their side.[9]

Walter Millis' *Road to War* (1935), a popular bestseller, makes similar points. Like Grattan, Millis ridicules Wilson for being "profoundly shocked by this revelation of the fact that one could not go to war with Germany without having the Germans fight back." He portrays the telegram as a purely defensive measure, comparing its terms to Allied territorial promises to Japan, Italy, and Romania. In the context of U.S. intervention, Millis wrote disapprovingly, the telegram served the unwholesome ends of "the Northeastern fire-eaters."[10]

One of the weightiest revisionist tomes, Charles C. Transill's massive *America Goes to War* (1938), as well as Alice Morrissey's *The American Defense of Neutral Rights, 1914–1917* (1939), addresses the telegram in less depth than do Grattan and Millis, but essentially argues in the same vein: the German overture to Mexico constituted no real threat to U.S. security and therefore did not warrant a serious response from the Wilson administration.[11]

In *Propaganda for War* (1939), Horace C. Peterson produces one of the most extensive revisionist analyses of the telegram. The author calls Britain's handling of the telegram "their most successful propaganda maneuver" and dismisses American outrage as naive: "Most probably these American statesmen had never thought of the idea that by taking part in Europe's wars their country's territory would run the risk of being considered spoils of war." Zimmermann, on the other hand, gets a free pass: "It was, of course, Zimmermann's duty as Foreign Minister to arrange for the eventuality of American entrance into the war. He was not at fault in trying to secure an ally; he was at fault for being found out. The episode must be now considered as one of history's classic stupidities—a blunder from which the British reaped great profit."[12]

Even the respectable *New York Times*, long past its interventionist days, joined the revisionist chorus two decades later. In Zimmermann's obituary of June 8, 1940, the *Times* portrays the former German foreign secretary good-naturedly as "a big, broad-shouldered East Prussian, with a determined will, a jovial manner and a keen sense of humor." As for the telegram, the *Times* reminds readers that many earlier accounts of the telegram had "failed to stress the words in the note which stated that Germany made the Mexican-Japanese alliance proposal only in case of America's entering the war."[13]

While Wilsonians cited the telegram as evidence of German conspiracies in the Western Hemisphere, thus justifying U.S. entry into war, revisionists by and large argued that the British had exploited a legitimate diplomatic German initiative in order to force Washington to engage in the conflict, a step that would serve Allied interests more than the United States'. Wilsonians and revisionists agreed, however, that the telegram's publication had a decisive impact on American public opinion. If anything, revisionists emphasized this point even more strongly than Wilsonians. Grattan and Transill diagnosed "war hysteria" in the United States upon the telegram's publication, and Millis observed that it "exploded with its maximum effect at precisely the point where it would do the Allies the greatest good." Peterson contended, "Great indignation was immediately aroused throughout the country, and most important was the fact that the West and Middle West joined in the expressions of anger. The fact that the Central Powers were supposedly threatening the West naturally made Westerners ready to fight back. It brought the war home to them and completely defeated the work of the pacifist."[14]

While American intervention in World War I remained controversial after the fact, the U.S. entry into World War II enjoyed near-unanimous approval. The Japanese attack on Pearl Harbor, subsequent declarations of war by Germany and Italy, and postwar revelations about Nazi horrors left little room for doubt about the justice of the cause. Early popular perceptions of the Cold War as a struggle between the totalitarian Soviet Union and the democratic West further shaped the memory of World War II as a battle of good versus evil. In the wake of the Second World War, contemporaries quickly projected this Manichean interpretation on World War I. Revisionism, which by and large had looked kindly upon imperial Germany, died practically overnight. In its stead emerged a stark, dichotomous worldview that depicted Germany under the kaiser as an evil empire, and its foreign policy as a harbinger of Nazi aggression. This paradigm shift directly affected perceptions of the Zimmermann telegram. Now, authors typically cast imperial Germany as a strategic threat to the United States, and Zimmermann's overture to Mexico as a manifestation of a long-standing master plan to challenge the United States in the Western Hemisphere. Likewise, Cold War authors tended to applaud American interventionists as righteous and to scorn isolationists as naive or misguided.

Samuel R. Spencer's *Decision for War, 1917* (1953), the first monograph on the telegram, was an early example of this post–World War II school. Publishing less than ten years after the war's end, Spencer uses the telegram to draw a straight line from Wilhelm II to Adolf Hitler: "[I]t is reasonably safe to assume that even if actual military assault upon the western hemisphere had proved impracticable, he [the kaiser] would have attempted the same type of politico-military penetration which Hitler later effected. In any case, the threat to the United States was not imaginary." At the same time, Spencer looks much more kindly on Hall than the revisionists had and explains Hall's hesitation about conveying the telegram to the U.S. government as motivated by an understandable desire to protect British intelligence's methods and sources. Yet Spencer concurs with previous authors about the effect of the telegram on American public opinion, comparing it to that generated by Pearl Harbor.[15]

Although Spencer's book foreshadows an interpretational pattern that would soon emerge as the dominant Cold War take on the telegram, Barbara Tuchman's *Zimmermann Telegram* (1958) stands out as the only major English-language monograph on the subject. The strength of her book lies not in the discovery of significant new facts, but in weaving many already available strands of the story into a compelling narrative. Her book provides an accessible account that derives its appeal from the author's considerable storytelling skills and a propensity to pass unambiguous moral judgment on the protagonists. Instead of focusing on historical processes, Tuchman hones in on individual actors and brings them to life with catchy descriptions—for example, the "clever Kaiser," the "suave Count Bernstorff," Hall's "brilliant blue eyes," and so on. Her inimitable style, dripping with irony and sarcasm, makes for a highly readable black-and-white tale that comes down harshly on representatives of imperial Germany and those Americans hesitant to join the war, while implicitly endorsing the interventionist cause and Hall's handling of the telegram.

Like Spencer, though more vividly, Tuchman portrays the telegram as a veritable challenge to the United States in the Western Hemisphere: "But the Prussian invasion plot, as the newspapers termed it, was clear as a knife in the back and near as next door," she wrote. "It was the German boot planted upon our border." Tuchman also subscribes to earlier notions about the extraordinary effect of the telegram on contemporary public opinion.[16] To her lasting credit, she acquainted a large audience with an important aspect of American intervention in World War I. The commercial success of her monograph, which has sold hundreds of thousands of copies to date, is testimony to both the author's narrative talent as well as the enduring appeal of her subject.

Few books manage to have the final word on a historical subject, and Tuchman's work is no exception. Her limited access to and use of primary sources eventually undermined many of her conclusions. The first major study to make extensive use of official German records in examining the telegram was Friedrich Katz's massive tome, *Deutschland, Diaz und die mexikanische Revolution* (1964), the product of a postdoctoral research project at Humboldt University in Berlin. Due to its publication in communist East Germany, the volume is occasionally couched in Marxist slang. Katz's study was later translated and expanded into *The Secret War in Mexico* (1981). Katz amends but largely supports and amplifies Tuchman's findings. He argues that beginning in the late nineteenth century, Germany had sought to expand its sphere of influence in Mexico. With the onset of World War I in Europe, Berlin wanted to provoke conflict between Mexico and the United States and, the author contends, from 1917 to 1918 sought to establish hegemony over Mexico. The telegram, Katz claims, represented "a new stage" in this escalating strategy of German domination over Mexico.[17] Like most authors before him, he concludes that the telegram "had its greatest impact in precisely those areas of the United States where isolationism and thus opposition to U.S. involvement in the war were particularly strong: the Southwest. People in this area," the author opines, "found the German offer to Mexico of annexation of Texas, Arizona, and New Mexico especially offensive."[18] Other authors have made the same point with regard to the telegram's impact in the United States.

Arthur Link, in *Wilson: Campaigns for Progressivism and Peace, 1916–1917* (1965), the fifth volume of his lengthy political biography of Woodrow Wilson, argues that the telegram greatly affected the president as well as American public opinion. "Wilson," he wrote, "was shocked and angry. It was almost incredible, he must have thought, that any government could be so evil and intriguing." Likewise, Link contends that the telegram's publication resembled "a gigantic bolt [that] had struck from the blue across the American continent. No other event of the war to this point, not even the German invasion of Belgium or the sinking of the *Lusitania*, so stunned the American people. . . . Excitement approaching panic raged all day in Washington."[19] Four years later, John Milton Cooper argued along similar lines. Zimmermann's alliance scheme, he wrote in *The Vanity of Power* (1969), constituted "a direct threat to American territory. Editorial anger not only flared at the Zimmermann telegram, but for the first time a large segment of the press called for war."[20]

American authors dominated the historiography of the telegram, but the Cold War view of Zimmermann's alliance scheme as a strategic threat to American security also found advocates on the other side of the Atlantic. Jürgen Möckelmann contended in his doctoral dissertation, "Das Deutschlandbild in den USA 1914–1918 und die Kriegszielpolitik Wilsons" (1964), that the "Zimmermann Telegram seemed to prove the threat to the Monroe Doctrine and the direct threat to the USA posed by Germany."[21] The British author Patrick Devlin, in his study of Wilson's wartime presidency, *Too Proud to Fight* (1974), likewise portrayed the telegram as a veritable military challenge, compared to which even German atrocities in Belgium and the sinking of the *Lusitania* paled.[22]

World War I narratives geared toward the larger public generally continued to adhere to the account popularized by Tuchman through the end of the Cold War and beyond. For example, the journalist Jules Witcover argues in *Sabotage at Black Tom* (1989) that Germany had been plotting for years to pit Mexico and Japan against the United States and that the telegram presented "clear-cut evidence that Germany meant to do harm to the United States in a direct and very tangible way." He contends, "Here was something to fight about that could be understood by the average American not convinced that the rights of wealthier Americans to sail the Atlantic was worth going to war over." By the same token, Witcover regards Hall's hesitation in handing the telegram to the Americans as necessary to protect his sources.[23] Another, more recent example of this trend is Gary Mead's *Doughboys* (2000), a popular account of the American World War I experience. In it, the author argues that the "telegram was regarded as devastatingly treacherous. . . . The view of Germany by most Americans as utterly perfidious was now complete."[24]

As the fall of the Berlin Wall, the reunification of Germany, and the collapse of the Soviet Union brought the Cold War to a close, yet another interpretation of World War I, imperial Germany, and the telegram emerged. While many Cold War authors had portrayed imperial Germany as an external threat to the United States, several post–Cold War authors began to try to understand why imperial Germany had pursued certain foreign policies. These historians, several of them Germans, made extensive use of German records, and their works appeared at a time when many observers assumed that Germany would expand its role in world politics. While these authors did not deny that imperial Germany's foreign policy had posed challenges to other powers, their views of German actors were more complex and occasionally more sympathetic to them than portrayals in the preceding decades.

In the year of German reunification, Friedhelm Koopmann published *Diplomatie und Reichsinteresse* (1990), a dense study of German covert operations in the United States during the period of neutrality. While Koopmann never explicitly challenges earlier treatises on the telegram, he suggests that

Zimmermann's proposal should not be dismissed simply as short-sighted or as outright stupid. Rather, he argues that the foreign secretary's initiative followed a certain logic if one accepts the premise—as the German military leadership had—that the United States by early 1917 had de facto joined the Allies and would be unable to provide significant additional support to Germany's enemies if its leaders decided in favor of intervention. Germany's gross underestimation of U.S. strength, he maintains, resulted from faulty intelligence about its military potential. Koopmann therefore considers the telegram first and foremost an intelligence failure rather than a Machiavellian scheme for domination of the Western Hemisphere.[25]

Two years later, Martin Nassua expanded on Koopmann's focus on German domestic politics in *Gemeinsame Kriegführung, Gemeinsamer Friedensschluss* (1992), his published master's thesis. Explicitly challenging Tuchman and Katz, Nassua argues that these two authors overemphasized the threat that the telegram posed to the United States. He portrays Zimmermann's alliance scheme as the result of domestic politics, rather than a vehicle for projecting German power into the Western Hemisphere. Nassua also offers the first methodical review of German American reactions to the telegram's disclosure in the U.S. press.[26]

David Paull Nickles, in *Under the Wire* (2003), a study of the effect of telegraphy on diplomacy, examines the telegram largely from Ambassador Bernstorff's perspective. The German envoy emerges as a tragic figure, a liberal at heart earnestly trying to keep the United States out of the war, while dealing with ever-more stringent directives from military-minded hardliners in Berlin. Nickles' study sheds significant new light on Bernstorff's work in Washington as well as State Department diplomacy vis-à-vis imperial Germany on the eve of U.S intervention.[27]

While Koopmann, Nassua, and Nickles examined the telegram from the perspective of German politics, and the motivations of German protagonists, another set of post–Cold War authors viewed the telegram against the backdrop of contemporary U.S. military interventions in the Middle East. Like the original revisionists, these neo-revisionist authors doubted the wisdom of American engagements abroad, deplored their cost, and with a critical eye examined the domestic processes that led to war. Some explicitly compared President George W. Bush's "freedom agenda" "to strengthen democracy and promote peace around the world" to Wilsonian notions of making the world "safe for democracy." For example, Geoffrey Hodgson, in *Woodrow Wilson's*

Right Hand: The Life of Colonel Edward M. House (2006), calls the Bush administration's foreign policy "unmistakably Wilsonian."[28]

In *Propaganda for War* (1996), Stewart H. Ross disparagingly likens American anti-German propaganda during World War I to U.S. propaganda during the Cold War and the Persian Gulf War. In all three conflicts, the author contends, human, material, and financial costs outweighed political or military gains: "Seventy-five years after Americans were assigned an alliterative 'Beast of Berlin' [Kaiser Wilhelm II], they were given a 'Butcher of Baghdad' [Iraqi president Saddam Hussein] as the hated-enemy symbol for the 1991 Persian Gulf war. As before, Americans were charged with fighting an enemy 'now' rather than 'later,' and the timeworn atrocities of 'rape and pillage' made headlines." Echoing pacifist and isolationist arguments from World War I, Ross reveals his contempt for the power of the modern media and war profiteering: "Crushing wartime news censorship by the Pentagon mocked America's press freedoms, and again, big-business communications media enthusiastically followed Washington's lead." Also like the original revisionists, Ross regards the telegram as a legitimate, if harebrained, initiative: "Absurd though it was, the German foreign minister's proposal was no less moral than the secret treaties already signed by the Allies to apportion conquered enemy territories among themselves."[29]

In *The Illusion of Victory* (2003), a passionate tour de force of America during World War I, Thomas Fleming deals harshly with Woodrow Wilson's policies, both domestic and foreign. He dismisses as illusory any advantages the United States might have gained from the war and deplores the more than 50,000 dead and 150,000 wounded soldiers who were sacrificed in the pursuit of this illusion. Perhaps with the impending U.S. invasion of Iraq in mind, he asserts, "I could only shake my head and hope the men and women who guide America's covenant with power in the world of the twenty-first century have the courage and the wisdom to manage our country's often perplexing blend of idealism and realism. God helping us, we can do no other." Though Fleming regards the telegram as an "effrontery," like the revisionists he also views it as a minor offense that helped Britain pull the United States into the war. He carefully balances, and by implication justifies, Zimmermann's initiative against U.S.-Allied arms deals in the period of American neutrality.[30]

The accounts reviewed above, from World War I into the twenty-first century, offer a wide range of assessments of the telegram's historical significance, yet they all approach the story within the framework of political history. Another group of authors has focused first and foremost on cryptanalytic aspects of the telegram, that is, modes and dates of transmission, codes and decryption, and the inner workings of Room 40, where the cryptanalytic work of British naval intelligence was done. There is necessarily an overlap between political and cryptanalytic aspects of the telegram, but overall the two kinds of studies have been conducted distinctly. While students of the cryptographic or intelligence elements have referenced political studies of the telegram, they have typically focused their analytic firepower on technical issues. Over the past decades, these historians have progressively unlocked virtually every cryptologic secret the telegram once held.

The cryptologic study of the telegram began in earnest when some of those with firsthand knowledge, along with an investigative journalist, made public some of the technical details of its encoding, interception, and decryption. Among the earliest are Ambassador Bernstorff in an account of his tour of duty in Washington (1920), Burton J. Hendrick in the third volume of his biography of Ambassador Page (1926), Hall in his affidavit before the Mixed Claims Commission (1926), and Alfred Ewing, Room 40's first director, in a public lecture (1927).

Hall's autobiography, written in the early 1930s, is another important source, but the text remained classified until long after World War II. Coming from the man at the center of the interception, decryption, and handling of the telegram, Hall's manuscript is a fountain of information, although its reliability is occasionally devalued by minor and major inaccuracies. For example, Hall obviously confuses the German codes 0075 and 13040, probably because of his weak grasp of cryptologic basics. For political purposes, he deliberately perpetuates the falsehood, first publicized by Hendrick (but based on information originally provided by Hall), that the Germans had relayed—and the British had intercepted—the telegram by multiple means, including radio and with the assistance of the Swedish government, rather than through U.S. State Department cables alone.[31] For all the insight Hall provides into the inner sanctum of Room 40, much of his memoirs must therefore be taken with a grain of salt.

In 1938 the American cryptanalysts William F. Friedman and Charles J. Mendelsohn produced the first systematic cryptologic study of the telegram, *The Zimmermann Telegram of January 16, 1917*. Commissioned by the War Department's Office of the Chief Signal Officer, their work remained classified until 1965. Carefully sifting through the evidence then available, the authors reached several important conclusions. By pointing to the insurmountable difficulties of wiring messages directly between Germany and Mexico, the authors debunk Hall's contention that the Germans had transmitted the telegram by wireless. They likewise dismiss Hall's claim before the Mixed Claims Commission that the British had decrypted the telegram by means of a captured German codebook. Perhaps most important, they reassess Hall's hesitation in handing the telegram, intercepted between Berlin and Washington, to the U.S. government: "To disclose the Berlin-Washington version of the Zimmermann telegram, which it will be recalled was sent via State Department channels, would have necessitated revealing the fact that the British Intelligence Service was intercepting and solving not only German code messages but also intercepting and perhaps solving diplomatic messages of the American government—a power whose aid they were desperately seeking at the time." This revelation would have added plenty of grist to the revisionist mill had it not remained classified at the time.[32]

In 1955 William "Bubbles" Melbourne James published *The Eyes of the Navy*, a narrative of Hall's intelligence work during the Great War. Hall had recruited James to run the day-to-day operations of Room 40 in 1917, based on Hall's autobiography; Bubbles admired his chief greatly. Though James did not quote Hall's (at that point still classified) autobiography, he followed it closely, occasionally verbatim. His book was the first to make Hall's recollections of the telegram available to a broader public. James, however, reproduced Hall's memoirs uncritically, and therefore perpetuated several inaccuracies, such as the alleged German usage of Swedish cables—the so-called Swedish roundabout—for transmission of the telegram to Washington.

In *The Codebreakers* (1967), a sweeping history of the usage and breaking of codes and ciphers, David Kahn presents the first systematic cryptologic study of the telegram by a non-government historian. Kahn goes to great lengths in describing the various German codes, and their decryption, and he clears up a number of then-prevailing misunderstandings about the telegram, such as the precise use of codes 0075 and 13040 and the techniques and timing of British decryption. Kahn was the first author to make use of the Göppert report, the German investigation of the telegram's disclosure, and he was the first historian to cast doubt on the alleged use of the Swedish roundabout.[33]

Patrick Beesly's *Room 40* (1982) contains a chapter on the telegram that relies mostly on James' *Eyes of the Navy*, and thus on Hall's autobiography, but in addition, Beesly made use of several declassified British documents, including Hall's correspondence with the British naval attaché in New York, Captain Guy Gaunt. While Beesly produced a readable overview of British naval cryptanalysis during World War I, he added little cryptologic insight to the story and, like James before him, perpetuated several of the inaccuracies originally introduced by Hall.

Although Nickles' *Under the Wire* focuses on the diplomacy of Ambassador Bernstorff, the author makes an important contribution to the cryptologic study of the telegram as well. Based on a careful examination of available sources, Nickles confirms and expands upon Kahn's earlier doubts about the Swedish roundabout: "I have found no evidence," Nickles states, "that the telegram traveled via the Swedish route, although many historians have claimed that it did. . . . I believe the claim probably testifies to the effectiveness of British misinformation. . . . Many historians have also repeated the claim of Hendrick and Tuchman . . . that the message went out on wireless. This is almost certainly incorrect."[34]

With "The Zimmermann Telegram Revisited" (2006), Peter Freeman produced a penetrating and comprehensive account of British cryptanalysis of the telegram. Then a historian for the Government Communications Headquarters (GCHQ), Britain's premier cryptanalytic agency, Freeman used his extraordinary command of British sources painstakingly to reconstruct the telegram's journey from Berlin to Mexico City via Washington and the British interception and decryption of it. Among many important findings, this fine study produces solid documentary corroboration of Kahn's supposition and Nickles' hypothesis that the Germans had sent the telegram via State Department cable alone. Joachim von zur Gathen, in "The Zimmermann Telegram" (2007), used German foreign office logs and the Göppert report to confirm Freeman's conclusion about the telegram's route. In 2008, David Ramsay published a political biography of Hall. The author makes no bones about his admiration for the subject of his study, though his findings are mostly derived from previously published works. *"Blinker" Hall* draws amply on James' biography and especially on Beesly's history of Room 40, but in incorporating Freeman's findings, the author omits many of the inaccuracies that plague these two earlier accounts.

The historiography of the telegram has shown a remarkable degree of fluidity and constancy. Research into the cryptology of the telegram has been largely progressive. It began in the 1920s on the basis of several false assumptions, most of which originated with several misleading claims made by Hall. Over the years, however, authors have peeled back layer upon layer of Hall's disinformation. Freeman's article on British cryptanalysis of the telegram may be considered definitive, but the debate over Hall's management of Room 40 is bound to continue. While most authors have dismissed as minor or acceptable Hall's transgressions in using the intelligence obtained by his code breakers, a case can also be made to the effect that Hall's utter secrecy and disregard for the proper chain of command were systematic and had long-term effects that proved detrimental to British democracy.

Assessments of the telegram's content have fluctuated wildly over time. If interventionists in 1917 portrayed it as a sinister German plot, revisionists during the interwar years regarded it first and foremost as an unpalatable British attempt to meddle in U.S. politics. World War II and the end of the Cold War produced additional interpretational swings back and forth. Often, judgments of the telegram's content have been tied to assessments of the U.S. rationale for intervention in the war. Thus it seems that as long as the debate over the causes of and reasons for American intervention in the Great War continues, so will varying interpretations of the telegram.

Interpretations of several aspects of the telegram affair have remained virtually static. For example, from the time U.S. newspapers published Zimmermann's scheme, contemporaries and other historians have contended that its disclosure mobilized the American public for war. This particular claim has become so widely accepted that many authors repeating it do not bother citing a source. Other assumptions about the telegram have also not received much historical scrutiny. To date, no work has examined the role of Hans Arthur von Kemnitz, the German foreign office official who conceived of the Mexican-Japanese alliance proposal, and few studies have sought to understand Zimmermann's reasons for embracing the project. Instead, both old and recent publications have been content to dismiss the German foreign secretary as "an archetypal Prussian bully,"[35] rather than examine his actions and policies in the context of wartime Germany. Yet even interpretations that have held remarkably steady over time can easily crumble or may require significant readjustment when checked on the basis of new evidence and a careful re-examination of available sources.

Chapter Two

ARTHUR ZIMMERMANN

rthur Zimmermann was born on October 5, 1864, to a local tavern proprietor in Marggrabowa, a small town on the periphery of East Prussia near the Russian border.[1] Growing up far away from progressive urban centers like Berlin or Hamburg, Zimmermann spent his adolescence in a sheltered provincial environment that infused loyalty to emperor and empire. In the 1880s, when a rejuvenated German nationalism came into its own, he studied law at the University of Königsberg and the University of Leipzig. Like many of his fellow students, he joined one of the popular *schlagende Verbindungen* (fencing corps), patriotic fraternities whose members battled each other with rapiers to prove their manhood. Having a scar (*Schmiss*) from such an encounter was considered a mark of honor, and Zimmermann always proudly sported his own.[2]

Zimmermann never entered the legal profession, having set his eyes instead on a career in the foreign service. This wish led him to apply for a job at the German foreign office, or Auswärtiges Amt, located at Wilhelmstrasse 76, a narrow street running south from Unter den Linden, the axis of imperial Berlin. As a commoner, Zimmermann wisely chose to apply for the mundane consular branch rather than the elitist diplomatic section that staffed German embassies around the globe, preferably with aristocrats, and that might well have rejected the middle-class Zimmermann. If he performed well in the consular service, he could expect eventual transfer to the diplomatic branch. In 1893 he joined the consular service, and from 1896 to 1901 he served as vice consul in Shanghai, Canton, and Tientsin, where he distinguished himself during the Chinese Boxer uprising.[3]

On his return from Asia to Germany, Zimmermann crossed the United States, from California to New York, spending two days in San Francisco and three days in New York City. This journey was his only firsthand experience of the United States. The American ambassador to wartime Berlin, James Gerard, claimed in his memoirs that Zimmermann "seemed to think that this transcontinental trip had given him an intimate knowledge of the American character."[4] Gerard personally disliked Zimmermann, and his antipathy probably inspired this disparaging remark. On the other hand, few of Zimmermann's Eurocentric colleagues had ever visited the United States, so Zimmermann may have prided himself in having seen the country for himself, albeit briefly.

Shortly after Zimmermann's return to Germany, Foreign Secretary Friedrich von Holstein invited the young consul to join the diplomatic service. Zimmermann eagerly accepted and following his transfer rapidly ascended from the commercial section to the legal division. In 1905 he entered the prestigious political division as counselor. Only five years later, the Wilhelmstrasse appointed him director (*Dirigent*) of the division, and in 1911 he became undersecretary of state, the second-in-command at the foreign office.[5]

Many contemporary observers agreed that Zimmermann deserved his rapid series of promotions because of his hard work and dedication to the tasks at hand. His bosses, colleagues, and fellow diplomats valued his diligence, attention to detail, and cooperativeness. Joseph Grew, a competent and perceptive diplomat at the U.S. embassy in Berlin who would be ambassador in Tokyo during the bombing of Pearl Harbor, wrote in a letter to Washington in 1916, "I think that Zimmermann may be regarded as a coming man and that he will rise high. He has been handicapped by not being of noble birth, a handicap which in Germany is difficult to overcome, but his personal ability and character have already brought him a great deal of influence."[6] Former foreign secretary Bernhard von Bülow, who liberally dispensed sarcastic comments about German politicians after being sacked by Kaiser Wilhelm II in 1909, remarked, "Zimmermann was still the best of the whole lot, audacious, an optimist, and an excellent worker."[7] In his postwar memoirs, an acerbic reckoning with imperial Germany's leadership, Bülow still found a few good words for Zimmermann, describing him as a "workaholic" (*Arbeitsbiene*) who was "rather conscientious, unlike [Foreign Secretary Gottlieb von] Jagow or [Chancellor Theobald von] Bethmann [Hollweg], an enemy of intrigue, honest and loyal."[8]

Good-humored and unpretentious, Zimmermann won over many of his official contacts with his willingness to bend the rules and cut through red tape.

"That favorite word of the average Prussian official—'ausgeschlossen' (Quite out of the question)—finds no place in his lexicon," penned an American journalist enthusiastically.[9] Grew wrote favorably of him,

> it is always a pleasure to take things up with him at the foreign office. He is a great big blond-haired giant with a charming and cordial manner and a sunny smile which goes a long way in gaining one's confidence; he speaks English well, works like a cart horse and shows a keen interest in everything which is taken up with him and a genuine desire to carry out one's requests—quite to the contrary of some of his colleagues who seem to look for red tape and reasons why a thing can't be done."[10]

Theodor Wolff, the editor of the liberal *Berliner Tageblatt*, was delighted when Zimmermann offered him rare insights into Germany's foreign policy, and the mostly non-aristocratic parliamentarians appreciated Zimmermann's straightforward oratory and plebeian manners.[11] Although one of Zimmermann's bosses, the reticent Jagow, lamented his subordinate turning his office into a "political barbershop," his remarks may have been tinged with envy at the fact that Zimmermann had managed to become the center of attention at the Wilhelmstrasse.[12]

Ever since his university years, Zimmermann had been a social drinker who bonded easily with other men. He could be charming in the presence of women, who generally found him physically attractive, though he remained a bachelor all his life. Despite his congeniality, Zimmermann possessed traits that limited his effectiveness as a top diplomat. For one, he did not respond well to stress. Although generally polite and cordial, he cracked easily when under pressure or faced with conflicting demands. When Grew appeared at the foreign office to discuss reports of German submarine attacks on merchant ships with American citizens on board, Zimmermann "immediately lost his temper, banging his fist on the table and exhibiting the utmost petulance and nervousness. He said, approximately, 'Do you dare to come to me, Herr Grew, believing these damnable Reuter reports which are aimed simply to stir up trouble between our Governments, and to tell me that you expect an immediate reply?'"[13] While journalists and foreign diplomats valued his eagerness to divulge insider information from the Wilhelmstrasse, his boss, Jagow, complained that Zimmermann spent far too much time socializing with all sorts of lobbyists, succumbed to their influence, and tended to spill the beans out of vanity and a propensity for indiscretion.[14]

Moreover, Zimmermann never quite outgrew his modest roots. Lacking the cosmopolitan background of many of his aristocratic colleagues, Zimmermann failed to acquire their level of worldliness, despite his consular service in China. Hence, Bülow's verdict may be exaggerated but can't be dismissed altogether: "He didn't comprehend European politics very well, and he didn't know the relevant people in St. Petersburg and Paris, in London and Vienna. . . . He belonged to the category of those Germans who, for all their willpower and unquestionable diligence, still don't understand that a diplomat must be, more than anything, skillful [*geschickt*], and has to know 'how to do it.'"[15]

To his credit, Zimmermann was aware of his shortcomings. In 1912, when Foreign Secretary Alfred Kiderlen-Waechter suddenly died, two men were considered to succeed him: Zimmermann and Jagow. Then ambassador to Rome, Jagow did not want to exchange his pleasant posting to the eternal city for the minefield of Berlin. Jagow fought the prospect of his appointment tooth and nail, pointing out that he was not a gifted orator and thus unsuited for representing the Wilhelmstrasse to the Reichstag. At the same time, Zimmermann refuted his own candidacy by pointing to his fragile health, his lack of proficiency in foreign languages, and the fact that he was a commoner. In the end, Berlin casually dismissed Jagow's objection about his lack of oratory— "no problem . . . several of your predecessors have not been great orators, either"—and "morally forced" him to accept the appointment. When he asked the kaiser a year later why he hadn't appointed Zimmermann instead, Wilhelm replied uncannily, "One should never make the scullion chef." [16]

Contemporary observers, especially Americans, made much of the fact that Zimmermann was a commoner and deduced that he must therefore be somewhat of a reformer. Even the skeptical Gerard considered him "at heart a Liberal and violently opposed [to] a system which draws the leaders of the country from only one aristocratic class." The New York *Evening Post* reminded its readers that Zimmermann was almost entirely surrounded by aristocrats who regarded him as a "rank intruder" and suggested that his advancement in the foreign office heralded fundamental, progressive changes at the Wilhelmstrasse.[17] The politically liberal former German ambassador to London, Karl Max von Lichnowsky, praised Zimmermann as "the only sensible man" at the foreign office.[18] Yet Zimmermann's supposed liberal leanings went only so far. Anyone pursuing a career at the imperial foreign office had to be a staunch monarchist, and Zimmermann was no exception. It is also true that the rising middle classes in imperial Germany tended to imitate the mores of the aristocracy, rather than challenge them; again, in this regard, Zimmermann appears to have been a follower rather than a rebel. As Jagow later remarked acerbically, "[H]e always swam with the stream and with those who shouted loudest."[19]

Though competent, Foreign Secretary Jagow was by nature retiring and sickly and thus inclined to leave his undersecretary significant room for maneuver. Therefore, Zimmermann exerted considerable influence over the Wilhelmstrasse even before he replaced Jagow in 1916. In fact, Zimmermann made several important decisions during the final years before the war and during the crisis in July 1914 that followed the assassination of Austrian archduke Franz Ferdinand in Sarajevo and triggered World War I. In October 1913, for example, Zimmermann defused a crisis between Austria-Hungary and Serbia that had pushed the two nations to the brink of war over Belgrade's drive to the Adriatic. By refusing to back Germany's old ally Austria unconditionally, and by negotiating furiously between Vienna, London, and Belgrade, Zimmermann eventually achieved not only a strengthening of the Austro-German alliance but also a confirmation of Albania's independence, blocking a hostile Serbia from the Adriatic.[20]

During the early stages of the unfolding crisis in the summer of 1914, Zimmermann's influence over foreign policy further increased because Jagow was absent from Berlin most of the time—first on his honeymoon and then at general headquarters on the western front. Just as he had done in October 1913, Zimmermann reacted with restraint to the unfolding crisis, at least initially. The Austrians were pressing for a military solution to deal once and for all with the meddlesome Serbians, yet Vienna knew it could not proceed without unconditional German support. Neither the German ambassador to Vienna, Heinrich von Tschirschky, nor Zimmermann were prepared, however, to acquiesce to the Austrians; instead they counseled moderation. Had Zimmermann persisted, it is not inconceivable that his diplomacy might have defused the July crisis and avoided the outbreak of World War I, but the undersecretary lacked the stamina to stick to his guns under pressure. Carried away by the war fever that gripped so many German leaders in July 1914, the emperor brushed away Zimmermann and Tschirschky's concerns, commenting curtly, "Tschirschky will be so good as to drop this nonsense. We must finish with the Serbs, *quickly.*"[21] A frantic Zimmermann, eager to please his monarch, turned on a dime and henceforth emerged as one of the most strident warmongers at the foreign office.

Shortly thereafter, news leaked to the German press corps that Japan had demanded the unconditional surrender of Kiau-Chow, the German colony in

China. The newspaper editor Theodor Wolff sought out Zimmermann to confirm the rumor, but the extremely nervous undersecretary pointed lamely to the possibility of U.S. mediation and refused to confirm or refute Wolff's story.[22] These episodes are telling examples of the undersecretary's style: As Europe plunged into war, Zimmermann failed to seize the initiative at the Wilhelmstrasse and appeared overtaxed and clueless at critical junctures. Even though he had considerable leeway to implement his own ideas, he did so only hesitantly and quickly abandoned them when exposed to criticism.

A similarly checkered pattern emerges with regard to Zimmermann's position on German war aims. As the German armies crushed the Russians in East Prussia and marched through Belgium and northern France, politicians and public figures outdid each other with fantastic territorial claims in expectation of imminent triumph. Notably, Zimmermann was not one of them. On September 1, 1914—before German reversals in France raised the specter of a drawn-out contest—he spoke earnestly of the "poor French" and expressed his concern that the military would make excessive claims in the West: "Mars rules the hour. Let's not fool ourselves, the military and the Pan Germans are riding high." He also warned against annexing French or Belgian territory, a demand very popular among the military and nationalists at this point in time.[23] Likewise, Zimmermann counseled against the outright annexation of Russian-controlled Poland and generally against "blindly following a policy of annexations." Instead, he urged the creation of a Polish buffer state and others in the east as a more viable and effective way to keep Russia at bay.[24]

Although Zimmermann appeared rather progressive on war aims, he held extreme views when it came to the conduct of the war. Vastly overestimating German capabilities, he rejected the possibility of a separate peace with either Britain or Russia in November 1914, advocating total victory over both. Naturally, he could not uphold this position when it became evident that Germany would be unable to win a two-front war.[25] Overall, there was little consistency in his views and decisions, other than his tendency to defer to strongly held views by colleagues or superiors.

Yet one theme runs through Zimmermann's career at the Wilhelmstrasse like a red thread. From his earliest days in the diplomatic service, he was involved in intelligence operations and covert activities. While on assignment in China, long before the war, Zimmermann had participated in a covert network of German consuls who used money in slush funds to bribe Chinese officials in order to procure classified government documents. Back in Berlin, he and his colleague Wilhelm von Stumm successfully pushed to allow the German navy's intelligence division to recruit agents from the Wilhelmstrasse's worldwide consular network.[26]

German intelligence expanded its operations significantly during World War I, and Zimmermann's involvement in covert actions grew with them. When war broke out, the Germans quickly devised a policy of fostering insurgencies as a means of creating distractions for the Allied powers, especially Great Britain. These efforts included activities in Ireland, India, North Africa, and Russia. Early on, Berlin displayed particular interest in an Islamic uprising in the Middle East and successfully lobbied the sultan of the Ottoman Empire for a declaration of a holy war (jihad), involving all Muslims, against the Allies. Zimmermann emerged as one of the chief executives of this policy. In a letter drafted by the undersecretary shortly after the outbreak of war, the kaiser asserts grandiloquently to the emir of Afghanistan, "It has long been . . . my wish to see the Mohammedan nations independent and to achieve for their states the maximum of free development."[27] The text amounted to a thinly veiled promise of support for Afghan endeavors to push back British influence. In late August 1914, Zimmermann took charge of an operation to infiltrate German agents from the Ottoman Empire into Egypt and Sudan to incite the native populations against British rule, liquidate the British officer corps in the Egyptian army, and block the Suez Canal by demolishing locks and waterworks, telegraph offices, railway bridges, barracks, and port installations in Suez, Port Said, and Alexandria. The plan ultimately disintegrated as a result of wrangling over competencies between Ottoman and German authorities and British countermeasures.

Zimmermann then turned his eyes to Russia. In August 1914, two Russian armies invaded East Prussia, but numerically inferior German forces decisively defeated the Russians at the battle of Tannenberg. Subsequently, the German forces began their invasion of the vast regions of the Russian Empire that included large numbers of non-Russian minorities. The Germans intended to exploit anti-Russian sentiment in these areas they sought to conquer. One group the Germans hoped to win over were Russian Jews, who had endured many years of discrimination and pogroms under the tsars. The German consul in Bucharest contacted Jewish agents who promised him "a rising in Bessarabia [today's Moldova] within ten days and later a general revolution against Russia." While the consul made substantial payments to the Jewish agents, Zimmermann, on behalf of the foreign office, issued a statement endorsing and approving Jewish emancipation in Russia. It did more harm than good, however, as it provoked the Russians to take immediate countermeasures. The Russian government cracked down hard on the Jewish population, while nationalist mobs took out their anger at the perceived enemy within. German troops were not within reach of areas of Jewish concentrations. This intelligence failure notwithstanding, Zimmermann continued to support revolutionary action against the tsarist regime, a policy that would ultimately lead to German support of Vladimir Ilyich Lenin, a Russian exile in Switzerland who would mastermind the Bolshevik Revolution in the fall of 1917.[28]

Zimmermann's support of covert action schemes extended to the Western Hemisphere as well. Early in the war, he had established contact with American Jews to elicit their support for Germany's cause. In the winter of 1914–1915, Zimmermann boasted to Ambassador Gerard of 500,000 fully trained German reservists in the United States and threatened the ambassador with the prospect of a combined German and Irish American uprising if Washington pursued an anti-German policy. In his memoirs, Gerard wrote that Zimmermann "worked himself up to a passion and repeatedly struck the table with his fist. I told him that we had five hundred and one thousand lamp posts in America, and that was where the German reservists would find themselves if they tried any uprising."[29]

Zimmermann's actions sometimes went beyond mere threats. In December 1914, the undersecretary urged the German ambassador to Washington, Johann Heinrich von Bernstorff, to lend financial support to a scheme of German military intelligence to destroy the Canadian Pacific Railway. Furthermore, the undersecretary had a hand in German schemes to support U.S.-based revolutionaries from British India, and he served as the Wilhelmstrasse's liaison between the German military and Irish revolutionaries. In this capacity, he drafted an official German declaration of support for Irish independence, published in November 1914.[30] Zimmermann also met with Captain Franz Rintelen von Kleist, an agent of the German military. In 1915 Rintelen spent several months in the United States organizing sabotage operations against the country's armaments industry.

Zimmermann's appointment to the top job at the Wilhelmstrasse occurred virtually by default. Foreign Secretary Jagow, as an old school diplomat, found himself increasingly at odds with military leaders during the war. In particular, Jagow resisted the pursuit of unrestricted submarine warfare by the German navy. If German submarines were given a free hand to sink any vessel they encountered in the North Sea and the Atlantic, the navy argued, Great Britain would quickly be starved and sue for peace. Unrestricted submarine warfare did not, however, distinguish between neutral and Allied ships, and Jagow feared U.S. intervention as a possible consequence. As the jingoistic press, nationalistic politicians, and military and naval leaders pressed ever harder to unleash the submarines, Jagow grew increasingly despondent. He resigned as foreign secretary late in November 1916, following a demeaning scolding from the kaiser over a bagatelle. Indicating the true reason for his departure, Germany's top diplomat remarked at the time that he was annoyed at the interference of the supreme army command with his work.[31] As Jagow's second-in-command, Zimmermann was his natural successor.

In the eyes of the German leadership, Zimmermann brought many desirable qualities to the table. Jovial and gregarious, he could be expected to handle the press more skillfully than the introverted Jagow, and his jaunty manner and unadorned oratory were popular, especially among influential right-wing parliamentarians and politicians. The kaiser, who appreciated a manly demeanor and forthright talk, liked the straightforward Zimmermann, who happened to be on friendly terms with the empress as well. Unlike the refined Jagow, the pushy Zimmermann had managed to impress the kaiser's rough-edged military entourage. Notably, Zimmermann had made some rather coarse remarks about submarine warfare, which military men regarded as an indicator of his likely support for such a war measure: In May 1915, a German submarine had sunk the British liner *Lusitania* off the coast of Ireland, killing more than a hundred Britain-bound American passengers. The attack provoked outrage in the United States, but not so in Germany. On his way to the Wilhelmstrasse, Zimmermann bumped into a journalist and remarked cheerfully, "Now, this will have quite an effect! The hatred towards us can't possibly increase, they will always hate us, but in this situation the only thing we can do is lash out at all sides, we have no room for any consideration whatsoever."[32] Such bellicose remarks gained the undersecretary respect within military circles. Jagow later wrote that Zimmermann "was in his heart always pro-U-Boat," but privately he acknowledged that Zimmermann was unsteady on this subject, shifting positions depending on whose advice he had just heard.[33] At any rate, the chancellor considered Zimmermann's popularity an asset for the government and appointed him foreign secretary on November 22, 1916.[34]

Zimmermann received accolades from all sides upon his appointment. The military cherished the prospect of working with a like-minded spirit at the helm of the Wilhelmstrasse, and moderate politicians found reason for rejoicing as well. Jagow told Hugo von Lerchenfeld, the Bavarian envoy to Berlin, that "the policy of the foreign office will probably remain the same since he [Jagow] and his successor always shared the same opinion."[35] American observers, too, expressed satisfaction, and sometimes enthusiasm, at Zimmermann's appointment. The U.S. embassy regarded him "as a warm and true friend of America," as an American diplomat put it in a report to the State Department. The journalist Gilbert Hirsch published a complimentary article titled "Our Friend Zimmermann" in the *Evening Post* on November 25, 1916.[36]

Popularity with the military, politicians, American diplomats, and journalists would appear to be an asset for the new foreign secretary. If the German leadership remained united and maintained good relations with the United States, Zimmermann could be expected to play his part well. In this ideal scenario, he would serve his superiors as an efficient facilitator domestically and goodwill ambassador vis-à-vis Washington in foreign affairs. But what if German leaders diverged on military strategy and foreign policy, and the United States adopted a hostile posture toward Berlin? In this case, the Wilhelmstrasse would need a resolute and principled leader to steer the nation with a steady hand through the crisis. Unfortunately for Germany, Zimmermann was neither.

Chapter Three

THE MEXICAN IMBROGLIO

The Mexican Revolution erupted in 1911, when a thirty-seven-year-old idealist, Felix I. Madero, ousted Mexico's octogenarian dictator, Porfirio Díaz, who had ruled the country with an iron fist for more than thirty years (the so-called Porfiriato). Though reform minded and well intentioned, Madero failed to establish effective control over the nation. Consequently, he called on a tough regular army officer, Victoriano Huerta, to suppress armed rebellions against his shaky regime by reactionary and revolutionary forces. Cunning and ruthless, Huerta scored several military victories over Madero's enemies, but in the process he developed an appetite for power. In February 1913, he forced Madero to resign and assumed the presidency himself. Four days later, Madero was shot in what Huerta's men described as an attempt to escape prison. Many contemporaries, however, held that Huerta had Madero killed.

The freshly minted president quickly set up a de facto military dictatorship and throughout his brief reign battled armed opposition in the south, led by Emiliano Zapata, and in the north, led by Venustiano Carranza and Francisco "Pancho" Villa. Carranza's forces called themselves constitutionalists, in reference to the Mexican constitution, which Huerta had violated by deposing Madero. With U.S. support, Carranza ousted Huerta in July 1914, and a German warship evacuated the fallen dictator. In Mexico, Carranza assumed power as the "first chief" and like his predecessors faced armed opposition from his erstwhile allies, Zapata and Villa, in the south and north. As World War I enveloped Europe, the Mexican Revolution entered another bloody stage.

The revolution continued and reinforced Mexican foreign policy trends initiated in the waning years of the Porfiriato. Economic development under Díaz had led to an influx of foreign capital, especially from the United States. As a result, Washington's leverage south of the Rio Grande grew. Díaz then sought to counter American influence by forging closer commercial ties with European powers, principally Great Britain and Germany. This policy, in turn, irritated the United States, which decided to back Madero against Díaz. As the Great War caused increasing friction between the United States and Germany, the Mexican government, under Carranza, turned to Berlin in its continuing effort to check U.S. influence.[1]

Germany appeared to have little interest in Mexico. The Eurocentric Wilhelmstrasse traditionally had treated Mexico as a diplomatic backwater and in 1911 appointed a retired naval officer, Rear Admiral Paul von Hintze, as envoy to Mexico City. Hintze had never held a diplomatic post, but his assignment turned out to be a stroke of luck. During his tenure, Hintze impressed his superiors in Berlin as a shrewd and wily diplomat. A Japanese military attaché described him as "a man of clever diligence."[2] Although a novice to the foreign service, the perceptive Hintze quickly grasped the dire political situation in Mexico and wisely counseled the Wilhelmstrasse against entanglement with any of the warring factions. After the outbreak of war in Europe, Berlin reassigned Hintze to what the foreign office considered to be a more important post, in China. In Mexico City in early 1915, Hintze left his assistant, Arthur Magnus, in charge until the new envoy, Heinrich von Eckardt, arrived.[3]

Previously minister to Cuba, Eckardt had a reputation as a mediocre diplomat; the confusing political environment in Mexico further undermined his effectiveness. In late 1914, German warships withdrew from the Western Hemisphere, leaving the new envoy with little force to back up his authority. The cutting of Germany's transatlantic cables by the Royal Navy early in the war complicated Eckardt's communications with Berlin. The distance between Mexico and Berlin prevented direct transmission by radio, so Eckardt communicated with the Wilhelmstrasse mostly through the German embassy in Washington or with the help of the friendly Swedish minister in Mexico City. Either way, the process of sending and receiving transatlantic messages proved lengthy and insecure. When Eckardt's reports did reach Berlin, they offered little to encourage the Wilhelmstrasse to pay more attention to the lands south of the Rio Grande. In early 1916, for example, he relayed the following bleak assessment of the Carranza regime: "Today's Mexico under the regime of the 'Constitutionalistas' presents a picture of unfathomable depredation, miserable ruins."[4]

At times, Mexico's turmoil affected German officials directly. In December 1913, for instance, the governor of Mazatlán ordered the arrest of a German businessman, Gustav Eimbcke, who had been doubling as a naval agent for the admiralty staff. The governor accused Eimbcke of supporting revolutionaries, confiscated his property, and threw him into jail.[5] Magnus, too, experienced the disintegrating law and order at first hand, reporting the following incident to Berlin: "Last night, 11 p.m., on my way home in the diplomatic quarter, about 150 meters from the Imperial Ministry, I was assailed by an individual who tried to steal my watch and chain." However, Magnus' ample body mass provided sufficient armor against the attacker: "Probably due to the lack of success and the beatings I administered with my stick, the individual thrust a knife at my heart, but [I sustained] only a laceration, three centimeters in length, four deep, midriff uninjured; neither danger nor fever; recuperation within two weeks. Diplomats use this incidence to point their governments once again to the untenable circumstances [in Mexico]."[6]

At the Wilhelmstrasse, Foreign Secretary Gottlieb von Jagow and his under-secretary, Zimmermann, spent much of their time dealing with the European neutrals and the United States, and it fell to Adolf Maximilian Maria von Montgelas, the foreign office counselor for American and Mexican affairs, to handle issues pertaining to Mexico. Montgelas hailed from a distinguished aristocratic Bavarian family of French descent. His grandfather, Maximilan de Garnerin de la Thuille, Comte de Montgelas, had fled France during the revolution at the close of the eighteenth century, settling the family in Bavaria, where he became the king's grand chamberlain, his most trusted confidant, counselor, and prime minister. Putting down firm roots in Bavaria, numerous members of the Montgelas family served their new home country as adminis-trators and diplomats. Count Adolf was no exception.

Born in Munich in 1872, Montgelas studied at the local university, and when barely thirty years of age, joined the diplomatic service. After a brief stint in Constantinople, he served as third secretary of the German embassy in Washington, from 1900 to 1903, while his later boss, Zimmermann, was plugging away as vice-consul in China. Montgelas moved on to fill, in rapid succession, posts at key German legations in Bucharest (1904–1905), St. Peters-burg (1906), and then in a variety of functions at the German embassy in Tokyo until 1911.[7] In March 1911, he reported on the improbability of a for-mal Mexican-Japanese alliance, a matter of some concern in the United States at the time.[8]

In Berlin, Montgelas rubbed shoulders with various American officials, most of whom held him in high regard. One diplomat of the U.S. embassy in

Berlin, Joseph Grew, described him as "one of my best friends . . . and I have a very high opinion of him. He has been in Washington, speaks English perfectly and might well be a future Ambassador to the United States." The count and his wife were frequent guests of Ambassador James Gerard, who valued him as "an extremely agreeable man." Montgelas would be one of only a handful of Wilhelmstrasse officials at the train station to see off the U.S. embassy staff after diplomatic relations between Germany and the United States were severed in 1917.[9]

Like so many other German officials, Montgelas was on summer vacation when the Great War erupted. On July 29, 1914, the foreign office informed him that there was no need to cut short his holidays in upper Bavaria, but in the evening he received a follow-up message, urging his return to Berlin.[10] As the drama of the war unfolded, the United States, though not Mexico, was very much on Montgelas' mind. "I only pray that America doesn't come in. If she does, we are lost," he reportedly told Ludwig Stein, foreign policy editor of the Berlin *Vossische Zeitung*, on the outbreak of war. Specifically, Montgelas worried about the consequences of unrestricted submarine warfare, and the sinking of the *Lusitania* by a German submarine in 1915 greatly disturbed him. Stein, who saw Montgelas shortly after this incident, "found him in a state of complete collapse with the tears streaming down his eyes. I said: 'This is a second Marne [a reference to the German reversals in France in September 1914].' He replied, 'It is far, far worse. I know American psychology, both because I lived in Washington three years and because my wife is American. She shares my grief and I hers. Personally and politically I am heartbroken.'"[11] Gerard had a similar impression: "I think [Montgelas] at all times had correctly predicted the attitude of America and had been against acts of frightfulness, such as the torpedoing of the *Lusitania* and the resumption of unrestricted submarine war."[12]

Behind the scenes, Montgelas actively participated in the wrangling over unrestricted warfare, and the tug-of-war found him firmly on the side of its opponents. In August 1915, when a German submarine sank the *Arabic*, another merchant ship with American citizens on board, Montgelas strongly urged the issuance of restrictive orders to U-boat commanders: "[As of now] a U-boat commander can at will cause a break between Germany and America. . . . This state of affairs is, in my opinion, untenable." In an insightful memorandum on the upcoming American presidential elections of 1916, Montgelas doubted whether U-boat war could be expanded without antagonizing Washington: "Whether the 'new measures' adopted by the navy will bring us such military advantage as to justify the risk of a break with the United States, seems rather doubtful to me."[13]

During the course of 1915, the United States began to tilt toward the Allies, and Montgelas developed an interest in scenarios that would create a diversion in Mexico and avert American attention from Europe. Against the backdrop of the Mexican civil war, such considerations did not appear unrealistic. On June 2, 1915, for example, President Woodrow Wilson sent a sharply worded note to the belligerent Mexican factions calling on them to come to terms as quickly as possible, otherwise Washington would be "constrained to decide what means should be employed to help Mexico save herself." Contemporary observers interpreted Wilson's note as a veiled threat of intervention, and the German ambassador in Washington, Johann Heinrich von Bernstorff, who relayed the remarks to Montgelas, made exactly this point: "Should [the Mexicans] refuse, intervention is threatened." Montgelas underlined this sentence.[14]

A large-scale American intervention in Mexico suddenly appeared at hand when more than 400 heavily armed Mexican horsemen crossed the U.S. border and raided the small town of Columbus, New Mexico, on March 9, 1916. The Mexicans torched the business district and attacked a detachment of the 13th U.S. Cavalry, garrisoned at Camp Furlong. After about two hours of ferocious fighting, including several instances of bloody hand-to-hand combat, the American soldiers drove the invaders back across the border. The Americans quickly identified the man in charge of the raiding party as "Pancho" Villa, the notorious leader of a constitutionalist faction in the Mexican civil war at the time opposed to the country's de facto leader, Carranza. Less than a week after the Columbus raid, President Wilson dispatched the famous "punitive expedition," a contingent of 4,000 men under General John J. "Black Jack" Pershing, to find Villa and disperse his forces.

Villa's cross-border raid had a strategic purpose. By 1916 he had lost ground against Carranza, who enjoyed U.S. support. By attacking the United States, he hoped to boost his popularity among Mexicans and provoke a U.S. intervention, which would, in turn, embarrass his rival, Carranza. His gambit bore fruit, at least in the short term. Over the next twelve months, Villa's successful evasion of Pershing's forces turned him into a Mexican folk hero of sorts. Although Villa had perfectly good reasons of his own to raid Columbus, rumors quickly spread to the effect that he had acted at Berlin's command. On March 29, Ambassador Bernstorff reported to Chancellor Theobald von Bethmann Hollweg: "It is not surprising that an attempt has been made to blame Villa's incursion on German intrigues, and to portray Germany as the real troublemaker. A substantiation of this nonsensical allegation is, of course, not forthcoming." One official scribbled the cynical comment "unfortunately" next to the word "nonsensical."[15] Since Mexico-related messages typically landed on Montgelas' desk, he was probably the person who added the "unfortunately." The written comment reveals two facts: first, some German officials would have been happy to support Villa's Columbus raid; second, Germany had had no hand in it.

Just a few days later, Captain Fritz Prieger, the director of the foreign division of German naval intelligence, forwarded a lengthy top secret report by one of his agents to the Wilhelmstrasse. The agent, apparently based in London and with access to Reuters journalists, waxed lyrical on Villa's prowess and pronounced, "What was going on in Mexico now, is not only an insurrection, but the beginning of a war between Mexico and the United States."[16] Montgelas' initials on this communication show that he avidly read incoming intelligence reports on the fallout of Columbus throughout March and April. He added a question mark next to the agent's bold prophecy, and on March 23, he put his thoughts on the Mexican situation in writing:

> There is little point, in my opinion, in sending *"money"* to Mexico. To the extent that anything can be achieved there with *money*, the Americans will always be able to outbid us easily, since they simply have more money and moreover because they have infinitely more channels at their disposal than we do, since the Americans have been working in this way for a long time in Mexico. It would be something quite different if we could get arms and ammunition (preferably *of American origin*) to Villa and his bands surreptitiously. This is, however, complicated by the fact that communications with northern Mexico from Veracruz are currently poor.[17]

At first glance, it may seem surprising that Montgelas—married to an American citizen and generally opposed to measures that might provoke Washington—sought to escalate the U.S.-Mexican crisis. If his overriding concern was the preservation of American neutrality in the European conflict, however, his hawkish proposals regarding Mexico appear quite rational. After the *Lusitania* and *Arabic* incidents, U.S.-German relations reached a nadir, and American intervention seemed a real possibility. If Wilson could be tricked into a Mexican adventure, however, the likelihood of U.S. intervention in Europe would decrease because Washington would be reluctant to wage war in two theaters simultaneously. In other words, Montgelas considered a U.S.-Mexican war the lesser of two evils. Not surprisingly, one of America's leading interventionists, Secretary of State Robert Lansing, held a diametrically opposing view. "Germany desires to keep up the turmoil in Mexico until the United States is forced to intervene," he noted in his diary on October 10, 1915. "[T]therefore," he concluded, "we must not intervene."[18] In Berlin, the excitement over Villa's Columbus raid and Pershing's punitive expedition blew over quickly. Other German officials read Montgelas' suggestion of sending money and materiel to Villa with interest, but without acting on it.[19]

The Columbus raid was not the only incident beckoning the Wilhelmstrasse to engage more directly in Mexican affairs. In December 1914, New Orleans–based Felix Díaz, the nephew of the toppled dictator, had approached German officials in Spain through a middleman who said that his boss planned an uprising to reestablish law and order. Capitalizing on his name, Díaz claimed backing from his exiled uncle and inquired whether Germany was willing to support him with $5 million. The German envoy, Hintze, had previously dismissed the younger Díaz as a theatrical personality incapable of organization, and a Wilhelmstrasse official—probably Montgelas—now jotted a curt "NEIN" (no) on the request.[20] That was the end of Díaz's quest for German support, but other Mexicans soon came knocking on Berlin's door.

Arnold Krumm Heller, also known as Arnoldo, was born in Salchendorf, Westphalia, in 1872. He left Germany at the age of eighteen, lived in Mexico and Chile, and traveled to Peru as an assistant to an American Inca scholar. Krumm Heller later touted the title "doctor" and claimed to have studied medicine in Paris. When the Mexican revolution erupted, he joined Madero, and after his murder enlisted with Carranza's forces, where he attained the rank of colonel. In early 1916, Carranza appointed him military attaché to Germany for one year, a move designed to capitalize on Krumm Heller's ethnic background and fluency in German, as well as his widely known ardently pro-German views. Eckardt, the German envoy in Mexico, drafted a glowing letter of introduction to the German chancellor, pointing out cheerfully that Krumm Heller was more interested in disseminating German propaganda in Latin America than in his official mission to study German military medical institutions.[21]

Krumm Heller's mission got off to a rocky start. British officials in New York (probably the naval attaché) learned about his trip before he embarked and informed London. When his ship, the SS *Oscar II*, passed through Kirkwall, British authorities seized him and brought him to London, where Scotland Yard's Special Branch director personally grilled him about the purpose of his trip. Compounding his misery, the Mexican minister to London denied any connection to him.[22] Fortunately for Krumm Heller, he had managed on board the *Oscar II* to pass off Eckardt's letter of introduction to a Swedish diplomat. The diplomat delivered it to Swedish officials, who, in turn, forwarded it to the German embassy in Stockholm. Although British officials remained ignorant of this potentially incriminating document, they nevertheless decided that Krumm Heller's "real mission was undertaken purely in the German interest" and sent him back to America. In Berlin, Montgelas noted that Krumm Heller's mission had become "irrelevant" due to his arrest, but the Wilhelmstrasse had not reckoned on the Germanophile attaché's persistence.[23]

In early September, Krumm Heller showed up at the German ministry in Berne and announced his imminent voyage onward to Berlin. Despite Eckardt's effusive commendation, the Germans remained wary. As foreign secretary Jagow cautioned the German envoy in Berne, "due to political considerations, anything has to be avoided that might provoke the impression in the United States that the Imperial Government supports directly or indirectly Mexico's anti-American tendencies."[24] Moreover, questions arose about Krumm Heller's credibility. The German envoy to Berne considered him "honest if a little bizarre." Others felt less ambivalent. A German diplomat formerly attached to the ministry in Mexico City warned that "the so-called 'Dr.' Krumm Heller had a very bad reputation in the German colony, and had no access to the higher classes of the Díaz regime. He called himself a medical doctor, but people deny he has medical knowledge. Utmost caution is warranted." Still, Krumm Heller's enthusiasm for Germany appeared authentic. As soon as he entered the country of his birth, he cabled the German envoy in Berne: "Having gladly arrived on German soil, I send you my innermost thanks. Long live Kaiser and Fatherland. Colonel Krumm Heller."[25]

After he set up shop at the Mexican ministry on Berlin's Kurfürstendamm, the new military attaché requested an interview with the foreign secretary. Jagow referred him to Montgelas, who met with Krumm Heller on October 30. Montgelas reported that according to Krumm Heller, Carranza wished to avoid war with the United States "as in the long run Mexico would come off second-best although it might take the Americans years—K. said ten years—to conquer Mexico." He added, "Carranza is awaiting confidently the victory of the German arms."[26]

At the same time, Krumm Heller made contact with German military officers to pursue the study of "military medical institutions," his official task. In December, he called on the director of the department for prisoners of war at the war ministry (*Kriegsministerium*), and in January 1917, a series of visits to various prisoner camps was arranged. The officer who accompanied Krumm Heller reported delightedly that "the basic streak of his character manifests itself in fanatical hatred for England and unlimited enthusiasm for Germany . . . therefore, Colonel Dr. Krumm-Heller seems very well suited to combat anti-German and promote pro-German propaganda. . . . It appears advisable to get to know his personality better, not least because, in pursuit of his goals he tends to give in to subjective exaggeration over objectivity, and therefore I don't feel that everything he says should be taken at face value."[27]

Krumm Heller did not stop at anti-British rants. On January 7, he discussed with a German naval officer the question of closer German-Mexican cooperation. Emphasizing his position as Carranza's "confidential man," Krumm Heller proposed the establishment of radio stations sufficiently powerful to enable direct contact between Germany and Mexico; sabotage of the seaport of Tampico to block the Royal Navy from access to Mexican oil; and the establishment of a German submarine station in Soto la Marina as a basis for anti-British operations. The naval officer reported, "The Mexican government would like to conclude an alliance with Germany as Mexico seeks backup against the United States. To this end, the Mexican government has already concluded an alliance in the form of an oral agreement with Japan. Our [Germany's] position vis-à-vis the United States would be substantially improved if we could come to an agreement with Japan." Krumm Heller suggested he sail to Mexico on board a German vessel in order to promote Germany's cause there.[28]

It is unclear whether Carranza had really instructed his military attaché to go this far. Given Krumm Heller's personality, and his naive enthusiasm for all things German, he may well have been carried away and in the moment exceeded his instructions. The German naval officer who drafted the memorandum did not explicitly state that Krumm Heller's proposal was an official initiative by Carranza's government. Be that as it may, the memorandum indicates the kind of discussions that Krumm Heller conducted with German officials. Although German authorities did not pursue any of his proposals, they must have taken note of the fact that Mexico's military attaché considered Japan's detachment from the Allies feasible and a German-Mexican alliance advisable.

During the following months, Krumm Heller completed his metamorphosis from Mexican military attaché to German propagandist. "One completely loses sight of the fact that he is officially a representative of a neutral power because of his strongly asserted interests in Germany," noted a German military officer in early January. When his one-year tour of duty ended, Krumm Heller was recalled to Mexico, in July 1917, but before his intended departure he asked Zimmermann how he could best "serve the German cause" at home. Zimmermann referred him to the intelligence division of the foreign office.[29]

Unable to return home by sea due to the British naval blockade, Krumm Heller remained attached to the Mexican ministry "on a special mission,"[30] advocating stronger German-Mexican bonds and lecturing widely on "the general prosperity of Mexico, and on the wonderful fertility of Mexican soil and the abundance of its harvest. The result is that his audience believes that Mexico is a kind of 'earthly paradise.'"[31] The German authorities were delighted, and in April 1918 arranged a visit for him to a German submarine in Bremen.[32] Just a few days before the war's end, Krumm Heller was invited to the residence of the industrialist Krupp family where he explained the long-range gun used in bombarding Paris.[33] The Americans and Allies were by now routinely intercepting cables from the Mexican ministry in Berlin and must have been particularly amused to read Krumm Heller's assessment, dated September 7, 1918: "The triumph of the Central Powers is certain; hence we must continue to remain neutral."[34] Eight weeks later, Germany surrendered, and Krumm Heller's "special mission" came to an end.

Krumm Heller was not the only Mexican emissary who aggressively pushed for a Mexican-German alliance. Early in the war, Franz von Papen, the German military attaché to Washington, met with a certain Gonzalo C. Enrile. Born in Guanajuato in central Mexico in 1867, Enrile passed himself off as a colonel, claimed to have a large following in Mexico, and offered the Germans advantages—"oil wells, etc."—in Mexico in exchange for German support against Carranza. Papen issued Enrile a letter of recommendation as an introduction to other German authorities.[35]

In 1915 Enrile moved on to Havana. In Cuba, as the Mexican consul in Havana reported, Enrile and a Spanish friend—probably a man called Humberto Islas—boasted about their plan to travel to Germany "in order to acquire money and support for the purpose of disrupting at any price the existing relations between Mexico and the United States." In February 1916, Enrile appeared at the German embassy in Spain, touting Papen's letter and requesting a passport to Berlin "for negotiations about . . . the relations between

Mexico and Germany." Ambassador Maximilian von Ratibor forwarded Enrile's request to the Wilhelmstrasse, where Montgelas and Zimmermann read it. They consulted Papen (by now back in Germany), who advised against Enrile's proposed trip to Berlin but also suggested that Enrile not be dismissed entirely. Hence, Zimmermann instructed Ratibor to string the Mexican along: "Here no interest in Enrile. Please inform him kindly that visit 'currently' not opportune, but hint at possibility that this may later be convenient."[36]

Unperturbed, the industrious Mexican headed for Berlin. On April 10, Enrile and Islas entered Germany from Switzerland and three days later took up residence in the Central Hotel on Berlin's Friedrichstrasse, just a few blocks from the Wilhelmstrasse. Over the next six days, Enrile and Islas penned their thoughts on a proposal for German-Mexican alliance. On April 19, they finished their memorandum, and Enrile began to besiege the German authorities for an audience. Islas, on the other hand, stuffed a copy of the memorandum into one of his boots, along with some other papers, and headed for Switzerland, in all likelihood to keep their middlemen in Spain abreast of developments in Germany. German authorities apprehended him on April 29 at the Swiss border, searched his belongings, and retrieved the documents. When informed of the find, Zimmermann requested that Islas be relieved of the papers but otherwise permitted to proceed with his voyage to Switzerland and Spain, which he did.[37]

Meanwhile, Captain Rudolf Nadolny, the director of the army's sabotage and covert action department, Sektion P, had gone through the reports on Enrile and informed the Wilhelmstrasse that he was not interested in working with the Mexican.[38] The foreign office, however, did not dismiss him as readily. With Papen's letter of recommendation in hand, Enrile showed up unannounced at Wilhelmstrasse 76 on June 15, met briefly with Montgelas, and handed him a lengthy memorandum, dated June 14. Montgelas told Enrile to return in two days to discuss its contents. The memorandum, as well as the papers seized earlier from Islas, purported that Enrile represented a "nationalist party," including such diverse leaders as Díaz, Villa, and Zapata, and outlined in intricate detail proposals for German support of this nebulous group to take over Mexico. In return, Enrile's junta would grant major concessions to Berlin, and notably operate as a spearhead against the United States. The April 19 memorandum offered Germany "an alliance or secret treaty against the United States of America." As a first step, Germany was to help end the "terror regime" of Carranza. In return, Enrile promised Berlin

1. A Mexican policy favorable to Germany and aimed against the interests of the United States.

2. The creation of a strong army, which would invade American territory at a time propitious for Germany and Mexico.

[. . .]

5. Support for the separatist movements existing in several southwestern states: namely—Texas, Arizona, New Mexico and the south of Upper California.[39]

Enrile also noted, "The total sum, required partially in cash, partially in arms, ammunition and other war material needed to get the movement well on its way and to invade the United States, amounts to *c.* 300 million marks."[40]

In the June 14 memorandum, Enrile elaborated on some of the above points. He argued that U.S. intervention was probable, in which case Mexico would be in a position to entangle American forces and keep Washington busy, as evidenced by Pershing's ongoing punitive expedition. Should the United States attack Germany in spite of its exposed southern flank, "the participation of the Mexican army, which can easily be augmented to 200,000 men, deployed on American territory, along an open border of 2,000 km, etc., will help seal the defeat of the States." Enrile closed his memorandum by pointing out that Mexico would prefer the German option but had an alternative with Japan which "for some time and also recently has made proposals to Mexico to aid our position through support of our aspirations against the United States." Montgelas carefully read the memorandum and its three appendices, underlining Enrile's request for German "support of Mexico" and "modern weapons and war materiel" and his insistence that Mexico required "purely financial" aid.[41]

Enrile did not know it, but his mission was doomed. Even if the foreign office had been interested in his scheme, the Germans couldn't be sure whom, if anyone, Enrile represented. It seemed highly unlikely that Díaz, Villa, and Zapata would have agreed to send an emissary collectively, and Enrile had no bona fides as proof that he spoke for any of them. Moreover, his own credentials were shaky; Montgelas wrote of "the somewhat strange 'military career' of Colonel Enrile." Also, Berlin harbored no hostility toward Carranza and had no intention of toppling him. Montgelas conferred with Jagow and Zimmermann, and when Enrile returned to the Wilhelmstrasse on June 17, the counselor told him, "German-U.S. relations are currently quite normal. Our interference in American-Mexican disputes is—at this point in time, at any rate—out of the question."[42]

From that point on, Enrile's career as a Mexican emissary went downhill. German military intelligence considered using him as a spy in France, but then balked when questions about his military career arose. To make matters worse, the military began to suspect him of being an Allied spy. In June, the Berlin police received a notice from a suitcase manufacturer that Enrile had ordered a piece of luggage with a hollowed-out compartment. The detective in charge of the investigation discovered that the Mexican intended to use the secret compartment to conceal a copy of his alliance proposal for his party in Mexico, as well as "pictures of the emperor, von Hindenburg, Tirpitz and letters from von Papen." The Berlin police concluded that Enrile was credible, and not a spy, so they released him.[43] Free to go but empty-handed, Enrile proceeded to Spain and pitched his project of a "Mexican revolution against the United States" one more time to the German ambassador in Madrid, Ratibor, who informed Berlin of Enrile's claim that he could "win over the Japanese for Mexican cause and sever them from Entente." Montgelas' colleague Hans Arthur von Kemnitz, the department chief (Referatsleiter) responsible for Latin American and East Asian affairs, delivered Zimmermann's verdict to "amicably decline" Enrile's offer.[44]

Having exhausted his funds, Enrile then began to besiege Ratibor for reimbursement of his various expenses. Zimmermann promptly forwarded the request to the war ministry because, he argued, Enrile's trip had originated with the German military attaché to Washington. When the war ministry contacted Papen, he replied that he had suggested "economic and political negotiations" to Enrile, not military discussions. Therefore, the war ministry concluded, it would not reimburse the Mexican. Montgelas wired Ratibor that the Wilhelmstrasse had consistently expressed their disinterest in Enrile's project and would therefore not reimburse him either. In February 1917, Enrile made a last, desperate attempt to excite the Germans about his project—"in view of the break with America"—but Zimmermann replied coolly, "No interest in Enrile's offer since he has no leverage with current Mexican government." Enrile returned to Havana. Several months after Cuba's declaration of war on Germany, on April 7, 1917, local authorities arrested him and confiscated all documents in his possession.[45]

Evidently, Enrile was a Mexican adventurer who may have been in touch with various revolutionary factions but truly represented no one but himself. He used his various German documents—Papen's letter of recommendation and his own memoranda that Islas tried to smuggle out of Germany—to augment his own standing with revolutionaries and counterrevolutionaries at home. Had Papen not issued him a letter of recommendation, Enrile may have never made it to Germany. The Wilhelmstrasse was well advised to keep him at arm's length. On the one hand, Enrile's trip to Germany amounted merely to a cloak-and-dagger story of little importance to the course of the war. On the other, his proposals introduced influential German officials to the notion that Mexico might be interested in an anti-American alliance in exchange for financial support and U.S. territory and the possibility of incorporating Japan in this alliance.

If Enrile did not represent the Mexican leadership, another Mexican overture demonstrated the Carranza regime's interest in closer ties with Germany. In October 1916, the constitutionalists approached Berlin, "seeking from Germany a declaration in Washington according to which an armed intervention in Mexico would not be viewed with favor. In return, the Mexicans offered extensive support for the German U-boats, should they desire to attack English oil tankers leaving the port of Tampico."[46] The Germans did not pursue this offer, but on November 3, 1916, the Mexican envoy to Berlin, Rafael Zubáran Capmany, submitted a memorandum to the Wilhelmstrasse with suggestions for closer ties between the two countries. In particular, he proposed the dispatch of German military instructors to Mexico, German assistance in setting up munitions factories in Mexico, Mexican acquisition of German submarines, and the construction of a powerful radio station on Mexican soil to establish direct contact with Berlin.[47]

In view of constant U.S. pressure and Pershing's ongoing military expedition to Mexico, Carranza's desire for German support was understandable, but the Mexicans had little to offer the Germans in return. Zimmermann, about to become foreign secretary, replied that his government viewed the proposals with sympathy and would look at them in detail, "however, the current moment does not appear to be the best for the conclusion of new, specific agreements. As soon as peace comes, we would energetically push for them." The Mexican envoy appeared satisfied with Zimmermann's dilatory response and added that he, too, thought the arrangement should be postponed until the end of the European war.[48]

Evidently, some Mexicans displayed a genuine interest in closer cooperation with Berlin in 1916, especially after U.S. troops under Pershing had begun operating on Mexican territory. The Wilhelmstrasse did register repeated calls for assistance from Carranza, but what precisely they sought was not always obvious, and not all of the emissaries could claim to speak on behalf of the "first chief" or another significant political faction. Berlin invariably rejected all advances in this regard or deferred the emissaries to the end of the war, since Germany stood little to gain from these offers.

While Carranza could hope to strengthen his hand against the United States with German backing, the foreign office was rightly afraid of jeopardizing its delicate relationship with Washington by dabbling in domestic Mexican affairs. The Germans' attitude would change only when relations with the United States appeared damaged beyond repair, and little would be lost by taking a more aggressive stance in the Western Hemisphere. Yet the various Mexican proposals were significant in that they left a paper trail in the Wilhelmstrasse, and familiarized a number of key officials with putative Mexican foreign policy goals, which the Germans would pick up on when the political situation changed due to the impending U.S. entry into the war. In this regard, they became an important building block of the alliance proposal Zimmermann would make to Carranza in early 1917.

Chapter Four

THE GERMAN QUEST
FOR JAPAN

T
hough first and foremost a European conflict, the Great War touched nations and peoples around the globe. One such area was the Pacific, where Germany had carved out a colonial empire of archipelagoes and footholds in Papua New Guinea and mainland China. After war broke out in Europe in July 1914, Japan saw an opportunity to expand its sphere of influence in Asia and the Pacific at Germany's expense. Bound to Great Britain by a bilateral alliance concluded in 1902, the Japanese government sent a harsh ultimatum to Berlin in August 1914 demanding German withdrawal from the Pacific. The Germans left the ultimatum unanswered, and on August 23, Japan declared war on Germany.

In the course of the next few months, Japan conducted a predatory military campaign against the numerically small and widely dispersed German colonial forces in the Pacific. In the process, Japan gobbled up much of Germany's far-flung possessions in the Far East, including the strategically valuable Chinese port city of Tsingtao, after a two-month siege. On November 7, 1914, the last German colonial forces in the Pacific surrendered to Tokyo.

Japan's conquest of the German possessions in the Far East removed a key motivation for Tokyo's participation in the war. When early German military victories against France and Russia appeared to portend a quick and comprehensive defeat of the Allies in Europe, Japan's allegiance to the Allied cause began to waver. In the spring of 1915, Japan's officially inspired press assumed an anti-British tone, while affording broad coverage to Germany's military victories. Pro-German military leaders as well as some intellectuals publicly voiced their preference for Japan to come to an agreement with the Central

Powers. Peace with Germany, these advocates hoped, would enable Japan to penetrate deep into China, a goal strongly resented by the Allies.[1]

Berlin duly took notice of Japan's vacillation. Fearing the transfer of Japanese troops to Europe and concerned about the growing volume of Japanese arms deliveries to Russia, the Wilhelmstrasse began to consider avenues for detaching Tokyo from the Allies. Less than two weeks after the fall of Tsingtao, the Wilhelmstrasse exhorted the German envoy to China to initiate negotiations for a separate peace with his Japanese counterpart. On January 12, 1915, Foreign Secretary Gottlieb von Jagow expounded his thinking vis-à-vis Japan in a lengthy memorandum to his deputy, Zimmermann. Tokyo had fulfilled its treaty obligations to Great Britain, and Japan was neither contractually obliged nor did it appear willing to send troops to Europe in support of the Allies. The war played to Japan's advantage, the foreign secretary argued, as it weakened and distracted the Entente powers from Asia. Germany could take advantage of this development if it accepted the loss of Tsingtao. Jagow regarded the precarious state of Japan's finances as a promising basis for future German-Japanese negotiations.[2]

From the very beginning, institutional and cultural peculiarities shaped the German quest for a separate peace with Japan. On an institutional level, the Wilhelmstrasse's department (*Referat*) handling East Asian affairs exerted an unusual degree of influence over Berlin's approaches to Tokyo. Two reasons accounted for the department's outsized importance. First, neither Chancellor Theobald von Bethmann Hollweg, nor Jagow, nor Zimmermann was well versed in Japanese politics. Second, Japan did not figure prominently in the Germans' thinking when compared to Europe or the United States. As a result, German leaders tended to rely on the foreign office experts for information and advice on East Asia. This delegation of authority gave particular influence on foreign policy to the men heading the East Asian department during the war: Adolf von Montgelas (until early 1916), Hans Arthur von Kemnitz (until late 1917), and Edmund Rhomberg (through the rest of the war).[3]

A condescending, not to say racist, attitude toward the Japanese also permeated German policy. A good number of Berlin policy makers and diplomats seemed to think that Japan "owed" Germany because Tokyo had modeled its modern bureaucracy and army partly on their German counterparts. Some German officials habitually used pejorative terms—such as "yellow peril" or "yellow fellows (*Gelbe Kerle*)"—in internal references to Japanese diplomats and policy. A German negotiator in Stockholm portrayed the local Japanese envoy's alleged "self-satisfaction" as "easily explainable, since one has to bear in mind that in earlier years he was general consul in New York, where he certainly had to endure countless minor insults [*Taktlosigkeiten*] on account of his short stature." The Japanese, in turn, sought to play these prejudices to their advantage. In February 1915, for example, the Japanese envoy to Sweden informed the Germans via his Austrian counterpart that "we admire this powerful country and its titanic battle, as well as its splendid army, which continues to serve us as model." The Wilhelmstrasse erroneously interpreted these remarks as a genuine Japanese desire to quickly strike a separate peace agreement with Germany.[4]

It is noteworthy that diplomats who had served in Japan, such as Montgelas and Rhomberg, by and large avoided succumbing to such stereotypes. They generally displayed a realistic grasp of the limits of Japan's willingness to reach a separate agreement with Berlin and repeatedly advised the political leadership against placing too much hope in these negotiations. Others, among them Zimmermann and especially Kemnitz, pursued Tokyo much more aggressively. Neither of the two had extensive or firsthand knowledge of Japan, and they readily based their assumptions about Japanese politics on platitudes rather than hard analysis. Kemnitz, for example, explored at great length the alleged importance of "the emotional" in Japanese politics in a 1916 memorandum. His recommendations, based on such pseudo-analysis, were therefore the result of wishful thinking rather than *Realpolitik*.[5]

German overtures to Japan began in earnest in early 1915. In January, Paul von Hintze, then ambassador to China, informed his Japanese counterpart of Germany's willingness, under certain conditions, to let Japan keep Tsingtao and the Pacific islands and to give Tokyo a free hand in China. Hintze launched several initiatives to lure the Japanese into peace negotiations, but he eventually failed, leaving neutral Sweden as the main venue for German-Japanese peace talks.

Tokyo's main protagonist in Stockholm was its envoy, Sadatsuchi Uchida. Uchida was an excellent tactician whom the British envoy described as an "active minded man who felt restive at lack of work." He would soon find a suitable challenge in his talks with the Germans who, characteristically, tended to underestimate him. One German negotiator who met Uchida dismissed him as a second-rate personality.[6] In January 1915, Uchida told a Swedish news agency that "Japan considered the war against Germany ended." In response to this ambivalent statement, Jagow drew up the above-mentioned memorandum for Zimmermann outlining Germany's position vis-à-vis Japan. In it, the foreign secretary envisioned a joint German-Japanese administration of

Tsingtao, or even complete cession of the territory to Tokyo, and carte blanche for Japan in the Far East in return for a separate peace. The chancellor sanctioned Jagow's proposals, and the German envoy in Stockholm, Hellmuth von Lucius, received instructions to contact Uchida through the Austrian and Ottoman envoys, Maximilian von Hadik and Mustafa Chekib Bey, whose nations were allied to Germany but not at war with Japan.[7]

Like Montgelas in Berlin, Lucius did not place high hopes in these negotiations, and he treated Jagow's instructions dilatorily. Zimmermann prompted him several times to make contact with Uchida.[8] When Lucius finally did so, Uchida expressed his interest in the German proposal. He also indicated that Japan would not send troops to Europe. Encouraged, Lucius communicated Uchida's statements to Berlin, and pursued his diplomatic endeavors through the services of his Austrian colleague. Shortly afterward, he reported that Uchida had told the Austrian envoy, Hadik, that Japan had been forced to take Tsingtao as the result of its obligations under the Anglo-Japanese alliance, but that this obligation had now been fulfilled. When Hadik suggested that Russia and Great Britain were Japan's real enemies, Uchida wholeheartedly agreed. A few days later, Uchida expressed his country's general admiration for Germany and his hope for the restoration of good relations between the two nations.[9]

The German leadership initially jumped at the bait. On May 15, 1915, the chancellor informed the Wilhelmstrasse of his intention to "conclude peace as soon as possible with Japan" and offer Tokyo Tsingtao as well as German support for Japanese ambitions in China. When Bethmann's memo reached Montgelas, however, the East Asian division chief balked. He pointed to the existing Japanese-British alliance as a formal obstacle to a separate peace and insisted that Germany had nothing tangible to offer, save Tsingtao (which the Japanese already had). He also reminded the German leadership of the pro-British proclivities of Japan's foreign minister, Takaaki Kato, who might immediately share the secret German terms with the Allies. Eventually, Jagow agreed with Montgelas and for the time being considered a separate peace with Japan neither possible nor feasible.[10]

Montgelas had accurately assessed the Japanese position. Since Tokyo already de facto possessed the German territories in the Pacific, Berlin had little with which to bargain. Japanese officials pursued the German overture chiefly in an effort to play off the Germans against the Allies and extract maximum concessions from the latter. The Japanese government communicated Hintze's as well as Lucius' proposals to the Allies, causing considerable consternation in Europe and sparking concern in the United States about German schemes.

As James Gerard, Washington's ambassador to Berlin, noted in his diary, "I think from underground rumours that the Germans and the propagandists will endeavour to embroil us with Japan."[11] Western insecurity over Japan's allegiance made the Allies much more amenable to Tokyo's demands in the Far East, precisely as Japanese policy makers intended. Japan's leaking of Germany's proposals to the Allies ultimately helped Tokyo secure a series of agreements with Russia, France, and Great Britain supporting Japanese claims to the former German possessions in China and the Pacific north of the equator.[12] As a result of Tokyo's double-dealing and Berlin's doubts about Japanese sincerity, the Japanese-German peace talks in Sweden petered out in late 1915.

While Foreign Secretary Jagow and Chancellor Bethmann grew disenchanted with the Japanese, German military leaders continued to call for a rapprochement with Tokyo. In December 1915, Admiral Henning von Holtzendorff, chief of the German naval staff, advocated a separate peace with Japan that, he argued, would undermine the Allies and compel Britain to divert precious naval forces from the North Sea and the Atlantic to the Pacific.[13] Holtzendorff and others who supported renewed efforts to engage the Japanese diplomatically soon found a valuable ally in Hans Arthur von Kemnitz,[14] who assumed responsibility for the foreign office's East Asian division in April 1916 and would play a leading role in events surrounding the Zimmermann telegram.

Born on August 17, 1870, in Charlottenburg, now a west Berlin neighborhood, Hans Arthur von Kemnitz hailed from a conservative, Protestant military family. His father, Albert von Kemnitz, was a Prussian officer, and respect for the military became a deeply ingrained trait of the younger Kemnitz. Seventy-five years of age at the end of World War II, Arthur still revered "our old Prussian and German military forces and the spirit they had. . . . [T]hat spirit was a spirit of Christianism [sic] and honor."[15] Politically, he sympathized with the chauvinistic Pan-German movement, and his narrow, ultranationalist views would remain basically unchanged throughout his life.[16]

Kemnitz attended prestigious public secondary schools (Gymnasien) in Charlottenburg and Tilsit, a town at the extreme northeastern tip of East Prussia, and then studied law and political science at universities in Freiburg, Berlin, and Leipzig. In 1890 he served one year in the elite Royal Prussian 2nd Guards Ulan Cavalry Regiment and eventually acquired the rank of cavalry captain of the reserve. In 1901 he entered the consular service and served briefly with the Prussian ministry at the Vatican. Like Zimmermann, he managed to transfer to the more prestigious diplomatic service two years later, in 1903. The two men developed close ties, and Kemnitz would eventually become Zimmermann's protégé.[17] In 1909, Kemnitz married Laura née Freiin von Rosenberg, the daughter of another aristocratic Prussian officer.

A federal salary typically did not cover all the costs incurred by a member of the diplomatic corps, and Kemnitz later complained that the switch put a heavy financial burden on his parents.[18] During his prewar career, he completed tours in Constantinople (1904), Lisbon (1905–1906), Beijing (1906–1908), and Madrid (1910–1912). In January 1913, he took over the South and Central America department at the Wilhelmstrasse while holding the title of permanent assistant (*Ständiger Hilfsarbeiter*). The department's responsibilities included Mexican affairs.[19]

By most accounts, Kemnitz's performance as a diplomat was subpar. In 1905, for example, a group of German politicians sought to open a casino on the Portuguese island of Madeira, in the Atlantic. Designed to rival the famed Monte Carlo, the project was to include gambling halls, hotels, parks, and swimming pools. Investors put significant funds into the scheme, but the land for the envisioned complex belonged to an Englishman who refused to sell. When local authorities threatened the English landlord with dispossession, he turned to the Portuguese government, which vetoed the looming expropriation and halted the project altogether. German investors and politicians then pulled some strings at the Wilhelmstrasse, and soon thereafter the German legation in Lisbon received a letter from Berlin with instructions to put pressure on the Portuguese government to withdraw its veto. The chancellor had not signed the instructions and probably was unaware of the situation. An experienced diplomat doubtlessly would have asked for clarification on this delicate affair, especially since Germany had just sustained a major diplomatic defeat at the hands of France and Britain at the Algeciras conference, whose participants agreed to turn Morocco into a French protectorate, against Germany's wishes. A clash with London over a casino in Madeira was the last thing Berlin needed at this point.

The German envoy in Lisbon was absent when the fateful foreign office dispatch reached Portugal, and Kemnitz happened to be the official in charge in his stead. Without further consultations, he immediately demanded from the Portuguese government the withdrawal of its veto, triggering a minor international crisis. Annoyed, Lisbon contacted Washington and London, and the infuriated British ambassador to Berlin demanded an explanation from the chancellor. The latter denied knowledge of the affair, effectively burying the casino project and exposing Kemnitz as naive and careless. When subsequently discussing the subject with a member of the German embassy in London, Britain's King Edward VII merely shrugged and smiled as if to say, "By God, what a small horizon that diplomat [Kemnitz] had!"[20]

In the summer of 1914, the Wilhelmstrasse chose Kemnitz to succeed Hintze as envoy to Mexico. However, the routine medical checkup performed in preparation for this posting revealed a heart condition that made him unfit for permanent residence and work in the high altitude of Mexico City. Kemnitz, therefore, remained at his desk job in Berlin. When war broke out, the armed forces enrolled all foreign office permanent assistants of appropriate age, and Kemnitz rejoined his old regiment, the 2nd Guards Ulan Cavalry. He served in the army for nearly two years, saw frontline duty, and received two medals, the Iron Cross, First Class, and the Iron Cross, Second Class. Eventually, the foreign office requested his return to Berlin, and he reassumed his job, now with the title *Referatsleiter* (department chief) of the Latin American division, on April 8, 1916. The geographical responsibility of this department had slightly changed, however. It now included East Asia but explicitly excluded Mexico, which was part of the North American division under Montgelas.[21]

Kemnitz's return to the Wilhelmstrasse coincided with the resumption of Japanese-German negotiations for a separate peace. The Germans had never entirely abandoned hope for an agreement with Japan. In 1915 the negotiations in Stockholm had been conducted exclusively by an intermediary, but when the Japanese envoy to Stockholm, Uchida, indicated his willingness to meet in person with his German colleague, Lucius, the Wilhelmstrasse forged ahead. On April 1, 1916, Uchida and Lucius met for a two-hour session at the Grand Hotel in Stockholm. The meeting had been arranged by Hugo Stinnes, a wealthy German industrialist, who also attended the meeting.[22] The three participants wrote diverging accounts of the discussions, but their statements agree on two points. First, Uchida explained that Japan did not want to conclude a separate peace because of its alliance with Britain. Second, the participants nevertheless discussed the possibility of initiating talks between Russia, Japan, and Germany. Whatever Uchida told the Germans, his remarks were sufficiently ambivalent to stoke hopes in Berlin for severing Japan, and possibly even Russia, from the enemy alliance. The chancellor's secretary expressed admiration for the "delightful brutality" of the negotiating skills of the "yellow fellows."[23] The Japanese envoy reinforced German expectations when he met with Lucius for a second time, on April 24, at the residence of the Japanese consul in Stockholm. As Lucius reported to Berlin, Uchida was much less reserved at this meeting than he had been three weeks earlier.[24]

Kemnitz did not initiate this second round of talks, but he wholeheartedly endorsed them and pushed them forward. Picking up on Uchida's tantalizing hints about a far-reaching agreement between Berlin, Tokyo, and St. Petersburg, Kemnitz on May 17 drafted detailed territorial concessions in the Pacific that Germany should make to Japan and Russia in an effort to pry both nations from the Allies.[25] Zimmermann agreed with Kemnitz. In his opinion, Germany's colonial possessions in the Pacific were a liability due to the difficulty of defending them in the case of war. Instead, "Africa must be our goal. . . . May the Japanese and Americans be left to themselves in the Pacific, England's days there should also be numbered."[26]

Yet the Japanese were up to their old game of playing the Germans off against the Allies. While encouraging the Germans to make concrete proposals, Tokyo leaked the substance of the talks to London in order to raise the Japanese bargaining position vis-à-vis the Allies. As they were not interested in a formal agreement with the Germans, the Japanese prevaricated in their negotiations with German diplomats, frustrating the Wilhelmstrasse, and led the exasperated foreign secretary to lament the difficulty of getting anything out of "these lying and taciturn Japanese." Sensing Tokyo's double-dealing, Jagow warned political and military leaders in early May that Japan would "seize the present opportunity, while the European powers' hands are tied by the war," to realize "its ambitious plans" in the Far East.[27]

Jagow was right on the mark. A few days after he had issued his warning, Tokyo instructed Uchida to inform the Germans orally that Japan could not enter into peace negotiations with Berlin and that any German peace proposal would have to be directed jointly to Japan, France, Russia, and Britain. Uchida informed Lucius accordingly. Infuriated, the Wilhelmstrasse terminated the negotiations, and Kaiser Wilhelm II, in one of his infamous outbursts, noted that there was no point in negotiating with the Japanese because "[o]ne can get more by thrashing them!"[28] Not all German officials drew the same conclusion, however.

Kemnitz noted that he had "expected" this response from Tokyo.[29] In hindsight, he laid the blame for the failure of the Stockholm talks at Berlin's doorstep rather than Tokyo's. "We were partially responsible" for the rupture, he wrote. "In spite of my continuous urging, our side had pursued [the talks] far too tepidly, and when Japan consequently declared that it could not conclude a separate peace, but that it would be ready, as the least involved Allied power, to bring about a general peace, this proposal was rejected by us, without even hearing me, 'because we did not need Japan for this purpose, but could have this every day cheaper from England.'" Had the Wilhelmstrasse only followed his counsel of pursuing Japan more vigorously, Kemnitz argued, the war could have been ended in 1916.[30]

In fact, some German officials continued to chase the Japanese mirage even after Uchida's notification of May 1916 and the conclusion of a separate Japanese-Russian agreement in July 1916. Military and naval leaders anticipated U.S. intervention in response to Germany's unrestrained use of U-boats, and they hoped that Japan could be used to neutralize the looming American threat.[31] While the chancellor and foreign secretary cautioned against the overestimation of Japanese power and the political consequences of unrestricted submarine warfare, not every foreign office official concurred with the civilian leadership. Kemnitz, for one, remained steadfast in his conviction that an agreement with Tokyo was the key to "a satisfactory conclusion of the war" and kept urging his superiors to restart negotiations with the Japanese.[32]

In a July 1916 memorandum, Kemnitz argued that Tokyo's next goal would be Japanese domination in the Pacific or the implementation of an "East Asian Monroe Doctrine." If Germany permanently abandoned all political aspirations in the Pacific, he reasoned, "we would over time become the wooed and it would be in our hands to side either with Japan or with England. I would recommend the former."[33]

In spite of the earlier frustrations of negotiating with the Japanese, the German leadership endorsed Kemnitz's proposal. In preparation for yet another overture to Tokyo, Berlin directed the German press to tone down criticism of Japan, omit racist buzzwords, such as the ubiquitous "yellow peril," and avoid taking China's side when reporting on Japanese activities in East Asia. Not surprisingly, these steps yielded no tangible results. By late 1916, Berlin realized the failure of its press campaign and appeasement policy vis-à-vis Tokyo and abandoned both.[34]

Stubborn as ever, Kemnitz remained undeterred. When his mentor Zimmermann succeeded the cautious Jagow as foreign secretary in November 1916, he saw yet another opportunity to resurrect his pet project. In view of the failure of the talks with Uchida in Stockholm, Kemnitz began to focus on neutral Mexico as an alternative route for engaging Tokyo. Even though Mexico did not officially fall into Kemnitz's purview, he had developed a certain expertise on it during the prewar years, and he continued to exhibit an interest in Mexican politics. Kemnitz's persistent pursuit of a separate peace with Tokyo now joined his old area of responsibility to his new one. As he explained in 1918, he was bent on "correcting" the Wilhelmstrasse's supposed bungling of the

German-Japanese talks: "[S]ince my repeated suggestions to approach Japan directly did not fall on a fertile soil with my superiors, because they did not want to 'chase after' Japan, I proposed to go through Mexico, which for over ten years had close relations with Japan."[35]

Indeed, Japanese-Mexican relations had traditionally been close and were molded by a mutual suspicion of the United States. As early as 1910, the German military attaché to Washington had reported that Mexican-Japanese relations had grown noticeably more cordial in response to alleged U.S. schemes to annex all of Mexico. A year later, Montgelas, then attached to the German embassy in Tokyo, discounted the possibility of such an alliance, but in May 1914, the German naval attaché to Washington, in a dispatch titled "Fear of Japan," reported American rumors that "the entire U.S. Navy strike force has been assembled in Mexican waters as a precaution against a third power. The country usually named is Japan, occasionally Germany."[36] Moreover, Japanese companies had developed certain economic interests in Mexico in the early twentieth century, and when the Mexican Revolution broke out, Tokyo called for a strong central government to stabilize the country. The Japanese also had to take into account the presence of a growing number of its citizens in Mexico, many of whom had ended up south of the Rio Grande due to restrictions imposed on Asian immigrants by the United States."[37]

It was Mexico, however, not Japan, that pushed for closer political ties between the two nations. In May 1916, shortly after General John Pershing's troops had entered Mexico, the Carranza regime approached Japan, probing for a possible alliance, the purchase of arms, and mediation with Washington. The Japanese chargé d'affaires, Tamekichi Ohta, remained non-committal to Carranza's foreign minister, Cándido Aguilar, and forwarded his inquiry to Tokyo. On May 13, the Japanese foreign ministry responded that Tokyo would neither arbitrate between Mexico and the United States nor provide arms to the Carranza regime.[38]

Undeterred, Venustiano Carranza assembled a secret military mission, under the direction of Colonel Rafael Vargas and Lieutenant Angel Guitiérez Astraege, and tasked them to travel to Japan for large-scale arms purchases. They arrived there in late July and received a mixed welcome. While the Japanese ministry of the navy went to great lengths to accommodate the Mexicans, the foreign ministry gave them the cold shoulder. Eventually, Vargas signed contracts with several Japanese companies for the purchase of 30 million cartridges as well as machinery for manufacturing gunpowder and a cartridge factory. The *New York Times* concluded that these purchases would ensure the Carranza regime's independence from foreign ammunition suppliers.[39]

As the *New York Times* coverage of the "secret" Mexican military mission's endeavors in Japan indicates, its operations remained hardly covert. As the desk officer responsible for handling Japanese affairs at the Wilhelmstrasse, Kemnitz closely followed this Mexican mission in Japan. He also simultaneously tracked the "mission" of the self-styled Mexican emissary Gonzalo Enrile in Germany, and thus became familiar with his proposals regarding an alliance with Japan. At the time, Kemnitz terminated Enrile's endeavors with the words, "no interest in Enrile here. Please decline amicably."[40] However, Enrile's various proposals evidently struck a chord with Kemnitz for he would subsequently use elements thereof in a diplomatic initiative of his own.

In reality, a formal Mexican-Japanese alliance against the United States remained as unlikely as Germany's quest for a separate peace with Japan proved elusive, yet both Mexico and Japan continued to loom large in the imagination of German officials. The kaiser himself suggested to Zimmermann that Germany approach Mexico in order to stir up trouble against the United States,[41] and military leaders continued to believe in the feasibility of a German-Japanese alignment. Kemnitz shared these views. Moreover, Japan was the only country within Kemnitz's regional responsibility at the foreign office that potentially allowed him to influence German war policy. The resumption of unrestricted submarine warfare in early 1917 would open a window for Kemnitz to turn his pursuit of a separate peace with Japan into a formal diplomatic initiative and override earlier objections to this scheme by the foreign office leadership.

Chapter Five

DRAFTING THE TELEGRAM

Before the outbreak of war, the German navy had high hopes for its vaunted surface battle fleet, arguably the most modern of its day and second only to Britain's in size. German and British vessels had occasional skirmishes in the North Sea and across the globe during the first months of the war, but London and Berlin were reluctant to risk their fleets in an all-out engagement for fear of irrevocably losing control of the sea to the enemy. Instead, the Royal Navy imposed a distant blockade on German seaports, with the goal of suppressing Germany's trade with neutral nations outside Europe. With their high seas fleet effectively bottled up in the North Sea, the Germans turned to the submarine to strike at British commerce. German naval leaders hoped that by attacking merchant ships sailing to and from British seaports, the U-boats would be able to throttle British trade and starve London into surrender.

Tactically, the submarine worked most effectively when U-boat commanders were given permission to attack indiscriminately and without forewarning, regardless of whether a ship was armed or the flag it flew. The unrestrained employment of U-boats would eventually be termed "unrestricted submarine warfare." Such stealth attacks, however, frequently resulted in the loss of neutral ships and lives and provoked angry protests from neutral nations. Hence, during the first years of the war, a debate unfolded in Germany over the pros and cons of unrestricted submarine warfare. Chancellor Theobald von Bethmann Hollweg, Foreign Secretary Gottlieb von Jagow, and Johann Heinrich von Bernstorff, German ambassador to Washington, consistently pointed out the political hazards of this tactic, especially its potential for antagonizing the

United States. Naval officers, on the other hand, routinely brushed aside the civilians' concerns, arguing that the submarines would vanquish Britain before U.S. intervention could become effective.

In late 1916, the debate over unrestricted submarine warfare entered its final stage. Whipped up by a skillful navy propaganda campaign, a war-weary public began to regard the submarine as a miracle weapon that promised to bring "perfidious Albion" to its knees and end the war in a few months' time. The new leadership of the army's supreme command (Oberste Heeresleitung, OHL) unreservedly embraced their naval colleagues' arguments, putting tremendous pressure on the chancellor and foreign secretary. With Bernstorff's encouragement, Bethmann floated the possibility of reaching a negotiated peace in a speech delivered to the Reichstag on December 12, but the Allies promptly rejected it. When, six days later, President Woodrow Wilson's offer of mediation between the warring parties also fell flat, the final showdown over unrestricted submarine warfare was at hand.[1]

The absence of a clear decision-making process at the top echelon of imperial Germany's leadership significantly aggravated the political crisis brought about by the debate over unrestricted submarine warfare. According to the German constitution, the kaiser had the final word on all issues of overriding strategic and political importance, but this seemingly impressive concentration of power in the hands of one man existed largely on paper. Even in times of peace, Kaiser Wilhelm II was neither a competent nor a strong monarch. Though intelligent and progressive in some respects, he was also insecure, arrogant, erratic, and enraptured by the medieval pomp and pageantry of his imperial court. His impulsiveness and saber rattling had contributed markedly to Germany's growing international isolation in the years preceding the war.

The war further diminished Wilhelm's standing. In late 1914, the kaiser took up residence variously at general headquarters at Charleville-Mézières, in northern France, or at the picturesque Pless castle, in Upper Silesia, an hours-long train ride from Berlin. He thus distanced himself from the political scene in Berlin and compounded his isolation from meddlesome politicians at times by refusing to receive civilian leaders and high-ranking diplomats—because they "made him nervous," as Gottfried zu Hohenlohe-Schillingfürst, the Austrian ambassador to Berlin, remarked.[2] Cut off from independent counsel, the kaiser grew increasingly detached from reality and more willing to bow to the military's wishes. By early 1917, monarchical rule relied de facto, if not de jure, on the military.

By law and by temperament, Chancellor Bethmann was ill-equipped to counterbalance the growing power of the military. Talented and somewhat of a progressive, he was also indecisive and prone to brooding. The constitution gave him no authority over the military, and he could not always count on the kaiser for support. In the absence of a mechanism to settle the differences of opinion that inevitably arose over tactics and strategy, the chancellor and military leaders sought to resolve issues by letter or, on important occasions, by conference. While a forceful personality might have been able to use these face-to-face meetings to retain some control over the military, the men in uniform more often than not upstaged the introverted Bethmann.

Military power in wartime Germany resided in the OHL, the highest echelon of command of the German armies. In August 1916, Field Marshall Paul von Hindenburg and his quartermaster general, General Erich Ludendorff, were appointed to direct the OHL. They proved a powerful combination. While Hindenburg, an old-school officer with a formidable mustache and crew cut, provided gravitas and respectability, the kinetic and pushy Ludendorff injected drive and energy. The two men had won a brilliant military victory over vastly numerically superior Russian forces invading in East Prussia in 1914 and were widely regarded as heroes in Germany.

General Ludendorff was the driving force of the OHL. If Hindenburg typified the traditional Prussian army officer, Ludendorff represented a new breed of technocratic soldiery, interested less in romantic heroism than in military hardware, less in loyalty to the crown than in logistics on the battlefield. Taking and turning on its head Clausewitz's dictum of war as the extension of politics by different means, Ludendorff advocated the subordination of politics to warfare, insisting that during wartime all resources of the nation must be made available to the military, a concept that would become infamously known as total war.

By most accounts, Ludendorff was not a likeable individual. People generally found him "tense, cold as a fish, a monocled humorless eye staring from a heavily jowled red face as he barked orders in a high, nasal voice, his second (later third) chin quivering from the effort. He was rigid and inflexible in thought, given to sudden rages, a table banger, frequently rude to subordinates, often tactless to superiors."[3] At the OHL, Ludendorff displayed little tolerance for opinions that differed from his own, especially if they came from civilians.

This was the toxic political environment that Zimmermann entered when he succeeded Jagow in November 1916. Even though the foreign secretary answered to the chancellor, the impatient Ludendorff expected Zimmermann to serve as a compliant tool of the OHL. After all, Zimmermann had earlier given the impression of sharing the military's viewpoint, especially with regard to unrestricted submarine warfare. Ludendorff was to be disappointed. On October 28, 1916, a German U-boat torpedoed and sank the British merchant ship *Marina* to the west of Ireland, killing several Americans. As Bethmann consulted with the chief of the admiralty staff, Admiral Henning von Holtzendorff, about the appropriate response to American protests, Ludendorff tried to insert himself into the talks. Zimmermann shut out the general by informing him pointedly that the text of the note to Washington had already been approved, leaving an irate Ludendorff exasperated by the new foreign secretary's abrasiveness.[4] Shortly thereafter, Zimmermann throttled the general again. On December 20, Ludendorff insisted that in view of British coolness toward a German peace initiative, "the U-boat campaign must now be inaugurated in full force." Zimmermann replied coolly, "At the moment there are serious objections to the unrestricted submarine campaign, not only on account of America, but with regard to European neutrals also."[5]

Bethmann, too, continued to express his reservation about the wisdom of unrestricted submarine warfare, but the relentless military pressure took its toll on the chancellor. As early as March 1916, a parliamentarian observed that the chancellor "was tense, tired, and nervous. He smoked one cigarette after another to quiet his nerves. To judge from the tempo at which he smoked during the committee proceedings, he must consume five or six dozen daily. His hair has become white, his face is lined with deep furrows. He seems the personification of despair."[6] An American diplomat gained a similar impression during an interview on November 22, with Bethmann "sitting at his desk, speaking slowly, deliberately and sadly of the horrors of war. He seemed to me a man broken in spirit, his face deeply furrowed, his manner sad beyond words."[7] By the end of December, events weighed so heavily on Bethmann that he largely withdrew from the decision-making process.

In early 1917, the military mounted its final push for unrestricted submarine warfare. On January 8, Holtzendorff met with Hindenburg and Ludendorff at Pless, and the three men reached an agreement. Should Bethmann continue to resist unrestricted submarine warfare, they would advocate for his replacement with a more compliant politician. After the meeting, Holtzendorff easily won over the kaiser at a personal audience, while Hindenburg informed Bethmann in a curt telegram that unrestricted submarine warfare could and therefore should be commenced on February 1. The chancellor immediately boarded a Pless-bound train. Suffering from a stubborn bout of bronchitis, he arrived the worse for wear after a tiring night journey. The chief of the naval cabinet, Admiral Georg von Müller, a friend of Bethmann and an erstwhile opponent of unrestricted submarine warfare, received him at the train station with the bad news that everything had already been settled in favor of U-boat war. A depressed Bethmann then headed for the castle where the determined military leadership awaited him.

The Pless crown council that convened at 6 p.m. on January 9 rubber-stamped the decision already made by the military men.[8] As Bethmann entered the room, the pale and distraught-looking kaiser, surrounded by his three cabinet chiefs, stood with one hand resting on a large table around which Holtzendorff, Ludendorff, and Hindenburg were gathered. Holtzendorff laid out confidently how the submarines would strangle England within six months, without a single American soldier reaching Europe. Thereafter, Hindenburg expressed his hope that the U-boats would restrict U.S. ammunition deliveries to the Allies. At last, Bethmann was permitted to say a few words. Agitated, he expressed his concern about American intervention, but he withdrew his opposition to unrestricted warfare in view of the navy's confidence in victory. The emperor listened impatiently to his chancellor and concluded that unrestricted submarine warfare was thus agreed upon. He went on to say that "it would be the diplomats' task to explain the necessity of this measure to America and the remaining neutrals." One participant commented succinctly in his diary: "Finis Germaniae."[9]

The decision for unrestricted submarine warfare taken at Pless left Zimmermann in an uncomfortable position. The political defeat of the chancellor heralded the final victory of the military over the civilian leadership that would dominate government decision making in imperial Germany for the remainder of the war. This was bad news for Zimmermann, who evidently had backed the wrong horse by siding with Bethmann on the question of U-boat warfare. Indeed, Ludendorff made no bones about his contempt for the new foreign secretary. On January 11, Ludendorff declared in a meeting with Hindenburg and Valentini that "in the long run they didn't think they could work with Bethmann and people like [Vice Chancellor Karl] Helfferich and Zimmermann." Evidently, Ludendorff very much associated Zimmermann with obstructionist "people like" Bethmann and Helfferich, the latter being one of the staunchest opponents of unrestricted submarine warfare among top government officials.[10]

Zimmermann reacted to the news of Pless by abruptly endorsing the new government policy. His radical turnaround failed, however, to appease the military and managed also to erode his standing with moderate civilians. A parliamentarian discussing the question of submarine warfare with Zimmermann at the time said he thought the foreign secretary acted "totally confused." Editors of several major Berlin newspapers began to describe him as a poor choice for foreign secretary,[11] and the chancellor's secretary, Kurt Riezler, privately lambasted him as a "frat boy and boor [*Korpsstudent und Prolet*]."[12] The liberal shipping magnate Albert Ballin, a personal friend of the kaiser, complained that Zimmermann "had not succeeded in breaking the aristocratic clique that now completely dominated him."[13]

One should not underestimate the psychological impact of such a sudden fall from grace on someone who thrived on working harmoniously with his superiors. Zimmermann's stress was on public display. On January 6, 1917, Zimmermann attended a reception with the Austro-Hungarian foreign minister, Ottokar Czernin, at the Austrian embassy, followed by a gala dinner at the Adlon Hotel for the U.S. ambassador, James Gerard, who had recently returned from the United States. At both events, Zimmermann's edginess got the better of him. At the Austrian embassy, he yelled and gesticulated wildly with his arms. Asked afterward about his impression of the foreign secretary, Czernin replied, "Well, we were always afraid that he would spit somewhere in the room."[14] By the time Zimmermann reached the Adlon, he was slightly inebriated. Toasting his friendship with Gerard, he praised their nations' good relations and added that he had always been convinced the ambassador would return "to the barbarians," a self-mocking reference to Germany.[15] Gottlieb von Jagow, who observed his successor's antics that evening with growing apprehension, called the dinner "inexpedient" and Zimmermann's toast "foolish," since Gerard was bound to feel let down when unrestricted submarine warfare—at this point a foregone conclusion—would be declared shortly thereafter.[16] Zimmermann's need to be in good standing with everyone, and his inability to steer a clear course, now turned against him, and the mental toll on him showed. A photograph taken at the Adlon dinner shows the foreign secretary looking haggard, aged, and weary.[17]

One historian observed that "the actions of some German leaders during these hectic days suggest nervous breakdown."[18] Evidently, the foreign secretary was one of these leaders, and his mental state must be considered a critical factor in his decision making during this time period.[19] When Zimmermann learned of the impending declaration of unrestricted submarine warfare, he had less than three weeks to prepare diplomatically for the measure. He needed to inform German envoys worldwide about the decision and send them instructions on how to deal with the political fallout from neutral powers, which would be severe. The Wilhelmstrasse awaited the American response with particular concern.

The facade of a united civilian leadership crumbled in the wake of the Pless decision. While Bethmann in Berlin resigned himself to his fate of playing second fiddle to the OHL, Bernstorff in Washington engaged in a round of desperate last-minute diplomacy to avert U.S. intervention. At the Wilhelmstrasse, an overtaxed Zimmermann relied mostly on his staff to hammer out instructions to German diplomats in the remaining neutral nations about the imminent submarine campaign.

The Zimmermann telegram was conceived amid this frantic scramble of German diplomats to prepare for the official announcement of unrestricted submarine warfare, set to begin on February 1. Although no official records on the origins of the telegram have survived, one participant—Hans Arthur von Kemnitz—left a detailed personal account, drafted a decade after the event, in 1927. Kemnitz's memorandum must be read with caution because it was composed with hindsight and for the purpose of putting the author in a favorable light. Since it remains the only firsthand account of the origins of the telegram and provides valuable insights into the foreign office decision-making process, it deserves to be quoted at length:

In early 1917, a decision was reached, initially in secret, in favor of unrestricted submarine warfare. Due to my familiarity with the prevailing sentiment in the United States, I could not doubt that the implementation of this decision would provoke war with America, and I realized that we were drifting into a political situation amounting to the epitome of the impossible: not only would our old enemies Russia and England fight against us as allies, now, also Japan and America, who were no less antagonistic towards each other, were supposed to oppose us in the field as allies. Therefore, I was considering options to approach Japan in the last hour.

It so happened that Mexico had proposed an alliance against the United States to us some time before, an offer that had been treated dilatorily until then. Since our relationship with America couldn't get any worse, I suggested at our daily joint conference of political advisors with the foreign secretary that we now accept this proposal in principle, and simultaneously tell the Mexicans that this offer would be significantly more valuable if they succeeded, in view of their 10-years old, intimate relations with Japan, to interest the latter in this issue. Even if I was not very optimistic for this initiative to succeed at this late hour, I still considered it my duty to leave no stone unturned in order to ameliorate our desperate military situation through diplomatic means.

I was instructed to conceptualize such a telegram, and did so. The draft was then submitted to Count Montgelas who . . . was responsible for Mexico.[20]

The document gives several important clues about the origins of the telegram: it was Kemnitz who came up with the idea for the Mexican-Japanese alliance scheme; he did so during a routine conference at the foreign office that took place shortly after the decision at Pless to proceed with unrestricted submarine warfare; his principal goal was not an alliance with Mexico, but with Japan; and he was aware of and made use of the earlier Mexican proposals to Berlin.

No minutes of this fateful foreign office conference have survived, but other contemporary sources confirm Kemnitz's central part in the scheme. In reaction to news reports about the telegram in American newspapers on March 1, 1917, Bethmann's secretary, Riezler, noted in his diary: "Kemnitz, this fantastic idiot, has done this."[21] Eleven days later, a foreign office official wrote to a colleague: "The father of this issue is Kemnitz, who pushed his idea through, against the resistance of the [foreign] office."[22] An internal foreign office report, completed shortly after the armistice, also confirmed Kemnitz's authorship.[23] Last but not least, Kemnitz himself repeatedly affirmed his intellectual ownership of the idea as well as his primary objective of the scheme, i.e., an alliance with Japan rather than Mexico.[24]

As instructed, Kemnitz drafted a proposal for alliance along the lines discussed during the conference (see Fig. 1). A careful study of this document corroborates and expands upon Kemnitz's 1927 memorandum. The text of Kemnitz's handwritten draft, with comments by several Wilhelmstrasse officials, translates into English as follows. Marginal comments, not included in the final draft, are indicated by brackets [ ]; italicized words indicate text subsequently added to the original draft; explanatory comments by this author are indicated by braces { }.

Berlin, 13 January 1917.

Minister {Heinrich} von Eckardt

Mexico

Most secret. Decipher yourself.

We intend to begin on the first of February unrestricted submarine warfare. We shall endeavor nonetheless to keep America neutral.

In the event of this not succeeding, we propose to Mexico an alliance on the following basis: Conduct war jointly. ~~and~~ Conclude peace *jointly*.

Substantial financial support and consent [No guarantee is expressed hereby] on our part for Mexico to reconquer lost territory in Texas, New Mexico, Arizona [California should be reserved for Japan]. ~~Defense treaty after conclusion of peace provided Mexico succeeds in drawing Japan into the alliance.~~ *The settlement in detail is left to your Excellency.*

Your Excellency will present to the President {Carranza} ~~immediately~~ the above most secretly *as soon as the outbreak of war with the United States is certain,* and add the suggestion that he should, on his own initiative, invite Japan to immediate adherence, and at the same time mediate between Japan and ourselves.

Please call the President's attention to the fact that ruthless employment of our submarines *now* offers the prospect of compelling England in a few months to make peace. . . .

{Initialed by Arthur Zimmermann, January 13; Wilhelm von Stumm, January 13; Baron Ernst Langwerth von Simmern, January 12; Count Adolf von Montgelas, January 12; Hans Arthur von Kemnitz, January 11.}[25]

The initials at the bottom of the text indicate that Kemnitz finalized his draft on January 11, two days after the fateful Pless meeting. It therefore took him only forty-eight hours, or less, to complete and submit the document. Given that the Wilhelmstrasse was comsumed with the diplomatic implications of unrestricted submarine warfare, one might assume that his idea was not the central item on the meeting's agenda and did not receive the careful attention it otherwise would have.

More interested in an alliance with Japan than with Mexico, Kemnitz was careful to explain that "California should be reserved for Japan." Moreover, he wanted to reward Mexico with a postwar defense alliance only if Carranza succeeded in bringing about a German-Japanese alliance, but another official subsequently deleted this provision. Kemnitz did not regard Mexico, unlike Japan, as an equal partner for Germany. Thus, he pointed out that the foreign office expressed "no guarantee" in promising financial support and consent for Mexico to conquer U.S. territory. In short, Mexico's main function was to build a bridge to Tokyo and attack the United States, but unlike Japan, it could not expect a binding wartime alliance or even financial guarantees from Germany in return.

Just as Kemnitz indicated in his 1927 memorandum, he almost certainly mined some of the Mexican papers at the Wilhelmstrasse for his proposal. In fact, there are striking textual similarities between his original draft and Enrile's

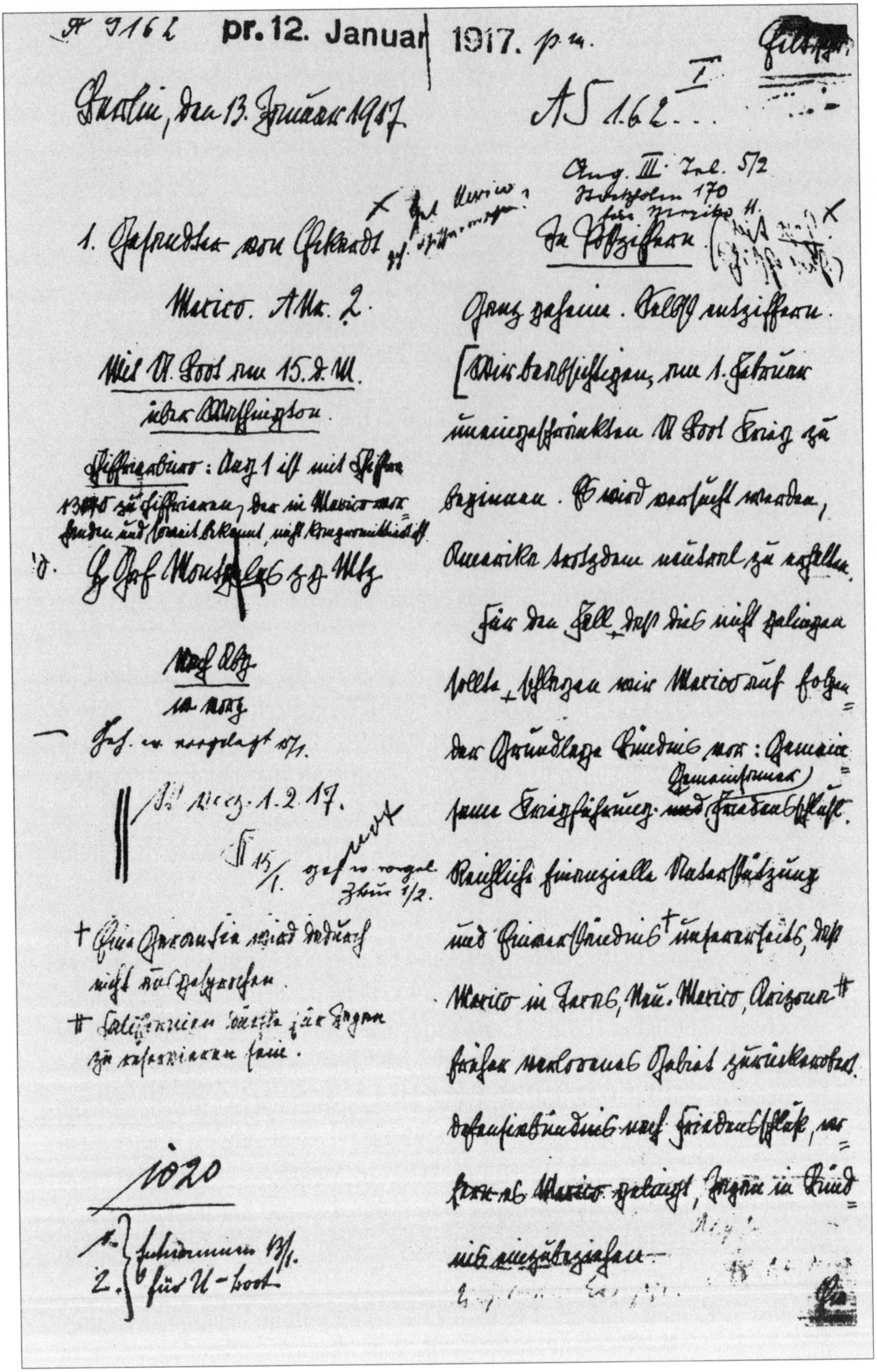

A 3162 pr. 12. Januar 1917. p.m.

Berlin, den 13. Januar 1917

A S 162

1. Gesandter von Eckardt

Mexico. Ang. 2.

Mit U-Boot am 15. d. M. über Washington

Ganz geheim. Selbst entziffern.

Wir beabsichtigen, am 1. Februar uneingeschränkten U-Boot Krieg zu beginnen. Es wird versucht werden, Amerika trotzdem neutral zu erhalten. Für den Fall, dass dies nicht gelingen sollte, schlagen wir Mexico auf folgender Grundlage Bündnis vor: Gemeinsame Kriegführung. Gemeinsamer Friedensschluss. Reichliche finanzielle Unterstützung und Einverständnis+ unsererseits, dass Mexico in Texas, Neu-Mexico, Arizona++ früher verlorenes Gebiet zurückerobert. [illegible]

+ Eine Garantie wird dadurch nicht übernommen.

++ Californien dürfte für Japan zu reservieren sein.

1020

1. } 2. } [illegible] 13/1. für U-boot

FIGURE 1. The original, handwritten draft of the Zimmermann telegram. (page 1 of 3) (Courtesy of the *Politisches Archiv des Auswärtigen Amtes*, Berlin)

The original, handwritten draft of the Zimmermann telegram. (page 2 of 3)

zwischen uns und Amerika zum Kriege
kommen, ein Bündnis anzubieten und
ihm gleichzeitig vorzuschlagen, Japan
von sich aus zum Beitritt einzuladen.

The original, handwritten draft of the Zimmermann telegram. (page 3 of 3) request for German financial support in exchange for a Mexican attack on the United States and the cession of U.S. territory to Mexico—specifically, Arizona, New Mexico, and Texas.[26] Enrile had also envisioned cession of "the southern part of Upper California" to Mexico, but Kemnitz preferred using this territory as bait for Japan.

The chronological sequence of initials at the bottom of the text indicates how the draft moved up the chain of command at the Wilhelmstrasse. Kemnitz passed it first to Montgelas, who signed it on January 12, and then again on January 15 (in its final form).[27] The draft gives no indication of Montgelas' take on the scheme, so one can only speculate based on circumstantial evidence. It is true that, in the wake of Pancho Villa's raid on Columbus, New Mexico, Montgelas had vainly urged the Wilhelmstrasse to intervene more aggressively in Mexico in order to distract Washington from Europe. However, the international framework had changed significantly since then, with the U.S. punitive expedition winding down and unrestricted submarine warfare about to commence. Most likely, Montgelas spent little time on the scheme as he was at this time hammering out an all-important note on behalf of the chancellor, who on January 16 would send it, along with the telegram, to Bernstorff in Washington, issuing the ambassador instructions in preparation for unrestricted submarine warfare.

The draft then passed to Ernst Langwerth von Simmern, who directly supervised Kemnitz and Montgelas. The scion of an aristocratic family from the Rhineland, Langwerth had entered the foreign service in 1899, working at the German legations in Athens, Lisbon, Tangier, and Berne before the war. In 1916 he became director of the political division of the foreign office.[28] Several contemporary sources report that Kemnitz's proposal met resistance as it traveled through the foreign office hierarchy, and Langwerth appears to be one of the critics.[29] While Kemnitz's original draft would have instructed Eckardt, the envoy in Mexico, to "immediately" approach Carranza, that is, even before an American declaration of war on Germany, Langwerth objected to this aggressive provision, deleting and replacing it with the phrase "as soon as the outbreak of war with the United States is certain." Thus, he gave the scheme a defensive character that Kemnitz had not envisioned.[30] Langwerth signed the draft on January 12, the same day he received it, and passed it on to Wilhelm von Stumm, who had succeeded Zimmermann as undersecretary of state.

"Reticent, conservative, but with lots of brains," according to the American ambassador, the eccentric Stumm was somewhat of a maverick.[31] In his mid-fifties, he had just become engaged to a twenty-year-old countess. A seasoned diplomat, Stumm had served in London, Washington, Paris, Vienna, and St. Petersburg prior to the war, but some of Stumm's colleagues considered him a malevolent éminence grise. A former German ambassador to London deplored his influence and described him as "forceful and a fantast."[32] A former foreign secretary denounced Stumm as "an evil spirit, a pathological human being who completely dominates Jagow."[33] Perhaps because of Stumm's alleged tendency to "dominate" his superiors, Zimmermann put him on a tight leash and excluded him from critical decision making.[34] Kemnitz's draft appears to be a case in point, as there is no indication that Stumm added much, if anything at all. According to the chancellor's secretary, Stumm simply "said yes," signed the document on January 13, and passed it on to Zimmermann.[35]

Like Stumm, Zimmermann spent hardly any time considering the scheme. He left no comment on the draft and signed off on the document the same day he received it. It remains unclear why the foreign secretary sanctioned this improbable alliance offer and what he hoped to achieve by it. The kaiser had suggested some sort of Mexican alliance scheme to Zimmermann earlier, and the foreign secretary, ever keen to please those in authority, naturally would have been eager to follow up on Wilhelm's suggestion when the possibility presented itself.[36] The idea of approaching Japan also likely appealed to Zimmermann, who in 1916 had supported Kemnitz's push for a separate peace with Tokyo. In the context of German domestic politics, the scheme could serve as tangible proof of the Wilhelmstrasse's commitment to supporting unrestricted submarine warfare, and Zimmermann may have hoped to take the edge off of Ludendorff's wrath against him by endorsing it.

Likewise, the idea of embroiling the United States in a guerrilla war along its southern border must have intrigued Zimmermann. As a long-standing proponent of Berlin's worldwide covert action program, and given his past management of such operations, Zimmermann would have been naturally drawn to the idea of tying up U.S. troops in this way. In fact, Wilhelmstrasse officials had avidly read intelligence reports about the failure of the U.S. punitive expedition to catch Villa, and Zimmermann thought Carranza could pull off a similar feat. "Mexico is not to be underestimated as an enemy," he declared before the Reichstag's budget committee on March 3, shortly after the alliance proposal had been published in the American press. Two days later, he elaborated "that the instruction aimed at prompting Carranza to attack after the outbreak of war in order to tie up the American mercenaries in America." At the same time, Zimmermann was careful to stress that Berlin incurred no obligations in return: "A proposal is not yet a treaty," he added. Hence, if Carranza attacked the United States, and the latter eventually prevailed, Germany would have no legal obligation to come to its partner's rescue.[37] To think that Carranza would fall for this ploy appears naive in retrospect, but Zimmermann was not alone in considering this possibility. The British envoy in Mexico, for one, noted in mid-February that Carranza "is contemplating taking Germany's side in case of war between US + Germany. All Carranza's generals besides being pro-German [are] ignorant enough to believe that they could defeat the United States + they are likely to be exceptionally confident if they have received promises of active support from Germany."[38]

Last but not least, Zimmermann's inability to perform well under stress and his frantic efforts to prepare diplomatically for unrestricted submarine warfare probably prevented him from reviewing Kemnitz's draft carefully. His lack of interest at the time is evidenced by both the short amount of time he took to sign off on it as well as the absence of original input. Yet, by signing it, he endorsed and assumed political responsibility for the scheme. The final document differed somewhat from Kemnitz's original draft in that the scheme's emphasis had tilted from Japan to Mexico and envisioned an alliance in response to, rather than in anticipation of, American intervention. The text as finalized on January 13 comprised four key elements:

First, the German envoy to Mexico was instructed secretly to propose an alliance to Mexico as soon as the United States' entry into the war on the Allied side was considered imminent. The precise moment was left vague, and the German envoy was given considerable leeway—"The settlement in detail is left to your Excellency"—probably because the Wilhelmstrasse anticipated the closing of the German embassy in Washington and, consequently, a communications breakdown between Berlin and Mexico City. The alliance proposal reveals that Zimmermann considered Washington's declaration of war in the near future possible, albeit not necessarily probable. Yet rather than try to prevent it, he began to plan for its eventuality.

Second, the Germans sought to lure Mexico with the prospect of unspecified financial assistance and conquest of U.S. territory. The text did not, however, name a specific sum of money, and Kemnitz's marginal note stated, "No guarantee is expressed hereby." The nature of German support for Mexico's conquest of Arizona, New Mexico, and Texas remained equally obscure. For one, the text spoke of "lost territory *in* Texas, New Mexico, Arizona," being non-committal about the extent of U.S. territory Berlin was willing to help Mexico conquer—be it a strip of land along the border or the entirety of the three mentioned states. Moreover, the text employed the non-committal phrase

"Einverständnis unsererseits, dass Mexico . . . zurückerobert" (consent on our part for Mexico to reconquer), though contemporary English translations, and subsequent authors, have given this passage a subtly different slant. For example, the text published in many American newspapers on March 1, 1917, read "it is understood that Mexico is to reconquer."[39] Barbara Tuchman, in her classic account, translates it as "an understanding on our part that Mexico is to reconquer."[40] Such faulty translations suggest erroneously that Germany encouraged Mexico to attack the United States, whereas the original document merely expressed Berlin's non-committal consent to what the Wilhelmstrasse perceived as Mexican ambitions.[41] Before the Reichstag's secret budget committee on March 5, Zimmermann made it clear that the three U.S. states were merely a carrot to egg on Carranza to attack the United States: "That the Mexicans were not in a position to make conquests in the United States, is clear to me, too. I merely wanted to prompt the Mexicans through this encouragement to invade the said provinces [i.e., states] in order to tie up American troops and thus prevent them from being sent to Germany."[42]

Third, the Wilhelmstrasse encouraged the Mexican president to approach Tokyo with a view to create a German-Japanese alliance. This had been Kemnitz's principal goal, and Zimmermann certainly did not rule out the possibility of a Japanese attack on the United States: "I do not know whether Japan has given America assurance that she will not stab her in the back. It is rumored, and I do not believe that it is impossible," he opined to the budget committee on February 22, 1917.[43] However, in his explanations before the budget committee on March 5, he clearly designated Mexico the main addressee of the proposal, with Japan merely an afterthought: "I considered the mentioning of Japan necessary since the Mexican-Japanese relations are old and well-founded. On the basis of top secret information on Japanese-German attempts to come to an agreement I concluded that an agreement with Japan cannot be ruled out entirely."[44]

Fourth, the German envoy was to emphasize his nation's confidence in a quick, victorious end to the war, thanks to unrestricted submarine warfare. The document's concluding statement that "ruthless employment of our submarines *now* offers the prospect of compelling England in a few months to make peace" may have been addressed as much to Carranza as to Ludendorff and the German military, in an effort to reestablish their confidence in Zimmermann. The foreign secretary probably had the same domestic audience in mind when he explained before the budget committee on March 5 that "it was important to me not to set new enemies on our brave field gray troops, and at least ensure that the American mercenaries . . . will immediately be employed against Mexico."[45]

When Zimmermann signed off on the draft, two practical issues needed to be resolved: Whom should he inform of the scheme outside the Wilhelmstrasse, and how should the text be conveyed to Eckardt in Mexico City? The foreign secretary was constitutionally required to consult the chancellor on major foreign policy initiatives. The telegram certainly fell within this category. Chancellor Bethmann maintains complete silence on the subject in his memoirs, but his secretary, Riezler, notes in his diary on March 4, 1917, "and the chancellor has approved the matter only orally." Riezler, however, later crossed out this sentence.[46] Why did he initially write that Bethmann had been informed, but later delete the statement? Evidently, Riezler was somewhat confused about when the chancellor had become aware of the scheme, but at some point he learned that Bethmann had *not* been informed of the matter *before* the Wilhelmstrasse had sent the telegram.

An anonymous German article, published shortly before the end of the war, sheds further light on this issue. In the *Nürnberger Nachrichten*, the author—obviously well connected in the foreign office—suggests that Zimmermann had informed Bethmann after the telegram had been dispatched, but before it was published in the American press on March 1.[47] In his memoirs, Jagow recalls that Zimmermann tended to execute "minor political business without asking me," and at this point, Zimmermann may well have considered the telegram "minor political business," as compared to the diplomatic preparations in advance of unrestricted submarine warfare.[48] Zimmermann's negligence in informing Bethmann immediately may have been encouraged by the chancellor's reclusion in the days following Pless. If so, the foreign secretary's failure to clear the proposal with the chancellor was less an act of deliberate disobedience than of sloppiness. The available evidence suggests that Zimmermann did inform Bethmann of the telegram before the American press reported on it.

What about the military? Constitutionally, Zimmermann had no obligation to inform Ludendorff or any other top military officer of a diplomatic initiative by the foreign office. Yet, this is what he did. Franz von Papen, Germany's wartime military attaché in the United States, wrote to his former naval colleague, Karl Boy-Ed, in 1919: "General Ludendorff personally reassured me that he was informed of the idea of the alliance proposal to Mexico only after the fact. State Secretary Zimmermann talked to him only of financial authorization regarding the insurgent war. This plan therefore stems exclusively from the brain of the then-adviser for Mexico and State Secretary Zimmermann.

Perhaps Mr. [Erich] Hossenfelder, on account of his in-depth knowledge of the American situation, advised Zimmermann in favor of this initiative."[49]

A military man loyal to Ludendorff, Papen understandably sought to distance the general from the unpopular telegram. His acknowledgment that Ludendorff had discussed insurgent warfare in Mexico with Zimmermann must therefore be taken as evidence that the foreign secretary did mention the Mexican scheme to the general, if only in passing. It appears that in the hectic days following the decision to launch unrestricted submarine warfare, Zimmermann relayed much of the information on this risky project orally and fragmentarily. That Zimmermann decided to inform Ludendorff at all about the scheme highlights his resolve to put himself in good standing with the general.

There remained the question of communicating the text to Carranza. An obvious channel would have been Carranza's envoy to Germany, Rafael Zubáran Capmany. However, Zubáran Capmany was in Switzerland at the time. Even if he had been in Berlin, Zimmermann probably would not have availed himself of his services because the envoy spoke no German, and the Wilhelmstrasse did not fully trust his translator.[50] Consequently, the Germans had to come up with another channel for communicating with Carranza.

This task initially fell to Kemnitz. His pertinent instructions on the original draft read as follows: "By U-boat on the 15th via Washington. To the cipher bureau: Document 1 is to be encrypted with code 13040, which is available in Mexico and, as far as is known, is not compromised."[51] In other words, Kemnitz wanted the document delivered by submarine to Washington, where Ambassador Bernstorff's staff would encrypt it, using code 13040, and wire it to Mexico City. A note, dated January 13, on the original document indicates that an official had indeed removed the document with the intention of taking it on board a U-boat, the merchant submarine *Deutschland*, at Bremerhaven. The *Deutschland* had already crossed the Atlantic twice, circumventing the British naval blockade, delivering diplomatic mail and a codebook to the German embassy in Washington, and carrying dyestuffs, chemicals, and medicines to Germany on its return. The boat was scheduled to sail for the United States a third time, but the formal decision in favor of unrestricted submarine warfare threw a wrench into its projected third voyage. The navy was considering requisitioning the *Deutschland* for war duty, so on January 20, the chief of the admiralty staff ordered preparations for the journey suspended. Shortly thereafter, the navy requisitioned the boat, outfitting it for combat.[52]

Kemnitz's plan to send the proposal by sea provides insight into the political considerations of the Wilhelmstrasse vis-à-vis unrestricted submarine warfare and the United States. As it would have taken the *Deutschland* roughly three weeks to cross the Atlantic, it would not have reached U.S. shores before mid-February. By this time, unrestricted submarine warfare would have been in full swing, therefore the foreign office did not consider a consequent rupture of diplomatic relations (let alone war) probable because the diplomats expected the German embassy in Washington to still be functioning normally in mid-February, enabling Bernstorff's staff to collect the document and forward it to Eckardt in Mexico City.

With the *Deutschland* out of the picture, the foreign office needed an alternative route. It was Montgelas who decided to attach the document to top secret telegram no. 157, containing instructions for Bernstorff regarding the imminent declaration of unrestricted submarine warfare.[53] The attached telegram received the running number "telegram no. 158," and an explanatory sentence for Bernstorff was added, asking him to encode and forward the message to Eckardt in Mexico City. Still, how were the two messages to be conveyed securely to Washington? The Wilhelmstrasse displayed both ingenuity and chutzpah in finding a solution.

Early in the war, the Royal Navy had severed Germany's transatlantic submarine cables, complicating communications between Washington and Berlin. At the instigation of Edward M. House, adviser to President Woodrow Wilson, the State Department then began to allow the transmission of enciphered German messages on its diplomatic cables between Washington, London, Copenhagen, and Berlin. Trusting in the Germans' good faith, the Americans accepted numerous encrypted messages without being knowledgeable of their actual content. The Wilhelmstrasse would submit an encrypted message in Berlin to the American ambassador, who would transmit it to Copenhagen to the American legation, which would then forward it to the State Department in Washington via the U.S. embassy in London. In Washington, the State Department would hand the encrypted message to the German embassy. The Germans used this route in both directions. Bernstorff availed himself of this option as early as November 12, 1914, and the volume of messages increased greatly in 1915, when the sinking of the *Lusitania* and the resulting high volume of diplomatic notes between the Wilson administration and the German government made a reliable means of communication for both governments imperative.[54]

Montgelas suggested the Machiavellian idea of using the U.S. diplomatic service to convey the instructions on unrestricted submarine warfare as well as the telegram to Bernstorff. The Wilhelmstrasse rolled the two messages into one encrypt, using the recently introduced diplomatic code 0075. On January 16, Montgelas forwarded the encrypt to the American ambassador, Gerard, who noted that he would only send it to Washington if the Wilhelmstrasse disclosed the content. Without missing a beat, Montgelas replied that the encrypt "included merely an instruction for Count B. for his personal information." He then advised Zimmermann and Stumm to toe the same line vis-à-vis the U.S. ambassador. This assurance was good enough for Gerard, who, blissfully unaware of the diplomatic bombshell in his hands, immediately had the encoded text wired to Copenhagen and on to London.[55] On January 19, the telegram reached the German embassy in Washington. On the same day, Ambassador Bernstorff's staff deciphered it, re-enciphered it in code 13040, and sent it to Eckardt in Mexico City, using the commercial cable company Western Union, which charged the embassy the princely sum of $85.27, more than $1,000 in today's dollars.[56]

Following dispatch of the telegram on January 16, the Wilhelmstrasse for more than two weeks did nothing to develop the Mexican or Japanese angle of the project. Zimmermann's failure to follow up on his original proposal indicates its low priority among the German diplomats. Only the rapidly deteriorating German-U.S. relationship prompted the foreign office to take up the scheme once again.

Despite the decision on unrestricted submarine warfare, key German players did not consider a diplomatic break, or war, with the United States a foregone conclusion. On January 12, the Bavarian military representative at general headquarters reported to Munich that his colleagues did not think "that forceful submarine warfare will automatically trigger the break of relations with America."[57] Zimmermann shared this naive assessment. On January 30, he informed the American ambassador about the imminence of unrestricted submarine warfare and added cheerfully, "But as you will see, everything will be all right. America will do nothing, for President Wilson is for peace and nothing else."

After the war, Zimmermann claimed that Gerard had not been upset about the declaration of unrestricted submarine warfare.[58] In fact, Gerard protested strongly against the German decision. A German parliamentarian who saw Zimmermann shortly after his January 30 meeting with Gerard described the foreign secretary as "completely shattered."[59] Still, Zimmermann continued to delude himself. When on February 3 the United States severed diplomatic relations with Germany, the foreign secretary was genuinely astonished. He broke down and wept in front of reporters and reacted with violent language and great emotion when Gerard informed him of his recall to the United States. On his way home to the United States, Gerard told the British envoy to Switzerland that there could be no doubt that Wilson's action took Zimmermann and the German government by complete surprise.[60]

Caught off guard, the Wilhelmstrasse reacted to the break of diplomatic relations as precipitously as it had to the decision for unrestricted submarine warfare. On the very same day of the break's announcement, Kemnitz suggested to the dejected Zimmermann the revival of the original idea of proposing an alliance to Carranza at once, rather than waiting for American intervention. Still reeling from Wilson's blow, Zimmermann and Montgelas both immediately signed off on Kemnitz's proposal, and on February 5, the foreign office sent instructions to Eckardt to "submit the proposal of an alliance to the President [Carranza] already now."[61] Once again, confusion at the foreign office and Zimmermann's inability to handle stress allowed Kemnitz to push through a reckless proposal.

In the same fashion, Kemnitz may have used the break in diplomatic relations to restart German-Japanese peace talks, his long-standing pet project. Likely prompted by Kemnitz, Zimmermann on February 17 instructed the German envoy in Stockholm, Hellmuth von Lucius, to resume his talks on a separate peace with the Japanese envoy, Sadatsuchi Uchida. Perhaps in a sign of a rapprochement between Zimmermann and Ludendorff over the telegram, the general on February 26 emphatically endorsed these talks from a military perspective in a memo to the chancellor. It is highly doubtful that the instructions to Eckardt and Lucius stood a reasonable chance of success even under more favorable circumstances. As it was, the disclosure of the telegram in the American press on March 1 buried both. On March 3, the chancellor replied to Ludendorff's memo, reminding the general of Japan's double-dealing in the past and counseling caution in approaching Tokyo once again on this subject.[62]

Chapter Six

"BLINKER" HALL

World War I witnessed the emergence of large, permanent intelligence organizations in many of the belligerent countries. Great Britain established and expanded several secret services, with varying fields of responsibility. MI5 (military intelligence, department no. 5) conducted counter-intelligence operations in the United Kingdom. Scotland Yard's Special Branch was in charge of arresting enemy agents, while MI6 (also known as SIS, Secret Intelligence Service) took the lead on espionage operations abroad. The War Office and the Admiralty both ran their own cryptanalytic or "code breaking" services. It was the Admiralty's agency—called the Naval Intelligence Division (NID), or naval intelligence—that would gain fame for its role in bringing the Zimmermann telegram to light.

In order to decrypt enemy messages, the British first had to intercept them. Due to a combination of good luck and skill, the Royal Navy quickly gained access to German naval communications. At the outbreak of war, an Admiralty wireless station sent a stack of coded signals to Rear Admiral Henry Oliver, the director of NID whose taciturnity had earned him the unflattering nickname "Dummy." The signals were believed to be of enemy origin. Not knowing what to do with them, Oliver handed them to Alfred Ewing, the soft-spoken, Scottish-born director of naval education (DNE) and an expert in radiotelegraphy.

As Ewing took charge of the Admiralty's fledgling cryptanalytic efforts, the stream of intercepted enemy encrypts expanded rapidly. On August 5, the British cable ship *Telconia* cut Germany's overseas telegraph cables in the North Sea, forcing the German foreign office to resort to the use of wireless messages to communicate with its overseas legations. The British could now simply pluck these messages from the ether. Two amateur radio hams and personal friends of Ewing informed the DNE that they were intercepting German radio signals, so Ewing obtained permission for them to establish a W/T (wireless telegraphy) station at Hunstanton. This arrangement eventually led to the establishment of fourteen intercept stations across the British Isles, all with direct landlines to the Admiralty.

Like all major powers, the Germans encrypted their military and diplomatic messages. Interception of enemy messages was one thing for the Admiralty, decryption quite another. The German encrypts proved too hard a nut to crack for Ewing alone. Therefore, he hired a handful of assistants, mostly mathematicians and German linguists. Ewing's team struggled initially but eventually made a breakthrough, when the British obtained several German naval codebooks, captured by British and Allied navies from German vessels in various places. Ewing handed these to Fleet Paymaster Charles J. E. Rotter, NID's foremost German expert, and asked him to work on the intercepted German encrypts. In November 1914, Rotter delivered the first decrypts. Although the German navy would change its method of encryption many times over the next four years, Rotter's initial success had opened a window into German cryptologic thinking, and British code breakers would produce a stream of German decrypts throughout the war.[1]

One of the first British politicians to grasp the significance of cryptanalysis was the young Winston Churchill, at that time first lord of the Admiralty. Enthusiastic about the possibilities of this comparatively new form of intelligence gathering, and keen to put the naval code breakers on a firm institutional footing, he issued the following directive on November 8, 1914:

> An officer of the War Staff, preferably from the ID [Intelligence Division], should be selected to study all the decoded intercepts, not only current but past, and to compare them continually with what actually took place in order to penetrate the German mind and movements and make reports. All these intercepts are to be written in a locked book with their decodes, and all other copies are to be collected and burnt. All new messages are to be entered in the book, and the book is only to be handled under direction from COS [chief of staff].

Churchill's directive provided the code breakers with a legal framework. It also foreshadowed two major characteristics of naval intelligence during the war: centralization and utter secrecy. Nobody informed the war cabinet of the unit's existence, and it is unclear whether Churchill even bothered to apprise the prime minister.[2]

Three weeks later, on November 29, Churchill issued further instructions regarding the handling of decrypts: "The telegrams when intercepted will go direct and exclusively to COS who will mark them 1st Sea Lord, [and Admiral] Sir A. K. Wilson, it being understood that deliveries are not to be delayed through the temporary absence of any addressees."[3] In other words, it was not up to the Admiralty's Director of the Intelligence Division (DID) to decide who should receive certain intercepts or when. Once decrypted, a message was to go straight to the next higher authority. This rule would soon be bent and eventually broken.

In contrast to Churchill's enthusiasm for cryptanalysis, military and naval officers typically did not regard intelligence as a desirable assignment. Service with the army in the field, or on board a battleship, promised quicker promotions than an obscure desk job in a stuffy office in London, and it was no coincidence that several wartime secret service directors received their appointments by default. Captain Vernon Kell became director of MI5 following his resignation from active service in the army because of severe asthma, and Captain Mansfield Smith-Cumming assumed control of SIS after being placed on the Royal Navy's retired list as "unfit for service"; the hapless Cumming had developed severe seasickness during his years of active naval duty. It was this type of "bad luck" that would bring about the consequential appointment of a new director of British naval intelligence.

Like his colleagues at MI5 and MI6, Captain William Reginald Hall had entered the intelligence business somewhat by chance. Born in 1870 as the son of Britain's first director of naval intelligence, Hall chose a naval career, specializing in gunnery. A reformer who thought outside the box, he introduced numerous innovations, at times crossing more traditional naval officers. His subordinates remembered him as a stern yet humane superior. In 1913 he reached the pinnacle of his seagoing career when the Admiralty assigned him captain of the new battle cruiser HMS *Queen Mary*. Hall participated in the August 1914 battle of Heligoland that inflicted heavy casualties on the German navy, but in October his days at sea came to an abrupt end. Since childhood, Hall had struggled with his weak physical condition, and in the early weeks of the war he became so ill that his executive officer feared for the captain's life. Hall had to give up command of HMS *Queen Mary*, which, incidentally, may have saved his life: German gunfire sank the ship during the Battle of Jutland in 1916. Realizing Hall's permanent unsuitability for life at sea, the Admiralty made him DID in November 1914.[4] (Oliver moved on to become chief of the Admiralty war staff.) One of Hall's earliest acts as DID was to provide the naval cryptographers with a proper office, Room 40 in the Admiralty's Old Building. Those few in the know would soon refer to the organization as Room 40 OB, or simply Room 40, a name that stuck.[5]

Hall was a conspicuous man, though not handsome. Prematurely bald with a dome-shaped head and a large hooknose, he "looked like a demonic Mr. Punch in uniform."[6] His false teeth clicked audibly as he spoke. When excited, his face began to twitch, and underneath a pair of bushy eyebrows, his piercing eyes took to frequent blinking, a habit that earned him the enduring nickname "Blinker." Hall put his peculiar physical features to effective use. When making a point, he clicked his false teeth horridly, and his icy stare and wiggling eyebrows were said to work wonders in negotiations, confrontations, and interrogations.

Those who knew Hall invariably described him as a charismatic man with an almost hypnotic personality, which seemed to be particularly attractive to the Americans. The young Franklin D. Roosevelt, then assistant secretary of the navy, met Hall in 1918 in London and continued to marvel about him a war later. The admiration of Walter Hines Page, American ambassador to London, was virtually boundless as evidenced by a letter to President Woodrow Wilson in 1918: "Hall is one genius that the war has developed. Neither in fiction nor in fact can you find any such man to match him. . . . I shall never meet another man like him; that were too much to expect. For Hall can look through you and see the very muscular movements of your immortal soul while he is talking to you. Such eyes as the man has! My Lord!" Hall's subordinates at the intelligence division also revered their chief: "When blinking incessantly, exuding vitality and confidence, he spoke to you, you felt that you would do anything, anything at all, to merit his approval," recalled one. Another remembered, "He was indeed an admirable chief to work for. He held us all together and kept the peace."[7]

While Oliver had been happy to let Ewing build and run the Admiralty's cryptanalytic unit, the ambitious Hall quickly moved to bring it under his authority. Churchill's memorandum of November 8 failed to define the exact relationship between the DID and Room 40, and over the next months a silent struggle for control over the organization pitted Ewing against the cunning newcomer. Engaging, winsome, and a master of intrigue, Hall gradually sidelined the DNE. In 1916 Ewing accepted the inevitable and then assumed the principalship of Edinburgh University, in Scotland. Hall thus became the undisputed master of Britain's naval cryptanalysts.

Having gotten rid of Ewing, Hall gradually expanded Room 40's staff to around thirty. Many of the code breakers were Eton, Oxford, or Cambridge graduates or were affiliated with these institutions at the time of their joining Room 40. Typically, they were academics specializing in German or classic philology and had a penchant for math. Many had a distinguished, upper-middle-class background, including Nigel de Grey, an Eton graduate who joined Room 40 in 1915 from the Royal Naval Air Service. Slightly built, good-looking, with dark hair and chiseled, movie star features, de Grey descended from the distinguished family of the fifth Baron Walsingham (no relation of Sir Francis Walsingham) and had worked for the prestigious William Heinemann publishing house prior to the war. He would become something of a favorite in Hall's Room 40.[8]

One of the cryptanalytic unit's first recruits was thirty-one-year-old Alfred Dilwyn "Dilly" Knox, the second son of the bishop of Manchester. An Eton and Cambridge graduate, Knox had written a dissertation on the prose rhythms of Thucydides and taught classics at King's College, Cambridge. Extremely forgetful, he reportedly kept his spectacles in his tobacco case to remind himself that he had put the tobacco in the spectacle case but had then exchanged the tobacco for a ham sandwich in case he should forget that he was hungry. He did some of his best thinking soaking in a bathtub, claiming that codes were most easily cracked in an atmosphere of soap and steam. Knox found professional as well as romantic fulfillment in naval intelligence, marrying a member of "Blinker's Beauty Chorus," the group of women hired by Hall for secretarial duties shortly after the war.[9]

Knox was not the only eccentric in Room 40. In fact, a pronounced quirk was as likely to be found on a Room 40 cryptanalyst's resume as a degree from Oxford or Cambridge. One code breaker delighted in wearing his naval cap back to front, and another entertained his colleagues as a comic actor and produced a humorous history of Room 40, *Alice in I.D. 25* (as the facility was officially named in 1917). Their somewhat childish behavior and idiosyncrasies render these otherwise rational men humane and likable. In those early days, the British intelligence services recruited their members exclusively through the "old boys' network," not by means of a transparent hiring process. Those on the inside of intelligence recommended former classmates and fellow students, who inevitably hailed from the same elite background. As a result of this restrictive hiring process, Britain's spooks represented an extremely small sector of upper-middle-class society and tended to share a narrow range of views. "This was reflected in trivial ways," as one historian observed, "like the silly names they used for each other: Woolly, Buster, Biffy, Bubbles, Blinker, Barmy, Tin-Eye, and so on; which reads rather like a roll-call of Snow White's Seven Dwarfs. This was normal public school practice, even when the former public schoolboys had become fully grown men. They liked 'japes,' 'wheezes' and 'mad-cap adventures,' which is another characteristic which to an outsider might be mistaken as arrested development, but was normal for that set."[10]

This upper-middle-class self-selection process produced a competent staff that could be relied upon to keep secrets among their small circle of like-minded fellow cryptanalysts. Yet Hall also used class and personality effectively to create an impregnable esprit de corps that kept outsiders and rivals at arm's length. His struggle with, and ultimate defeat of, Ewing was a case in point. As Knox remarked, Room 40's staff "was lent or, more accurately, stolen by Hall." And de Grey recalled, "Blinker had made a compact with a few of the 'research party' that if ever we dug out anything of real importance we were to take it direct to him without showing it to Ewing whom he mistrusted as a chatter-box (and rightly)."[11] In other words, the cryptanalysts' loyalty lay first and foremost with the great man, not with the institution of naval intelligence, and they asked no questions about process and procedure. As the only meaningful link between his code breakers and the government, Hall assumed a critical position vis-à-vis his nominal superiors, who were, at best, dimly aware of Room 40's range of activities, if even knowing of its very existence.

As soon as he took over as DID, Hall took a series of steps that elevated him from mere officeholder to a political player in his own right. First, he expanded his purview from interception and decryption of wireless messages to intelligence gathering by the means of human agents or spies. This process started early in the war. In autumn 1914, Hall and Basil Thomson of Scotland Yard's Special Branch staffed the American yacht *Sayonara* with Royal Navy officers masquerading as pro-German Americans and sent the ship on a cruise along the Irish coast to gain the confidence of disloyal Irishmen and gather information about (nonexistent) German submarine bases. They informed neither the Irish authorities nor the admiral commanding Queenstown. The *Sayonara* venture produced no intelligence of any value, but it stoked a spy scare that had seized the United Kingdom at the outbreak of war.[12]

Despite its failure as an intelligence gathering operation, the *Sayonara* episode set an important precedent. Shortly thereafter, Hall began to build up an intelligence network in neutral Spain, a hotbed of Allied and German spies. Hall's man on the ground was Gibraltar-based Colonel Charles Thoroton, known by his colleagues as Charles the Bold. Thoroton's DID-sponsored network eventually extended to the Baleares, North Africa, and Greece and "became immensely powerful," according to Edward Bell, Hall's liaison at the U.S. embassy in London. Thoroton's operations remain somewhat murky because he destroyed most of his papers, but his reasoning for retaining a few select items gives an idea of his gloves-off methods: "[I retained] those [papers] which I thought necessary to defend myself in case of an attack being made on me for some of my more questionable activities."[13]

Moreover, Hall made a number of useful connections with British officials inside and outside the Navy. He carefully developed relationships with British naval attachés around the globe, most notably with Captain Guy Gaunt, in New York. Under Hall's direction, Gaunt directed intelligence and propaganda activities against the Germans, quite often without the ambassador's knowledge. Hall also established personal ties with his colleagues at MI5 (Vernon Kell), SIS (Mansfield Smith-Cumming), Scotland Yard's Special Branch (Basil Thomson), the War Office (Colonel George Cockerill, director of special intelligence and in charge of censorship), the press, and the U.S. embassy. All of these connections would come in handy over time.[14]

In the summer of 1915, Hall made the momentous decision to let Room 40 attack encrypted German diplomatic messages in addition to naval messages, their original target. For this purpose, he set up a diplomatic section within Room 40, headed by George Young, a Middle East expert who reported directly to Hall. Ewing was cut out of the loop completely. Hall assigned to his brainchild some of his most competent code breakers, including Knox and de Grey. Initially, Room 40's diplomatic cryptanalysts found German diplomatic encrypts more challenging than their naval counterparts, but eventually they hit their stride and provided Hall with a regular stream of messages to and from the German foreign office. When Room 40 discovered in September 1916 that the Swedish foreign ministry and the U.S. State Department allowed Berlin occasionally to use their transatlantic cables to communicate with the German embassy in Washington, they began to attack German messages embedded in intercepted Swedish and U.S. diplomatic traffic as well. By late 1916, the British regularly intercepted and decrypted communications between the German embassy in Washington and the Wilhelmstrasse.[15]

These diplomatic encrypts were, in the words of Admiral William "Bubbles" James, Hall's wartime deputy and biographer, "the sole concern of the Foreign Secretary." In the spirit of Churchill's instructions of November 29, 1914, they should have gone "direct and exclusively" to the Foreign Office, but from the outset, Hall retained the right to distribute the resulting diplomatic intercepts as he pleased.[16] Although he forwarded many of "his" decrypts to interested government branches (after omitting references to his sources), he frequently made judgment calls as to when and with whom intercepts were to be shared.

Hall's propensity to use decrypts for his own purposes manifested itself in early 1916, when Edward M. House, President Woodrow Wilson's adviser, visited Europe. House had convinced the president to send him on a trip to London, Berlin, and Paris to promote the idea of a peace conference under U.S. aegis. Though in line with Wilson's desire to end the war, House's plan had a distinctly pro-Allied flavor. If each nation responded favorably to his initiative, "we would then have accomplished a masterstroke of diplomacy," House noted in his diary, but if "the Central Powers refused to acquiesce, we could then push our insistence to a point where diplomatic relations would first be broken off, and later the whole force of our Government, and perhaps the force of every neutral—might be brought against them."[17] Getting carried away in the course of his mediation mission, House told the French foreign minister that "inevitably, America will enter the war, *before the end of the year*, and will align herself on the side of the Allies."[18]

House spent nearly two months shuttling among the three European capitals, but he passed most of his time in London, where he discussed his project at length with British foreign secretary Edward Grey. As a result of these talks, House returned to the United States with the so-called House-Grey memorandum for the president. In it, Grey states, "Colonel House told me that President Wilson was ready, upon hearing from France and England that the moment was opportune, to propose that a Conference should be summoned to put an end to the war. Should the Allies accept this proposal and should Germany refuse it, the United States would probably enter the war against Germany." The document goes on to reveal that "if such a conference met, it would secure peace on terms not unfavorable to the Allies; and, if it failed to secure peace, the United States would leave the Conference as a belligerent on the side of the Allies, if Germany was unreasonable." In the end, House's efforts came to naught. Wilson effectively defanged the memorandum by inserting the modification "probably" before the words "leave the Conference."[19] The British government never asked Wilson to launch his mediation offer.

Hall had little use for a peace conference, even if the United States promised to throw its diplomatic weight behind the Allies. Instead, he mused that "there is a satisfactory killing of Germans" on the western front, "but it takes a long time to kill two million, and I do not see much chance of peace until we have done it."[20] Therefore, he followed House's moves in Europe with great interest and a considerable amount of suspicion. In all likelihood, the cryptanalytic bureau of military intelligence, MI1(b), intercepted and decrypted telegrams sent by House to Washington via the U.S. embassy. The bureau's director, Captain Malcolm Hay, then probably handed the decrypts to his naval colleague,

Captain Hall.[21] In turn, Hall appears to have shown the House decrypts selectively to other British officials with a view to mobilizing fellow hardliners and nip the American initiative in the bud.[22] As Maurice Hankey, secretary of the war cabinet, noted in his diary in early 1916: "I saw Captain Hall again first thing in the morning. He showed me more of [President Wilson's adviser] Col. House's telegrams sent from Berlin . . . I found that Hall had not shown these telegrams even to the First Lord [of the Admiralty, then Arthur J. Balfour]. This information is of course priceless."[23]

Many Foreign Office officials resented Hall's handling of intelligence. As Herbert Yardley, an American cryptologist on wartime liaison duty in Britain, observed, the "Foreign Office was extremely jealous of [Hall's] position for it was almost wholly dependent on him for information revealing the secret political intrigues of enemy and neutral governments. . . . It is no wonder then that he was feared by the Foreign Office."[24] Even Admiral James, a great admirer of his former boss, conceded that Hall "had no right to handle the political messages himself and that he should have sent them without comment to the Foreign Office."[25]

The crafty Hall did not stop at hogging intelligence and dispensing it as he saw fit. He also deployed his secretly collected information in covert operations aimed at discrediting London's foes and swaying the war in Britain's favor. Often, he did so on his own authority, as was the case during the ill-fated Gallipoli campaign of 1915 aimed at opening a sea route to Russia. Early that year, Hall had sent secret emissaries to Constantinople with instructions to offer up to £4 million to secure the passage of the Royal Navy. He did so without consulting the Foreign Office, the cabinet, or the Admiralty.[26] In his memoirs, Hall left a candid account of the ensuing interview with Churchill and Jackie Fisher, the first sea lord of the Admiralty:

> [Churchill] was frowning. "Who authorised this?" he demanded.
> [Hall replied:] "I did, First Lord."
> "But—the Cabinet surely knows nothing about it?"
> "No, it does not . . ."
> It was one of the moments when dropped pins are supposed to be heard. Then Mr Churchill turned to Lord Fisher. . . . "D'you hear what this man has done? He's sent out people with four millions to buy a peaceful passage! On his own!"[27]

Hall also did not hesitate to exploit his access to intelligence for personal vendettas when it suited him. Though the following account is probably too good to be true, it nevertheless accurately reflects Hall's attitude toward his sense of entitlement to the intelligence produced by Room 40: Sometime during the war, a British judge allegedly handed down a light sentence for a German spy in whose arrest Hall had played a part. The judge ruled on the grounds that the agent had only reported to his spymasters in Germany the location of British factories that the judge considered to be "targets of no military importance." Furious, Hall reportedly sent a report to Germany in the spy's name, giving the position of the judge's country house as the site of another factory. Shortly thereafter, Hall ended up at dinner next to the judge, who told him and the other guests that Zeppelins had bombarded his house and that he had only narrowly escaped with his life. To this Hall supposedly replied with delight, "Well, it was not a target of any military importance, was it?"[28]

A reshuffling of the British government in 1916 greatly strengthened Hall's position. In December 1916, the then-secretary of state for war, the Liberal MP David Lloyd George, formed a coalition government. The new prime minister appointed the first lord of the Admiralty and eminent Tory, Arthur J. Balfour, foreign secretary. Although Balfour's appointment added much-needed gravitas and expertise to Lloyd George's cabinet, political, generational, and temperamental differences caused latent friction between the two men. For Hall, Balfour's nomination to the top spot at the Foreign Office was a stroke of luck. As the first lord of the Admiralty, Balfour had been one of the DID's immediate superiors, and Hall, who preferred to work along personal rather than institutional lines, had collaborated harmoniously with Balfour, whose conservative political views he shared and whose laissez-faire style suited him well. Their disdain for Lloyd George further bound the two men.[29]

Balfour's appointment as foreign secretary allowed Hall to consolidate the invisible empire he had created over the preceding two years. His power derived from the procurement, exclusive access, and arbitrary dispensation of secret information. Hall was the first British executive official to read intercepted diplomatic messages between Washington and Berlin, and he alone decided when and with whom to share the decrypts. "He had unbounded confidence in his ability to decide how much of the information in the messages should be passed on to other Government departments," wrote his biographer.[30] Hall's information monopoly gave him a degree of leverage over British foreign policy that far exceeded the authority formally vested in him as DID. As Edward Bell of the U.S. embassy in London remarked: "So powerful did Admiral Hall become, that he was often in a position to influence the conduct of Great Britain's foreign policy in the most important matters, and actually did so on several occasions."[31]

Chapter Seven

INTERCEPTION AND DECRYPTION

How did the British intercept the Zimmermann telegram? Finding the answer begins with German transatlantic communication.

Following the cutting of Germany's submarine cables by the Royal Navy early in the war, Berlin had developed a number of alternative techniques for contacting its diplomats in Washington. These included by submarine, by courier, by inserting secret text into ordinary news dispatches, by radio, and by using Swedish and American cables. The Wilhelmstrasse had planned initially to send the Zimmermann telegram via the submarine *Deutschland*, but the German navy then requisitioned the vessel for its own purposes, before it launched for the United States.[1] Delivery by courier would have been lengthy and uncertain, and insertion of the secret text into ordinary news dispatches seemed impractical. Wireless communication, on the other hand, represented a viable option for the German foreign office.

The Wilhelmstrasse and the German embassy in Washington frequently used the powerful long-range radio stations in Sayville, Long Island, and Tuckerton, New Jersey, as well as in Nauen, outside Berlin, to send transatlantic telegrams. During the war, however, the Germans were unable to fully master the technical challenges of sending and receiving wireless messages over such a long distance. Moreover, the U.S. government supervised the two stations on U.S. soil and insisted that the Germans hand them a copy of the code used for wireless telegrams sent to and from Sayville and Tuckerton. Hence, in the words of the German ambassador to Washington, "[t]his course was not suitable for handling negotiations in which the American Government was concerned."[2]

The pro-German Swedish government offered a more reliable means of wireless communication across the Atlantic. Shortly after the outbreak of war, Stockholm had agreed to assist the Wilhelmstrasse in maintaining contact with its overseas legations. The German foreign office would give an encrypted message to the Swedish foreign ministry in Stockholm, which would then relay it to its envoy in Buenos Aires. There, the Swedish envoy would hand it to his German colleague, who, in turn, would forward it to the addressee, for example, the German embassy in Washington. British cryptanalysts referred to this route as the "Swedish roundabout." The British Admiralty discovered and began plucking telegrams from the Swedish roundabout in early 1915. Room 40 started decrypting the intercepts in late 1916.[3]

One other option was the U.S. State Department.[4] Beginning in late 1914, the Wilhelmstrasse began sending encrypted telegrams to the German embassy in Washington via U.S. diplomatic cables. The German foreign office continued to use this route intermittently until diplomatic relations were broken in February 1917. All the messages sent across the Atlantic passed through London, giving British intelligence ready access to them. Room 40 began eavesdropping on the cables to and from the U.S. embassy in London in May 1915, or perhaps earlier, intercepting U.S. diplomatic messages as well as the occasional embedded German messages.[5]

The German foreign office files indicate that the Wilhelmstrasse sent the Zimmermann telegram through the State Department channel. An official German report from April 1917 states that Berlin handed the encoded telegram "to the American ambassador [to Germany], with the request of conveying it to the imperial embassy in Washington." The report goes on to reveal that the "American ambassador received the dispatch from the foreign office on January 16 at three o'clock in the afternoon and sent it immediately by way of the American legation in Copenhagen." On January 19, "the State Department handed the Telegram to the German embassy in Washington," which forwarded it to Mexico.[6]

The German records mention neither the Swedish roundabout nor long-distance radio with regard to the telegram. Yet in 1926, William Reginald Hall, since retired from British naval intelligence, filed an affidavit for the German-American Mixed Claims Commission settling wartime compensation claims by Americans against the German government. In it, the former director of naval intelligence states that the telegram was "sent from Berlin to Washington by cable via the Swedish foreign office. It was intercepted by us en route to Washington."[7] Hall repeated this claim in his unpublished autobiography, adding that the Germans "probably use[d] other routes as well."[8] He does not say what those "other routes" might be, but Hall does refer readers to the journalist Burton Hendrick's multivolume biography of Walter Hines Page, the U.S. wartime ambassador to London. In the third volume, published in 1926, Hendrick claims that the Wilhelmstrasse had indeed used three routes for the Zimmermann telegram: the Swedish roundabout, a radiogram to Sayville, and the U.S. embassy in Berlin. For confirmation, Hendrick points readers to the proceedings of an official German parliamentary investigation into the causes of Germany's defeat. There was indeed such an investigation in 1920, but its records make no mention of the Swedish roundabout or long-distance radio. Instead, the investigation stated merely that the Wilhelmstrasse had sent the telegram "through the offices of the American Embassy in Berlin . . . to Count Bernstorff [German ambassador in Washington] by way of the State Department in Washington."[9]

If not from the records of the German investigation, where had Hendrick picked up the notion that the Wilhelmstrasse had sent the telegram by way of Sweden and long-distance wireless? In preparing his biography of Ambassador Page, Hendrick collaborated closely with Hall. The old spymaster generously provided Hendrick with background material, and the latter boasted to the American diplomat Edward Bell in 1921, "Admiral Hall has given me the complete story of the Zimmerman [sic] Mexico telegram. He has . . . given all details about the ways [it was] sent, decoded, etc."[10] Although Hendrick does not state explicitly that Hall had told him that the Germans had sent the telegram via Sweden and by wireless, his statement to Bell strongly suggests it. If so, Hendrick's claim about the Germans' use of three different channels for sending the telegram originates with Hall.

For quite some time, the Page biography provided the main source for research on the Zimmermann telegram, and it took historians years to refute Hendrick's, and thus Hall's, assertions about the Wilhelmstrasse's use of multiple routes. In 1938 two American cryptanalysts, William F. Friedman and Charles J. Mendelsohn, argued that technical difficulties would have prevented the Germans from sending the telegram as a transatlantic cablegram.[11] Their findings did not reach the public until 1965, when the government declassified their study, and they did not question Berlin's use of the Swedish roundabout. Only in 1967 did cryptology historian David Kahn question the Germans' use of this route, for the first time. Kahn noted that the German foreign office records gave "only the American route for the message, which may mean that the Zimmermann telegram did not go by the Swedish roundabout."[12] Nearly four decades later, in 2003, State Department historian David Nickles cast further doubt on the use of the Swedish roundabout.[13] Subsequently, historian Peter Freeman, in 2006, and mathematician Joachim von zur Gathen, in 2007, confirmed Kahn's and Nickles' suspicions, based on British and German records, respectively.[14]

Despite painstaking historical and cryptologic research, and a gradual correction of Hall's disinformation, myths about the Zimmermann telegram's transmission have persisted. Barbara Tuchman's popular account of the telegram, in particular, has cast a long shadow over this issue.[15] Tuchman uncritically accepted and reproduced the falsehood of the Wilhelmstrasse's use of three routes, and several subsequent in-depth studies of the telegram failed to correct her. Friedrich Katz, in *The Secret War in Mexico* (1985), reiterates the claim of the telegram's threefold delivery by quoting Tuchman and Hendrick, as does Martin Nassua in his master's thesis on the telegram, published in 1990.[16] A popular history of cryptography claims as recently as 1999 that "Zimmermann was forced to send his encrypted telegram via Sweden and, as a back-up, via the more direct American-owned cable."[17] All of these erroneous claims go back ultimately to disinformation originating with Hall.

Why did Hall produce this smoke screen about the method by which British naval intelligence intercepted the telegram? The British were understandably loath to reveal to their American allies the interception and decryption of State Department cable traffic by Room 40 during the period of U.S. neutrality, but why did Hall continue to obfuscate the truth long after the war even though the German parliamentary investigation and Hendrick disclosed it in 1920 and 1926, respectively? The reason for Hall's persistent refusal to acknowledge British eavesdropping on U.S. communications lay in the longevity of these operations and their continuity long after the United States had entered World War I.

The British found U.S. codes easy to break. The American cryptanalyst Herbert Yardley had also found U.S. diplomatic codes shockingly simplistic when he joined the State Department as a code clerk in 1913. When he tried his hand at an encoded message from adviser Edward M. House to President Woodrow Wilson about a meeting with the kaiser in Berlin in 1914, he managed to decrypt it, without key, in less than two hours. "Imagine my amazement," he recalled. "This message had passed over British cables and we already knew that a copy of every cable went to the Code Bureau in the British Navy. Colonel House must be the Allies' best informant! No need to send spies into Germany when they have Colonel House's reports of interviews with the Emperor, Princes, Generals, leading industrial leaders."[18]

94 Chapter Seven

Over the next years, the British continued to prey upon the State Department's diplomatic communications. In early 1917, Yardley's boss told him, "We already know by our telegrams from London that England maintains a large bureau for solving diplomatic correspondence." He asked Yardley whether he believed the British could solve the State Department's code. Yardley replied in the affirmative, and a few weeks after the U.S. declaration of war, he handed his boss a stack of messages he had solved. His boss, however, "seemed content to let the matter drop, assuming the hopeless view that nothing is indecipherable."[19]

The United States' entry into the war did not change British attitudes toward attacking U.S. diplomatic communications, as evidenced by several intercepted messages in the British archives dating from August 1917.[20] In other words, His Majesty's code breakers not only read State Department messages during the period of U.S. neutrality, they continued to do so *after* the U.S. intervention. This appears to have been Hall's main rationale for continually and falsely playing up Berlin's use of the Swedish roundabout and long-distance radio for the transmission of the telegram. For fear of losing an important intelligence source and antagonizing a critical ally, Hall sought to obscure his agency's eavesdropping operations on U.S. diplomatic cables even after the United States entered the war. American cryptologists nevertheless suspected the truth. On liaison duty in London in August 1918, Yardley "did not dare communicate with Washington, since the British would decode every word I sent."[21]

The British continued their cryptanalytic campaign against the United States without a hitch into the postwar period. In 1921 a U.S. Senate hearing revealed that the British were eavesdropping on all American cable communications, commercial as well as governmental.[22] When called upon to assess the security of American diplomatic messages in 1926, Yardley once again found them highly vulnerable.[23] As late as 1944, in a posthumously published account of Hall's war work and postwar career, the former director of naval intelligence failed to acknowledge the fact that the British had obtained the telegram by spying on U.S. diplomatic cables.[24] It is a fair guess that Hall did so in order not to complicate his successors' ongoing interception and decryption of American messages. Indeed, there are indications that the British intercepted and decrypted U.S. communications during World War II, and a history of post–World War II American cryptanalysis, published in 1982, claims that British eavesdropping on U.S. diplomatic messages "continues to the present."[25]

Whatever the scope of British snooping on U.S. communications after April 1917, London began intercepting U.S. diplomatic traffic early in the war, and British intelligence started decrypting the intercepts in the spring of 1915.[26]

Hence, by the time the telegram crossed the Atlantic on State Department cables, the British had been reading American diplomatic messages for two years. The telegram's interception was therefore a matter of routine. As soon as British eavesdroppers had plucked the encoded message from the ether, they needed to decide where to send it for decryption.

The task of sorting U.S. intercepts to the appropriate cryptanalytic agency—naval or military—fell to MI8, the War Office agency in charge of cable censorship. Since Room 40 was responsible for attacking German encrypts, and the army's cryptanalytic unit, MI1(b), for all non-German encrypts, MI8 first had to determine whether an intercepted U.S. cable contained an embedded German message. The identification of an encrypt's provenance was easy because the Americans used letter codes, whereas German codes were numeric. When MI8 procured Ambassador James Gerard's lengthy message to the State Department that included the Zimmermann telegram on the morning of January 17—two days before Ambassador Johann Heinrich von Bernstorff would receive his copy in Washington—the censors immediately recognized that the embedded numerical code groups were German and forwarded the message to Room 40 for decryption.[27]

The message Gerard forwarded on behalf of the Wilhelmstrasse consisted of about a thousand numerical code groups. Date (January 16) and addressee (the German ambassador in Washington, Bernstorff) were given en clair, but the main body of the text was encrypted by means of a highly sophisticated codebook that the Germans called 0075 and the Americans and British referred to as 7500. Berlin had first distributed the code in July 1916 to its missions in Berne, Bucharest, Constantinople, Copenhagen, Kristiania (Oslo), Lugano, The Hague, Sofia, Stockholm, and Vienna. In November 1916, the merchant submarine *Deutschland* delivered the code to the German embassy in Washington; Room 40 began intercepting messages to the embassy encoded in 0075 in the same month. The British code breakers learned from their analyses that 0075 was a two-part, four-digit code. Its numerical groups consisted of two zeros and two digits, the two digits always showing an arithmetical difference of 2. The groups were allocated entirely randomly to the vocabulary. Due to this deliberate randomness, the Germans called 0075 a *Lotteriechiffre* (lottery cipher). A fifth digit was prefixed to some groups to indicate the definite article and one or two other grammatical reflections.[28]

"Dilly" Knox, the cryptanalyst who first attacked the encoded message, did not get very far. He therefore turned to his colleague Nigel de Grey, arguably Room 40's most talented cryptanalyst. With Knox's assistance, de Grey went to work.[29] Since Room 40 knew only a few elements of code 0075, the task resembled solving a puzzle without all the required pieces and without knowing what the final product would look like. Yet de Grey and Knox quickly realized that the message consisted of two German telegrams, no. 157 (informing Bernstorff of the impending unrestricted submarine warfare) and no. 158 (the actual Mexican dispatch). Since no. 158 was shorter, and therefore more quickly solvable, the cryptanalysts tackled it first. De Grey recalled:

> We could at once read enough groups for Knox to see that the telegram was important. Together he and I worked solidly all the morning upon it. With our crude methods and lack of staff no elaborate indexing of groups had been developed—only constantly recurring groups were noted in the working copies of the code as our fancy dictated. Work therefore was slow and laborious but by about mid-day we had got a skeleton version, sweating with excitement as we went on because neither of us doubted the importance of what we had in our hands. Was not the American-German situation our daily bread?[30]

Beaming with excitement, de Grey took this skeleton version to Hall (see Figs. 2 and 3). In his autobiography, Hall vividly recalled the moment when he first learnt of the telegram: "I am not likely to forget that Wednesday morning, January 17th, 1917," he wrote a little more than ten years after the event. "There was the usual docket of papers to be gone through on my arrival at the office, and [Hall's assistant] Claud Serocold and I were still at work on them when at about half-past ten de Grey came in. He seemed excited." A dramatic exchange ensued. "'D.I.D.', de Grey said, 'd'you want to bring America into the war?' 'Yes, my boy,'" Hall replied. "'Why?'" De Grey explained: "'I've got something here which—well, it's a rather astonishing message which might do the trick if we could use it. It isn't very clear, I'm afraid, but I'm sure I've got most of the important points right. It's from the German Foreign Office to Bernstorff.'" De Grey then handed Hall the message.[31]

Since Hall did not read German, the cryptanalysts had translated the partial decrypt into English. This is the text of the message de Grey showed Hall that morning:

W. 158
16th Jan. 1917
Most secret for Your Excellency's personal information and to be handed on to the Imperial Minister in ? Mexico with . . . . . . by a safe route.
Tel. No. 1.

We propose to begin on the 1st February unrestricted submarine warfare. In doing so however we shall endeavour to keep America neutral . . . . . ? If we should not (succeed in doing so) we propose to (?Mexico) an alliance upon the following basis.

(joint) conduct of war

(joint) conduct of peace

Your Excellency should for the present inform the President secretly (that we expect) war with the U.S.A. (possibly) (. . . . . . Japan) and at the same time to negotiate between us and Japan. . . . .

(Indecipherable sentence opening please tell the President) that. . . . .our submarines. . . . . . will compel England to peace in a few months. Acknowledge receipt.

Zimmermann[32]

This fragmentary decrypt does not mention Germany's consent for Mexico to reconquer U.S. territory, but it still contained several bombshells, including the imminence of unrestricted submarine warfare, the possibility of a German-Mexican alliance directed against the United States, and evidence of Germany's intention to pry Japan away from the Allies.

Room 40's standing orders required Hall to promptly share the message, or its content, with the Admiralty and the Foreign Office so that the government could take appropriate military and diplomatic action. In this case, appropriate measures might have included naval preparations for the onslaught of German submarines, securing British interests in Mexico, and ensuring Japan's loyalty to the Allied cause. Hall, knowing full well that he was acting counter to instructions, did the opposite of his orders. "This," he told de Grey, "is a case where standing orders must be suspended. All copies of this message, both those in cypher and your own transcripts, are to be brought straight to me. Nothing is to be put on the files. This may be a very big thing, possibly the biggest thing of the war. For the present not a soul outside this room is to be told anything at all."[33]

Be it deliberate disinformation, a guilty conscience, or simply a faulty memory, Hall claimed a quarter of a century later that he had sent the telegram "promptly upon its interception to the British Prime Minister with a notation written across its corner calling to its importance in the relations between the Allies and the United States."[34] This statement is demonstrably incorrect. As noted, when Room 40's code breakers showed Hall a partial decrypt of the telegram, the DID told his staff that "not a soul outside this room is to be told anything at all."[35] Furthermore, neither the British archives nor Hall's auto-

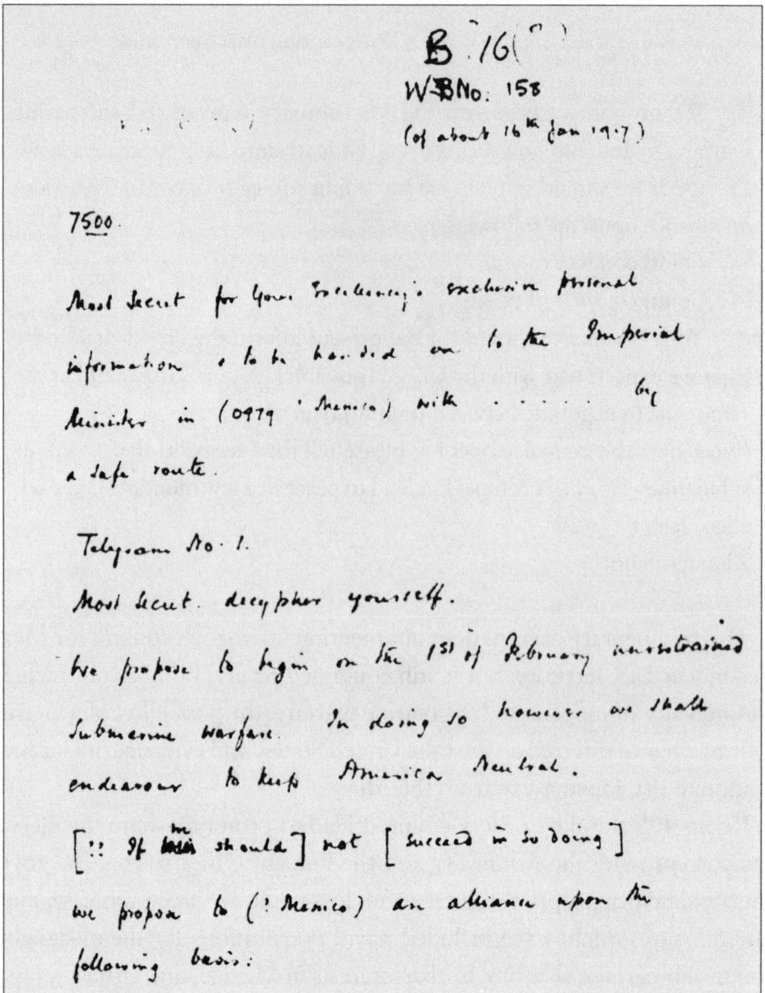

B. 16( )
W$No. 158
(of about 16ᵗʰ Jan 1917)

7500.

Most Secret for Your Excellency's exclusive personal
information . to be handed on to the Imperial
Minister in (0979 'Mexico) with . . . . . by
a safe route.

Telegram No. 1.
Most Secret. decypher yourself.
We propose to begin on the 1ˢᵗ of February unrestrained
Submarine warfare. In doing so however we shall
endeavour to keep America Neutral.
[:: If we should] not [succeed in so doing]
we propose to (: Mexico) an alliance upon the
following basis:
  (joint) conduct of the war
  (joint) conclusion of peace.
[an obscure passage]
Your Excellency should (for the present) inform the President
secretly (that in expect) war with the USA (possibly)
[a sentence in which Japan is mentioned] and at the
same time to negotiate between us & Japan.
[undecypherable sentence meaning please tell the President
that . . . our submarines . . . . will compel England to
peace in a few months. Acknowledge receipt.   Zimmermann

FIGURE 2. The start of Nigel de Grey's handwritten decrypt of the
Zimmermann telegram. (Courtesy of the *National Archives*, London)

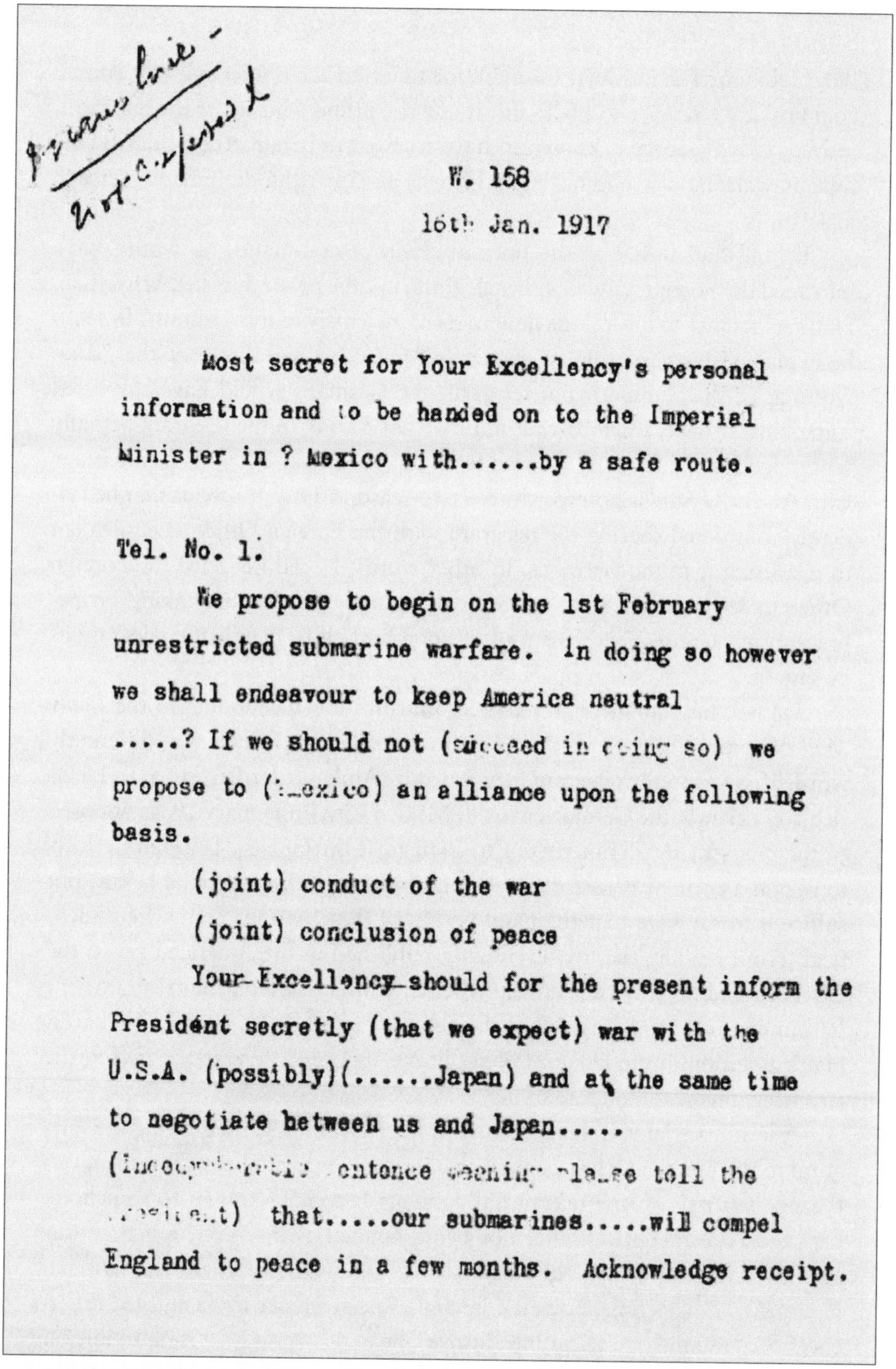

FIGURE 3. The typed version of de Grey's decrypt, with annotation by Captain William Reginald Hall across top left: "main line—not exposed." The term *main line* refers to Germany's use of the U.S. State Department route, and the term *not exposed* means "not published." (Courtesy of the *National Archives*, London)

biography nor David Lloyd George's memoirs nor any other relevant source contains any reference to Hall's informing the prime minister of the telegram. Indeed, Lloyd George is known to have received only one decrypt during his time as wartime prime minister, and it was an American diplomatic message in 1916.[36]

If Hall had followed the normal chain of command, he would have informed the Foreign Office of the telegram, not the prime minister. Why, then, Hall's reluctance to inform the diplomats immediately of the telegram? In 1926 he explained his hesitation to the *Daily Mail*: "If I had disclosed the actual wording of the Zimmermann telegram the Germans would have suspected something at once. I had to wait until we got a copy of the telegram actually sent, which was differently worded from the one in Berlin."[37] Hall's interview with the *Daily Mail* is noteworthy for two reasons. First, it reveals that he evidently considered sharing the telegram with the Foreign Office as equivalent to disclosing it to the Germans. In other words, he did not trust the Foreign Office to keep the telegram secret or to disclose it only after taking proper precautions. Consequently, he took it upon himself to handle the telegram as he saw fit.

Second, his statement contains an untruth. His mentioning to the *Daily Mail* of getting "a copy of the telegram actually sent, which was differently worded" refers to the telegram forwarded by Ambassador Bernstorff to Heinrich von Eckardt, the German envoy in Mexico City, on January 19, as opposed to the one sent by Zimmermann to Bernstorff on January 16. Hall's efforts to obtain a copy of Bernstorff's telegram in Mexico are described below, but suffice it to say here that the main bodies of these two telegrams were identical. From reading the text eventually published in the American press, the Germans had no way of knowing whether it was based on the telegram sent by Zimmermann to Bernstorff or the one forwarded by Bernstorff to Eckardt. Hall's assertion in the *Daily Mail* about the supposed difference between the two telegrams was therefore disingenuous.[38]

A few years later, in his autobiography, Hall still regarded giving the telegram to the Foreign Office as equivalent to making it public: "Why, then, run the smallest risk of [the telegram's] contents becoming known to somebody [i.e., the Foreign Office] who, not being familiar with every branch of our activity, might all unwittingly compromise some part or all of the work in Room 40?"[39] This time, however, he makes no reference to the alleged differences between the two telegrams. Instead, he explains his hesitation to inform the Foreign Office by citing his concern that publication of the telegram might alert the Germans to the existence of Room 40 and cause them to change their codes. Furthermore, he wrote, he had not yet obtained sufficient proof to convince President Wilson that the telegram was genuine, and not "a British-made hoax."[40] These justifications ring hollow, as well. The Germans were bound to wonder how the telegram ended up on the front pages of U.S. newspapers, regardless of when the disclosure occurred. When Hall eventually informed the Americans of the telegram, on February 19, he told them that the British had obtained it through cryptanalysis.[41] Yet this information he could have given them already in January.[42]

In fact, Hall did not worry that the Americans would consider the telegram a British hoax or that the Germans would find out about Room 40's activities. Rather, he feared that the Americans might discover Room 40's eavesdropping on their communications. If he had informed the Foreign Office of the telegram as soon as Room 40 had produced a partial decrypt on January 17—and per his unspoken assumption, the diplomats would carelessly share this intelligence with their American colleagues—the British would have been hard-pressed to explain their source—U.S. diplomatic cables—to the Americans.

If the Americans had made an educated guess, the telegram would not only have caused a diplomatic scandal between Washington and London, but the State Department would probably have changed its codes, depriving Room 40 of an important intelligence source. If, on the other hand, Hall held on to the telegram for a few weeks, he could be reasonably sure that he would eventually be in a position to provide the Americans with the complete text of the telegram *and* a safe explanation as to how the British had obtained it. Hall knew from the partial decrypt of Zimmermann's telegram to Bernstorff that the German ambassador would forward the alliance offer to his colleague in Mexico City, Eckardt. From past experience, Hall also knew that Bernstorff would have to use an older, more vulnerable code to communicate with Mexico, since Eckardt did not possess a copy of codebook 0075. If Hall managed to obtain a copy of Bernstorff's telegram to Eckardt, he could expect his staff to decrypt the encoded message in toto and fill in the remaining lacunae. If he then decided to share his intelligence with the Americans, he would be in a position to tell them that the British had obtained it in Mexico rather than from U.S. cables. In short, this ruse would enable him to conceal British eavesdropping operations from the Americans as well as afford Room 40 continued access to U.S. diplomatic messages.[43]

Prompt U.S. intervention in response to Germany's public declaration of unrestricted submarine warfare would have relieved Hall of his dilemma. In this case, which he considered likely, Hall reasoned, "the Zimmermann telegram need never be used at all."[44] In expectation of Washington's impending entry into the war, Hall sat on the partially decrypted telegram for more than two weeks, patiently awaiting the submarine deadline, while his government, ignorant of the bombshell in Hall's possession, struggled to bring about U.S. intervention on the Allied side. After the war, Hall asked self-critically, "What, then, was there to prevent me from immediately handing it [the telegram] over to the Foreign Office authorities?" In response, he conceded that a "naval officer is not trained for foreign politics, and surely there were those who were far better able to deal with the matter than myself. Yet, so far, it would seem, from taking the obvious course, I deliberately withheld [the telegram] from those best entitled to receive it until a dangerously late date, and assumed a responsibility which ought never to have been mine."[45]

Hall's stated intention to keep the telegram permanently under wraps, in case the United States responded to Germany's declaration of unrestricted warfare by joining the Allies, conjures up an interesting alternate historical scenario. The telegram's non-disclosure would have meant that Zimmermann's alliance scheme probably would not have been exposed in the press in March 1917. This, in turn, would have given the Germans time to make headway with their Mexican alliance scheme, while at the same time the United States would have remained utterly ignorant of these efforts. Whether Carranza would have eventually joined the Germans and attacked the United States remains hypothetical of course, but Hall's decision to keep the telegram secret in case Washington entered the conflict in response to unrestricted submarine warfare potentially exposed the United States to an attack on its southern flank.

In the event, the United States did not precipitously enter the war. When Germany declared unrestricted submarine warfare, President Wilson decided to sever diplomatic relations with Berlin, rather than join the Allies. Still, the rupture took Zimmermann by surprise, and on February 5, he followed up the original telegram with another message, instructing Eckardt to enter into negotiations with Carranza "even now," that is, without awaiting American intervention (Fig. 4). The Wilhelmstrsasse encrypted this message in an old code, 13040, and sent it by way of the Swedish roundabout. On the evening of February 8, the message passed through London, and Room 40 decrypted it two days later. Its content indicated a radicalization of German strategy, but it remains unclear when Hall forwarded Zimmermann's February 5 dispatch to the Foreign Office or whether he did so at all.[46]

British naval intelligence learned of Wilson's decision to sever diplomatic relations with Germany through private channels even before the British Foreign Office or the U.S. ambassador in London did. On February 2, Wilson's adviser, House, informed Captain Guy Gaunt, the British naval attaché in New York, that the administration had decided to send Bernstorff home. Exhilarated, Gaunt relayed the news to Hall, and added, "I'll probably get soused." The next morning, Hall showed up at the U.S. embassy, at Grosvenor Square, and proudly reported the news of the imminent rupture of diplomatic relations between Berlin and Washington to Ambassador Page. In a celebratory mood, the embassy staff promptly invited the DID for "generous whiskies and soda." Though effusive on the outside, deep down Hall was disappointed because he had hoped for an American declaration of war. His decision to personally appear at the U.S. embassy may well have been the opening gambit to relay the telegram to the Americans in order to put pressure on Wilson. Before he

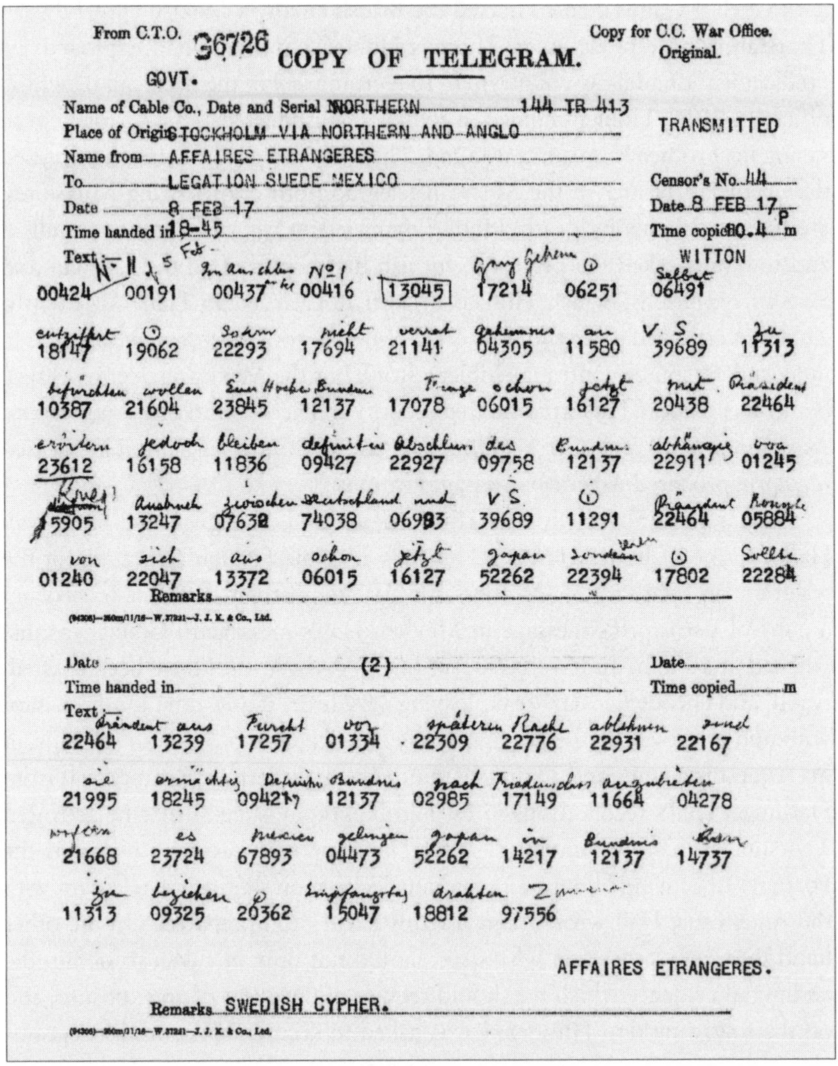

From C.T.O. 36726 **COPY OF TELEGRAM.** Copy for C.C. War Office. Original.

GOVT.

Name of Cable Co., Date and Serial No. NORTHERN 144 TR 41.3

Place of Origin STOCKHOLM VIA NORTHERN AND ANGLO — TRANSMITTED

Name from AFFAIRES ETRANGERES

To LEGATION SUEDE MEXICO — Censor's No. 44

Date 8 FEB 17 — Date 8 FEB 17 P

Time handed in 18-45 — Time copied 10.4 m

Text: — WITTON

00424	00191	00437	00416	13045	17214	06251	06491	
18147	19062	22293	17694	21141	04305	11580	39689	11313
10387	21604	23845	12137	17078	06015	16127	20438	22464
23612	16158	11836	09427	22927	09758	12137	22911	01245
15905	13247	07632	74038	06983	39689	11291	22464	05884
01240	22047	13372	06015	16127	52262	22394	17802	22284

Remarks

(2)

Date — Date

Time handed in — Time copied m

Text:

22464	13239	17257	01334	22309	22776	22931	22167
21995	18245	09427	12137	02985	17149	11664	04278
21668	23724	67893	04473	52262	14217	12137	14737
11313	09325	20362	15047	18812	97556		

AFFAIRES ETRANGERES.

Remarks SWEDISH CYPHER.

FIGURE 4. British intercept and decryption of Zimmermann's telegram to Heinrich von Eckardt, German envoy in Mexico, sent February 5, 1917, via Sweden. (Courtesy of the *National Archives*, London)

could share the telegram with the embassy, however, Hall needed to ensure that the Americans would remain unaware of the ongoing British eavesdropping operation on their diplomatic cables.[47]

Getting his hands on the Washington-Mexico version of the telegram now became the cornerstone of Hall's strategy, and he moved with habitual alacrity and independence. On Monday, February 5, he cabled Gaunt in New York "to try and get copies of all telegrams from German Embassy Washington to German Minister Mexico since Jan 18th. If procurable wire in original to me."[48] Gaunt then contacted the British envoy in Mexico City, Edward Thurstan, whose predecessor, Thomas Hohler, reportedly had exploited the predicament of a fellow countryman to recruit a spy in the Mexican telegraph office: In 1916, Hohler claimed, a fellow Englishman had asked for help in saving his brother from a firing squad. The Mexican government had accused the brother, a printer in the Mexican telegraph office, of forging banknotes, a crime punishable by death. Hohler managed to get the sentence annulled, and in return asked the printer to furnish him copies of all the German and Swedish telegrams, which Hohler, in turn, forwarded to Hall. Apparently, Thurstan arranged to extend this service when he took over from Hohler.[49] No independent source confirms Hohler's story, but the Mexican telegraph office by no means posed insurmountable security barriers to those seeking access. According to a British-German double agent, the German legation in Mexico regularly procured American messages from it.[50]

Apparently, Hall activated Thurstan without Foreign Office approval. Hall informed Charles Hardinge, his liaison at the Foreign Office, about the telegram on February 5. On the same day, he instructed Gaunt to procure a copy of Bernstorff's message in Mexico. Hall's message to Gaunt was dispatched at 10 a.m. To have been sent out so early, it must have been drafted, typed, and encoded at daybreak, leaving very little, if any, time for discussion with and approval by the Foreign Office. Hence, it is possible that Hall sent his request to Gaunt and Thurstan and then sought retroactive approval from Hardinge. Hall's recollections in his autobiography suggest that he activated Thurstan on his own initiative. After Hardinge had informed him that the Foreign Office would take no immediate decision on sharing the telegram with the Americans, Hall wrote, "but for this I had been prepared. On the other hand there was no reason why steps should not now be taken to obtain the additional evidence which we should require in the event of an exposure, and on the following day T[hurstan] was asked to secure copies of all telegrams sent by Bernstorff to Eckhardt [sic] since Jan. 18th. These were to be sent on to Gaunt, who was to forward them on to me as he received them, but put into our own cypher."[51]

Per Hall's instructions, Thurstan procured a copy of the encoded telegram from the Mexican telegraph office on February 8 and sent it to New York. From there, Gaunt forwarded a copy to London. It arrived at Room 40 on February 19.[52] As Hall had anticipated, the German embassy in Washington had used an obsolete code, 13040, for encryption. This code consisted of about 25,000 plaintext elements with a fair number of homophones and proper names, each of which was assigned a four- or five-digit code group. The Wilhelmstrasse had introduced 13040 to its missions in Central America and South America between 1907 and 1909 and to Washington and New York in 1912. The German embassy in Washington replaced code 13040 with 0075 in 1916, but Bernstorff had to use the older 13040 code for communications with the German legation in Mexico, which had not received code 0075 from the Wilhelmstrasse.[53]

In historiography, the decryption of code 13040 by the British has long been the stuff of mystery and lore. In one popular story, the British managed to capture the baggage of a German secret agent in the Middle East that contained a copy of the relevant codebook. The story involved an actual wartime event in Persia—the narrow escape of Wilhelm Waßmuß, the "German Lawrence of Arabia," from his British pursuers[54]—but Waßmuß did not carry a German codebook with him, and his colorful adventures had no bearing on the breaking of 13040.[55] Another account asserted that an Austrian wireless engineer in German employ smuggled a copy of the codebook to the British military attaché in The Hague. Later in the war, Hall supposedly arranged to have the engineer silenced: "I paid £1,000 to have that man shot," he allegedly said.[56] This story, too, cannot be corroborated. Ruthless as Hall may have been, his bag of tricks did not include assassination.

The prosaic truth is that the British broke 13040 not by means of a fanciful cloak-and-dagger operation, but through tedious, painstaking cryptanalysis. Room 40 had received German messages encoded in 13040 from early on in the war and therefore had a wealth of German crypto-material to practice on. Eventually, the code breakers reconstructed this German codebook,[57] and by 1917, Room 40 was routinely and quickly decrypting messages encoded in 13040.[58] Thanks to Room 40's fluency in 13040, de Grey was able to receive a copy of the Bernstorff-to-Eckardt cable on February 19, produce a complete decrypt of the telegram, and hand it to Hall on the same day (see Figs. 5 and 6).[59] On this day, a little over a month after the Wilhelmstrasse had sent the telegram, Hall had assembled all the elements he needed in order to inform the Americans about the Mexican-Japanese alliance scheme without revealing to them the ongoing British eavesdropping on U.S. diplomatic communications.

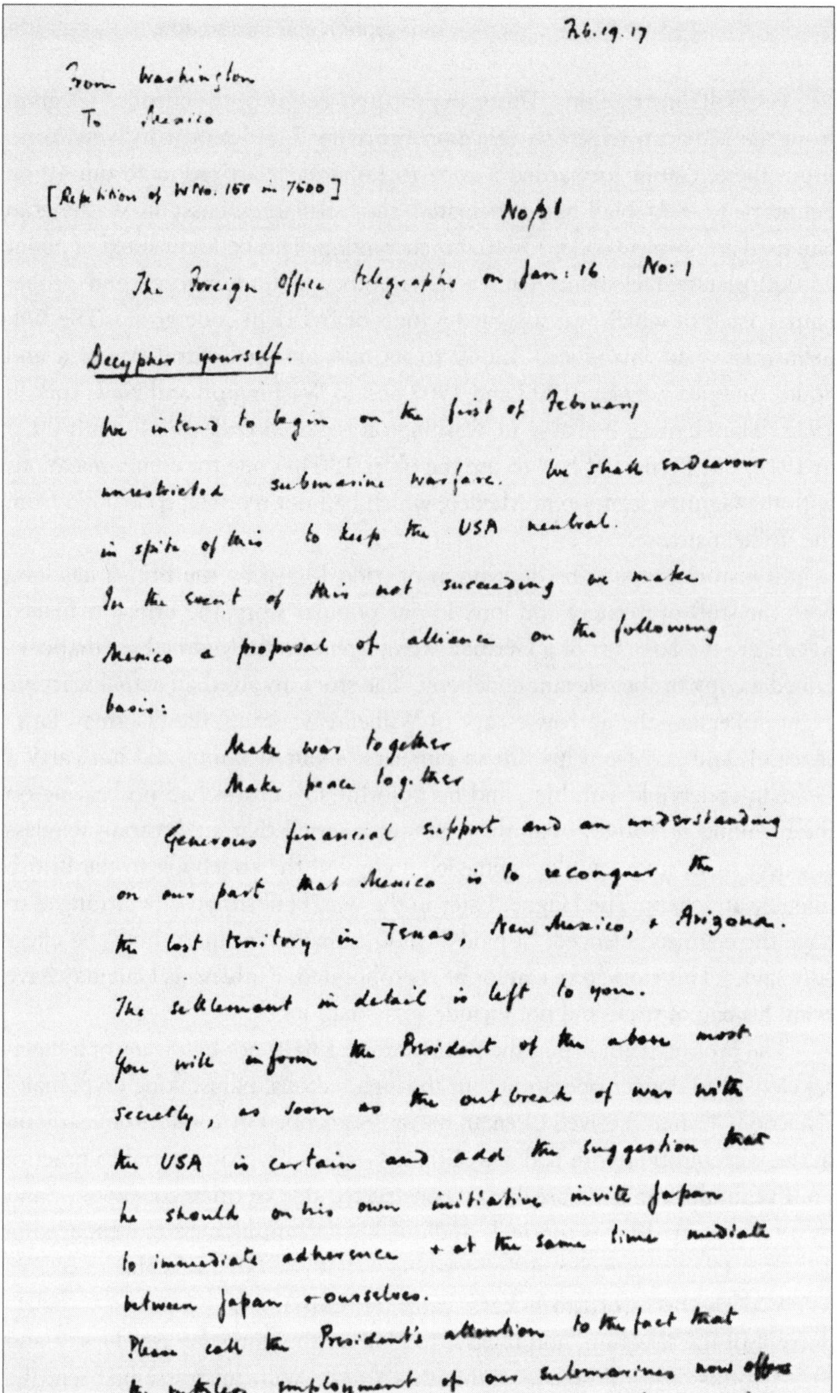

26.19.17

From Washington
To Mexico

[Repetition of tel. No. 158 in 7500]

No 1

The Foreign Office telegraphs on Jan: 16. No: 1

Decypher yourself.

We intend to begin on the first of February unrestricted submarine warfare. We shall endeavour in spite of this to keep the USA neutral.
In the event of this not succeeding we make Mexico a proposal of alliance on the following basis:

    Make war together
    Make peace together

Generous financial support and an understanding on our part that Mexico is to reconquer the lost territory in Texas, New Mexico, & Arizona.
The settlement in detail is left to you.
You will inform the President of the above most secretly, as soon as the outbreak of war with the USA is certain and add the suggestion that he should on his own initiative invite Japan to immediate adherence + at the same time mediate between Japan + ourselves.
Please call the President's attention to the fact that the ruthless employment of our submarines now offers the prospect of compelling England in a few months to make peace.
Acknowledge receipt

                               Zimmermann

FIGURE 5. The start of de Grey's handwritten complete decrypt of the Telegram. (Courtesy of the *National Archives*, London) *[handwritten annotation top left, partially illegible]* Inland cable on American soil—this was the one handed to Dr. Page and exposed by President.

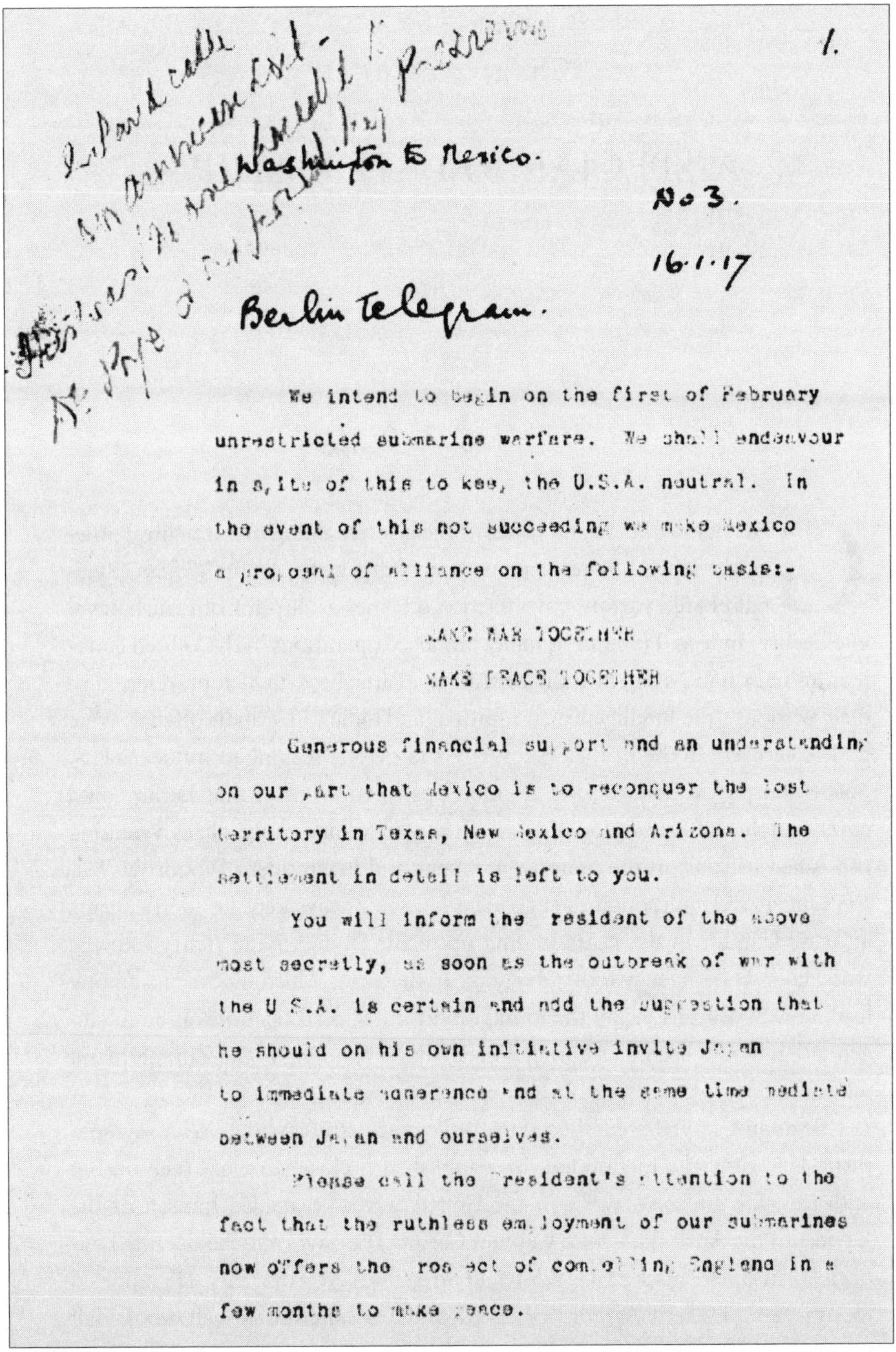

[handwritten top right] No 3.

16·1·17

[handwritten] Washington to Mexico.

[handwritten] Berlin telegram.

We intend to begin on the first of February unrestricted submarine warfare. We shall endeavour in spite of this to keep the U.S.A. neutral. In the event of this not succeeding we make Mexico a proposal of alliance on the following basis:-

MAKE WAR TOGETHER

MAKE PEACE TOGETHER

Generous financial support and an understanding on our part that Mexico is to reconquer the lost territory in Texas, New Mexico and Arizona. The settlement in detail is left to you.

You will inform the President of the above most secretly, as soon as the outbreak of war with the U S.A. is certain and add the suggestion that he should on his own initiative invite Japan to immediate adherence and at the same time mediate between Japan and ourselves.

Please call the President's attention to the fact that the ruthless employment of our submarines now offers the prospect of compelling England in a few months to make peace.

FIGURE 6. The typed version of de Grey's decrypt, with annotation, probably by William James, Hall's wartime deputy, across top left: "Inland cable on American soil—this was the one handed to Dr. Page and exposed by President." (Courtesy of the *National Archives*, London)

Chapter Eight

A SPECIAL RELATIONSHIP

Given its size and significance as the last remaining major neutral power, the United States was the prime target of Captain William Reginald Hall's various covert action schemes as director of British naval intelligence. Indeed, Hall ran so many influence operations in the United States that his liaison in New York, the British naval attaché, Guy Gaunt, referred to their work as "the Intelligence-cum-propaganda line."[1] German officials were no less active than the British in covertly and overtly seeking to influence U.S. policy and public opinion, but London possessed an asset that Berlin could never match: the British could count on the active assistance of high-ranking pro-Allied officials in the State Department and in President Woodrow Wilson's inner circle (although the president himself always kept London's agents at arm's length). In the years leading up to the United States' entry into the war, Hall and his agency took advantage of these pro-Allied sentiments among leading U.S. officials to lay the foundation for a special relationship in intelligence that would become a cornerstone in Hall's handling of the Zimmermann telegram.

Beginning in 1915, Hall worked a two-track strategy to cultivate sympathetic U.S. officials. In London, he established a close personal relationship with the U.S. embassy, while in the United States he availed himself of the services of the Australian-born Captain Gaunt. The naval attaché operated out of the British consulate at 44 Whitehall Street in New York City. He reported to Ambassador Cecil Arthur Spring Rice in Washington as well as to Hall in London. Flamboyant and bohemian, but also vain and egocentric, Gaunt was well-connected in American society and quickly developed a range of influential contacts, including former president Theodore Roosevelt, Assistant Secretary of the Navy Franklin D. Roosevelt, J. P. Morgan partner Edward Stettinius, and General Lionel Wood of the U.S. Army.[2]

Two of Gaunt's most important contacts were the journalist John R. Rathom and President Wilson's confidential adviser, Edward M. House. Rathom, the editor of the *Providence Journal*, had volunteered his services to Gaunt early in the war. Subsequently, the two men met almost daily. While Gaunt gave Rathom the details about secret German operations in the United States, the editor reciprocated by regularly publishing stories embarrassing to the Germans. Rathom also occasionally managed to get his fare into the pages of his old employer, the *New York Times*. Rathom, it seems, was motivated both by patriotism—like Gaunt, he was an Australian by birth—as well as dislike of President Wilson.[3]

Gaunt met regularly with House beginning in 1915. He flattered the American by imparting confidential (although mostly inconsequential) information to him, soliciting his opinion on many matters, and generally making him feel important. Gaunt's ego would occasionally get the better of him, such as when he boasted to House that "the British Intelligence Service is marvellously [*sic*] good. They have reports of everything going on in Berlin."[4] Such hyperbole notwithstanding, House generally appreciated Gaunt's efforts, and he even commended him warmly to First Lord of the Admiralty Arthur J. Balfour: "I want to express my high regard and appreciation of Captain Gaunt. I doubt whether you can realize the great service he has rendered our two countries. His outlook is so broad and he is so self-contained and fair-minded that I have been able to go to him at all times to discuss, very much as I would with you, the problems that have arisen."[5]

Hall could also count on pro-Allied sympathies in the State Department and its intelligence branch. An amorphous organization during the early years of the war, the department's secret service was formally set up as the Bureau of Secret Intelligence (BSI) in April 1916. Tasked with collecting information by nontraditional means and coordinating intelligence activities of other U.S. agencies, the extralegal BSI had a permanent staff of two officials in Washington. Counselor Frank K. Polk, a former New York lawyer and distant relative of President James K. Polk, headed the bureau, reporting directly to the secretary of state, while day-to-day operations were handled by Special Agent Leland Harrison, "positively the most mysterious and secretive man I have ever known," according to a colleague.[6] The bureau did not run independent agents or spies outside the United States, but drew on the vast network of

U.S. embassies and consulates. Numerous embassy secretaries, consuls, and customs officials doubled as intelligence gatherers and liaisons for special operations on behalf of BSI.[7]

Virtually all the top positions in the State Department were held by ardent interventionists, starting with the secretary, Robert Lansing. A Yankee corporation lawyer with a compact figure, dapper dress, silver hair, and immaculately trimmed moustache, Lansing had concluded as early as 1915 that a German victory was not in the United States' interest. Polk, Harrison, and American diplomats around the globe shared Lansing's sentiment. Not surprisingly, the department's pro-Allied bias colored its intelligence operations. During the period of U.S. neutrality, the BSI utilized American diplomats posted to Allied nations as well as diplomats serving with embassies in nations affiliated with the Central Powers. The intelligence assignments of diplomats in Allied and Central Power nations were diametrically opposed. American diplomats reporting to BSI from Germany and its allies generally worked against their host nations, while those assigned to Allied countries liaised closely with local intelligence agencies. For example, Allen Dulles, Lansing's nephew and later CIA director, was posted to the U.S. embassy in Vienna in 1916 with the assignment to covertly work for Austria's detachment from its alliance with Germany. On his way to Austria, Dulles probably met with British intelligence officers in London and received rudimentary training in basic spycraft.[8] On the other hand, the U.S. embassy in London and its BSI component became a citadel of pro-Allied sentiment and support.

Located in an elegant building at Grosvenor Square, behind Buckingham Palace, the U.S. embassy in London surpassed all other American legations in importance and size. By 1915 it employed eighty staff, several of whom worked for the State Department's intelligence branch. One of the embassy's most active BSI agents was the second secretary, Edward "Ned" Bell. Born in 1882, Bell hailed from an old New York family and attended Harvard, where he became good friends with the young Franklin Roosevelt. After entering the diplomatic service, he worked in Tehran and Havana before joining the U.S. embassy in London in 1913. A man of average height, brown eyes, and dark hair, Bell also had a quick mind; his enthusiasm and likeability endeared him to his British friends, who called him "Eddie." Bell had a penchant for cloak and dagger stories that predisposed him for intelligence work. A colleague of his later recalled that Bell held a conspiratorial view of the world, noting, "[H]e seemed to feel that sinister forces were at work to undermine the United States." In London, Bell was assigned the task of liaising with British intelligence. Hall quickly became his most important contact.[9]

On intelligence matters, Bell reported directly to Special Agent Harrison in Washington.[10] In London, he worked with several embassy staff members. Third Secretary Eugene Shoecraft, a career Foreign Service officer in his early twenties, often helped Bell with routine matters, and Bell's superior, the competent if finicky first secretary and later counselor Irwin B. Laughlin, was also in the know about Bell's special assignment. Most important, Bell had the wholehearted support of Ambassador Walter Hines Page.

Page was a particularly striking example of an unabashedly pro-Allied American diplomat, even by Lansing's standards. Page had assumed his post before the war, and like for most prewar U.S. ambassadors, his assignment had stemmed from his personal friendship with the president and donations to the Democratic Party, not his professional qualifications. A large, rawboned North Carolinian with a homely, big nose, Page was intelligent and articulate, and in the early stages of the war was closer to Wilson than perhaps any other ambassador in Europe. As the war progressed, Page identified ever more closely with his host country. As early as September 6, 1914, he warned Wilson that the Germans were "another case of Napoleon—even more brutal; a dream of universal conquest." After the sinking of the *Lusitania*, he came out openly for American intervention. The result of Page's unconcealed, fervent partisanship was a rapid decline in his standing in Washington. By fall 1915, Wilson and House considered Page "utterly hopeless." Even the staunchly pro-Allied State Department leadership began to have doubts. In November 1915, Polk told House that Page was "so pro-British that his judgment is of no value"; Lansing sought his recall. Disappointed and disenchanted, Page considered resigning at the beginning of Wilson's second term in March 1917, but in the end stayed on, mainly for lack of a suitable alternative.[11]

The British relished the fact that the top U.S. representative in London supported them so vigorously, yet they could not fail to notice Page's declining fortunes in Washington. "If President is angry at Page, can we do anything to help the latter?" the foreign secretary asked his staff in January 1917. A seasoned diplomat replied, "I am afraid not: The accusation against Mr. Page is that he is too pro-British + anything we say will only I fear strengthen this impression." His faltering reputation in Washington notwithstanding, Page's blatant pro-Allied leanings made him a first-rate conduit for Hall to channel pro-Allied and anti-German material to the U.S. government.[12]

The detection of German plots in the United States constituted one of the main foci of the British-American intelligence axis. The exposure of German naval captain Franz Rintelen von Kleist was an early example of such a joint operation. The "Dark Invader," as Rintelen styled himself in his postwar memoirs, was a dashing naval officer in his mid-thirties, sent to the United States by the German war ministry in April 1915. There, he was to interrupt the flow of U.S. arms and munitions to the Allies by purchasing large quantities of materiel to prevent the Allies from buying them or by sabotage.

Rintelen's can-do attitude quickly revived the German covert action program in the United States. He and his men set up a scheme to foment strikes in ammunition factories, and they ran a dangerous but highly successful operation of placing time-delayed explosive devices on board vessels leaving New York Harbor with cargo for the Allies, sending many of them to the bottom of the ocean. But Rintelen's arrogance and his reckless exploitation of the limited covert funds at the disposal of German officials in the United States antagonized the German military and naval attachés, Captain Franz von Papen and Captain Karl Boy-Ed. Only four months after Rintelen's arrival in New York, the two attachés had so successfully lobbied Berlin for Rintelen's recall that on August 3 the "Dark Invader" embarked for Holland under the name Emile Victor Gaché.[13]

Since Room 40 routinely intercepted and decrypted German transatlantic diplomatic traffic, the British knew about Rintelen's return trip beforehand. British officials quickly identified and arrested him during a routine search of his ship off Ramsgate on August 13 and delivered him to Hall. The British also seized Rintelen's papers, which revealed many of his covert schemes in the United States. On August 23, Hall informed Bell, of the U.S. embassy, of his findings, and Bell promptly forwarded them to his superiors. The Rintelen papers provided documentary proof to the Wilson administration of several illegal German covert operations in the United States, and they implicated the naval and the military attachés (but not the German ambassador, Johann Heinrich von Bernstorff).[14]

Only a few days after Rintelen's arrest, British-American intelligence cooperation scored another success. With Hall's knowledge and approval, the British naval attaché in New York ran a spy ring of Czech Americans under Emmanuel Voska. Some of Voska's men were Austrian citizens who had managed to find employment with the Austrian embassy. There they discovered that German and Austrian officials in the United States occasionally used the American journalist James F. J. Archibald as a courier, to carry confidential correspondence to Europe. In the summer of 1915, they learned that Archibald was planning a trip to Europe and would later that year embark on a Dutch steamer, carrying top secret Austrian documents with him. (On a hunch, the

German ambassador had declined to entrust documents to Archibald, but the German military attaché exerted less caution.)

Gaunt informed Hall of Archibald's impending voyage a month before his departure, giving the Royal Navy ample time for preparations. On August 30, British naval officers searched Archibald's ship at Falmouth, arrested the startled journalist, and sent him to London for interrogation. They also impounded the papers in his possession and delivered them to Hall, who immediately recognized their value as a propaganda tool. One document implicated the Austrian embassy in a scheme to instigate strikes among workers of Hungarian descent in U.S. arms munitions factories. In another paper, the Austrian ambassador, Constantin Dumba, describes President Wilson as obstinate. The German military attaché Papen, in a letter to his wife, refers to Americans as "those idiotic Yankees."[15]

Hall wanted to share the papers immediately with the U.S. embassy, but the Foreign Office balked for diplomatic reasons. Hall got into a major fight with the Admiralty (then under Balfour as first sea lord) over the issue. Without awaiting formal authorization from either department, Hall forwarded copies of the pertinent documents to Bell. Later, he nonchalantly informed the Foreign Office that the Americans already had the papers; he also had an altercation with Balfour, insisting that the first sea lord give a press conference to American journalists on certain naval issues touched upon in the Archibald papers. Balfour refused.[16]

The Rintelen and Archibald papers caused quite a commotion in the United States. The U.S. government released excerpts of the Archibald papers to the press, causing public outrage and stoking American concerns over German espionage and sabotage operations in North America. The State Department declared Austrian ambassador Dumba persona non grata, and Vienna recalled him in September 1915. The Rintelen and Archibald papers also eroded the standing of the German service attachés, Papen and Boy-Ed, and the U.S. government declared them personae non gratae in December 1915.[17] When Papen's ship called at Falmouth on January 3, 1916, Hall had his papers confiscated, Papen's protests of diplomatic immunity notwithstanding. The papers revealed further evidence of German plots in the United States, and Hall promptly handed copies to Page, who forwarded them to Lansing in Washington.[18]

The U.S. embassy also played an important role in Hall's efforts to destroy the reputation of Roger Casement in 1916. Casement was an Irishman with a distinguished career in the British colonial service. In the years leading up to World War I, he had become involved with the Irish independence movement and on the outbreak of war had traveled to Germany to lobby for German military support of an armed Irish uprising. In Berlin, he met with military officers as well as Undersecretary Zimmermann and Chancellor Theobald von Bethmann Hollweg. As the Irish Easter rebellion gained steam, Casement asked the Germans to send him to Ireland, and on the evening of April 20, 1916, the German submarine U-19 dropped him and two companions at Tralee Bay, an isolated coastal strip on the western tip of Ireland.[19]

Casement's mission was doomed before he even set foot on Irish soil. Room 40 had intercepted and decrypted several German messages about his impending return. British authorities arrested him on the morning after his landing and transferred him to London. There, Hall and Basil Thomson of Scotland Yard's Special Branch interviewed him. Casement demanded publication of his capture in order to call off the rebellion and avoid unnecessary bloodshed in Ireland, but Hall refused, quite possibly because he wanted the rebellion to proceed so the government could crush it and deal with the Irish question once and for all.[20]

British forces subdued the ensuing uprising on Easter Monday after heavy fighting in Dublin. Casement was tried for high treason, found guilty in July 1916, and sentenced to death by hanging. The case, however, presented a serious perception problem for London. Casement had a large number of supporters, especially in the United States, where the execution of Irish insurrectionists following perfunctory courts martial generated widespread disapproval. As a distinguished novelist and leading Anglophile wrote, "Nothing more lamentable in the course of the war now raging has come to pass than this act of bloody vengeance by the English Government."[21] London's determination to carry out the death sentence against Casement antagonized President Wilson, and the U.S. Senate adopted a resolution appealing for clemency. Aware of Casement's high moral standing in the United States, Hall and Thomson hatched a plot to destroy the Irishman's reputation and blunt objections to his execution.

Casement was homosexual and kept detailed diaries of his amorous encounters. The entries were interspersed with graphic details about his sexual adventures.[22] Upon his arrest, these explosive documents fell into the hands of Hall and Thomson. Neither man had much tolerance for anybody who strayed from his set of values. (Thomson was an anti-Semite who called humanitarians "sub-human.")[23] Both men strongly disapproved of Casement's homosexuality, but more important, they recognized the diaries' potential for destroying Casement's public image as a valiant servant of a just cause. As early as April 23, Hall and Thomson copied some of the most graphic extracts of Casement's diaries and began circulating them in London clubs.[24] Copies also reached members of the cabinet, Foreign Office, and the Admiralty.

Since Casement had many sympathizers in the United States, Thomson and Hall set about spreading the news to America. Thomson discreetly showed some of the excerpts to Ambassador Page, who professed to be suitably shocked: "Forgive me, but I have a luncheon engagement today and, if I read any more, my host and his other guests will think that I have been taken seriously ill! One needs a strong stomach to eat anything after reading this." Despite his ostensible discomfort, Page did not miss a beat in adding, "Still I suppose that it will be my duty to send it to the State Department."[25]

Meanwhile, Hall showed extracts of Casement's diary to Ben Allen of the Associated Press and forwarded copies to Gaunt, who released them to American newspapers. By June 30, when Foreign Secretary Edward Grey ruled that no further distribution should take place, friend and foe were already well acquainted with Casement's "sins." The U.S. Senate passed a motion of regret about Casement's death sentence in July 1916, but the Foreign Relations Committee judged it too critical of the British government and sent a blander version to the White House. There, it was "unaccountably" held up for several hours, and thus did not reach London in time to affect the prisoner's fate. Casement was executed on August 3.[26]

When it became obvious that the United States would not enter the war in response to Germany's declaration of unrestricted submarine warfare in February 1917, Hall activated his connections with pro-Allied American officials to place an explosive piece of information in the American press. This time Hall decided to inform the U.S. government of Zimmermann's Mexican-Japanese alliance scheme, with a view to "rouse the whole of the United States and . . . force the President to declare war."[27]

In order to execute this operation, Hall needed the help of Arthur Balfour, even if the foreign secretary would play no more than a supporting role. As Hall wrote in his autobiography, "I wanted Mr. Balfour's assistance, whether in his official capacity as Foreign Secretary or privately as the impeccable 'elder statesman' I did not mind."[28] On February 5, nearly three weeks after he had first learned of the telegram, Hall informed his liaison at the Foreign Office, Permanent Undersecretary Charles Hardinge, of the telegram in general terms and recommended that Balfour personally hand over a copy to the Americans. Hardinge, a seasoned old-school diplomat who had just returned from his post as viceroy of India, "remained his usual cool self, interested but cautious. He asked for my views and promised to lay them before Mr. Balfour. No immediate decision, he thought, could be taken, but for this I had been prepared."[29]

About a week later, Hall began seeing Hardinge's secretary, Ronald Camp-bell, on a daily basis to discuss the feasibility and possible pitfalls of sharing the telegram with the Americans. For every suggestion Hall made, the Foreign Office raised an objection. Apparently, the Foreign Office feared that the U.S. government might surmise the source of Hall's intelligence. As Hall conceded in his autobiography, Hardinge "very properly" shunned "any step which could possibly convey the impression to Washington that there was a chambre noire in the Foreign Office [eavesdropping on American communications] or that the British Government was endeavouring to influence a neutral State in its favour."[30]

Following his meeting with Hall, Hardinge immediately informed Balfour of Germany's covert overtures to Mexico and Japan, and the foreign secretary promptly took steps to ascertain Tokyo's loyalty to the Allies and prepare for the eventuality of Mexico joining the enemy camp. On February 13, Balfour sounded out the Japanese ambassador who emphasized that "there were not any relations of interest between Japan and Mexico and that the Japanese had been most anxious to remove suspicions which Americans were always ready to entertain of Japanese intrigues in Mexico."[31] The Japanese ambassador to Washington assured his British colleague in the same vein that Tokyo "had no intention of disturbing [U.S.-Japanese relations] in order to please the Mexi-cans or to seek chimerical advantages in a country in which Japan has no vital interests."[32]

Although Balfour could feel reasonably certain about Japan's loyalties, he was rather anxious about Mexico's position. "In the opinion of the For-eign Office," Balfour wrote to the Admiralty, "if the United States go to war with Germany, the last vestige of restraint on [Mexican leader Venustiano] Carranza's action will be removed, and the [British-owned] oilfields will be in greater danger than ever."[33] Britain's envoy to Mexico, Edward Thurstan, reit-erated these fears in late February,[34] and Ambassador Spring Rice in Washing-ton regarded the telegram as proof that "a real practical danger is imminently threatening."[35] The diplomats' growing concern about the possibility of a hos-tile German-Mexican combination added to the Foreign Office's interest in giving Hall carte blanche on all issues regarding the telegram.

While the Foreign Office deliberated, Hall acted. Immediately after he had informed Hardinge of the telegram on February 5, he instructed Gaunt in New York to procure a copy of the telegram in Mexico City.[36] Hall also took the momentous decision to inform the U.S. embassy about the telegram before the Foreign Office authorized him to do so. On February 19, he called Bell at the embassy and invited him over to his office. Bell arrived half an hour later, and Hall showed him a decrypt of Ambassador Bernstorff's relayed telegram to Heinrich von Eckardt, the German envoy in Mexico City. Bell received the message in the spirit in which it was provided, and Hall gleefully listened to his infuriated American colleague: "Mexico to 'reconquer the lost territory'! Texas and Arizona?" He added, according to Hall's autobiography, "Why not Illinois and New York while they were about it?"[37] The American diplomat wondered briefly whether the telegram might be a hoax, but quickly came around to accepting its authenticity.[38]

In the course of their conversation, Hall candidly told Bell that the Foreign Office had not authorized him to share this information with him:

> I explained that the Foreign Office had not yet been able to come to a decision. There were difficulties in our way. Information which I had no objection to giving him privately would have to be given officially to his Government. It had still to be settled whether the dispatch should be shown only to the President or given to the American public. "What I want you to do . . . [i]s to tell your Ambassador what you have seen and beg him to make no use of the information until Mr. Balfour has made a decision."

Bell agreed to "sit tight . . . for as long as you say."[39] Both Hall and Bell surely understood, however, that it was highly unrealistic to expect the embassy not to inform Washington of the telegram, even if Balfour subsequently refused to authorize Hall's initiative. In other words, the director of naval intelligence had unilaterally made the decision to share a highly sensitive piece of information with a foreign power without proper authorization from his own government.

Why did Hall inform the Americans of the telegram before the Foreign Office gave him the green light to do so? According to his memoirs, he simply sought to ensure "that at the first possible moment our friends at the American Embassy should share, unofficially, in what was so essentially an 'American' secret."[40] This was not a convincing argument coming, as it did, from someone who had professed his intention not to disclose the telegram at all if the United States joined the war in reaction to Germany's declaration of unrestricted submarine warfare.

Hall's true motivations for proceeding as he did were threefold. First, Hall had concluded that President Wilson would not respond to Berlin's declaration of unrestricted submarine warfare by declaring war on Germany and therefore required further prodding. Second, Hall finally possessed a full (rather than a partial) decrypt, and he could truthfully tell the Americans that the British had intercepted the telegram between Washington and Mexico, rather than Berlin and Washington. Avoiding reference to the Berlin–Washington intercept would divert American attention from possibly contemplating that Britain might be eavesdropping on U.S. transatlantic cables. Third, by bypassing the Foreign Office, Hall retained control of an operation that was shaping up to be his greatest intelligence coup and one of the most consequential of the war. Although he could be reasonably sure that Balfour, eager to bring in the United States, would approve the operation, he effectively forced his government's hand by informing the U.S. embassy of the telegram's full text before the Foreign Office chose to do so. If the Foreign Office were to drag its feet for diplomatic reasons, Hall could drop a hint to the Americans, and Page would take up the issue directly with Balfour.

After Hall had shared the telegram with Bell, he "felt that the time had come for immediate action, and formally pressed for a decision" in a discussion with Campbell, Hardinge's secretary. On February 20, Campbell sent Hardinge a memo putting forth Hall's suggestion that the telegram be given to the Americans. This could be done, in Hall's opinion, by giving the telegram to the American government or by leaking it directly to the American press. Either way, the memo explained, Hall expressed confidence that he could keep Britain's role secret. Rather than inform Campbell about his meeting with Bell the day before, Hall created the false impression that he was still waiting for Foreign Office authorization to go ahead: "[Hall] would suggest that he be authorized to give the substance to Mr. Bell of United States Embassy who after informing the Ambassador would see that it reached the President."[41]

At this point, things could have gone seriously wrong for Hall, because Hardinge expressed strong reservations about sharing the telegram with the Americans. The seasoned British diplomat pointed to the central dilemma of Britain's continued eavesdropping on U.S. cables: "it seems to me that it would be difficult to explain to Mr. Bell how we came to be in possession of this news, and how to convince him of its authenticity." Furthermore, Hardinge maintained that the telegram should only be released to the U.S. press if Britain's role could be effectively concealed. [42] Hardinge did not advise a decision one way or the other to Balfour, but he had raised two important issues. In the event, Balfour brushed all objections aside. "I think Captain Hall may be left to clinch this problem. He knows the ropes better than anyone," he determined.[43]

With Balfour's retroactive approval, Hall's gamble had paid off, and he was free to wrap up the greatest intelligence coup of his career.

Hall lost no time. On February 20, he visited the U.S. embassy, this time "officially" to hand the telegram to Bell's boss, Irwin Laughlin. As Laughlin read the text, he started patting his bald head, a nervous habit he exhibited when excited. Obviously more concerned with a pretext for war than the seriousness of the Mexican or Japanese threats to the United States, he exclaimed, "This is wonderful!" The two men then went to see Page, who read the telegram several times, banged his fist on the desk, and reportedly declared that the document must be sent immediately to Washington.[44] The ambassador appears to have put on a show to obscure the fact that the preceding day, Bell likely had bypassed his immediate supervisor, Laughlin, and informed Page of the telegram.[45]

Over the next three days, Hall, Page, Bell, and Laughlin discussed the most effective method of delivering the telegram to Washington. Hall used this exchange primarily to plant red herrings as to how the Germans had sent the telegram. He insinuated that the German foreign office had used several methods of transmission, rather than a single route (that is, the American transatlantic cable), and that the British had decrypted the telegram by means of a captured German codebook, rather than through the efforts of a team of skilled cryptanalysts (which might make the Americans wonder what else these people did).

Page, for one, was completely taken in by Hall's yarns: "What a story is here!" he noted in his diary on February 24. Much of his esteem for, and even idolization of, Hall originates from this period. "If there be any life left in me after the war," he wrote to President Wilson about a year later, "and if Hall's abnormal activity and ingenuity have not caused him to be translated, I wish to spend a week with him at some quiet place, and then spend a year in writing out what he will have told me. That's the shortest cut to immortality for him and for me that has yet occurred to me."[46] Page and Hall quickly agreed that the most effective method of relaying the telegram was for the widely respected Balfour to officially hand it over to Page. Both sides regarded Balfour's role in the scheme as largely ceremonial. Nigel de Grey, who had deciphered the telegram, referred to the foreign secretary as Hall's "mouthpiece," and Bell called Page and Balfour "intermediaries" who were subsequently to be dispensed with. It was almost as if the Anglo-American intelligence community had assumed a life of its own.[47]

Following the prearranged script, Page met with Balfour in the foreign secretary's office on the afternoon of Friday, February 23. Balfour ceremoniously

handed Page an English translation of the telegram, emphasizing that it had
been "bought in Mexico" and omitting the fact that it had first been intercepted on the American transatlantic cable.[48] Balfour expressly authorized the
Americans to publish the telegram, but in the excitement of the moment he
apparently failed to impress on Page the necessity of keeping certain aspects
of the operation strictly secret; the Foreign Office reminded the American
ambassador in a brief note to this effect shortly afterwards.[49] Both Balfour and
Page were deeply moved by the scene. "As dramatic a moment as I remember
in all my life," the British foreign secretary later recalled.[50] Page returned to
the embassy "with blood in his eye."[51] Even though the two diplomats were
evidently overcome with emotion, their encounter at the Foreign Office had a
farcical element to it since both Balfour and Page had known for several days
exactly what to expect.

At the embassy, Page began furiously crafting an accompanying note for
Lansing and Wilson. This task took him longer than anticipated, and in order
to ensure proper attention to his message, he sent off a telegram at 2 a.m. on
Saturday morning, announcing his forthcoming scoop: "In about three hours
I shall send a telegram of great importance to the President and Secretary of
State."[52] Meanwhile, Bell and the embassy's third secretary, Shoecraft, spent
all night encoding Page's message,[53] which was finally dispatched at 1 p.m.
on February 24. The ambassador transmitted an English translation of the
telegram, adding, "The receipt of this information has so greatly exercised the
British Government that they have lost no time in communicating it to me to
transmit to you, in order that our government may be able without delay to
make such disposition as may be necessary in view of the threatened invasion
of our territory." (As we have seen, "the threatened invasion" of U.S. territory
was the furthest thing from Hall's mind when he plotted his coup.) Page also
reiterated the misleading story about sole procurement of the telegram in Mexico and pointed out Britain's request to keep the telegram's source confidential.
However, "they put no prohibition on the publication of Zimmermann's telegram itself," which was precisely what both the British government as well as
the U.S. embassy wanted. Finally, Page asked that Balfour be thanked officially
"for the service his government has rendered us."[54]

With the dispatch of the telegram to the State Department, the initiative
shifted to Washington. British politicians, intelligence officers, and the U.S.
embassy staff in London now largely assumed the role of anxious observers.
As Hall recalled in his memoirs:

After [the dispatch of the Telegram to Washington], I suppose, there came what was for me personally the most anxious time of the whole war. I had assumed this new responsibility: would it be justified? Had we done all that was possible to safeguard Room 40? Even so, was there a chance that the Zimmermann Telegram would misfire? I was, I admit, dreadfully worried. America's entry into the war within the next few weeks was of the greatest possible importance to the Allies. I was, indeed, staking everything upon it. But suppose there were further delays: suppose something went wrong! Both Dr. Page and Eddie Bell were confident, but I confess that for about three days I lived in a kind of nightmare.

Hall does not explicitly state the source of his concern, and what he meant by the telegram "misfiring" or "something [going] wrong!" Yet his anxiety during these three days has never been sufficiently explained. He nebulously pointed to the possibility that Room 40 might be compromised and that the telegram would fail to bring America into the war, but in fact, his anxiety was closer to home. Although he had done his level best to make the Americans believe that the British had procured the telegram in Mexico, he could not count on the Americans drawing the desired conclusion. President Wilson, who tended to take personal offense at diplomatic slights and was extremely sensitive to allegations of being influenced by others in his political decision making, surely would not have appreciated the fact that the British were regularly reading his messages. Also, untimely revelations about the British connection in the American press could take away the telegram's propagandistic thunder and might even cause it to boomerang on the Allies. Hall was therefore understandably relieved when Page informed him on February 28 that the U.S. administration had thanked Balfour for information "of such inestimable value" and announced Washington's decision to publish the telegram on March 1.[55]

Some loose ends remained. In order to convince the Americans of the genuineness of the telegram, and to further divert attention from the fact that British naval intelligence had first intercepted it by eavesdropping on the United States' transatlantic cable, the British advised the Americans to procure a copy of the Bernstorff–Eckardt telegram in Washington. Since Bernstorff's message was encrypted, and therefore illegible to the Americans, the British provided Page with information as to how to identify the relevant copy. Page relayed this information to Lansing in his message of February 24: the telegram "was sent via Washington and relayed by Bernstorff on January 19. You can probably obtain a copy of the text relayed by Bernstorff from the cable office in Washington. The first group is the number of the telegram 130, and the second is 13042, indicating the number of the code used. The last group is 97556, which is Zimmermann's signature." The British also provided Page with a complete copy of the encoded text of the telegram, which Page promised to send by mail, so that the State Department could compare it to any encrypted telegram obtained from the Washington office of Western Union, which the German embassy used to send telegrams to Mexico.[56]

The State Department sought to avail itself of this opportunity not only to confirm the British information about the telegram but to procure other German diplomatic messages from Washington to Latin America as well.[57] Lansing's deputy, Polk, took the lead in obtaining these messages from privately owned American commercial telegraph companies. After applying considerable pressure on the company's director, Polk managed to hector Western Union into handing over several copies of telegrams from the German embassy to Mexico City, including a decrypt of the telegram.[58] In mid-March, Polk confidentially requested copies of German diplomatic cable traffic from his personal friend, Clarence Mackay, the director of the Commercial Cable and Commercial Pacific Cable companies. Despite reservations, Mackay eventually agreed to pass the telegrams to the State Department. Among these were messages sent by Bernstorff to Cuba, Guatemala, Haiti, and various South American countries in January and February 1917.[59]

All the Western Union and Commercial Cable dispatches obtained by Polk were encoded, and the Americans had no means of decrypting them. Hence, Lansing sent Page three encoded telegrams from Bernstorff to German legations in Latin America (not including Zimmermann's) on February 28 and instructed the American ambassador to "endeavor to obtain copy of German code from Mr. Balfour, decode the following messages and telegraph translations." Lansing sought to encourage British cooperation by adding, "Contents of messages decoded here would of course be communicated to the British Government."[60] The British refused, however, arguing "the actual code would be of no use to us as it was never used straight, but with a great number of variations which are known to only one or two experts. They cannot be spared to go to America." Instead, the British would "gladly decipher" any of Bernstorff's messages given to them by the Americans.[61]

The British reply was disingenuous. It was true that the cryptanalytic process was more complex than the Americans imagined, because the German embassy in Washington employed at least three different codes (13040, 5950, 7500) and often used superencipherment, enciphering an already encoded message. Yet the telegram was not superenciphered and could have been read by anyone in possession of a reconstructed 13040 codebook. The actual reason for Hall's declining the Americans' request was his categorical refusal to transfer any cryptographic intelligence to Washington.[62] As Hall wrote in his autobiography, "My views, however, remained unchanged. Any deciphering which had to be done must be carried out in London and under my immediate supervision."[63]

The question of verification assumed additional urgency when American newspapers published the text of the telegram on March 1. On the evening of that day, Lansing informed Page that members of Congress were (accurately) charging that the British had provided the telegram to the Wilson administration as a way to influence U.S. policy. Lansing therefore asked Page to obtain British permission for the ambassador or one of his staff to personally decrypt a copy of the encoded telegram (obtained from Western Union) and send the decrypt to Washington (Fig. 7). As he explained: "[T]this course will materially strengthen [the U.S. government's] position and make it possible for the Department to state that it had secured the Zimmermann note from our own people."[64]

On Friday, March 2, Bell took an encoded copy of the telegram to the Admiralty, where de Grey awaited him with the reconstructed 13040 German codebook. The two men retired to Hall's office and got to work. According to Bell, he "did the job myself and it was all correct, and Eugene [Shoecraft] and I sent back the true reading (in German) of the decode by telegraph much to the Department's joy."[65] Hall supports this version of events: "And there in the presence of de Grey, Claud Serocold and myself, an American citizen [Bell] decyphered for himself the message as received from his own Government."[66] De Grey, on the other hand, gives a more flowery account of the episode. Though lengthy, de Grey's recollection bears reprinting in full because it differs from Bell's and Hall's accounts in that he claims that he deciphered the telegram all by himself, with Bell merely looking on:

Being in a hurry I grabbed my own version of 13040 without thinking and went off to the D.N.I.'s room. There Edward Bell produced a copy of the telegram and invited me both to decypher it in his presence and to explain the system as I went along. I gaily proceeded and all went well with the first few groups but then on coming to the next I found my book blank and realized with horror that I hadn't done my homework. I had not written up my book and this was by way of being a demonstration

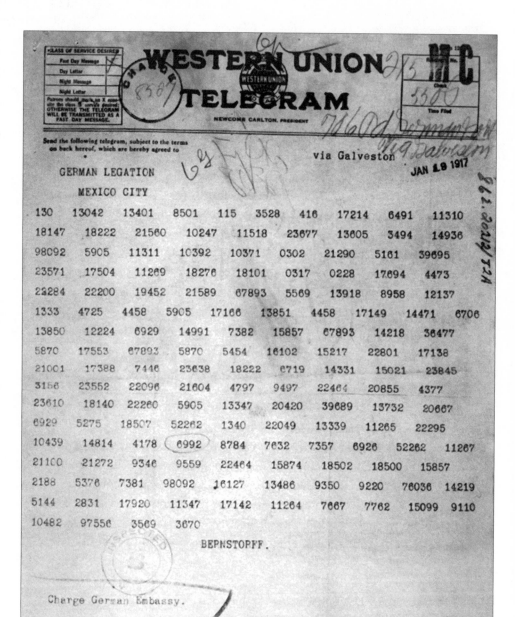

FIGURE 7. Copy of German ambassador Johann Heinrich von Bernstorff's Western Union telegram obtained by State Department counselor Frank Polk. (Courtesy of the *National Archives and Records Administration*, College Park, Maryland)

to the Americans of the absolute castiron certainty of our story, good enough to carry firm conviction to their hesitating hearts.

If I stopped and fetched another book he would suspect at once that we had faked it up for his benefit. If I let him see that I was writing it down out of my head he would not have believed me. If he did not believe me we should fail and have lost the greatest opportunity ever presented to us. Several seconds of bloody sweat. Then I bluffed. I showed him all the groups when they had been written in my book and passed quickly over those that were not, writing the words into the copy of the telegram by heart.

Edward Bell, most charming man, was thoroughly convinced—the more easily I think that he wanted to be convinced and anyhow regarded the whole thing as black magic. A more unconvincing demonstration could never have been given.[67]

Who decrypted the telegram—Bell or de Grey? The truth may be somewhere in the middle. The first page and a few pages of the second of the original decrypt produced that day are in Bell's handwriting, but the remainder is in de Grey's (Fig. 8).[68] This would suggest that Bell started the process but quickly deferred to the more experienced de Grey, who professionally decrypted the rest.[69]

"That's torn it," Bell said according to Hall when the full decrypt was produced.[70] Page cabled the State Department at 4 p.m. that day: "Bell took the text of the German message contained in your 4494 of yesterday to Admiralty and there, himself, deciphered it from the German code which is in the Admiralty's possession."[71] The Wilson administration was now fully equipped to parry potentially embarrassing questions about the telegram's origins or a German denial of its authenticity.

The British wrapped up their coup by seeking to maximize the telegram's effect in the United States and to prevent exposure of their own role in its interception and communication to the U.S. government. The Foreign Office sought to accomplish the former by stoking American concerns about Mexican intrigue. Thomas Hohler, having transferred from Mexico to the British embassy in Washington, where he pursued propaganda and liaison duties, warned Chandler Anderson of the State Department that the Germans had obtained such a strong influence over Carranza that armed conflict with Mexico might be unavoidable, even if Washington refrained from declaring war on Germany.[72] On February 27, Balfour asked Britain's envoy in Mexico, Edward

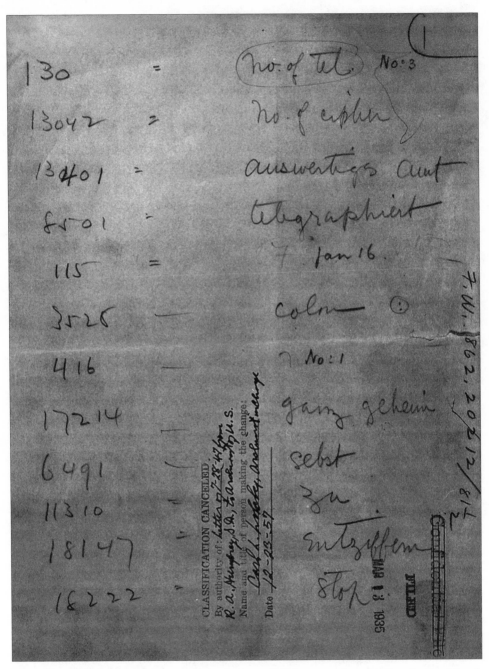

FIGURE 8. The first and last page of the Bernstorff decrypt produced in London on March 2, 1917. Note the different handwriting on page 1 (Bell's) and 4 (de Grey's). (Courtesy of the *National Archives and Records Administration*, College Park, Maryland)

4458 gemeinsam
17149 Friedenschluß.

14471 ⊙
6706 reichlich
13850 finanziell
12224 unterstützung
6929 und

14991 einverständnis
7382 unsererseits.
158(5)7 daß
67893 Mexico.
14218 in
36477 Texas
5870 ⑤
17553 neu
67893 Mexico..
5870 ①
5454 AR
16102 IZ
15217 ON
22801 A

Thurstan, whether he could confirm "strong rumours" about German activity in Mexico. The foreign secretary specifically requested information on "suspicious concentration of Germans" in that country.[73] On the same day, Thurstan replied that he felt "no doubt as to German movement" and would enquire further.[74]

This was good enough for Balfour, who on March 1 informed Page that Thurstan "has telegraphed that the Germans in large numbers are arriving there daily from the United States and that he has good reason to fear impending German activities in that country."[75] The foreign secretary thus reported a mere rumor as hard fact to Page since Thurstan had never confirmed that Germans were crossing the U.S.-Mexican border in large numbers. Two weeks later, Balfour sent a telegram to Thurstan inquiring whether New York press reports were correct in stating that up to 150,000 Germans had already arrived in Mexico. A Foreign Office official scribbled in the margin of Balfour's message: "well under 10000, that very liberal."[76]

Other Foreign Office officials were prepared to go further than merely providing the Americans with inflated estimates of German citizens in Mexico. Both Ambassador Spring Rice and Hohler suggested to the U.S. adviser Edward House that a Mexican faction acceptable to the United States and Britain be provided with arms and money so they could overthrow Carranza's government. "Such a method would be far cheaper and promised far better results than a policy of intervention," Spring Rice concluded.[77] House appeared interested but remained noncommittal.[78] A few Foreign Office diplomats continued to contemplate a coup against Carranza to, in the words of Thurstan, bring to power "white men by blood and education."[79] Only later in the war were such covert action plans definitively shelved.

As Hall's operation unfolded across the Atlantic, the director sought to restrict knowledge of his agency's involvement to a tight circle of confidantes. He even kept the British naval attaché in New York out of the loop, until Gaunt learned about the telegram from House. On February 26, Gaunt inquired whether Hall could provide "any information which would make announcement fuller and more decisive."[80] The next day, Hall outlined the telegram's content to Gaunt, adding, "Do not use till Aaron [Hall's code name for President Wilson] announces it, premature exposure fatal."[81] Three days later, when the telegram was published in the American press, Hall warned the naval attaché "that knowledge of this affair shall never be traced to British sources." Yet for all his talk of secrecy, Hall could not help boasting to Gaunt: "Alone I did it."[82]

Chapter Nine

THE SMOKING GUN

On January 19, 1917, the State Department delivered an encoded telegram from the German foreign office to the German embassy in Washington. The Americans had agreed to send this message on behalf of the Wilhelmstrasse because the Germans had assured them that it contained instructions of a harmless and personal nature for Ambassador Johann Heinrich von Bernsdorff in Washington.[1] Nothing could have been further from the truth.

The encrypt consisted of two separate dispatches: a lengthy telegram (no. 157), consisting of 856 cipher groups, and a short annex (no. 158). Seven German embassy clerks immediately began deciphering the encoded text. When they were done, they had produced two plain texts—in telegram no. 157, Chancellor Theobald von Bethmann Hollweg informs Ambassador Bernstorff of Germany's intention to declare unrestricted submarine warfare and issues instructions for Bernstorff to inform the U.S. government of this decision on February 1 (which the Germans would subsequently change to January 31); in telegram no. 158, Zimmermann makes the German offer of alliance to Mexico and Japan and gives instructions for Bernstorff to forward the proposal to the German envoy in Mexico City. Two German clerks re-enciphered the second message and on the same day dispatched it through Western Union to Mexico.[2]

In his memoirs, Bernstorff emphasizes that his embassy served merely as an intermediary for the telegram, adding that he "disapproved of its contents."[3] There is no reason to doubt the sincerity of the ambassador, whose primary goal had always been the preservation of peace with the United States, not preparation for war. At the same time, Bernstorff had very little time to consider the German alliance offer to Mexico. Telegram no. 157 was of far more immediate concern to him since the imminence of unrestricted submarine warfare was bound to have major and immediate repercussions on U.S.-German relations. The ambassador realized that this decision left him little room to maneuver and would in all probability push the United States into the Allied camp. "War inevitable in view of the proposed action," he cabled back to Berlin on the same day while urging postponement of unrestricted submarine warfare.[4] On January 26, he again strongly counseled against unleashing the U-boats, adding perceptively "that we will now reach a better peace through conferences than if the United States joins our enemies." The German leadership dismissed Bernstorff's advice out of hand. "Regret suggestion impracticable," Berlin informed Bernstorff curtly on January 29.[5] Two days later, on the afternoon of January 31, Bernstorff proceeded to Robert Lansing's office at the State, War, and Navy Building (today's Eisenhower Executive Office Building) and with a heavy heart handed the secretary of state the text of Germany's declaration of unrestricted submarine warfare.[6]

The note did not come as a complete surprise to Lansing and the State Department. On January 8, the American ambassador in Constantinople, Abram I. Elkus, had reported that Germany was planning for "pitiless submarine warfare" by the end of February.[7] Two days later, the American ambassador to Berlin, James Gerard, submitted a similar report.[8] On January 24, Lansing drafted a "[N]ote on the Probable Renewal of Submarine Warfare." This report was apparently partially based on information derived from wiretaps at the German embassy, since Lansing references a conversation in which a prominent member of the German embassy berates a friend, telling him that he should not have let a mutual acquaintance sail for Europe "now."[9] Lansing later noted that he was merely surprised at the early start of the submarine campaign, not the announcement itself.[10] Lansing immediately informed President Woodrow Wilson of Bernstorff's note. The secretary of state hoped that unrestricted submarine warfare would trigger U.S. intervention, but the president's verdict was not a foregone conclusion, as Wilson's political decisions were closely intertwined with his complex personality.

Wilson was a man of many contradictions. Tall, slim, with angular facial features, a square jaw, and piercing gray eyes, Wilson projected an aura of determination and authority, but underneath his constitution he was fragile; his failing health would cloud the final years of his presidency. He was a deeply religious and well-educated idealist, yet he could be remarkably stubborn, petty, and vengeful. Wilson believed profoundly in the democratic process but had little patience for those who failed to see things his way. "[H]e does not seem to have the slightest conception that he can ever be wrong," the French ambassador, Jean Jules Jusserand, acerbically remarked.[11] While he encouraged his advisers to share their thoughts with him, at the end of the day, he preferred to make decisions alone.[12]

The one person who had a certain degree of influence on U.S. foreign policy was the president's only close male friend, "Colonel" Edward Mandel House.[13] A wealthy Texas Democrat, House was in many ways Wilson's opposite. Small, pale, self-effacing, and frail, the "colonel" loved to operate and manipulate behind the scenes. House understood that Wilson craved affection and gave it to him in abundance. Wilson, in turn, rewarded House with his trust: "Mr. House is my second personality," the president once said.[14] Though House gained Wilson's trust chiefly by acting as the president's sounding board and amplifier, not by persuading him of his own views, his unparalleled access to and understanding of the president made him one of the most influential men in Washington. House's penchant for operating behind the scenes and his closeness to Wilson provoked resentment in some corners; the son of Secretary of the Navy Josephus Daniels referred to House crassly as "that devious son-of-a-bitch" and "a porcelain chamber pot full of shit."[15] Like Lansing, House sought to steer Wilson to the side of the Allies, albeit in a more discreet manner.

Germany's announcement of unrestricted submarine warfare amounted to a severe blow to presidential policy. Although philosophically and emotionally Wilson had long felt closer to Britain than to Germany, his overriding interest for the first couple of years of the conflict had been the restoration of peace, not the United States joining the Allies. In fact, he was reelected in November 1916 on the slogan "He kept us out of the war." With his second term secured, and no end of the war in sight, Wilson launched a carefully prepared peace initiative. On December 18, he sent identical peace notes to the Central Powers and the Allies, asking them to state their war aims, with a view toward kick-starting negotiations. Wilson's initiative was stillborn, since neither side was ready to settle for less than total victory. The British, recognizing their dependency on the United States, wisely chose not to reject Wilson's overture outright. In stark contrast, the German leadership in effect told Wilson to mind his own business, brusquely informing him that only direct negotiations between the belligerents would do. Still, the president did not give up. On January 22, 1917, he criticized the war aims of both sides, drawing no moral distinction between the Central Powers and Allies, and called for a "peace without victory."

As Wilson persisted with his goal of bringing about peace, he swam against a rising tide of war fervor inside his administration, much of the Republican Party, and the East Coast elite. The most ardent interventionist in his cabinet was Lansing. Frustrated about the United States' continued neutrality and being shut out of major foreign policy decisions, Lansing acted in a way that bordered on insubordination. When Wilson's peace missive appeared in the newspapers, Lansing called in a group of journalists and told them, in complete contradiction to Wilson's intentions, that the "sending of this note will indicate the possibility of our being forced into the war." According to House, Wilson came close to demanding Lansing's resignation, and the president's leading biographer asserts that the president "should have fired [Lansing] on the spot." Instead, Wilson merely ordered Lansing to tell reporters that his statement "had been radically misinterpreted."[16] Germany's declaration of unrestricted submarine warfare a few weeks after this incident further strengthened the pro-war parties and threatened to box in the president.

Confident that Germany's note meant war, an elated Lansing conferred with the president on the evening of January 31 from 8:45 p.m. to 10:30 p.m. During their meeting, Wilson expressed resentment at the German note, but he also bristled over British disregard for neutral rights, such as London's refusal to allow commerce with the Central Powers and the blacklisting of U.S. companies suspected of trading with Germany. In a somewhat bizarre aside he noted that "white civilization" and its domination over the world would rest largely on the ability of the United States to rebuild the ravaged European nations after the war; in other words, he still deemed neutrality the best policy. Yet he agreed to have Lansing tentatively draft a note informing Ambassador Bernstorff of a break in diplomatic relations.

The next morning, House found Wilson "sad and depressed" at the White House. Disappointed about Berlin's forceful step, the president spoke of Germany as "a madman that should be curbed," but when House asked whether it was fair to let the Allies do the curbing, Wilson allegedly winced but insisted he would not go to war if it were humanly possible.[17] Later in the morning, the two were joined by Lansing, who harangued Wilson about the necessity of establishing democratic institutions throughout the world and extirpating the evils of Prussian militarism. As soon as the three men parted, the secretary fired off two more letters to Wilson, one indicting Germany's "merciless and inhuman" submarine warfare, the other outlining two policy options for the administration: a mere break with Germany or a break accompanied by an appeal to Congress for a declaration of war. Lansing clearly advocated the latter.[18]

For the time being, however, Wilson withstood the pressure of the pro-war advocates. On February 2, the cabinet met for a little more than two hours to discuss a response to Germany's declaration of unrestricted submarine warfare.[19] When asked by one of the participants which side he wished to see win, Wilson replied bluntly "that he didn't wish to see either side win—for both had been equally indifferent to the rights of neutrals—though Germany had been brutal in taking life, and England only in taking property." The president went on to ask whether he should sever diplomatic relations with Berlin, but he prejudiced the question by telling his surprised cabinet that U.S. inaction would keep "the white race or part of it strong to meet the yellow race." Wilson thus made it clear that he preferred continued neutrality. Several cabinet members disagreed, and Secretary of Agriculture David F. Houston made an impassioned plea for a declaration of war on Germany.[20] At the end of the session, Lansing, too, came out openly for intervention, pleading "that it was for our interest and the interest of the world that we should join the Allies." Wilson rebuffed him coolly: "I am not so sure of that." The president argued that greater justice would be done if the conflict ended in a draw.

Although Wilson eventually agreed to breaking off relations with Germany—Bernstorff was handed his passports the next day—his decision came with a twist. The president observed that Germany had hitherto not committed an "overt act," and unless this happened, nothing else should be done. In the context of submarine warfare, the term *overt act* implied the sinking of an American ship, but the term was sufficiently flexible to include a range of interpretations, such as non-naval forms of aggression. For the time being, Wilson had shifted responsibility and initiative back to Berlin. As long as German submarines steered clear off U.S. vessels, it seemed, a U.S. entry into war would be postponed.[21]

It quickly became evident that Wilson had maneuvered the United States into a blind alley by yielding the initiative to Berlin. The Germans had, of course, no intention of sparing American ships, but the mere declaration of unrestricted submarine warfare quickly cleared the Atlantic of U.S. vessels. Insurance for Europe-bound ships skyrocketed, and transatlantic commerce slowed to a trickle, with cargoes and vessels clogging East Coast seaports. By mid-February, Anglo-American trade was down by 75 percent—without the Germans having fired a single torpedo at an American vessel.[22] The pro-Allied, interventionist *Washington Post* grudgingly conceded in an editorial, "The merchant marine of the United States has been terrorized and driven from the seas. To all intents and purposes Germany has put into effect an embargo on

American exports and passenger traffic with England and France. So long as our shipping is suspended the submarine campaign is as successful as if American vessels had been torpedoed."[23]

The economic consequences of the German navy's threat caused the administration great concern. At a cabinet meeting on February 6, Secretary of War Newton D. Baker urged Wilson to arm or convoy American vessels, otherwise "Germany would have us effectively locked up by her threat."[24] Three days later, the cabinet observed that the U.S. merchant fleet showed every sign of internment. By mid-February, several cabinet members had grown desperate.[25] Houston told Baker that the United States should join the Allies at once: "I would rather see this nation side with the Allies, go down to destruction with them if necessary, and disappear from the map as a nation, than to see it exist and prosper subject in the slightest degree to the dictation of an arrogant maediaeval [sic] tyrant and his supporters."[26] Baker agreed. Even Wilson eventually became concerned about the decline in transatlantic trade and the spectacular initial accomplishments of the U-boats against Allied shipping; in February 1917, German submarines destroyed nearly half a million tonnage of Allied shipping.[27]

Wilson worried about the Royal Navy's refusal to escort merchant ships by convoy (a tactic that would eventually thwart the submarine threat), but without an "overt act," the president had neither the option nor the inclination to join the Allies. Instead, he began to contemplate the arming of American merchantmen as an alternative to, not a stepping stone toward, intervention. "[Wilson] will avoid war as long as possible," cautioned Cecil Arthur Spring Rice, the British ambassador, to his government in London.[28] In fact, "armed neutrality" quickly became the rallying cry of anti-interventionists. While the economic and strategic situation of the Allies rapidly deteriorated, the American public began to sink back into indifference over Germany's latest campaign, which did not seem to threaten American lives after all. For the time being, the collapse of commercial profit affected merely a small community of businessmen and bankers who had long favored intervention anyway. Thus Wilson proceeded along his course of neutrality in the face of growing pressure from the hawks in his administration.

Matters came to a head at a cabinet meeting on February 23. Secretary of the Treasury William McAdoo emphatically demanded the arming of merchant ships so they could venture into the war zone. "[S]omewhat nettled by McAdoo's insistence and emphatic manner and language," Wilson sharply rebuffed him.[29] Others equally incurred the president's wrath. In an obvious attempt to vilify Germany, Secretary of the Interior Franklin K. Lane asked if reports were true to the effect that the wives of American consuls upon leaving Germany had been stripped naked, given an acid bath to detect writing on their flesh, and subjected to other indignities. Lansing replied in the affirmative. Lane then suggested that if Americans knew of this, they would favor intervention. Wilson asked Lane brusquely if he was recommending that they "work up a propaganda of hatred" against Germany. Lane denied this but maintained that in a democracy the people were entitled to know the facts. Other cabinet members supported him. At this point, Wilson ended the discussion by categorically ruling out such a campaign. Furthermore, he insisted that the country was not willing to risk war. After the meeting, several cabinet members considered resigning.[30]

For all intents and purposes, the administration had reached an impasse. Wilson had committed the United States to continued neutrality, but the initial success of the U-boat weapon began to conjure up the possibility of an all-out German victory, precisely the opposite of what Wilson had hoped to achieve by remaining neutral. Wilson had pinned the possibility of American intervention on an overt act, but in the absence thereof he was hard-pressed to change his policy. As the public stoically accepted Germany's latest campaign, the momentum for the United States' entry into the conflict seemed to have passed. This was the political equation in Washington when the administration learned of Zimmermann's secret Mexican alliance proposal.

Ambassador Walter Hines Page's message, including the text of the telegram, reached the State Department on Saturday, February 24, at 8:30 p.m., but the decoding process took the staff some time. Only the next evening, at 6:00 p.m., did the acting secretary of state, Frank Polk—Lansing was vacationing in Sulphur Springs—show the telegram to the president.[31] Neither Wilson nor Polk left testimony of the president's immediate reaction. According to Lansing, Polk told him a few days later that "the President . . . had shown much indignation and was disposed to make the text public without delay, [but] Polk had advised him to await my return which he had agreed to do."[32] That Wilson, who had recently been negotiating for peace with Berlin, should have been offended by the contents of the telegram sounds reasonable enough, but Lansing's suggestion—that the president nearly lost his head and would have published the telegram immediately but for Polk's advice to await Lansing's wise counsel—sounds preposterous and self-serving. For all his morality and emotionality, Wilson was a shrewd politician who hardly would have implemented such a far-reaching decision without due consideration. Wilson may well have said something to Polk to the effect that the telegram should be published—which, in the end, it was—but it seems unlikely that Polk exerted decisive restraint on the president. On February 26, Polk told House merely that the president "was much disturbed over this development and a plan is being considered as to what is best to do."[33] Polk's sober statement seems closer to the truth than Lansing's dramatic account.

Polk made several key decisions prior to Lansing's return. First, he sought an avenue to corroborate the telegram's authenticity. So far, the administration had only the word of Captain William Reginald Hall, British director of naval intelligence, to rely on. Page had conveyed Hall's suggestion for the Americans to procure a copy of the telegram forwarded by Bernstorff to Mexico. As director of the State Department's Bureau of Secret Intelligence, Polk knew that the key to verification lay in the offices of Western Union. The German embassy routinely used the company's services to send telegrams to the German envoy in Mexico City, so if Zimmermann's alliance proposal to the Mexican leader Venustiano Carranza was in fact made, an encoded copy would be in Western Union's files. By February 27, he had pressured Western Union into turning over the encrypt. Apparently, he took this action on his own initiative, and Lansing endorsed Polk's efforts when he returned to Washington.[34]

Moreover, Polk sought to determine whether Japan or Mexico was inclined to respond favorably to Germany's proposal. On Monday morning, February 26, he informed Ambassador Henry P. Fletcher in Mexico City of the telegram and instructed him to confront Carranza or his foreign minister, Cándido Aguilar, and tell him that the telegram would soon be published in the American press. Fletcher was to suggest to the Mexicans that they issue a statement of their disinterestedness.[35] On the same day, Fletcher responded that with Carranza being away in Jalisco, he had talked to Aguilar, who denied any knowledge of Germany's alliance offer.[36] Aguilar's statement was untrue (see chapter 15), but a message from Lansing to Page on February 27 indicates that the Americans believed him.[37] Only after the telegram's publication on March 1 was Fletcher able to meet with Carranza, in Guadalajara. The first chief disingenuously denied having received an alliance offer from Berlin, but he avoided saying directly that such a proposition would be rejected. Fletcher concluded that Carranza's and Aguilar's sentiments "inclined somewhat toward Germany," although he did "not think Mexico would under any circumstances accept alliance referred to."[38] Although Mexico's position seemed somewhat ambivalent, the Americans swallowed the Mexican leadership's key contention that they had not received Germany's alliance proposal prior to Fletcher's inquiry.

Secrecy was, of course, a key component in Zimmermann's proposal, and it was hardly conceivable that Carranza would now contemplate an alliance with Berlin, knowing full well that the United States was aware of the plot.

The threat from Japan appeared smaller still. The Japanese ambassador to Washington, Sutemi Chinda, repeatedly assured his British colleague, Spring Rice, that rumors about Japanese clandestine activities were groundless, and Spring Rice told Polk that he believed Tokyo's envoy.[39] On Lansing's instructions, Polk sent for the Japanese ambassador on February 28 and read him the telegram's portions concerning Japan. The ambassador "expressed great amusement and said it was too absurd to take seriously."[40] Likewise, after the telegram was published, the Japanese foreign ministry denied previous knowledge thereof and refuted an alliance with Germany as "absurd" and "preposterous.... This plot shows what mental delusion Germany is laboring under."[41] In short, within a few days of the telegram's arrival in Washington, the administration could be reasonably sure that the plot posed no security threat at all.

Polk also informed House, to whom he owed his appointment as counselor two years earlier. On February 26, Polk called Colonel House in New York and imparted the news of the telegram to him, albeit apparently without mentioning Germany's offer of U.S. territory to Mexico.[42] On the same day, Wilson sent House a copy of the telegram and told him that the administration intended to publish it.[43] House immediately tipped off the British naval attaché and then replied to Wilson the next day that he was "not surprised to read the dispatch concerning the German proposal," a comment replete with irony since he had, indeed, already heard about it from Polk. House went on to urge immediate publication as it would "make a profound impression both on Congress and on the country."[44]

House's recommendations to the president represent an example of interventionists close to Wilson viewing the telegram first and foremost as a useful tool in the struggle over the U.S. role in the war. Neither Polk nor Lansing nor House expressed genuine concern about a German threat to the Western Hemisphere, but all emphasized the propagandistic potential of Zimmermann's message. Wilson, too, has been accused of using the telegram as a political tool, to push his armed ships bill through Congress. As early as March 1, 1917, Senator Thomas Hardwick, an agrarian progressive Democrat from Georgia, argued, "[T]he real purpose of it [the telegram's publication], simply giving my opinion, was to hasten the passage of certain legislation during the closing hours of this Congress."[45] Yet, Wilson had told Lansing as early as February

22—that is, before Hall had informed the Americans of the telegram—that he would ask Congress for powers to arm merchantmen in four days. The president had the constitutional authority to do so without congressional approval, but Wilson viewed the vote as an important indicator of public attitude toward intervention. This, and not knowledge of the telegram, prompted him to introduce the armed ships bill.[46]

As noted earlier, when Wilson made the decision to ask Congress for a vote, he had viewed the arming of merchantmen as an alternative to intervention, rather than a step toward it. By the time Wilson addressed Congress, on February 26, however, he had learned of the telegram and of the likely explosive effect its disclosure would have on Congress and the public. In addition, while he was delivering his address, news of the German attack on the British liner *Laconia*, resulting in the death of two American women, reached the Capitol. These two factors—the telegram's impending publication and the death of American citizens at sea—inevitably cast the president's call for defensive measures against German submarine attacks in a much more belligerent light.[47] Given the sequence of events, Wilson cannot be accused of deliberately using the telegram to force Congress' hand, but he certainly must have anticipated increased pressure on Congress due to the telegram's publication, and he could not have been oblivious to the possibility that mixing his request for arming merchantmen with Zimmermann's alliance proposal might push the nation closer to war. In fact, he shared with House his concern that the telegram might bring about a crisis that he could not control.[48] Senator William F. Kirby, a Democrat from Arkansas, verbalized precisely this point in the Senate debate about the telegram on March 1: "[I]s not war the thing we are discussing now . . . ?"[49]

In fact, the telegram significantly accelerated the administration's drift toward war. On the morning of Tuesday, February 27, Lansing returned from his long weekend at Sulphur Springs. At 9:10 a.m. he arrived at his office in the State, War, and Navy Building and began going through his personal mail, but Assistant Secretary of State William Phillips soon interrupted him with the news of Zimmermann's "amazing message."[50] Phillips later recalled that the telegram caused "a decided change in Lansing's attitude."[51] Since the secretary of state had long been a leading hawk in the administration, Phillips' comment probably referred to Lansing's newly invigorated determination to push the president toward intervention. Later on that morning, Polk showed up and reported his delivery of the telegram to Wilson and the president's anger. Polk also mentioned Wilson's intention to make the scheme public, and Lansing took the liberty to instruct Polk to inform Democratic senator Furnifold McLendel Simmons of North Carolina, a leader of the white supremacist movement, of the telegram and its intended publication. Lansing then proceeded over to the White House, where he met with Wilson at 11:30 a.m.[52]

For fifty minutes, the two men discussed the content of the telegram and the appropriate way of handling it. Voicing concerns about the telegram's authenticity, Wilson wondered how Bernstorff had received the message, given the absence of secure communications between Berlin and the German embassy in Washington. Lansing must have relished answering this one. In early January, he explained, the State Department had granted the Germans access to their transatlantic cables in order to allow them to negotiate directly with Washington on possible peace terms. Lansing added that the State Department had granted this access very reluctantly and only at the insistence of House, a thinly concealed jab at the man who kept the secretary's role in foreign policy firmly subordinate to his own. On January 17, Lansing continued, the German foreign office had filed an exceptionally long message for Bernstorff, who received it one day later. Lansing inferred correctly that this message included Zimmermann's alliance proposal to Carranza. While listening to Lansing's no doubt persuasive account, Wilson exclaimed several times "Good Lord" and said he agreed with the secretary's conclusions. Overall, the president "showed much resentment at the German Government for having imposed upon our kindness in this way and for having made us the innocent agents to advance a conspiracy against this country."[53]

Although one has to rely entirely on Lansing's account of Wilson's reaction to the news that the Germans had abused American assistance, the president's subsequent change of mood vis-à-vis Germany is confirmed by other sources. On February 27, the cabinet decided to send a division of American soldiers to Cuba to prop up the government there against insurgents. Probably with the telegram in mind, Wilson argued that "so many things are happening we cannot afford to let Cuba be involved in G[ermany's] plots."[54] The next day, the president met with representatives of several peace societies. After one of them, William I. Hull, a former student of Wilson's, exhorted the president to pursue additional peace efforts with Germany, the president responded, "Dr. Hull, if you knew what I know at this present moment, and what you will see reported in tomorrow morning's newspapers, you would not ask me to attempt further peaceful dealings with the Germans." Jane Addams, another peace activist, later recalled that the "president's mood was stern and far from the scholar's detachment as he told us of recent disclosures of German machinations in

Mexico and announced the impossibility of any form of adjudication."[55] Both comments suggest the telegram's considerable effect on Wilson's thinking: "It was almost incredible, he must have thought, that any government could be so evil and intriguing," concluded one historian.[56]

Yet the strongest response the telegram elicited from Wilson was not heightened presidential concern over a German threat to the Western Hemisphere, but a feeling of personal insult over Germany's nonchalant disregard for his peace efforts and Berlin's chutzpah in using U.S. cables to transmit an anti-American alliance offer. In itself, the telegram did not convince Wilson of the necessity of intervention, but it left little doubt that Germany anticipated war and thus destroyed his remaining hopes of working with the German government. Since the president was the last significant holdout in political Washington contemplating continued neutrality, the consequence of the telegram's disclosure was significant. From that point on, Wilson's decisions would move the nation progressively closer to war.

Although House and Lansing notably urged immediate publication of Zimmermann's note, the decision had originated with Wilson. Keeping the message under wraps was hardly an option, as numerous officials on both sides of the Atlantic already knew about it. An eventual leak to the press was probable and would have subjected the administration to charges of deception by the Republican opposition. At any rate, Wilson never considered the possibility of keeping the telegram secret. It will be recalled that he had mentioned his inclination to publish it to Polk when first confronted with the telegram, before Lansing or House knew about it. His comments to the peace delegation on February 28 demonstrate that he had all but given up on any hope of reaching a peaceful agreement with Berlin. The only remaining questions were when and how the telegram would be made public.

In his conference with the president on February 27, Lansing advised against having the State Department issue the telegram officially, as this method might be construed as an attempt to influence opinion over the armed ships bill. Instead, he suggested making it public "indirectly," by leaking it to the press. This method, Lansing explained, "would avoid any charge of using the document improperly and would attract more attention than issuing it officially." The president concurred, and on Wednesday morning, February 28, he called Lansing to suggest a conference with Treasury Secretary McAdoo and Postmaster General Albert S. Burleson to discuss the most suitable venue for publication. Later in the morning, according to Lansing's account, Wilson again called him to report that Burleson and McAdoo could not be reached, because they were at the Capitol attending to pending bills.[57] This seems odd given that the president surely had the authority to pull members of his cabinet from meetings. Barbara Tuchman has argued that Wilson deliberately did not try very hard to summon Burleson and McAdoo because he preferred to act alone.[58] If true, it demonstrates the president's growing determination to control the telegram affair personally, to the exclusion of anybody else. He notably did not ask Lansing for advice.

Shortly before 4:00 p.m. Wilson called Lansing again and told him to have the telegram appear in the next morning's papers. The president also ordered Lansing to summon Nebraska senator Gilbert M. Hitchcock and read him the telegram.[59] This was a clever move on Wilson's part. A member of the Senate Committee on Foreign Relations, the aloof, dandyish Hitchcock was in charge of the armed ships bill. He was also considered a pacifist. Although himself not of German extraction, he had studied in Germany in his youth, had introduced a resolution to ban American munitions exports to Europe in December 1914, and was considered close to the large German community in his state. Yet, he was also known as a party loyalist. If Hitchcock's principled opposition to war could be weakened by sharing news of the telegram with him, congressional isolationism would be dealt a severe blow.[60]

Lansing called the senator, who arrived within twenty minutes, read him the telegram, and vouched for its authenticity. The shocked Hitchcock responded "that it would cause a tremendous sensation to make public such a dastardly plot." Lansing added that Hitchcock might inform Democratic senator William J. Stone of Missouri, the chairman of the Committee on Foreign Relations, who had temporarily stepped down due to his opposition to the armed ships bill. Based on Lansing's memorandum and diary notes, it appears that he told Hitchcock to contact Stone without Wilson's knowledge. If so, Lansing doubtlessly made this move to further weaken the isolationists.[61]

According to Lansing's desk diary, the secretary of state and his deputy, Polk, discussed the "method of making [the telegram] public."[62] Although Lansing insists in his March 4 memorandum that he advised Wilson to use the AP for leaking the telegram to the press,[63] his desk diary entry leaves open the possibility that the idea of using AP correspondent Edwin Milton Hood for this purpose had originated with Polk. Ever the loyal informant, Polk immediately called House in New York to report the telegram's forthcoming publication via AP the following day.[64] Meanwhile, Lansing prepared a publishable adaptation of the telegram for Hood, who visited the secretary's home at 6:00 p.m. "[B]inding him to secrecy as to where he obtained it," Lansing handed Hood a paraphrase of the telegram. The AP correspondent agreed not to release it before 10:00 p.m. so that reporters would not learn the news before midnight, and Lansing would not receive any late night phone calls.[65] At 9:20 p.m., Wilson called Lansing about the secretary's conversation with Hitchcock. Whether the secretary informed the president that he had advised Hitchcock to inform Stone about the telegram is not known.[66]

The text published in virtually every major American newspaper on the morning of March 1, 1917, did not wholly conform to the original telegram. For one, Lansing had stripped the intercepted text of anything not content related, such as the telegram number and Zimmermann's instruction to "confirm receipt." Also, the published version was not dated January 13 (the date of the original telegram intercepted by the British) but January 19 (the date of Bernstorff's message to Heinrich von Eckardt, the German envoy in Mexico). Furthermore, the published text made no mention of Bernstorff, thereby suggesting that the telegram was sent directly by Zimmermann to Eckardt. By obscuring the fact that the telegram was sent via Washington, Lansing sought to conceal the administration's source of the telegram, an issue that would soon roil the Senate. Furthermore, the AP version erroneously spoke of "general financial support" rather than "generous financial support" from Germany to Mexico. Since Room 40 had provided the U.S. embassy in London with the correct translation, and Page had in turn forwarded the text accurately to Washington, Lansing or Hood must have unintentionally introduced this textual error. Moreover, the AP version perpetuated a subtle but significant inaccuracy in translation committed by Room 40. In the original telegram, Zimmermann had merely consented (*Einverständnis unsererseits*) to Mexico's reconquest of territory in Arizona, New Mexico, and Texas, but Room 40 had turned this rather weak endorsement into the more aggressive "an understanding on our part." The published version read, "it is understood that Mexico is to reconquer the lost territory," implying Germany's active goading rather than passive consent.[67]

An explanatory note by AP, based on Lansing's conversation with Hood, put the telegram in context and was meant to amplify its effect. It reviewed various German espionage and sabotage operations and proclaimed that the telegram provided the "missing link" to a number of rumored German schemes, such as Berlin's alleged goal to establish submarine bases in Mexico, which was never proven. This was vintage Lansing.

Although State Department agents in Mexico had repeatedly failed to corroborate hearsay of German plots in Mexico,[68] the secretary stubbornly insisted that the Germans had hatched a series of anti-American schemes south of the border. The telegram, he now claimed, proved this point: "I have said that for a year and a half I have been receiving these rumors of German activities in Mexico and other places. Occasionally a definite fact would come and these we have been patching together, keeping them very secret so as not to cause German apprehensions and close our sources of information. Only the Zimmermann telegram was proved beyond question."[69] Thus, Lansing portrayed the telegram as the proverbial "smoking gun." As such, it assumed far more sinister proportions than Zimmermann's half-baked, ad hoc diplomatic initiative warranted.

Worried that the press might find out about the British connection, Lansing immediately embarked on a disinformation campaign to deflect suspicions about the administration's source for the telegram. In an interview with a journalist, the secretary insinuated that a daring spy had obtained the telegram, and he flatly refused to elaborate since further probing would "endanger the lives of those concerned."[70] Speculation in the press exploded. From London, Hall watched with delight:

> [I could not] help smiling at some of the tall stories about the acquisition of the Telegram which I was at some pains not to contradict. Secret codes, it was hinted, had been stolen in the unlikeliest places and bought by the Americans for the most colossal sums. Heroic backwoodsmen from Arizona searching for excitement in France had broken through the enemy line disguised as Church Army padres, obtained jobs in Brussels, discovered 'the German cipher-book' in the Governor-General's own house, and hurried back with the precious code to astounded officials in Washington. There were weird stories of German submarine captains being robbed on Broadway and Mexican revolutionaries who had captured wireless stations which never existed, and even one of a German agent in New York who . . . successfully burgled the German Embassy.[71]

Overall, publication of the telegram constituted a major triumph for the pro-war lobby. Polk told Lansing on the morning of March 1 that he did not see how the president could now avoid asking for a declaration of war.[72] A satisfied Colonel House noted in his diary that journalists "have called and telephoned constantly because of the exposé of the Zimmermann cable."[73] More than any other person in Washington, Lansing could claim responsibility for the telegram's orderly disclosure in the American press. His agents had ably collaborated with Hall in London, and the secretary had guided the president in choosing an appropriate venue for publication of the explosive document. At the same time, Lansing had effectively managed to conceal Britain's role from the public. No doubt, there was much to be proud of, and in his memoirs, Lansing waxes lyrically about the consequences of his contribution to Hall's coup: "The proposed alliance with Mexico and possibly with Japan, if it materialized, would affect the entire West. It needed but some disclosure of this sort to transform popular indifference into intense hostility to Germany, to convert pacifism and a desire for continued inaction into demands for war."[74]

Chapter Ten

CONGRESS DEBATES
THE TELEGRAM

In the presidential elections of 1912, Woodrow Wilson and the Democratic Party triumphed over a Republican Party divided into a progressive renegade faction, led by Theodore Roosevelt, and its traditional base, under Howard Taft. As a result, the Democrats captured not only the presidency that year, but they also built solid majorities in the House of Representatives and the Senate, allowing Wilson to push through an ambitious agenda of domestic reform during his first term. As the Republican rift healed, however, the Democrats' electoral advantage evaporated.

In 1916 Republican presidential candidate Charles Evans Hughes lost only narrowly to Wilson, and the Democrats' majority in Congress decreased significantly. In the Senate, Wilson's party lost two seats, shrinking its majority to twelve. In the House, the losses were steeper. Going into the election, the Democrats had held a solid majority in the House, but they lost sixteen seats, while the Republicans gained nineteen. In the final tally, the Republicans outnumbered Democrats by one representative—215 to 214—but with some horse-trading involving Progressives and the defection of a few Republicans, the Democrats retained control of the House, though only barely.[1] The emergence of a distinct isolationist bloc in both chambers further complicated President Wilson's already tenuous relationship with Congress.

Isolationism transcended party lines, and as the United States edged closer to war, the movement grew more pronounced and became more vocal. When the administration severed diplomatic relations with Germany, legislators from both parties expressed distinctly isolationist sentiments. For example, Rep. Henry Stanley Benedict, a Republican from California, warned that America must not surrender its position as "the hope of the oppressed and the refuge of all liberty-loving people" for the sake of "fighting to maintain the oppression of monarchies." Rep. George Huddleston, a Democrat from Alabama, charged that big business was seeking to push the country into the war "for its promotions, its profits, and its influence on our social and political life."[2]

How did isolationist lawmakers react to the publication of the telegram? In his memoirs Robert Lansing, Wilson's secretary of state, claimed that its "effect on Congress was marked."[3] It is true that, initially at least, the disclosure appeared to sideline congressional isolationists, as it railroaded the House of Representatives into approving Wilson's bill to allow American merchant ships to be armed in order to defend against possible German attack. The House passed the bill by an overwhelming margin of 403 to 14 after a few hours of debate. Half of the bill's opponents had previously voiced isolationist sentiments; most of them were Progressives or radicals who preferred social reform at home over military intervention overseas. Nine of the opponents were midwestern representatives whose constituencies included strong German American (Wisconsin) and Scandinavian American (North Dakota and Minnesota) populations.

The landslide vote resulted largely from a lack of time for reflection on the lawmakers' part. A subsequent House vote quickly revealed cracks in the seemingly united patriotic front. An amendment to the armed ships bill introduced by Republican Henry Allen Cooper of Wisconsin proposed to prohibit armed American merchant vessels from transporting munitions to belligerent countries. The pro-German lobby had long lamented munitions shipments to the Allies, and the amendment would have defanged Wilson's original bill. Although 293 representatives voted against it, 125 voted in favor, a manifestation of growing congressional opposition to intervention. The supporters included nearly all the Progressives, half of whom represented midwestern districts with significant German American or Scandinavian American constituencies. Nearly two-thirds of those approving the amendment were Republicans.[4]

Isolationist senators resisted the armed ships bill more forcefully than House representatives did because they had the benefit of more time to reflect on the bill as well as on the Zimmermann telegram. As Oscar W. Underwood, a Democrat from Alabama, noted, "I must say for the moment that I thought with those who were about me, we were swept off our feet, but since the hours have gone by and I have had the opportunity to think and analyse [sic] and read the note [the telegram] that is in discussion, I am not so sure that it is as serious as we imagine it is in itself."[5] In the end, twelve senators voted against the armed ships bill. Most of them did so on isolationist grounds, though one or two may have been motivated by sympathy for the Central Powers. Many represented midwestern states; seven were Republicans. Several of the bill's opponents perceived a link between intervention and big business. One of the most committed and eloquent isolationists, Wisconsin Republican senator Robert M. "Fighting Bob" La Follette, argued, "[W]e should not enter an aggressive war for humanitarian ends, much less for commercial profits, in carrying munitions."[6]

Anti-interventionist senators were determined to filibuster the bill until Congress adjourned on March 4. In a tactical alliance, they received tacit support from the pro-war party and the Republican leadership, which did not want to leave Wilson in sole control of foreign policy either, for fear he would further postpone the United States' entry into the war. Following the telegram's disclosure, many isolationists viewed the armed ships bill as a vote about intervention, so the bill became a rallying point for the antiwar movement inside and outside Congress. Under La Follette's leadership, twelve senators—seven Republicans and four Democrats—began to filibuster the armed ships bill. With an isolationist victory in sight, Republican senator George W. Norris of Nebraska exulted on March 3, "We've got them beaten. We can hold them now: we've got enough speakers to filibuster from tomorrow on."[7] Indeed, Congress adjourned without a vote on the armed ships bill, and the successful filibuster ensured that the president would not be freed from congressional supervision. In a fit of temper, Wilson branded his opponents "a little group of willful men, representing no opinion but their own."[8] In fact, the filibusterers had strong backing from their constituencies. Their offices had received hundreds of letters of support, and Norris was greeted with an enthusiastic reception when he returned to Nebraska in late March to explain his position. On March 9, Wilson issued an executive order to arm American merchant ships anyway.[9] Although the isolationists failed to thwart the arming of ships, they had become a force to be reckoned with, as evidenced in a Senate debate about the Zimmermann telegram on March 1.

The Wilson administration did not officially comment on the telegram when U.S. newspapers published the document. Seeking to exploit this fact, Senator Henry Cabot Lodge, a hawkish Republican from Massachusetts, requested confirmation of the telegram's authenticity from the president on the same day. Though ostensibly concerned with the telegram's authenticity, Lodge was really trying to tie Wilson to his interventionist agenda. As he wrote his friend Theodore Roosevelt, "As soon as I saw it I felt sure it came from the Administration. I felt that it would arouse the country more than anything that has happened, that it would widen the breach with Germany and drive us toward the Allies. The one thing lacking was a declaration from the President as to its authenticity, and with his endorsement on it I knew the country would be bound to accept it and that he would be tied up. It seemed to me of almost unlimited use in forcing the situation."[10]

On the Senate floor, Lodge declared, "We must not act on a newspaper publication. . . . [W]e ought to have the authentic statement of the President of the United States. He is asking for great powers, and I for one think he ought to have them; but we ought to know the evidence on which we are proceeding." Kicking off a lengthy Senate debate, Lodge then submitted a resolution asking the Senate to resolve that "the President be requested to inform the Senate whether the [Zimmermann] note . . . is authentic and in the possession of the Government of the United States, and when it came into possession of the United States, and if authentic to send to the Senate, if not incompatible with the public interest, any further information in the possession of the Government of the United States relative to the activities of the Imperial German Government in Mexico."[11]

According to Barbara Tuchman, the ensuing debate unfolded exactly as Lodge would have wanted, with all "pacifist senators promptly" voicing "the most sinister suspicions as to the origins of the telegram" and several of them denouncing the telegram as a lie. "There was no lack of senior statesmen," Tuchman concluded, "to thus rush in who were soon to wish they hadn't."[12] This, however, is a serious mischaracterization of what really occurred. As the Senate nominally discussed the telegram's authenticity, few senators actually voiced doubts in this regard. Two senators, Republican William E. Borah of Idaho and Underwood of Alabama, stated in the course of the debate that they initially had considered the telegram a forgery but now accepted it as genuine, early evidence of the telegram's transient effect. Only two senators went on record explicitly condemning the telegram as a forgery. Democrat Michael Hoke Smith of Georgia argued cautiously that "up to this point," he "preferred" to believe "that this so-called letter is a forgery and a sham, born in the brain of a scoundrel and a tool." Only the last speaker, Democrat "Pitchfork Ben" Tillman of South Carolina contended that "we have wasted a great deal of valuable time here in discussing a lie—a forgery." Since "Japan hates Germany worse than the devil is said to hate holy water," Tillman considered a Berlin-Tokyo axis inconceivable. The seventy-year-old Tillman, a notorious leader of the white supremacy movement with no expertise in foreign relations, stood virtually alone with his unconditional declaration that the telegram was a forgery.[13] The debate in the Senate would not only upend Lodge's resolution, but would come dangerously close to revealing Britain's hand in the telegram's disclosure as some isolationists had hoped to do.

Lodge and his supporters sought to emphasize the seriousness of the German threat and yoke the publication of the telegram to the administration in the hope that Wilson would then have to bend to public pressure to go to war.[14] Lodge himself claimed boldly during the course of the debate, "If the President, of his own motion, were to send those papers [the telegram] in to the Senate without comment, according to our precedents, it would mean that we could do nothing diplomatically, and he wrote to Congress for war."[15] Democratic senator Charles S. Thomas of Colorado, an isolationist turned interventionist, seconded Lodge by asserting that since the telegram was probably authentic, it should be viewed in the context of a pending Army and Navy bill. In other words, the telegram should be regarded as an act of German aggression to which the United States ought to respond by preparing for war. Democratic senator Atlee Pomerene of Ohio claimed that the telegram constituted the first documented instance of a German plot—as opposed to earlier rumors—in the Western Hemisphere and that if true, "it creates a very grave situation."[16]

Others downplayed the significance of the telegram. Republican senator Miles Poindexter of Washington argued that the telegram hardly constituted news: "I have been reading in the newspapers for a month about the very situation of which this Zimmermann letter would be a mere incident. . . . [W]hat is the occasion for excitement about it? What change in the situation is it going to make?"[17] He added quite plausibly "that it is impossible for Germany to send an army to Mexico at the present time, or to send a navy there."[18] Senator Gilbert M. Hitchcock, wavering between loyalty to Wilson and Nebraska's German American voting bloc, pointed out that the telegram was a defensive, not an offensive measure, since the Mexican government was not to be approached until after the United States and Germany were at war. Senator Underwood argued in the same vein, asserting "that the Imperial Chancellor of Germany would have been derelict in his duty to his own Government if he had not carefully informed his minister abroad what he should do in the happening of every contingency."[19]

Others raised questions about the intentions behind the telegram's publication. On March 1, the Associated Press (AP) had erroneously reported that the administration had been in possession of the telegram for a month.[20] At the beginning of the debate, La Follette demanded to know "exactly how long the

Government of the United States, or any branch of it, has been in possession of such information." The Wisconsin senator suggested that Wilson had coolly kept the telegram under wraps until it was politically opportune to release it, a thinly veiled suggestion that Wilson had used the telegram to try to push his armed ships bill through Congress. Senator John D. Works, a progressive Republican from California, drove his colleague's point home by accusing the president of playing politics with national security. Because the Senate was being asked, Works expounded, "to place in the hands of the President the power to determine practically whether or not we go to war," the administration should have informed Congress before Wilson submitted his bill. Later on, Democratic senator Thomas Hardwick of Georgia asked why the State Department had released the telegram, and then he provided the answer himself: "I think the real purpose of it, simply giving my own opinion, was to hasten the passage of certain legislation during the closing hours of Congress."[21]

Lodge's resolution was referred to the Committee on Foreign Relations, which adopted a slightly revised version and then submitted it to the full Senate. Lodge boasted to Roosevelt that since the "militant party was in complete control of the committee . . . we brought out a resolution entirely in accord with the one I introduced." When Democratic senator Claude A. Swanson of Virginia informed Lodge that Wilson had confirmed to him the note's authenticity, and that the president would be happy to respond to the resolution,[22] the pro-war lobby appeared to head for an easy victory. Instead, however, the debate took an ominous turn for the interventionists. The one countermeasure the isolationists could adopt to blunt, and even turn, Lodge's resolution into an instrument against intervention, was to shift the focus of the debate to the administration's source for the telegram. They did precisely that.

Senator William J. Stone emerged as the leading isolationist voice during the ensuing debate. A Democrat from Missouri, Stone was a professional politician who had earned the nickname "Gumshoe Bill" for his effective behind-the-scenes maneuvering in Missouri politics. A pragmatic reformer, Stone had loyally supported Wilson until he broke with the president over the armed ships bill and, subsequently, the United States' entry into the war.[23] There is no record of the deliberations of the Committee on Foreign Relations, but according to Stone, the possible involvement of a third government—read, Great Britain—and the method of the telegram's interception had been at the core of the committee's debate. In the full Senate debate, he put the spotlight on these issues. As soon as the committee's resolution had been read, Stone dropped a bombshell amendment that would completely reframe the Senate debate. It asked the president "also to inform the Senate as to whether the information in his possession respecting the letter signed 'Zimmermann' originated with any Government or official of any Government engaged in the present European war, and if so, to inform the Senate as to the facts relating thereto."[24]

Interventionists and isolationists alike realized that Stone was referring to Great Britain, without saying so explicitly. Stone's move threatened the objectives of Lodge and his supporters, because it would taint the cause of intervention, as well as those of the Wilson loyalists, for it might cast the president as a British pawn and the United States' entry into war as having been masterminded by London. As a consequence, the two factions joined in an unusual alliance to blunt the impact of Stone's amendment. While Lodge and other interventionists insisted time and again that only the telegram's authenticity mattered, Democrats close to the administration categorically repeated their mantra that Stone's amendment was "likely to be embarrassing to the President," as William Hughes of New Jersey cautioned.[25]

Stone plowed ahead, nonetheless. First, he noted, "Reading the newspaper accounts of the sources of information they had, the inference is unavoidable that it was obtained from the executive officials of this Government."[26] Though he still refrained from naming Great Britain explicitly, he contended that "it was given publicity to affect either public opinion or legislative opinion, or both, in the United States. We are passing through strenuous and dangerous days just now. A publication of this nature is calculated, however intended, to excite public opinion and to inflame the public mind of the country, and thus develop a tendency toward working up a spirit of belligerency on our part."[27] He then moved in for the kill:

It must have been derived from some outside, independent source. It is not to be presumed that this Government, as a neutral power, has been in such close touch with the Government of any of the belligerent powers as would justify it in sending its special agents to confer confidentially with any such Government and to collaborate with it. I hear some Senator ask, "Why not?" Why not? Because I hold, and I hope truly hold, that the attitude which we have declared on more occasions than one, of absolute and impartial neutrality between the warring powers, would make confidential and secret cooperation of that kind impossible. Mr. President, the news, so called, which comes to the United States from Europe is filtered, as we all know, through the London news bureau presided over and managed by Lord Northcliffe, supplemented by the exacting censorship of the British Government, the managing Government of the entente allies. . . . For example, did this information come from London? Was it given to us by that Government? I want to know about that, and that is all I am asking at this time.[28]

Even with that, Stone was far from finished. When George Sutherland, a Republican from Utah, questioned the wisdom of asking the president to name the source of the telegram, "because if he answers that question the effect of it may be to close that particular source in the future,"[29] Stone brushed him aside, arguing that one could "easily differentiate between asking the President as to the source of information in cases wherein he secured his information through instrumentalities of his own, for the employment of which the Congress has granted its authority, and cases like this, wherein I ask to ascertain whether this particular information was derived from a belligerent power."[30] In order to lend force to his argument, Stone elaborated on his source for Britain's alleged involvement: "I never heard of it until last night, or late yesterday afternoon. At that time some news reporters came to me and told me about it, as, I have no doubt, they told others of you. I could give them no information, for I had none; but I turned interviewer, being deeply interested, and asked them what they knew about it, and some of them told me that they understood that this letter came from high officials of the British Government to the Government of the United States."[31]

Here was another remarkable revelation. Throughout the war, Washington and London would officially maintain that the United States had obtained the telegram through its own efforts, but on the day of the telegram's publication, Stone named not only Britain as the source, but he also revealed that this knowledge was apparently well known to a number of American journalists. This leads one to speculate about what information, other than the text of the telegram, Lansing might have given Edwin Milton Hood, the AP journalist, on February 28. Stone concluded his remarks by elaborating on the double standard applied by his interventionist colleagues to information coming from the Central Powers and the Allies, respectively:

Mr. President, let us reverse the case. Suppose the Imperial Government of Germany had made a charge of something done by England which would have been offensive to the United States, and which would of itself have strained the diplomatic relations of the United States with that country, would the Senators who are urging the adoption of this resolution without amendment have been willing to accept the facts relating to the charge on the mere assurance even of so exalted a personage as the President that he thought the information to be correct? Would you not have said: "Before we act upon that we want information as to the sources; at least we want to know whether the information which you convey to us came from Berlin, from the Kaiser, to Washington"? And I would be with you on that with the same zeal and insistence that moves me now. Mr. President, I have said enough. I think there can be no harm in asking the President to tell the Senate whether his information respecting this letter came from a foreign Government engaged in this war. If the information conveyed to me by the news purveyors here, that it came from the British Government to us, is accurate, I think we are entitled to know that fact officially.[32]

When Stone had finished, Wilson's loyal lieutenant, Senator Hitchcock of Nebraska, swung into action with an attempt to thwart the amendment by contending that national security trumped the public right to know certain facts. By doing so, he subtly sought to create the impression that the telegram had been procured directly by American intelligence, not by the British:

[President Wilson] has in his hands more information than anyone else could possibly secure. Much of the information which comes to the President of the United States through the Diplomatic Service and through secret agents is in its very nature confidential. Our country is not alone in gathering this confidential information. Every great nation in the world makes it a regular business to gather it; every Government in the world places a secret fund at the disposal of its authorities for gathering it, and our own Government places at the disposal of the President of the United States a secret fund to pay for gathering secret information. For this reason the President is in a better position than anyone else to express an opinion as to whether or not information which has come to him or the Department of State is authentic. . . . [I]t is very evident that it would be a gross indiscretion on the part of the Senate of the United States, which is brought in close contact with international affairs, even to ask the source of the information that the President may have secured.[33]

Hitchcock's argument cut no ice with the isolationists. Senator Hardwick of Georgia asked him point-blank: "Does not the Senator think that if it is true in point of fact, that this note came to our Government from the Government of one of the belligerents that fact also ought to be called to the attention of the Senate and of the country in weighing this note and in deciding whether or not it really is authentic and genuine?"[34] In response, Hitchcock, who had earlier admonished his colleagues about their duty to protect America's sources of intelligence, accidentally came close to revealing the method by which the telegram was obtained:

> No. . . . I believe that the simple question for the Senate to decide now is whether to ask the President for a definite statement as to the authentic-ity of that note, and I say this because we have some knowledge of the methods adopted by which information of this sort is secured. If that note was sent it was sent by telegraph. If that note was sent it was sent in code. There are a number of different ways in which the information involved in establishing the authenticity of that note might have been gathered. There are telegraph records, there is the wireless telegraph, there are code books which sometimes get lost.[35]

Both Stone and Hitchcock had been informed by administration officials about the telegram, before it was published, and both probably knew details about how it was obtained. Curiously, Stone, who was keen on exposing Brit-ain's manipulative hand, was always careful to avoid references to interception and decryption, whereas Hitchcock, who sought to thwart Stone by stonewall-ing, came close to revealing just those intelligence sources.

When Hitchcock had finished, John Sharp Williams, a Democrat from Mississippi, rose to speak. A member of the Committee on Foreign Relations and a loyalist of the Wilson administration, Williams, like Hitchcock and Stone, surely knew a great deal about the telegram's origins, and he cleverly used his speech to draw attention away from the fact that it had been obtained by the British through interception and cryptanalysis. Like Hitchcock and Lodge, he emphasized the importance of content over origins:

> The sole question is this: Is there a letter like this signed by Zimmermann, the German secretary of foreign affairs, in existence in the possession of our Department of State, and secondly, is that letter authentic? The instrumentality whereby the United States got possession of the letter does not bear in the remotest degree either upon its authenticity or its exis-tence. The two questions simply are, Does it exist, and is it authentic? . . . It is totally irrelevant how it got out of [the] German Embassy—how it got into the hands of the American Government. Somebody might have

stolen it. Some careless fellow in packing up some day the papers for the files might have left a copy out. Some man who makes money out of such things might have gotten it and found that it was valuable. . . . You can suppose a thousand ways of its getting there. Suppose that it was caught upon the body of a German spy by the British Government and sent to us to hurt Germany. It seems to be rather a difficult supposition under the circumstances; but suppose that was the case, then the question is still not either the character of the spy or the character of the captor; the question is, "[I]s it an authentic letter, and did it proceed from the secretary of state of the Royal Imperial German Government?" You may suppose that it was caught coming on its way by wireless to Sayville, where Ambassador [Johann Heinrich von] Bernstorff received his communications, and that it might have been caught by a naval officer of the United States or by a Secret Service man of the United States who was watching.[36]

While seeking to shield the Wilson administration from attempts to reveal the source of the telegram, Williams simultaneously rebuffed the interventionists, who emphasized the alleged threat to the United States posed by Zimmermann's alliance offer. According to Williams, the telegram "will be but one of the many other circumstances tending to corroborate a belief that [Germany] has been at least careless about whether she would have war with us or not, and that she—while diplomatizing with us—has been making preparation to strengthen her hand when the war should come, if it should come. Gentlemen will notice that this letter itself, if it be authentic and true, was not to be delivered to the Mexican Government 'until there was a break with the United States,' but they were merely preparing their way."[37]

At this point, the debate had veered far off the course Lodge had intended it to take. The senator from Massachusetts therefore thought it necessary to jump into the fray with a speech of his own, though he was unable to add anything of substance to the points made earlier by Hitchcock. Lambasting Stone's amendment, Lodge reiterated his two key contentions—the German alliance proposal posed a veritable threat to the United States, and establishing the telegram's authenticity was all that mattered: "In that [news]paper was disclosed, if it is authentic, a plan on the part of one great Government to join with two other Governments in war on the United States. It went so far as to suggest parceling out some of our territory. It seems to me a very serious thing."[38] Citing a distant historical precedent, he argued against revealing the government's sources:

I think nothing would be more unfortunate than to inquire of the President the sources of his information. . . . The President is charged with the duty of preserving the interest of the United States. We give him a large fund to be spent on the voucher of the Secretary of State alone. Those sources of information would be cut off if he were to disclose them; and in a newspaper of this afternoon it is said that Mr. Secretary Lansing stated to the newspapers that under no circumstances could the sources of the information be disclosed, for it might involve the lives of those concerned. No Government can possibly make such a disclosure.[39]

By referencing Lansing's allusion to "the lives of those concerned," Lodge sought to throw off his isolationist colleagues whose line of questioning threatened to disclose the hand of the British code breakers. Predictably, he failed. Senator James A. O'Gorman, a Democrat from New York of Irish background, expansively reviewed past British propaganda activities in the United States and, with a view to the telegram, asked whether "this information [was] derived from one of the belligerent nations involved in this European war? The value of any evidence in any court of justice is dependent more or less upon the source from which it comes." He continued: "Suppose, Senators, in this situation you were satisfied that officers of the British Government handed this alleged document to the United States Government, would you not want some further evidence of its authenticity? Might it not be a fabrication? Might it not be a forgery? More than once in the history of our own country a belligerent nation has resorted to deceit and forgery in an effort to induce us to become involved in a contest in which we were not concerned."[40] By suggesting that the telegram might be a forgery, O'Gorman dared his opponents to prove him wrong by disclosing the method by which the administration had obtained it. But he also knew that if the administration admitted Britain's role in order to prove the telegram's authenticity, British intelligence and propaganda operations vis-à-vis the United States would become the focal point of public attention.

By now, the debate had settled into a predictable back-and-forth between those who wanted to expose Britain's role and those who sought to keep the focus on the telegram's content. In this contest, the latter group clearly had the weaker hand, because all they could do was reiterate their emphasis on authenticity and source protection. Anytime an interventionist or Wilson loyalist made these points, an isolationist would follow up by expanding on Britain's propaganda activities in the United States and suggest London's hand behind the telegram. Keeping Britain's involvement a secret was essential for the administration as well as for the interventionists, but each verbal exchange in the Senate chipped away at the mystery surrounding the telegram's origins.

While prolonging the exchange initially had served the isolationists' cause, after a while neither side was able to offer anything substantially new to their arguments, and the debate reached an impasse. Since Stone's amendment, asking the administration specifically for its source of the telegram, evidently was anathema to the interventionist cohort as well as administration loyalists, Michael Hoke Smith, the Democrat from Georgia, offered the following more general amendment as a substitute: "That the President be requested to furnish to the Senate whatever information he has concerning the note published in the press of this date, purporting to have been sent January 19, 1917, by the German secretary for foreign affairs to the German minister in Mexico, which, in his opinion, is not incompatible with the public interest."[41]

Stone responded at length. First, he openly came out in favor of continued neutrality, while refuting charges of disloyalty to the administration that had been raised by the Wilson loyalists: "Mr. President, I am against this country entering into this war—I do not disguise that—and shall use whatever power I have to prevent it until I feel that the honor and vital interests of this country and people have been assailed in such a way and to such a degree that there is no honorable escape from the dernier resort to war. . . . Do I assail the President in saying that? Do I insinuate aught [sic] against the President by that statement? No." Having made his point, Stone concluded his speech by endorsing Smith's amendment on the ground that it "asks for all information the President has respecting this matter which he thinks he can send to the Senate compatible with the public interest."[42]

Eventually, Smith's amendment was incorporated into the resolution from the Committee on Foreign Relations and agreed to. It completely changed the thrust of Lodge's inquiry. While the original resolution had asked only for "any further information in the possession of the Government of the United States relative to any activities of the Imperial German Government," the amendment asked the administration "to furnish to the Senate whatever information he [the president] has concerning the note." During the debate, Stone and his supporters had made it abundantly clear that they intended this passage to be understood as a reference to British involvement.

The administration responded promptly. Lansing instructed Ambassador Walter Hines Page in London to have the telegram deciphered by a member of the embassy to enable the administration to claim that the German alliance offer was procured from an American source (see chapter 7). On the same day, March 1, Wilson sent the Senate a statement from Secretary Lansing to the effect that "the Government is in possession of evidence which establishes the fact that the note referred to is authentic, and that it is in the possession of the Government of the United States, and that the evidence was procured by this Government during the present week." In the same statement, Lansing invoked national security in order to stop the hemorrhaging of further information: "[I]t is, in my opinion, incompatible with the public interest to send to the Senate at the present time any further information in the possession of the Government of the United States relative to the note mentioned in the resolution of the Senate."[43]

It should be noted that although State Department counselor Frank L. Polk had indeed obtained a copy of the telegram from Western Union on February 27, Second Secretary Edward Bell in London, with significant assistance from Nigel de Grey of British naval intelligence, deciphered the German encrypt only on March 2. Lansing was therefore stretching the truth in his statement of March 1, but evidently the administration felt the need to respond quickly, even precipitously, to the Senate, so as to preempt further embarrassing probing of the method by which the telegram had been obtained.

Still, the Senate debate of March 1 came dangerously close to exposing Britain's hand. Anyone who cared to attend the Senate session could make an educated guess about the source (British intelligence) as well as the means (cryptanalysis) by which the telegram had been purloined from the Germans. The debate also showed how quickly and widely knowledge of these facts had spread. British and American officials knew about the origins of the telegram, but so did several senators and journalists. British intelligence and the American pro-war lobby had to consider themselves fortunate that Bernstorff had left Washington on February 14, for the perceptive German ambassador surely would have used his connections to reporters and politicians to get to the bottom of the story.

Moreover, congressional debates on March 1 were an indicator as to how quickly the effect of the telegram's disclosure would dissipate, and they revealed strong crosscurrents in Congress regarding the U.S. position vis-à-vis the European war. The House passed the armed ships bill, but the Senate failed to follow suit, and then isolationists quickly turned an attempt by interventionist senators to use the telegram for their cause into a debate over Britain's meddling with U.S. neutrality. In the case of Congress, the telegram failed to become a unifying factor. As the Wilson administration edged ever closer to intervention, the issue became whether the telegram would rally the public for war.

Chapter Eleven

THE AMERICAN PUBLIC

By early 1917, interventionists on both sides of the Atlantic were claiming that the Zimmermann telegram's disclosure was galvanizing Americans for war. On March 4, Secretary of State Robert Lansing wrote of "the profound sensation" the telegram had created "throughout the country."[1] In a much-quoted passage from his memoirs, he elaborated that the publication of the telegram had "resulted in unifying public sentiment throughout the United States against Germany, in putting the people solidly behind the government and in making war inevitable."[2] Wellington House, the British propaganda arm responsible for the United States, reported in the same vein on March 7: "The timely revelation of the proposed German alliance with Mexico, and the gift to Mexico of these states of the Union, appears to have aroused feeling considerably, and it seems to have stirred precisely that part of the country which was most indifferent to American rights at sea."[3] In his autobiography, William Reginald Hall, director of British naval intelligence, stated that the publication of the telegram on March 1 had "created, as we hoped and expected, the most tremendous sensation."[4]

Most historians agree with these contemporary voices about the enormity of the telegram's effect on the American public. For example, Barbara Tuchman contends, "[t]he kick that did it, to the people whether or not to the President, was the Zimmermann telegram. It awoke that part of the country that had been undecided or indifferent before. . . . It was not a theory or an issue but an unmistakable gesture that anyone could understand."[5] Others have argued along similar lines. Arthur Link, in his monumental political biography of Woodrow Wilson, asserted, "[i]t was as if a gigantic bolt had struck from the blue across the American continent. No other event of the war to this point, not even the German invasion of Belgium or the sinking of the *Lusitania,* so stunned the American people."[6] For German historian Martin Nassua, "the public effect, which was caused [by the publication of the telegram] constitutes its historical significance."[7] John Milton Cooper concluded in his sweeping biography of Woodrow Wilson that the telegram "stirred up the furor that the British hoped for. . . . Editorial indignation flared across the country. Many newspapers called the Zimmermann Telegram an act of war, and some called for war in response."[8]

Cooper's reference to newspaper editorials points to an ongoing challenge for students of public opinion in the World War I era. No scientific polls exist that gauged Americans' attitudes toward the war. Therefore, historians must consult a range of contemporary records for this purpose, and newspapers are the most significant and abundant source material in this regard. In an effort to measure the telegram's effect on public opinion, a sample of twenty-one English-language and ten German-language newspapers has been examined here.[9] The sample represents all major regions of the United States, covers urban and rural areas, and includes papers that advocated intervention as well as those that favored continued neutrality in early 1917. Democratic- and Republican-leaning newspapers are both included in the sample. Contemporary reports and memoranda by politicians and embassy personnel, as well as memoirs, also have been reviewed to round out the picture derived from the analysis of the newspapers.

During the period of American neutrality, public opinion did not tilt gradually and inexorably toward war. Rather, interventionism ascended in fits and starts. Revelations about German espionage and sabotage in North America as well as the antics of the German military attaché, Captain Franz von Papen, offended many Americans in 1915, and Britain's disregard for U.S. interests in 1916 had a similar effect on American perceptions of the Allies. In particular, London's blacklisting of U.S. companies trading with Germany and its brutal repression of the Irish uprising enraged many Americans. Ambassador Cecil Arthur Spring Rice captured the effect of these events in late December when he expressed his worries about a decline of pro-Allied sentiment and suggested measures to reverse the trend: "Feeling on the whole is becoming less favorable to the allies and more favorable to the germans [*sic*] and I am continually being asked why the British do not organise a more intensive propaganda." In this memorandum, Spring Rice suggests that even unrestricted submarine warfare might not suffice to reverse this trend: "The feeling of the country is so pacific that it is very difficult to see how the country could consent to go to war on the question of sinking a foreign ship."[10]

In the event, Berlin's declaration of unrestricted submarine warfare on February 1, 1917, temporarily overrode public reservations about intervention. Initially, newspaper editors reacted forcefully to the German declaration. Twelve of the twenty-one sampled newspapers condemned Germany's decision in the most sweeping terms. Newspapers from the pro-Allied Eastern Seaboard predictably produced the most outspoken editorials in this regard. The *New York World* declared, "If Germany wants war with the United States, let Germany have war with the United States." The *New York Times* wrote, "[T]his is a declaration of war upon the trade, the rights, the sovereignty of all neutral nations."[11]

Seven papers adopted a middle ground. Acknowledging Germany's wrongdoing, they either counseled caution or emphasized that Berlin's declaration of unrestricted submarine warfare did not inevitably mean war. Most urged that nothing be done until the United States "is specifically injured," as the *San Francisco Chronicle* put it, unknowingly prefiguring the "overt act" policy that Wilson would soon announce. William Randolph Hearst, the owner of the powerful Hearst newspaper chain, which included the *New York American*, cautioned, "Notes are better than bullets; ink is cheaper than blood, and if there had been more writing in Europe there would have been less fighting." Two Texas dailies, the *Dallas Morning News* and the *Houston Post,* adopted stands similar to the *Chronicle,* even though their rhetoric was less sympathetic to Germany. Remarkably, the largest German-language U.S. newspaper, the *New Yorker Staats-Zeitung,* also belonged to this group. Far from defending Berlin's latest move, the *Staats-Zeitung* wrote that Germany's declaration had come "quite unexpected" and withheld judgment until it became evident what "the practical execution of the announced measure will look like."[12]

Only two papers challenged the conventional wisdom that Germany had put itself in the wrong. Favoring continued U.S. neutrality, both argued that unrestricted submarine warfare was merely a reaction to, and morally no different from, the British naval blockade. The *Milwaukee Sentinel* concluded, "A Boston brand of Americanism that bristles up over the Belgian deportations (which we are by no means upholding) and at the same time is as meek as Moses when Mother England treats our cargoes and our mail sacks as if they belonged to a dependency does not strike one as the sort that animated the great 'tea party' in 1773 America first!" The *Florida Times-Union* of Jacksonville editorialized that "both parties of the European belligerents have been

guilty of breeches of law heretofore accepted." The editor pointed to his newspaper's long-standing advice "that our safety must consist in a proclamation
of embargo and non-intercourse; the contrary policy has brought us nearer
to war after a waiting of two years." While the *Sentinel*'s stance reflected the
sentiments of Milwaukee's sizable German American population, the *Times-
Union*'s editorial may be regarded as an indicator of southern reservations
about intervention.[13]

Given the telegram's reference to Arizona, New Mexico, and Texas, newspapers from these states deserve special attention. With regard to Germany's
declaration of unrestricted submarine warfare, their reaction differed little
from the interventionist attitude of the Northeast press. Five out of the seven
sampled southwestern papers denounced the German declaration strongly.
The *Tucson Citizen* wondered if the remaining neutral nations were "going to
sit idly by and let their women and children die, the victims of ruthless slay-
ers, or are they going to be drawn into the war?" The *Santa Fe New Mexican*
asked, "[w]ill the United States run for cover before a bandit?"[14] The similarity
of editorial opinions from the East Coast and Southwest highlight the latter's
dependence on the Associated Press (AP) and United Press (UP) agencies for
foreign news. New York–based editors dominated AP and UP, and the two news
agencies composed their reports first and foremost for the largely pro-Allied
newspapers of that city. Whoever controlled the New York press therefore also
exerted strong influence over the foreign news in the rest of the country.[15] The
Southwest was no exception.

Throughout February, pro-war editors lambasted Germany's submarine
war—and the administration's supposed inertia—while a smaller group of
anti-war papers urged continued neutrality. The pro-interventionist *Washington Post* maintained on February 20 that the "attempt by Germany to deny
the use of the high seas to neutral nations is essentially an act of war," while
the *Florida Times-Union* editorialized on February 25, "[W]hen two outlaws
are fighting neither should be favored." The sinking of the *Laconia* by a German submarine on February 25 hardened the position of the pro-war parties.
The *Washington Post* editor made a case for the *Laconia* being the "overt
act" that President Wilson had cited earlier as a necessary precondition for
intervention. The *Arizona Republican* declared, "[i]t's War or Nothing." The
war opponents stuck to their guns, however, with the *San Francisco Chronicle*
expressing the hope that Wilson's drive for armed neutrality "will not lead to
war if he can help it," and the *Florida Times-Union* professing its continued
advocacy of neutrality and comparing Germany and Britain to "two struggling
cocks in a barnyard."[16]

Arthur Zimmermann,
German foreign secretary.
(Courtesy of the Politisches
Archiv des Auswärtigen
Amtes, Berlin)

Hans Arthur von Kemnitz,
director of the East Asian
and Latin American
division of the German
foreign office. (Source:
Bureau des Reichstags,
*Reichstags-Handbuch III:
Wahlperiode 1924*
[Berlin: Nordeutsche
Buchdruckerei, 1925])

Photograph taken after a banquet given by U.S. ambassador James W. Gerard in Berlin in early January 1917. *Sitting, left to right:* Adolf Wermuth, mayor of Berlin; Ambassador Gerard; Zimmermann; Reinhold von Sydow, Prussian minister of commerce. *Standing, left to right:* Unknown; Consul General Julius G. Lay; Lt. Cdr. Walter R. Gherardi, U.S. naval attaché; Joseph C. Grew, first secretary; unknown; Adolf von Montgelas, director of the North American and Mexican division of the German foreign office; Wilhelm von Solf, German colonial secretary; General Emil von Friedrich, in charge of prisoners of war; Isaac Wolf, president of the American Association of Commerce and Trade; John B. Jackson, former U.S. envoy to Cuba; unknown. (Source: James Gerard, *Face to Face with Kaiserism* [New York: Doran, 1918])

Otto Göppert, the German foreign office official tasked with investigating the Zimmermann telegram's disclosure. (Courtesy of the Politisches Archiv des Auswärtigen Amtes, Berlin)

Johann Heinrich von Bernstorff, German ambassador to Washington. (Courtesy of the Library of Congress, Washington, D.C.)

From left to right: Field Marshall Paul von Hindenburg, Kaiser Wilhelm II, General Erich Ludendorff. (Courtesy of the Library of Congress, Washington, D.C.)

Theobald von Bethmann Hollweg,
German chancellor. (Courtesy of the
Library of Congress, Washington, D.C.)

Heinrich von Eckardt, German envoy
to Mexico. (Courtesy of the Politisches
Archiv des Auswärtigen Amtes, Berlin)

President Woodrow Wilson.
(Courtesy of the Library of
Congress, Washington, D.C.)

Robert Lansing, U.S. secretary of state. (Courtesy of the Library of Congress, Washington, D.C.)

Edward Bell, second secretary of the U.S. embassy in London. (Courtesy of the Library of Congress, Washington, D.C.)

Walter Hines Page, American ambassador to London. (Courtesy of the Library of Congress, Washington, D.C.)

"Colonel" Edward M. House, President Wilson's advisor and confidant. (Courtesy of the Library of Congress, Washington, D.C.)

Senator William J. Stone. (Courtesy of the Library of Congress, Washington, D.C.)

Frank L. Polk, counselor of the U.S. Department of State. (Courtesy of the Library of Congress, Washington, D.C.)

Captain William Reginald Hall, director of British naval intelligence. (Courtesy of the Library of Congress, Washington, D.C.)

Nigel de Grey, British cryptanalyst. (Source: Colin Simpson, *The Lusitania* [Boston: Little, Brown, 1973])

David Lloyd George, British prime minister. (Courtesy of the Library of Congress, Washington, D.C.)

Captain Guy Gaunt,
British naval attaché
to Washington. (Source:
Colin Simpson, *The
Lusitania* [Boston: Little,
Brown, 1973])

Arthur James Balfour,
British foreign secretary.
(Courtesy of the
Library of Congress,
Washington, D.C.)

As the editorial war of words bogged down, the public gradually became accustomed to the notion of continued neutrality in spite of Germany's naval campaign. The pessimistic reports of Ambassador Spring Rice captured well the waning public anger over unrestricted submarine warfare. One day after the German ambassador, Johann Heinrich von Bernstorff, had informed the State Department of the impending submarine campaign, Spring Rice noted confidently that public opinion had changed much in favor of the Allies, and that indignation at Germany's latest measure was greater even than it was over the sinking of *Lusitania*.[17] Only one week later, he cautioned Foreign Secretary Arthur J. Balfour that the country "certainly does not desire war."[18] On February 23, Spring Rice conjured up a subsequently much-quoted metaphor to the effect that the situation in the United States "is much that of a soda water bottle with the wire cut but the cork unexploded." Most historians quoting this line forget, however, to add that the ambassador himself had serious doubts about the cork popping off. In the same letter, he cautioned that there would be no war without a major incident. In fact, he observed "an immense amount of indifference in the country" and concluded that it would be extremely unwise to count on the United States entering the war.[19] By late February, Spring Rice had reverted to his habitual pessimism, writing to the Foreign Office that 80 percent of the population did not want war, that the West and Midwest were not growing more warlike, and that the administration would face great difficulty in unifying the country for war.[20]

President Wilson's interventionist advisers shared Spring Rice's pessimism. William Durant, director of the General Motors Co., reported to House that he had met but one war enthusiast on a trip from California to New York.[21] House, in turn, told Spring Rice on February 23 that the West and Midwest were "difficult to get in line."[22] Four days later, Lansing wrote to a friend that the "psychology of the situation is the real problem which has to be solved."[23] Such comments indicate that by the end of February, the public was divided and tense, rather than determined and eager to go to war. One historian has argued that political isolationism had crystalized precisely in response to the threat of intervention posed by the resumption of unrestricted submarine warfare.[24] If so, the pendulum of public opinion was swinging toward neutrality, rather than war, when Americans learned of the telegram in early March.

The Zimmermann telegram made front-page news across the nation on March 1. At first glance, the media sensation created by its disclosure appears to suggest a dramatic turnaround in public opinion in favor of war. According to Barbara Tuchman, the telegram "brought down neutrality like a dead duck."[25] Indeed, the majority of editorials during this time condemned Zimmermann's alliance proposal, and several declared it a casus belli. Under the headline "An Infamous Alliance," Wilson's mouthpiece, the *New York World*, editorialized, "Germany under a desperate and criminal autocracy has made itself the enemy of mankind, and in such circumstances there is only one course for a Nation to take which is strong enough to assert its own rights and which retains sufficient moral courage to appreciate its responsibility toward its own civilization." The *Los Angeles Times* fumed, "There is no longer any doubt of Germany to make war upon us—and the proposed alliance with Mexico and Japan is no dream. The thing long dreaded has come. We are virtually at war today." Back on the East Coast, the *Boston Globe* announced defiantly, "[w]e can never be made to bow before threats." Altogether ten from the sample here concurred that Zimmermann's alliance proposal constituted a hostile act.[26]

The implications of this analysis should not be pushed too far. Nine out of these papers had previously issued strongly worded anti-German editorials, in early February. Therefore, it would be inaccurate to state that the telegram had caused them to *change* their opinion. The disclosure merely pushed them further in the direction of intervention. Moreover, the remaining papers of the sample responded much less unequivocally to the news of Zimmermann's Mexican alliance proposal. The typically warmongering *New York Times* uttered little surprise at the plot—"precisely what might have been expected"— but in view of Washington's fairly satisfactory relations with Mexico's government, the *Times* advocated a wait-and-see policy. The *Arizona Republican* responded similarly, recalling that rumors of German plots south of the border had been in circulation for some time and therefore labeling the telegram "interesting rather than momentous." In view of the impracticability of a German-Mexican-Japanese axis, the paper argued, "[W]e have nothing immediately to fear from such an alliance not because the supposed parties would not in any circumstances enter it, but because in the present circumstances they cannot."[27]

A second group of papers focused on Zimmermann's ineptitude rather than the content of his scheme. For the *Houston Post*, the telegram revealed a hitherto unsuspected "degree of stupidity" in Berlin, and under the headline "Germany's Proposed Suicide Pact," the *Washington Post* likewise proclaimed the project a product of Germany's "incurable stupidity" and "sheer lunacy." In a rare expression of appreciation of the departed Ambassador Bernstorff, the *Post* observed, "One may imagine with what disgust such an intelligent man as Ambassador Bernstorff was forced to participate in the harebrained German effort to spur Mexico into an attack upon the United States in the hope of recovering Texas, New Mexico and Arizona." Far from justifying the telegram, the *New Yorker Staats-Zeitung,* too, expressed utter bewilderment at Zimmermann's project—it was "beyond human comprehension."[28]

A small but vocal group of isolationist papers remained unimpressed by the telegram and dismissed the implied territorial threat as chimerical. In an editorial titled "Working Up the War Fever," the *San Francisco Chronicle,* the biggest West Coast paper, argued that the Germans had picked up the idea of separating Japan from the Allies from the American anti-Japanese press, and contended that the scheme posed no threat to the United States: "[I]t must not be forgotten that American newspapers and magazines have for a long time been printing articles, the object of which has been to create the impression in this country that the Japanese are itching to embroil themselves with us and that the Mexicans are ready to make common cause with them. . . . If the German Foreign Office seriously encouraged the implied intrigue, it argues a degree of desperation hitherto not suspected." The *Florida Times-Union,* the staunch southern advocate of neutrality, dismissed the telegram in the same vein: "[T]he most insulting suspicion of all is that Japan, in alliance with England against Germany, would attack the United States if our country should become involved in a war with Germany. It is unworthy of consideration."[29]

A number of contemporaries and historians have claimed, as exemplified in the words of Friedrich Katz, that "the note had its greatest impact in precisely those areas of the United States where isolationism and thus opposition to U.S. involvement in the war were particularly strong: the Southwest."[30] Indeed, most of the southwestern papers examined here condemned Zimmermann's scheme unequivocally, and some considered it a casus belli. The *Santa Fe New Mexican* editorialized on March 1 under the headline "Unmasked!": "The last utterly convincing demonstration and irrefutable proof of the villainous treachery of Germany has come to light. The United States of America has been handled by Germany like an innocent child. We have been the fatuous dupe of her 'diplomacy' while she has planned to stab us in the back. This is the last warning. If any considerable element of the population of the United States desires to parlay and vacillate longer we might as well abandon any attempt to be a nation. Sooner or later we are going to have to face this international desperado and criminal." All of the examined Texas, New Mexico, and Arizona newspapers that denounced the telegram had displayed strong pro-interventionist tendencies before March 1, so their critiques after the telegram's publication do not mark a change in opinion. Their reactions were in line with the rest of the American pro-Allied and interventionist press.

A few southwestern papers put the telegram in a local context. The *Arizona Republican* pointed out on March 1 that "[r]econquered Arizona [is] to be part of Mexico's reward for participation in dark plot." On the same day, in "Dangers Nearby," the *Houston Post* reminded its readers that "Texas has already felt called upon to use State means for the protection of its people against the raids from Mexico. It is not likely that should such means be employed again, the State troops will be as careful to avoid complications with the Mexican government as the United States troops have been. The fact is, Texas has about enough of that trouble on the border; and if the war department desires that present policies be continued there it would be well for Uncle Sam to keep a sufficient number of United States troops there to maintain order." The *Tucson Citizen* opined on March 3, "[a]ll of those who live on the border well know that German agents have been busy in Mexico and that [Mexican leader Venustiano] Carranza would only too eagerly grasp an opportunity to join a strong alliance of foreign powers against the United States."

By and large, however, southwestern papers framed the telegram in a national rather than local context. The majority of the examined Arizona, New Mexico, and Texas dailies denounced the telegram for the same reasons that interventionist editorials in the rest of the nation did—for German duplicity and as evidence of American naiveté. Several used it to lambast the pacifist movement, which hardly constituted a key element in local southwestern politics. Even the *Houston Post*, which on March 1 had warned its readers of "dangers nearby," partially retracted its alert one day later: "Foreign Minister Zimmermann must have been utterly ignorant of conditions in Mexico to have assumed that the flimsy Carranza government was able to conduct a campaign for the reconquest of Texas, New Mexico and Arizona. While the temptation of money might make an eloquent appeal to Carranza, nevertheless the old man has not quite gone crazy."

In general, the southwestern newspapers' commentary on the telegram strongly resembled national coverage. The similarity between southwestern and eastern editorial opinions in particular serves, as noted above, as a reminder of the former's dependence on the latter for international news, but it must also be regarded as evidence of southwestern editors' reluctance to see the telegram as a particular regional threat.

A review of contemporary cartoons regarding Zimmermann's alliance proposal confirms the findings from editorials and news reports on the telegram's shallow and transient effect on Americans. For example, a caricature entitled "Exploding in His Hands," depicts a dumbfounded Kaiser Wilhelm II (metaphor for Germany) with a bombshell (the telegram) prematurely going off in his hands (Fig. 9). The emphasis of the image is on the Kaiser's bafflement, not the threat posed by the telegram. The cartoonist notably omits any reference to Mexico or the notion of Mexico invading the United States.

"The Harmony Trio," published in Britain, focuses as well on German ignorance, rather than the Mexican peril (Fig. 10). Zimmermann, the kaiser, and Field Marshal Paul von Hindenburg are singing "another little war won't do us any harm"—a reference to the looming entrance of the United States into the conflict. Reminding readers of earlier derogatory comments about Americans by Papen, the German military attaché in Washington, the back side of their sheet music displays the sentence "War Plot Against Those 'Idiotic

FIGURE 9. William F. Kirby, "Exploding in His Hands," *World* (New York), March 2, 1917.

FIGURE 10. "The Harmony Trio," *Evening News* (London), March 2, 1917.

Yankees.'" Wearing evening suits rather than military uniforms, and perform-
ing on a stage, the three Germans appear comical, rather than menacing. As in
"Exploding in His Hands," the drawing omits any reference to Mexico.

The cartoon "Pie" depicts a burlesque kaiser offering a plate with sliced
pie in the shapes of Arizona, New Mexico, and Texas to a clownish-looking,
diminutive Mexican (Fig. 11). While pointing to an imposing Uncle Sam in the
background, the kaiser says, "All y'got to do is beat the stuffin' out of that old
guy there an' the pie is yours!" This illustration conveys no threat at all, but
rather a message of German insincerity and ignorance, for it is inconceivable
that the tiny Mexican would be capable of "beating the stuffin'" out of the
towering Uncle Sam—and receiving the proffered reward in return.

FIGURE 11. "Pie!" *Atlanta Journal*, March 2, 1917.

Clifford Kennedy Berryman's cartoon, likely published in the Washington *Evening Star* in early March 1917, depicts a hand inside an imperial glove carving up the southwestern United States (Fig. 12). At first glance, the illustration appears to cast the telegram as a direct territorial threat to the United States,

FIGURE 12. Clifford Kennedy Berryman, "For Myself," attributed to the *Evening Star* (Washington, D.C.), March 1917.

with Arizona, New Mexico, and Texas marked "For Mexico" and California labeled "For Japan (?)." The feasibility of the kaiser's plan is undermined, however, by the utterly unrealistic designation of the rest of the United States as "For Myself." The point of Berryman's cartoon is the grotesqueness of the telegram, not any territorial threat posed by it.

"Some Promise!" a cartoon distributed by Joseph Pulitzer's Press Publishing Company, depicts the kaiser and his potential Mexican partner-in-crime in a less cartoonish manner than the previous images (Fig. 13). While whispering conspiratorially in the ear of his prospective ally, the kaiser shows the Mexican the written alliance offer, "Join with Germany and you get a bit of United States." Although the Mexican is pondering the German offer, the seriousness of the situation is undercut by the cartoon's title—"Some Promise!"—which emphasizes the unfeasibility, and perhaps the insincerity, of the kaiser's scheme.

With "The Temptation," the *Dallas Morning News* produced the only political cartoon of the sample that does not in some way poke fun at Germany and Mexico (Fig. 14). The kaiser is depicted as the devil offering an undecided

FIGURE 13. "Some Promise!" distributed by the Press Publishing Company, likely originally published in early March 1917.

Mexican a sack of gold in return for the states of Arizona, New Mexico, and Texas. As in "Some Promise!" the Mexican appears to ponder the offer seriously, but here its effect is not mitigated by the title or some other humorous detail. Of the reviewed cartoons, "The Temptation" comes closest to casting the telegram as a serious territorial threat to the United States.

But even "The Temptation" appears tame in comparison with the numerous American propaganda images about the "rape" of "little Belgium" (Fig. 16) or those depicting the sinking of the *Lusitania* and the horrors of submarine warfare (Fig. 15). While American propagandists drew liberally on these two subjects throughout the war, they made virtually no use of the telegram after March 1917. The absence of a telegram theme in American wartime propaganda suggests that Zimmermann's Mexican overture did not have a profound emotional impact on the American psyche.

FIGURE 14. "The Temptation," *Dallas Morning News,* March 2, 1917.

According to Lansing, many Americans doubted the telegram's authenticity until Zimmermann admitted his authorship on March 3. He also contends that many anti-interventionists and pro-Germans denounced it as a British forgery. Consequently, Lansing argues, Zimmermann's admission deeply embarrassed and politically eviscerated those who had earlier staked their reputation on the telegram being a forgery.[31] If this were the case, the telegram would have played a significant part in crushing pro-German and anti-interventionist sentiment. Indeed, many historians have followed the secretary's line of argument, portraying the telegram as the death knell of anti-interventionism.[32] Interestingly, not a single newspaper from the sample dismissed the telegram outright as a forgery.

FIGURE 15. "Enlist!" poster issued by the Boston Committee of Public Safety, June 1915.

FIGURE 16. "Remember Belgium," poster advertising U.S. war bonds,
September 1918.

The *San Francisco Chronicle* saw "no good reason to challenge the authenticity of the letter signed 'Zimmermann.'" For the *Houston Post,* Lansing's vouching for the telegram's authenticity "duly established" its genuineness. In the same vein, the *Dallas Morning News* commented that the "President has certified to the authenticity of the Zimmermann note which betrays one of the intrigues of the German Government against the peace of the United States. But such a certification could hardly have been needed by any one who has observed the methods of the German Government with any attentiveness." The *New York Times* opined, "We need not recount every unverified rumor of German machinations in the countries south of us to show that the proposal of the German Foreign Minister, so far as it concerns Mexico, is precisely what might have been expected."[33] Other English-language papers did not even debate the question of authenticity, choosing to only discuss the telegram's political implications.

Although the vast majority of American newspapers cast no doubt on the telegram's authenticity, the British naval attaché in New York, Captain Guy Gaunt, reported to Hall on March 6 that "nineteen out of twenty men believed it was a forgery, and had not Zimmermann come out with his statement [acknowledging responsibility] on Saturday [March 3], I think it would have done us a great deal of harm." To illustrate this contention, Gaunt recounted his visit on March 2 to the select Round Table Dining Club, "the hottest stuff in New York in that line." Chaired by former U.S. ambassador to Britain Joseph Hodges Choate, the approximately eighteen attending members that evening included former attorney general George Wickersham, lawyer-cum-businessman John G. Milburn (at whose house President William McKinley had died in 1901), Senator Elihu Root, "and other men of that type." In sum, the roll call read like a who's who of prominent interventionist Republicans.

As the men gathered around the fire after dinner, Choate cornered Gaunt and bluntly denounced the telegram as a forgery. Virtually everybody present concurred with the former ambassador. When Gaunt pointed out that President Wilson had given his word to vouch for its genuineness, Choate retorted that a committee of representatives and senators should be given proof. Gaunt countered that it was unwise to give any details to "men like [anti-interventionist senators] Stone, [La] Follette, O'Gorman etc.," especially where "men's lives were involved." This jibe at the anti-war party immediately satisfied everyone, and the inquisition took a new turn. In a thinly veiled reference to Britain's involvement, Root asked Gaunt whether he personally considered the telegram genuine, and Choate asked him "point blank whether [he] knew anything about it." Gaunt "objected to the latter question," and his evasiveness left everybody present "fairly convinced that [he] did know." The naval attaché hastened to add that "information had been conveyed to me by U.S. authorities" (not by the British government), and he asked in apparent indignation why they were cross-examining him and not the president. According to Gaunt, this side blow at the Democratic president closed the ranks and "carried the day completely."[34]

To the extent it can be trusted, Gaunt's account casts a revealing light on the thinking of the conservative pro-war faction in early March. Although expressing skepticism about the telegram's authenticity, the Round Table Dining Club members quickly threw their doubts overboard at Gaunt's generic replies. The ease with which they came around suggests that they did not harbor suspicions about the telegram's authenticity in the first place and that their main interest lay in discovering more about the administration's source of the telegram—a natural reflex if the British naval attaché is the guest of honor. That they suspected Britain's involvement was not unusual. Numerous journalists and politicians knew about the British role, and Senator Stone had made exactly this charge the previous day in the Senate. Unlike Stone, however, Choate and his fellow interventionists had no problem with the notion of Britain pulling the Wilson administration into the war by conspiratorial means. To the contrary, they shared with Britain's representatives a disdain for the isolationists and the president's perennial hesitation and wavering. The Round Table dinner of March 2 represented a dialogue between two parties that essentially wanted the same thing—the United States' entry into the war—but could not say so openly to each other for political reasons.[35]

How did German Americans respond to the telegram? Assessments of German American reactions to the telegram have long focused on one individual, the outspoken German American propagandist George Sylvester Viereck.[36] An ardent believer in the German cause and purportedly the offspring of an illegitimate son of Emperor Wilhelm I, the young Viereck had joined the propaganda staff of the German embassy as early as 1914. An accomplished writer fluent in German and English, he brought passion and literary skill to the job. Throughout the period of U.S. neutrality, he heralded the Germans and blasted the British in his outspoken weekly titled the *Fatherland*, which was partially funded by the German embassy. Viereck's radical editorials and biased reports made the *Fatherland* unattractive to moderate Americans, and his increasing radicalization embarrassed the embassy. In October 1916, the German ambassador informed the Wilhelmstrasse that the *Fatherland* "has proved a failure" and that he would like to free himself from this noisy publication.[37]

To his own subsequent regret, Viereck took a "shoot first, ask questions later" approach to the telegram. On the day that American newspapers disclosed Zimmermann's scheme, Viereck fired off an open letter to Postmaster General Albert Sidney Burleson, newspaper publisher William Randolph Hearst, and leading editors across the nation. His missive left no room for ambivalence: "The alleged letter of Alfred [sic] Zimmermann published today is obviously faked; it is impossible to believe that the German Foreign Secretary would place his name under such a preposterous document. The letter is unquestionably a brazen forgery planted by British agents to stampede us into an alliance and to justify violations of the Monroe Doctrine by Great Britain."[38]

The American press immediately picked up on and reprinted Viereck's statement on March 2, but no newspaper of significance endorsed it. Several years after the war, Viereck nevertheless claimed that his brash dismissal of the telegram as a forgery was "adopted by the Hearst newspapers, and re-echoed by every foe of war in the United States."[39] This statement amounted to a gross exaggeration, if not an outright lie. Although Hearst himself privately expressed doubts about the authenticity of the telegram on March 2,[40] he published an editorial on the same day in all his major newspapers urging his readers to "prepare" for war, but without actually advocating intervention.[41] No Hearst paper endorsed Viereck's dismissal of the telegram as a British forgery nor did any other American English-language paper of significance.

When Zimmermann confirmed his authorship of the telegram on March 3, Viereck was greatly embarrassed and abruptly ceased his pro-German agitation. Still reeling from his public humiliation more than a decade later, he suggested that a large number of German Americans in early March 1917 had dismissed the telegram as a forgery and abruptly turned their back on Berlin when Zimmermann acknowledged its authenticity. In other words, many others had shared his folly, therefore perhaps making it pardonable. "Zimmermann's admission ended pro-Germanism in the United States," he wrote.[42] Viereck's claim to be one of many German Americans who suddenly lost faith in Berlin has been taken at face value by some,[43] but was his personal embarrassment and overnight disillusionment truly representative of German American reactions to the telegram at the time?

According to British historian Patrick Devlin, the "German-American press of course was unanimous in denunciation" of the scheme as a forgery.[44] Indeed, German Americans made up the only segment of the population that initially expressed a degree of skepticism about the telegram's authenticity. On March 1, a prominent German American from New York called it "bunk."

Another opined that "it was forged for the purpose of driving this country into war with Germany. There are thousands of paid English propagandists in this country who would do anything to drive the United States into war with Germany and thus earn their pay."[45] These were not isolated voices. A careful review of coverage in German American papers reveals a complex and occasionally contradictory response to the publication of the Mexican alliance proposal on March 1 and to Zimmermann's confirmation of its authenticity two days later.[46]

When the Associated Press released news of the telegram on March 1, all of the surveyed German American newspapers expressed doubts about its genuineness. Some did so more forcefully than others. For example, on March 2 *Der Deutsche Correspondent* of Baltimore argued, "[j]udging by the choice of words, this document was not composed by a German official; he would never have permitted himself to promise possession of Texas and Arizona to the Mexicans." The *New Yorker Staats-Zeitung,* on the other hand, merely noted that hard evidence was lacking. Only two papers, the *Volksblatt und Freiheitsfreund* of Pittsburgh and the *Germania Herold* of Milwaukee, openly contested the telegram's authenticity.

While several German American editors initially withheld judgment on the content of the telegram, two papers conceded that American criticism of the alliance offer was justified—if in fact the document were genuine. Under the headline "Wenn!" ("If!") the *Illinois Staats-Zeitung* wrote on March 2 in English: "Germany is fighting for her national existence . . . BUT THAT WILL NOT BE SUFFICIENT TO PERSUADE AMERICANS THAT GERMANY IS JUSTIFIED IN PROPOSING AN ALLIANCE WITH MEXICO TO THE INJURY OF THE UNITED STATES OR THE VIOLATION OF THE MONROE DOCTRINE" (emphasis in the original). The *Telegraph und Tribüne* made the same point but cautioned its readers that "external and internal evidence suggests that this is a malicious fabrication of British cowardice."

Zimmermann's admission of his authorship on March 3 provoked a range of reactions. One of the most despondent came from the *New Yorker Staats-Zeitung,* the nation's largest German American paper. With a nod to non-German readers, the paper commented in English on page 1 of its March 4 edition: "Dr. Zimmermann's instructions to the German Minister in Mexico constitute a mistake so grave that it renders the situation almost hopeless." With a view to German-language readers, the paper denounced the plan as "absurd" and "rubbish" and accused Zimmermann of "completely misconstruing the situation on this side of the Atlantic." The socialist *New Yorker*

Volkszeitung issued an even more scathing assessment on March 3, asking sarcastically, "when did Herr Zimmermann commit a greater stupidity: back then, when he dispatched this narrow-minded, idiotic 'letter' across the ocean or now, as he solemnly acknowledged his authorship yesterday?"

Other papers combined criticism of Zimmermann with sympathy for certain aspects of his scheme. The *Telegraph und Tribüne* argued on March 7 that the imminence of American intervention justified Berlin's quest for potential allies, although the paper conceded that Mexico would have been too weak for this purpose and that the telegram's disclosure had damaged Germany's case in the United States. *Der Deutsche Correspondent* called Zimmermann's alliance offer "ridiculous" and "a bad joke." At the same time, the *Correspondent* expressed understanding for Germany's attempt "to cause difficulties for the United States on this continent." The *Tägliche Volkszeitung*, in its March 5 edition, called the telegram an "unpardonable stupidity" but contended that some good might yet come of it, for the threat to their southern border would make Americans think twice before going to war with Germany.

Several papers that on March 1 or 2 had voiced strong skepticism of the telegram's authenticity sidestepped taking a position on Zimmermann's admission by reporting it without further comment. This group included the *Volksblatt und Freiheitsfreund* and the *Abendpost*. A couple of papers went so far as to endorse the position of the foreign secretary. On March 3, the *Germania Herold* uncritically and extensively reported Zimmermann's depiction of the Mexican scheme as a fully justified protective action (*gerechtfertigte Schutzmaßnahme*). The strongest endorsement of Zimmermann's stance came from the *Volksblatt und Freiheitsfreund* on March 4. Under the headline "Right of Self-Defense!" the article argued that the "Germanophobe American intrigues" justified "German preventive measures."

Judging from this newspaper sampling, the telegram strained German Americans' goodwill for their homeland, but it did not cause a sudden collapse of German American support for Germany, as Viereck claimed. Like their English-language colleagues, German American editors dropped coverage of the telegram after a few days. By mid-March, references to Zimmermann's Mexican scheme in the German American press had virtually disappeared. The debate about the telegram, as tempestuous and agonizing as it was for German American newspapers, proved short-lived and left no discernable mark on their coverage of the European war.

In the final analysis, there is little evidence to support Lansing's contention about the "profound sensation" the telegram supposedly provoked. While the American press hotly debated the implications of Zimmermann's scheme, this controversy passed quickly and did not fundamentally alter the stance of any editor of significance vis-à-vis the European war. Even after Zimmermann's acknowledgment of the telegram's authenticity on March 3, several English-language newspapers continued to advocate non-intervention. Likewise, numerous German-language newspapers retained their hope for peace, and a small group continued to endorse Berlin's policies. The limited impact of the telegram on American public opinion is further evidenced by the fact that by mid-March, coverage of Zimmermann's scheme had virtually disappeared from all American newspapers. When the United States went to war, few if any editors cared to quote the telegram as a justification for intervention. If the U.S. press can be taken as a reflection of public opinion, the telegram's effect on American attitudes vis-à-vis intervention was ephemeral.

Chapter Twelve

WAR

When the American press released the text of the Zimmermann telegram, the director of British naval intelligence, William Reginald Hall, felt certain that the United States would immediately enter the war. On March 1, he cabled Captain Guy Gaunt, the British naval attaché in New York, to inquire whether Gaunt had access to a secure channel of communication with the U.S. chief of naval operations in the event of a U.S. intervention.[1] Gaunt replied on the same day that Hall's was "a very difficult question," but in his opinion, the Americans were "so badly scared and aware of their ignorance and incompetence that if I had information and arrangements to trade I believe I could shift any doubtful character." He added that "[Assistant Secretary of the Navy] Franklin Roosevelt I know well and thoroughly trust and can speak very plainly to him."[2] The British naval men's planning proved premature, however. It would take the United States more than a month following the telegram's disclosure to join the Allies.

Why did the United States not join the Allies in early March? The basic answer is because the telegram failed to quash Americans' doubts about intervention. Citizens, members of Congress, and even President Woodrow Wilson continued to question the wisdom of going to war in spite of the alleged German threat described in the telegram. As a report for Wellington House, the British propaganda arm targeting the United States, observed in April 1917, "Travelling through the country one discovers an extraordinary ignorance and confusion of thought about the war prevailing in the masses."[3] The telegram had left the controversy over the United States' role in the European war unresolved. The closer the United States moved to the brink of war, the more obvious these fissures became in the fabric of American society.

President Wilson arrived neither promptly nor easily at his eventual decision to take the United States to war. Germany's launch of unrestricted submarine warfare presented Wilson with a stark choice—(1) do nothing and let Anglo-American relations wither as a result, which would have amounted to an abdication of three years of benevolent neutrality toward the Allies, or (2) keep the sea lanes open by force, which would inevitably lead to war. Before the telegram's release, Wilson had sought to steer a middle course by arming American merchant ships, but the realities of unrestricted submarine warfare and the disclosure of the telegram on the day the armed ships bill was introduced turned this policy into a step toward intervention. Even when taken together, Germany's declaration of unrestricted submarine warfare in addition to the telegram could not convince the president of the necessity of immediate intervention. These events, however, provoked presidential decisions that would ultimately lead to war, despite Wilson's persistent pangs of conscience.

A little more than a week after the press had first reported the existence of the telegram, Wilson took his first decisive step toward intervention. Suffering from a severe cold, on March 9 he issued an executive order from his sickbed to arm merchant vessels with navy guns and crews, regardless of the Senate filibuster led by Robert La Follette of Wisconsin against a bill doing the same and the absence of German submarine attacks on American ships. Although Wilson had originally intended this measure to serve as a means for supporting continued American neutrality, he surely realized that encounters of armed U.S. vessels and German submarines would inevitably lead to a clash at sea and eventually to war. In the event, the order had no practical significance. Before it could be implemented, the Germans sank four American ships—the *Algonquin*, the *City of Memphis*, the *Vigilancia*, and the *Illinois*—in rapid succession, on March 12, 17, 18, and 19, respectively. In the last three cases, the loss of American lives compounded the destruction of U.S. property.

Still, Wilson hesitated. To the despair of Secretary of State Robert Lansing, the president told him on March 19 that he did not consider the German submarine attacks a cause for war.[4] On the same day, Wilson, allegedly using stark language, expressed to Frank Cobb, editor of the *New York World*, his misgivings about the United States' likely entry into war. Historians disagree on whether this interview actually took place,[5] but it is true that the proponents of war deplored Wilson's lack of enthusiasm. Theodore Roosevelt wrote to his friend, the interventionist senator Henry Cabot Lodge, that Wilson's foreign policy was unworthy of support as it was "99 per cent wrong,"[6] and Thomas

Hohler of the British embassy in Washington wrote to Charles Hardinge, permanent undersecretary at the British Foreign Office, around the same time that the president was "the most agile pussy-footer ever made, and when any serious decision is taken, always tries to unload the responsibility on to someone else, and has been doing so this time again."[7]

In mid-March, several weeks after learning of the telegram, Wilson came around to fully accepting the idea of intervention. On March 20, he told his cabinet that he abhorred Germany's militarism on land and England's militarism at sea. When he then solicited the thoughts of his advisers, Wilson could hardly have expected them *not* to advocate intervention. As it turned out, every single speaker, including the pacifist Secretary of the Navy Josephus Daniels, advised him to declare war on Germany. "Well, gentlemen, I think that there is no doubt as to what your advice is," Wilson stated, concluding the meeting without voicing an opinion of his own.[8] The following day, Wilson requested that Congress convene for a special session on April 2. Most observers accurately predicted that on that date the president would announce to the world his decision to go to war.[9]

Even at this point in time, Wilson remained a reluctant interventionist. On March 27, he asked his adviser Edward M. House whether he should request from Congress a declaration of war or tell Congress that a state of war existed and ask lawmakers to grant him adequate means to respond. Fearing an acrimonious debate in Congress, House counseled in favor of the latter. When Wilson went on to say that he did not think he was fit for the presidency in war, House privately agreed. War, he wrote in his diary, called for a man of "coarser fiber and one less of a philosopher" than Wilson.[10] In the same vein, Secretary of the Interior Franklin K. Lane recorded on April 1 that Wilson went to war unwillingly.[11] On April 2, the president reportedly "sobbed as if he [were] a child" over his decision to go to war.[12]

With the choice for war made, even if reluctantly, Wilson sought to give the U.S. intervention direction and meaning. His war message to Congress on April 2, including his famous appeal that the "world must be made safe for democracy," has been hailed as one of the finest presidential orations ever delivered.[13] As Congress listened in complete silence, the president reviewed U.S. policy during the period of neutrality and the various reasons for his decision to ask legislators for their concurrence that a state of war existed between the United States and Germany. In Wilson's catalogue of grievances against Berlin, the telegram did not occupy a central position. He did, however, mention it explicitly in the third part of his speech:

One of the things that has served to convince us that the Prussian autocracy was not and could never be our friend is that from the very outset of the present war it has filled our unsuspecting communities and even our offices of government with spies and set criminal intrigues everywhere afoot against our national unity of counsel, our peace within and without our industries and our commerce. Indeed it is now evident that its spies were here even before the war began; and it is unhappily not a matter of conjecture but a fact proved in our courts of justice that the intrigues which have more than once come perilously near to disturbing the peace and dislocating the industries of the country have been carried on at the instigation, with the support, and even under the personal direction of official agents of the Imperial Government accredited to the Government of the United States. Even in checking these things and trying to extirpate them we have sought to put the most generous interpretation possible upon them because we knew that their source lay, not in any hostile feeling or purpose of the German people towards us (who were, no doubt, as ignorant of them as we ourselves were), but only in the selfish designs of a Government that did what it pleased and told its people nothing. But they have played their part in serving to convince us at last that that Government entertains no real friendship for us and means to act against our peace and security at its convenience. That it means to stir up enemies against us at our very doors the intercepted Zimmermann note to the German Minister at Mexico City is eloquent evidence.[14]

The fact that Wilson mentioned the telegram explicitly only in one sentence of his war address indicates that he did not regard it as a chief rationale for going to war. That he included it at all, however, proves that he considered it to be one of several reasons for going to war. Given that the war message was a comparatively short presidential speech—less than 3,500 words, delivered in only thirty-six minutes—and that long-standing American grievances, such as the sinking of the *Lusitania* and atrocities in Belgium, were not included, Wilson's brief reference to the telegram cannot be dismissed as insignificant. It is also noteworthy that Wilson chose to conclude his litany of German plots with a reference to the telegram and that he called it "eloquent evidence" of Germany's mischievousness. In thus structuring his accusations against Berlin's plotting in the United States, he implicitly endorsed Lansing's contention that the telegram was a smoking gun and confirmed allegations about a host of other conspiracies. As such, the telegram's inclusion in the war message represents an alignment of Wilson's thinking with that of his bellicose secretary of state.

If the president had eventually come to accept intervention, citing the telegram as one reason for going to war, the same could not be said for all of Congress. When Wilson concluded his address by asking Congress to endorse the
status of a belligerent nation, Supreme Court Justice Edward Douglass White
began cheering hysterically, and most of the chamber rose to its feet, screaming
and applauding wildly.[15] Senator La Follette of Wisconsin, among those who did
not join in the celebration, stood by motionless, arms folded tight and high on
his chest, chewing gum with a sardonic smile. Others shared his defiant stance.

When the Senate Committee on Foreign Relations convened to discuss
Wilson's war message on April 3, Chairman William J. Stone startled everyone
by casting a negative vote. Once Wilson's faithful lieutenant, Stone now refused
to follow the president. The senator from Missouri was convinced that a cabal
of newspapers and "big money" had pushed the United States into war, and
he said so openly. When Stone's colleague, Gilbert M. Hitchcock, asked for
a unanimous vote to have the war resolution presented to the full Senate, La
Follette objected to his request. Fuming pro-war senators could do nothing
but adjourn for several days before voting on the resolution, as La Follette had
made use of Senate rules established to prevent precipitous votes on important
topics such as the one at hand.

The pro-war party lambasted La Follette for his recalcitrance. Participants
of a local war rally responded to his name with hisses, and students from the
Massachusetts Institute of Technology burned him in effigy. A newspaper from
Wisconsin declared his home state "disappointed, chagrinned, indignant" and
wondered, "Is La Follette mad?"[16] The Senate reconvened on April 4 in an
angry mood, but even in the face of almost toxic adversity, the anti-war party
did not fold. Explaining his stance, James K. Vardaman of Mississippi gravely
doubted that "organizing the parliament of man" was worth sacrificing millions of American lives and spending billions of dollars.[17] Stone bluntly declared
U.S. involvement in the war "the greatest national blunder in history." Republican George W. Norris from Nebraska lambasted Wilson for the pro-Allied
nature of U.S. neutrality and denounced the war profiteers as the driving force
behind current policy: "We are going into this war on the command of gold.
. . . I feel we are putting the dollar sign on the American flag."[18]

Shortly before four o'clock came La Follette's turn.[19] Point by point, he
picked apart Wilson's war address. If Germany's unrestricted submarine warfare
was "a war against all nations," why was the United States the only neutral
nation that objected to it? If the United States intervened to make the world
safe for democracy, how did this premise square with the fact that its principal

ally-to-be, Great Britain, had not shown the slightest inclination to extend democracy to Egypt, India, Ireland, or even tens of millions of its own citizens who were denied the right to vote by the oligarchy that ran the country? Wilson's distinction between Germany's government and its people made little sense, La Follette argued, since far more Germans seemed to back the kaiser than Americans did the president, and so on. At 6:45 p.m., La Follette stopped speaking, tears streaming down his cheeks. In the audience, the journalist Gilson Gardner said to the reformer Amos Pinchot, "That is the greatest speech we will either of us ever hear."[20] Later in the evening, at 11:11 p.m., the Senate voted. Six lawmakers came out against war: Republican Asle Jorgenson Gronna of North Dakota and Democrat Harry Lane of Oregon joined Vardaman, Stone, Norris, and La Follette. Of the eight absentees, Democrat Thomas P. Gore of Oklahoma sent word that he also would have voted "no." When the clerk announced the final tally of 82 to 6, no one cheered, in marked contrast to the enthusiastic response to Wilson's speech in the Capitol just two days earlier. As La Follette returned to his office, a man handed him a rope.

The House met to discuss Wilson's resolution the following morning at 11 a.m. Fred A. Britten, a Republican from Ohio, caused a ruckus when he claimed that 75 percent of the representatives secretly opposed the war but were afraid to say so openly. Regardless of whether his estimate was exaggerated, a number of representatives spoke out against war. Illinois Republican William Ernest Mason declared, "I am against this war because I know the people in my state are not for it." To great and general surprise, the Democratic majority leader, Claude Kitchin of North Carolina, joined him, denouncing Wilson's failure to maintain even-handed neutrality toward the two hostile alliances. A parade of pro-war speakers sought to rebut the non-interventionists, and at one point the debate degenerated into a shouting match between the two sides.[21]

The Zimmermann telegram played virtually no role in the congressional debates on President Wilson's war message. It surfaced merely once, when Clarence B. Miller, a pro-war Republican from Minnesota, read a supposedly unpublished paragraph of Zimmermann's alliance proposal: "Agreeably to the Mexican government, submarine bases will be established in Mexican ports, from which will be supplied arms, ammunition and supplies. All [German] reservists in the United States are ordered into Mexico. Arrange to attack all along the border."[22] None of Miller's fellow representatives picked up on his claim. Four days later, the German foreign office's intelligence service reported Miller's remarks to the Wilhelmstrasse, where a German official, probably

Zimmermann or the department chief responsible for Mexico, Adolf von Montgelas, scribbled the word "rubbish" (*Quatsch*) in the margin.[23]

One of the most emotional testimonies in support of the antiwar position occurred when the lawmakers were asked to announce their vote. Representative Jeannette Rankin of Montana, the first woman elected to Congress, remained mute and virtually paralyzed when her name was called the first time around. On the second call, she struggled to her feet and said, "I want to stand by my country, but I cannot vote for war. I vote no." Sinking back into her seat, she began to sob. The final tally was 373 to 50 in favor of war.[24]

Although both chambers of Congress had given Wilson a firm mandate, legislative support for American participation in World War I was by no means rock solid. In times of crisis, legislatures tend to rally behind their elected leader, so a block of fifty-six congressional antiwar votes out of a total of five hundred eleven, or more than one out of ten, therefore constitutes a remarkably high number. By comparison, only one member of Congress (Jeannette Rankin) would vote against war in 1941. Until the Iraq War resolution of 2002, no other U.S. military engagement saw as many dissenting congressional voices as World War I. Opposition to intervention was concentrated in several geographical areas. While the Northeast produced a single negative House vote (the Socialist Meyer London from New York City), more than half of the nays came from the Midwest, including nine of Wisconsin's eleven representatives. In the South, four Democrats from Mississippi voted "no." Several observers reported in early April that Wilson could have carried majorities in both houses for any foreign policy he chose. Either way, he would have offended the hard core of lawmakers on the opposite end of the political spectrum. [25]

Public opinion regarding intervention mirrored the divisions in Congress. On the surface, interventionists had won a brilliant victory with the United States' entry into the war. The triumphant pro-war party dominated the public discourse, and many Americans had contracted war fever in the heady days of early April. Former president Theodore Roosevelt articulated the war enthusiasm on public display when he observed with relief that the United States wasn't "quite as anaemic" as he had feared.[26] Pro-war rallies attracted thousands while anti-interventionists appeared hesitant and dejected. Staunchly anti-war papers like the *San Francisco Chronicle* and the *Chicago Tribune* resigned themselves in late March to intervention. In Thermopolis, Wyoming, a local mob hung a man who had allegedly shouted, "Hoch der Kaiser" (long live the emperor), cut him down, revived him with cold water, forced him to kiss the American flag, and finally kicked him out of town.[27]

In private, American politicians and British observers expressed concern about the extent and depth of Americans' enthusiasm for war. In late March, Secretary of State Lansing fretted about the peace movement, and Wilson feared a lack of support on the West Coast.[28] The British ambassador, Cecil Arthur Spring Rice, stated bluntly, "[T]he vast majority of the country desire peace."[29] Also in March, Edward House and William Wiseman, the freshly minted station chief of the British foreign intelligence service in New York City, prepared an ominous memorandum for Prime Minister David Lloyd George. According to this document, only a slim section of the population supported the Allied cause while the mass of the people "wish to be entirely neutral as far as the European war is concerned." By praising the administration's "sympathy" with the Allies, the memo implicitly acknowledged the growing division between the president and the public over the question of intervention.[30]

The pro-war parties' concerns were by no means unwarranted. In early April, hundreds of antiwar protesters rallied in Washington, D.C. One group marched down Pennsylvania Avenue to the Capitol, led by a young woman carrying a banner with the inscription, "Is This the United States of Great Britain?"[31] Another group ventured into the Senate Office Building, and half a dozen activists from Massachusetts managed to find the offices of their senior senator, the interventionist Henry Cabot Lodge. They insisted on speaking to him, and eventually the sixty-seven-year-old politician relented. The ensuing meeting resulted in a shouting match, followed by fistfights between the pacifists and the senator and his aides. Eventually, the pro-war contingent badly mauled one of the pacifists. As the Capitol police carried the injured man into custody, Lodge basked in the glory of personally having beaten up a "German."[32]

Meanwhile, many antiwar congressional representatives could count on support from their constituencies, as isolated opinion polls from North Dakota, Wisconsin, and Minnesota indicate. Numerous letters expressed similar sentiments to antiwar Representative Kitchin of North Carolina.[33] Even after the United States had entered the war, Ambassador Spring Rice cautioned the Foreign Office, "There is no doubt that this country desires peace" and joined the Allies "with the greatest reluctance."[34] To what extent these disparate voices can be generalized is difficult to say, but several historians doubt that the majority of Americans wholeheartedly embraced war in April 1917. Some have argued that war enthusiasm significantly diminished between the time of the publication of the Zimmermann telegram and the U.S. entry into the war, and a recent study on this subject concludes that a sizable portion of the southern rural population resisted the war as much as many immigrants, German Americans, leftists, pacifists, and isolationists did.[35] Therefore, one historian opines, the "concept of overwhelming public support for the war becomes less and less tenable."[36]

In retrospect, the public response to the prospect of intervention appears confused and contradictory rather than uniformly supportive. The president probably could have carried public opinion either way amid this general uncertainty, just as he could have done so in Congress.[37] The reverse side of this observation is, of course, that Wilson would have faced opposition no matter what course he chose. The division of public opinion gave the president several options, but each was fraught with risk.

Unlike Wilson, most Americans failed to see the telegram as an argument in favor of war. If the U.S. press is an indicator of public opinion, Americans had by late March 1917 largely forgotten about the telegram. By that time, no major newspaper mentioned the telegram more than in passing or in the context of some other aspect of German intrigue. One of the last articles in a major U.S. newspaper to make the telegram a centerpiece of its reporting before intervention was a March 16 editorial in the pro-war, pro-Republican *Washington Post*. Under the heading "Plotting in Mexico," the paper reported uncorroborated allegations about German reservists streaming into Mexico and attempts by Berlin to stir up trouble for the United States across Latin America. As to Zimmermann's alliance offer, the *Post* contended, "[Mexican leader Venustiano] Carranza is evidently under the thumb of the German Minister to Mexico, and Germany is now financing the de facto government. Herr Zimmermann's attempt to make an alliance with Mexico, although exposed, seems to be going forward swimmingly."[38] The *Post* offered no evidence for its assertions and did not follow up on them.

To the extent that the Zimmermann telegram contributed to the United States' entry into the war, its effect was twofold. First, it appears to have prodded the president in the direction of war and helped to accelerate intervention, if only by a few weeks. Even though this had no discernible impact on the outcome of the conflict, it held important implications with regard to the United States' relationship with the cash-strapped Allies. From May to September 1916, the British treasury spent on average $207,500,000 (more than $3 billion in 2011 dollars) each month for war-related purchases in North America, and by the end of the year, British reserves were heading quickly to the point of exhaustion.[39] Fully aware of the perilous state of affairs, Prime Minister Lloyd George discussed Britain's delicate financial situation with members of his war cabinet during their first formal meeting on December 9. Sir Robert Chalmers of the treasury explained that Britain was at that point spending an unsustainable $60 million a week (more than $1 billion in 2011 dollars) in the United States, so the war cabinet resolved to quietly curtail orders to avert financial collapse.[40] U.S. intervention in early April 1917 saved London from bankruptcy, or at least from fully disclosing its financial plight to the United States, a situation that may have tilted the relationship between the two Anglo-Saxon powers during the following years decidedly in favor of Washington.

Second, by pushing the country closer to war, the telegram helped muffle the controversy about intervention rather than resolve it. As a consequence, the United States entered World War I less unified than Britain, France, or Germany had in August 1914. Also, unlike the Japanese attack on Pearl Harbor in 1941, the telegram in 1917 failed to persuade Americans of the moral righteousness of the cause. If the telegram did not gain traction with isolationists while at the same time pushing the administration closer to war, it contributed to a widening rift between the president and a large segment of the population. Hence, turning on its head Secretary of State Lansing's statement about the impact of the telegram, it resulted not in "putting the people solidly behind the government," but in further separating the administration from many of them. To be sure, when the United States entered the war, discussion in Congress and the press over the pros and cons of American participation largely ceased, but the underlying rifts in society by no means disappeared. A sense of patriotic duty muted skepticism about the war, but doubts festered beneath the surface. As the *Florida Times-Union* concluded on the day the United States entered World War I, "The adoption by congress of the resolution declaring that a state of war exists between the United States and Germany closes all discussion. Prior to the passage of the resolution Americans had a right to entertain any opinions on the subject that appealed to them, and to express their opinions. . . . The one object [now] is success and a debating society is not conducive to success."[41]

Chapter Thirteen

FALLOUT IN BERLIN

N ews of the Zimmermann telegram's disclosure quickly crossed the
Atlantic. On March 2, newspapers in the neutral Netherlands
reported on Zimmermann's scheme, and a Rotterdam-based staff
member of the *Berliner Lokalanzeiger* called foreign office counselor Adolf
von Montgelas in Berlin. The journalist relayed the published text of the Mexican alliance proposal as well as the contextual comments of the Associated
Press (AP), including Secretary of State Robert Lansing's disinformation that
the press could not publish all the pertinent facts for fear of endangering the
lives of those involved in obtaining the telegram.[1]

The disclosure came as a complete surprise to the Germans. While British
intelligence and the U.S. government had weeks to ponder the implications
of making public the alliance scheme, and devise an appropriate policy, the
Wilhelmstrasse needed to make a series of rapid decisions on how to deal with
the political fallout. Zimmermann faced a stark choice as foreign secretary.
He could either refute the story as a forgery and challenge the Wilson administration to back up its claim in the hope that the Americans would be unable
to do so, or he could own up to his authorship and explain the rationale for
approaching Mexico. Within a matter of hours, he settled on the latter. On the
evening of the same day, Zimmermann issued a statement to Wolff's Telegraph
Bureau, the semi-official German news agency run by Bernhard Wolff, admitting his authorship and defending the scheme:

> The American press contains reports about instructions from the ministry
> of foreign affairs to the German minister in Mexico City, in the event

that Germany, after the proclamation of unrestricted submarine warfare, failed to keep the United States neutral. These reports are based on the following facts:

After the decision had been taken to begin unrestricted submarine warfare on February 1 we had to reckon, in view of the previous attitude of the American government, with the possibility of conflict with the United States. That this calculation was right is proved by the fact that the American government severed diplomatic relations with Germany soon after the proclamation of a barred zone and asked other neutrals to follow her example.

Anticipating these possibilities it was not only the right, but also the duty of our government, to take precautions in time—in the event of a military conflict with the United States—in order to balance if possible the adhesion to our foes of a new enemy. The German minister of Mexico therefore was instructed in the middle of January that in the event of the United States declaring war he should offer to the Mexican government an alliance and arrange further details. These instructions, by the way, expressly directed the minister to make no advances to the Mexican government unless he knew for a certainty that America was going to declare war. How the American government received information of the instruction sent by a secret way to Mexico is not known. It appears, however, that the treachery—and it [surely] must have been treachery—was committed on American territory.[2]

Contemporaries and historians alike have dismissed Zimmermann's immediate and blunt admission as unstatesmanlike and naive. Secretary of State Lansing called it a "blunder" in his memoirs, and Barbara Tuchman referred to it as a "historic boner."[3] However, the foreign secretary had little choice. When he learned of the disclosure, Zimmermann was in no position of knowing how the Americans had obtained the telegram, and he had to consider the possibility that the U.S. government would be able to back up its claim with further evidence if he denounced it as a forgery. Thus, he would be exposed not only as a plotter but also as a liar. Remaining silent, on the other hand, would have been taken as an implicit endorsement of the AP story, while accomplishing nothing in the way of deflating mounting public pressure in Germany. At British naval intelligence, Captain William Reginald Hall, who at the time probably grasped the complexity of the telegram better than anybody else, had fully appreciated Zimmermann's decision. His admission was "by no means the stupid move that some people held it to be," judged Hall. "He took what in my opinion was the wisest course."[4]

Contemporaries and historians also have claimed that a clever journalist coaxed the foreign secretary into admitting his responsibility. According to this thesis, Hearst's pro-German press correspondent in Berlin, William Bayard Hale, suggested to Zimmermann on March 3 either at a press conference or one-on-one in front of the foreign office that he should deny his involvement. Zimmermann reportedly responded matter of factly, "I cannot deny it. It is true." The story may contain a kernel of truth in that Zimmermann did confirm his authorship vis-à-vis an unspecified member of the German Overseas News Agency on March 3. In any case, this conversation, or any other Zimmermann may have had with Hale or another journalist on the telegram, occurred *after* the foreign secretary's initial statement to Wolff's Telegraph Bureau on March 2. Also, whatever Hale's relationship with Zimmermann, the foreign office's first response to the disclosure was the above-quoted written statement, not a news conference. In all likelihood, the Wilhelmstrasse chose this course precisely to avoid probing questions.[5]

Zimmermann's prompt admission amounted to more than a mere acknowledgment of responsibility. In fact, the foreign secretary had already begun to put a very careful spin on the emerging controversy over the telegram. First, he stressed the defensive character of the plot by claiming that he had instructed Heinrich von Eckardt, Germany's envoy in Mexico City, to approach the Mexican leader Venustiano Carranza only after the United States had declared war on Germany. This contention was true with regard to the original telegram but ignored Zimmermann's follow-up message of February 5, exhorting the envoy to start negotiations "even now." In London, Hall could have easily called Zimmermann's bluff by publishing the secretary's intercepted February 5 telegram. The director of naval intelligence had not, however, released this message to the Americans, so Zimmermann's contention went unchallenged at the time, handing advocates of his scheme in Germany and abroad an argument for defending the plot.[6]

Second, Zimmermann omitted any reference to Japan. In all likelihood, the foreign secretary sought to focus the public debate exclusively on Mexico because at this point in time the Germans still held out hopes for an understanding with Tokyo. On February 17, Zimmermann had instructed the German envoy in Stockholm to resume discussions of a possible separate peace with his Japanese counterpart, and nine days later, General Erich Ludendorff informed Chancellor Theobald von Bethmann Hollweg that a German understanding with Japan was desirable from a military standpoint.[7] On March 3, Bethmann reminded the general of earlier frustrations in negotiations with Tokyo, but he agreed that Berlin would be well advised to remain receptive to Japanese feelers in this regard.[8] In the summer of 1917, Wilhelmstrasse counselor Hans Arthur von Kemnitz would successfully push for another diplomatic overture to the Japanese.[9] German-Japanese negotiations petered out eventually, but Zimmermann achieved his short-term goal in that the public debate over the telegram would largely ignore the issue of Japan.

Third, even before an investigation into the affair had been initiated, Zimmermann, in his admission, endorsed Lansing's suggestion that the telegram had been revealed to the Americans by a traitor, rather than through an insecure code. It amounted to a veiled attempt to blame the German embassy in Washington, and therefore Ambassador Johann Heinrich von Bernstorff. Although the U.S. secretary of state and the German foreign secretary were in pursuit of separate agendas, both men found it convenient to implicate Bernstorff. While Lansing sought to divert attention from the British connection, Zimmermann sought to find a scapegoat for the bungled plot.

On all three counts, Zimmermann's spin helped establish a framework in which the telegram would be discussed for many years. The initial phase of this debate played out in the pages of German newspapers in March 1917 and was remarkably frank. By and large, the liberal and socialist press, which had opposed unrestricted submarine warfare, denounced the telegram. "We cannot accept it. . . . [W]ith the methods of state policy used up to now, which are being so drastically illustrated by the German-Mexican affair, only a further intensification of the war and a further extension of the world conflagration is to be attained," wrote the radical socialist *Leipziger Zeitung*. Of note, the *Leipziger* chose not to include Japan in its reference to the "German-Mexican affair."[10]

The mainstream socialist *Vorwärts* called the telegram a "highly explosive bomb" that made a perfect gift to American hawks. The paper professed to be "astonished" by the offer of U.S. territory to Mexico and the notion of Carranza as mediator to Japan. It also criticized that the offer was made at a time when, according to the foreign office, relations with the United States had been excellent and admonished that the note should never have been sent if the diplomats could not guarantee secure transmission. The Social Democrats, the front-page article concluded, "decline any responsibility for this sort of foreign policy."[11] In the same vein, the editor Theodor Wolff, in the liberal *Berliner Tageblatt*, denounced the telegram as "naïve beyond belief" and took Zimmermann to task in a scathing, sarcastic editorial: "No gem of statesmanship has been lost between Berlin and Mexico."[12]

A particularly insightful critique appeared in the liberal *Frankfurter Zeitung*. First, the *Frankfurter* stated that it was far too early to point to any specific person for betraying the note, and regardless of the individual(s) responsible for the telegram's disclosure, secure transmission remained the responsibility of the foreign office in Berlin. Second, if unrestricted submarine warfare promised to bring Britain to its knees within a few months, as Zimmermann had claimed repeatedly in public as well as in the note to Carranza, why would Germany burden itself with an alliance with Mexico as a U.S.-Mexican war surely would drag on for years? Third, Carranza effectively ruled only a small part of Mexico, diminishing his value as a potential ally. Fourth, the paper noted the absence of Japan in the foreign office's official acknowledgment and questioned Tokyo's willingness to switch sides in the war. Fifth, the *Frankfurter* argued that Mexico, weak and torn as it was, would be unable to tie up a significant amount of U.S. forces. Overall, the editorial delivered a perceptive and damning analysis of Zimmermann's scheme.[13]

Several key German officials shared the *Frankfurter Zeitung*'s critique. The chancellor's secretary, Kurt Riezler, noted in his diary, "What rubbish regarding Mexico. It would have been better, even if the scheme is not betrayed, to do without this minor [Mexican] assistance, and let the Americans, if they are bent on war, deal with their strong domestic opposition" (and not provide the Wilson administration with an excuse for intervention). Riezler also correctly identified the scheme as originating with this "fantastic idiot" Kemnitz and harshly criticized Zimmermann as a spineless "yes man."[14]

Hugo Phillip von Lerchenfeld, Bavaria's representative to Berlin, was equally taken aback by Zimmermann's initiative. When the chancellor and the foreign secretary visited him on March 20, Lerchenfeld expressed his "surprise" about the initiative. Zimmermann replied that the alliance would have taken effect only in the event of war with the United States. He further explained that Carranza had been seeking a rapprochement with Germany for some time and that it would have been irresponsible on his part not to look for ways to stir up trouble on the Mexican border in the eventuality that the United States joined the Allies. Zimmermann's lengthy justification of the telegram left Lerchenfeld unconvinced. He regarded the incident as evidence that "people at the foreign office still cannot resist using completely unsuitable means. What have our operations [*Agitation*] in India, Ireland, Morocco and with the Senussis cost us in terms of men and money, without yielding any results. How badly have the attacks on munitions factories in America affected public opinion there, and how insignificant was the result. These examples should have advised against an operation in Mexico."[15]

Even Ernst zu Reventlow, a nationalist politician and opinion maker, initially condemned the telegram. In an editorial in the conservative *Deutsche Tageszeitung,* he wrote that the alliance proposal would have had a 95 percent chance of failure even if it had not fallen into American hands because Mexico was far too weak either to win over Japan or capture and hold U.S. territory. Reventlow ascribed the flawed alliance offer to a lack of expertise on Mexican-American affairs at the foreign office. At the same time, he conditioned his critique by contending that only those hoping to keep America neutral would brand Zimmermann's note a "policy of a fuse to a powder keg." He thus left himself the option of reversing his stance in case conservative opinion swung behind Zimmermann.[16]

It is worth noting that none of Zimmermann's critics publicly called for his resignation. Theodor Wolff and Colonial Secretary Wilhelm von Solf agreed privately that Zimmermann should have stepped down, and Lerchenfeld considered the lack of repercussions on Zimmermann's political career "strange."[17] Preferring graphic language, Franz Friedrich Andreae, brother-in-law of the liberal industrialist Walther Rathenau, asserted that "the whole nation feels like throwing up."[18] At the same time, moderates who had come to feel uneasy about Zimmermann due to his propensity of kowtowing to the military sensed there was no alternative to him. The leadership of the comparatively liberal state of Bavaria concluded that the liberal parties feared that his dismissal would only lead to replacement by a more conservative aristocrat.[19]

On the other side of the political spectrum, Zimmermann's supporters jumped into action. Most of the conservative, nationalist, and government-affiliated press quickly endorsed the telegram. The *National-Zeitung* contended that "Mexico is quite capable of mobilizing five hundred thousand men in an emergency, while the United States has previously been incapable of raising even a third of that number." The article continued, "The mood in Mexico during the war has been extremely pro-German. The students, for example, wore emblems with little pictures of Kaiser Wilhelm in their buttonholes to show their sympathies. The mood was such that it can be said that people were generally expecting an alliance with Germany." In the same vein, the semi-official *Kölnische Zeitung* wrote that it "was simply self-evident that we would make an effort, in the event of a war with the United States, to bring the natural enemies of the Union over to our side and to prompt them to attack."[20]

As the nationalist press rallied behind Zimmermann, Reventlow, too, quickly rejoined the flock and abandoned his earlier criticism of the telegram. On March 6, he wrote in the *Deutsche Tageszeitung* that his earlier comments had only expressed the opinion of those "who were placing great hopes on the maintenance of peace with the United States." He went on to express his unreserved support of Zimmermann's Mexican alliance scheme.[21]

For the popular national-liberal *Vossische Zeitung*, the telegram served not so much as evidence of Zimmermann's ineptitude as of his energy and drive. The real problem, the paper suggested, was not the telegram's content but its detection; it mused whether the German cipher key or the document itself had been purloined in Washington. Ambassador Bernstorff was, the editorial suggested ominously, not the epitome of diplomatic wisdom, and it reminded its readers of the carelessness that led to the loss of secret documents by other members of the German embassy in Washington, notably by Heinrich Albert and military attaché Franz von Papen.[22] The editorial fed directly into Zimmermann's strategy of shifting public discourse from the wisdom of his Mexican policy to the technical issue of communication security.

How well Zimmermann's blame-shifting strategy worked became evident in the secret sessions of the Reichstag's budget committee.[23] On March 3, Zimmermann read the telegram aloud before that body. He incorrectly stated that Eckardt was to open negotiations only in the event of war with the United States and claimed that Mexico was potentially a valuable ally. He said he regretted the "inexplicable" disclosure of his instructions. Disregarding the outrage over the telegram in the American press, he argued that actually some good would come of its publication since the American people now knew how perilous a war with Germany would be for them. Whether Zimmermann really believed his preposterous statement or whether he counted on his audience's ignorance of American affairs remains an open question.

The debate about the telegram during the budget committee session on March 5 demonstrated that the foreign secretary's strategy of damage control and blame shifting had worked. Only two speakers—both Social Democrats—came out against the telegram. Eduard David criticized the lack of secure communication, questioned Mexico's ability to seize U.S. territory as well as Japan's willingness to switch sides, and concluded that thanks to the telegram, peace prospects with the United States were now practically zero. After politely thanking David for his "calm and objective" speech, Zimmermann launched into a lengthy explanation of his ostensible motives, concluding once again that his plan had been feasible, had it remained secret, and that he could not be blamed for the disclosure. In a not-so-subtle maneuver to shift the debate to Bernstorff's responsibility, Zimmermann stated maliciously, "How the indiscretion was committed, I can today still not say. I cannot imagine that the Imperial Ambassador, as I read in a newspaper yesterday, gave the instruction to his valet in order that he might deliver it to Mexico. I cannot believe Count Bernstorff has acted so carelessly." He implied, of course, precisely that. David ventured no reply. His colleague Georg Ledebour lamented that Mexico could not be considered a valuable ally. Furthermore, Ledebour pointed out, the offer of U.S. territory to Mexico was incompatible with the self-determination of peoples, as postulated in an earlier German note to President Woodrow Wilson.

Zimmermann did not respond to Ledebour's brief speech, and the remaining seven speakers endorsed the telegram either partially or in its entirety. Six of them pointed to the disclosure of the telegram as the key weakness of the project and picked up on Zimmermann's red herring regarding Bernstorff's alleged role. Deputy Adolf Gröber of the Catholic Center Party demanded that the official responsible for the telegram's disclosure be identified and that the German embassy in Washington receive particular scrutiny. Deputy Siegfried Heckscher of the left-of-center Progressive People's Party flatly stated his belief that the German embassy in Washington bore responsibility for the disclosure.[24]

When the Reichstag discussed the telegram in an open session a few days before the United States' entry into the war, the debate developed along similar lines. Deputy Gustav Noske of the conservative wing of the Social Democratic Party lamented that thanks to the telegram, "for a while the war mongers in the United States were able to stir the passions of the American people, which has so much German blood in it, to the boiling point." Taking a jibe at Zimmermann, he called the telegram "not exactly a master piece." In short order, Kuno von Westarp, leader of the Conservative Party, came to the foreign secretary's aid. He and his political associates, Westarp explained, approved of Zimmermann's initiative because the foreign secretary needed to look for allies in the face of "America's threatening steps. I cannot judge the effect of the publication of the note negatively, as regrettable it is that it became known. Because of it, America was able to realize the seriousness of the situation, and the seriousness of our determination not to bow unconditionally to her commands." This was precisely the argument Zimmermann had used in the secret session of the budget committee on March 3.[25]

While Zimmermann's dealings with parliamentarians were key to managing perceptions of the telegram, his political survival depended on the continued goodwill of his political masters, Kaiser Wilhelm II, Chancellor Bethmann, and General Ludendorff of the OHL. He handled all three of them well. The Austrian ambassador to Berlin, Gottfried zu Hohenlohe-Schillingfürst, reported on March 3 that the kaiser had requested the foreign secretary "to account for this affair, and Herr Zimmermann [did so] in a fairly long presentation." Zimmermann successfully blunted reproaches about the fallout of the telegram by reminding the monarch that the Mexican alliance initiative was in line with the kaiser's earlier suggestions for such a scheme: "It had been his self-evident duty," Zimmermann told the monarch, according the ambassador, "to attempt to secure Mexican aid for the eventuality of war, which the Kaiser himself had previously suggested to him."[26] Zimmermann's justification apparently carried the day.

Having assuaged the emperor, Zimmermann on the same day proceeded to Bethmann's residence, where he conferred with the chancellor and top foreign office officials.[27] Since Bethmann in all likelihood had known about the telegram before its disclosure, the principal purpose of this meeting was probably for Zimmermann to report on his conference with the kaiser and to engage in damage control rather than assignment of responsibility. If Bethmann had wanted to fire Zimmermann over the telegram, this would have been an appropriate occasion to do so. The fact that the two men continued to work together for several months implies that Bethmann had no major disagreement with Zimmermann on the issue or that he considered the telegram too insignificant to let his foreign secretary go.

There was no need for Zimmermann to discuss the telegram with Ludendorff. Since he had informed the general about the Mexican alliance offer before its disclosure, at least in general terms, Ludendorff should not have been surprised when he learned of the precise content from the press. In fact, the general may have welcomed it as evidence of Zimmermann's support for unrestricted submarine warfare, a policy that the chancellor and foreign secretary had earlier criticized.[28] In his memoirs, Ludendorff is careful not to mention Zimmermann by name when dealing with the telegram. He acknowledges the telegram's detrimental effect on American public opinion but also contends that the United States was bound to join the Allies anyway, especially after Germany's declaration of unrestricted submarine warfare. His description of the telegram as an "attempt on the part of the Foreign Office to establish military relations with Mexico" cast the project as a reasonable endeavor. Ludendorff criticized the foreign office for its lax cipher security, a point the military made repeatedly in the months following the telegram's disclosure, but the general did not take issue with the substance of the Mexican-Japanese alliance scheme.[29] Several months after the telegram's disclosure, Lerchenfeld, the Bavarian representative, noted that Zimmermann continued to be in good stead with Ludendorff, a fact that would appear to imply the general's tacit approval of the foreign secretary's alliance proposal.[30]

When Zimmermann resigned in the fall of 1917, Wilson's adviser Edward M. House congratulated Captain Hall in London on "the great work" he had done and expressed his belief that the foreign secretary's "downfall was brought about by the exposé of his note to the German Ambassador in Mexico."[31] In fact, Zimmermann resigned over an entirely different issue. On July 19, 1917, a majority in the Reichstag consisting of Social Democrats, left-wing liberals, and the Catholic Center Party had passed a peace resolution. "The Reichstag strives for a peace of understanding and the permanent reconciliation of the peoples," it announced. "With such a peace, forced acquisitions of territory and political, economic, or financial oppression are inconsistent." The resolution flew in the face of Ludendorff's policy of military conquest and territorial expansion. Although Bethmann opposed Ludendorff's imperialist goals, he worked hard to block the resolution in order to maintain an outward facade of a united government. When it became clear that a majority in parliament would pass the declaration, Bethmann gave in to Ludendorff's pressure and resigned. He was replaced with a political nonentity, Georg Michaelis, a Prussian aristocrat closely aligned with the supreme army command.

Zimmermann did not outlast Bethmann by much. In the summer of 1917, he had loyally supported Bethmann in opposing the OHL's ever-growing territorial demands, thus alienating the political right and the military, the very groups that had seen him through the aftermath of the telegram scandal. Having earlier disappointed the liberals, the foreign secretary now found himself stuck between all the chairs.[32] Behind his back, his opponents criticized him as incompetent,[33] and the day before Bethmann stepped down, he had privately expressed his desire to resign.[34] His political fate was sealed ultimately when a German covert action in a neutral country was disclosed and traced to the foreign office.

In the summer of 1917, Norwegian police had discovered a number of explosive-filled boxes in the homes of suspected German agents. Since the boxes bore the insignia of the German embassy, the Wilhelmstrasse could hardly deny its involvement. The ensuing investigation revealed that German intelligence had run a scheme of planting explosives on Allied ships in Norwegian seaports. The findings led to the roll-up of German agent networks in Norway, multiple espionage trials, a marked deterioration in German-Norwegian relations, and the resignation of the German ambassador to Christiania. Zimmermann assumed political responsibility for the affair and, almost with relief, stepped down as secretary of state on August 5, 1917.[35] He was never again to hold public office.

Zimmermann's retirement brought about a turn for the worse for Kemnitz, his protégé at the East Asian and Latin American division. With Zimmermann gone, the foreign office had reassigned Kemnitz from his cushy desk job in Berlin to the German-occupied territories of Russia, where he served as liaison with the military's supreme command of the East. Just prior to his reassignment, Kemnitz made another push for the pursuit of a separate peace with Japan, his pet project. He would not return to the Wilhelmstrasse until the end of the war.[36]

As a retiree, Zimmermann played no political role in the turbulent days at the end of World War I, which toppled the monarchical system in Germany, saw the kaiser flee into exile in the Netherlands, and sent Ludendorff scrambling to Sweden. Yet the German revolution had an immediate effect on the former foreign secretary, because the new republican government opened an investigation into the causes of Germany's defeat. Its principal legal instrument was the Commission of Inquiry, established by the German national assembly on August 21, 1919. The commission was divided into four subcommittees, addressing the origins of the war, opportunities for a negotiated peace, war measures that violated the laws of nations, and economic war measures that violated the laws of nations.[37]

The second subcommittee investigated President Wilson's peace overtures of 1916–1917 and in the process subpoenaed Bernstorff, Bethmann, Zimmermann, and other imperial officials. If there ever was to be a wide-ranging official investigation into the origins of and political responsibility for the telegram, this would have been it. In fact, the text of the dispatch was appended to the transcript of the proceedings. Zimmermann's alliance proposal never became a subject of discussion, however. Two eminent historians have suggested that this was the case because "German leaders all seem to have joined a conspiracy of silence about the subject in their memoirs."[38] It is an attractive hypothesis, but the subcommittee probably glossed over the telegram for more mundane reasons. For one, the subcommittee correctly identified unrestricted submarine warfare, not the telegram, as the primary reason for the United States' declaration of war. This conclusion did not call for scrutinizing the telegram. Also, the foreign office had already identified and dealt with the official who originally proposed the Mexican alliance scheme, Hans Arthur von Kemnitz (see chapter 15). Why, then, waste precious time grilling Zimmermann on an issue of secondary importance?

It is also worth noting that of the four investigatory subcommittees, the one addressing peace overtures was the most critical of the old regime. Social Democrat Eduard David minced no words when accusing Zimmermann to his face as having been disloyal to Bethmann.[39] Aware of the subcommittee's inclinations, Zimmermann appeared harried and agitated on the stand, according to one observer. Solf, the former colonial secretary, noted that the "democrats' darling" Bernstorff received much more favorable treatment than the former imperial chancellor, Bethmann.[40] At the end of the hearings, the subcommittee de facto censured Zimmermann by resolving that the imperial government had missed an opportunity for peace by not responding more positively to Wilson's peace initiative. Given the subcommittee's critical distance from the old regime, its members are unlikely to have tried to protect the imperial government by circumnavigating the telegram. Rather, the dispatch was not central to its proceedings and therefore not investigated.[41]

In the following years, Zimmermann discussed his involvement with the telegram on several occasions. Visitors from the United States displayed a particular interest in this issue. The German American journalist and World War I propagandist George Sylvester Viereck, who interviewed Zimmermann sometime in the late 1920s or early 1930s, asked the former foreign secretary why he had not denied his role after the American press disclosed the telegram. Since Viereck had immediately declared the disclosed telegram a forgery, Zimmermann's confirmation of its accuracy had been a lingering source of embarrassment for the writer. Zimmermann told Viereck that he had had no other option since the "Allies had the goods on him." Viereck was evidently not satisfied with this explanation, because in his subsequently published memoirs, *The Strangest Friendship,* he continued to consider the telegram as well as Zimmermann's admission of its authenticity "a stupidity."[42]

A few years later, Zimmermann penned a brief exposé on the telegram in response to the memoirs of former foreign secretary Bernhard von Bülow, who had portrayed Zimmermann's handling of the scheme as naive and inept. Zimmermann argued that Germany's declaration of unrestricted submarine warfare, not the telegram, had provoked the U.S. entry into the war. As soon as the German leadership had taken this decision, "all that remained for me to do was, true to Count Bismarck's maxim, to make an attempt to create difficulties for our prospective new enemy. That my relevant instructions [the telegram] fell into enemy hands, was a misfortune, for which I cannot be held responsible."[43] By this time, the revelations about British wartime code breaking had established the fact that the telegram had been intercepted through cryptanalysis, not through lax security at the German embassy in Washington. Since cipher security fell into the purview of the foreign office, one can take issue with Zimmermann's flat-out refusal to accept responsibility.

A couple of years later, the American journalist David W. Hazen interviewed Zimmermann. Hazen, who visited Berlin in the summer of 1933, expected to find a "very stern, inflexible man," but he was pleasantly surprised to meet with "a delightful gentleman, so kind and amiable that I wondered how Americans could have thought so harshly about him in those furious days of 1917." Zimmermann let off some steam over prewar Chancellor and Foreign Secretary Bülow but otherwise engaged in small talk and proudly showed Hazen his rose and vegetable gardens. After the exchange of pleasantries, Hazen broached the subject of the telegram. Once again, Zimmermann portrayed the telegram as a defensive measure in the face of the United States' impending entry into the war. He compared his offer of Arizona, New Mexico, and Texas to the Allies' territorial promises to Italy. Both were equally legitimate, Zimmermann argued: "All fair [sic] in war and love." Elaborating, he once again ascribed the scheme's failure to the telegram's premature disclosure, not to inherent deficiencies of the project:

> I told my colleagues in the cabinet we should make Mexico our friend so it would make war with the United States and that would keep the American soldiers busy fighting Mexico so they could not come and fight us. I knew Mexico was not a strong military country, but I was sure it would take a very large army to conquer her and that America would have to keep very large patrol forces on the border. Then I thought if Mexico was at war with the United States, maybe America would hesitate about going into the war in Europe. I sent the message to Von Eckardt, our minister in Mexico, by code over the wireless but the English copied the message, deciphered the code and gave it to your government, so our plan failed.[44]

As the interview wound down, the discussion turned to the current political situation in Germany, and Zimmermann offered exuberant praise for Chancellor Adolf Hitler: "He is a great political leader, and a very fine orator. And since he has become chancellor, we see he is a statesman as well as a politician." Zimmermann's unabashed admiration of the Führer was, of course, not uncommon in those days, but it betrayed his intrinsic tendency to go with the flow, as well as a lack of political reflection and critical distance that had been so characteristic of him throughout his career.[45] Zimmermann's interview with Hazen was one of the last occasions for the former foreign secretary to go on the record about the telegram. Seven years later, on June 7, 1940, he died of pneumonia in Berlin.[46]

Chapter Fourteen

SCAPEGOAT

W hen the United States severed diplomatic relations with Berlin, the German embassy in Washington shut down, and the ambassador, his family, and the German staff began preparing for their departure to Germany. On the morning of February 14, Ambassador Johann Heinrich von Bernstorff and his party boarded the Norway-bound Danish liner *Frederik VIII* in New York City. A large crowd of curious onlookers, journalists, and personal friends of the Bernstorffs and other embassy personnel made for a friendly atmosphere, and the daily press published several benign farewell articles. Bernstorff's final press release expressed "heartfelt gratitude" for the "cordial hospitality" he had received in the United States. A testimony to the goodwill that Bernstorff had generated in the United States, the warm send-off raised eyebrows in Germany, where sentiment toward the United States had long ago turned hostile. Bernstorff's popularity in the United States thus played into the hands of Zimmermann and other German officials who were looking for a scapegoat in the telegram affair.[1]

In Halifax, Canada, where the *Frederik VIII* called in order to obtain Royal Navy clearance for its journey across the Atlantic, Bernstorff's German detractors received unexpected assistance from the British. Vastly overestimating Bernstorff's cache in Berlin, the British feared that the ambassador might be able to halt the United States' slide toward war by making a last-ditch appeal to Berlin for accommodation with Washington after his return to Germany. They resolved therefore to delay his return to Germany as long as possible. Through a mix of lengthy examinations, personal searches, and other chicanery, such as the careful sifting of the vessel's coal supplies for contraband, the British held up the *Frederik VIII* for twelve days. They also impounded a trunk with diplomatic papers from the Swedish minister to Washington and forwarded it to the Admiralty and Captain William Reginald Hall, director of naval intelligence, in London.

The confiscated trunk contained perfectly legitimate Swedish diplomatic correspondence, but Hall quickly realized its propagandist value. He leaked the news of a trunk with secret documents seized on board the *Frederik VIII* to the press, and when American journalists confronted him with the theory that the U.S. secret service had found the telegram in this mysterious trunk, Hall slyly responded that he "had to admit that all the evidence pointed to the seals having been broken before we took the chest."[2] His ambivalent reply planted yet another red herring, pointing to lax security at the German embassy in Washington as the source of the telegram's disclosure. Possibly as a result of Zimmermann's innuendo, the kaiser himself came to believe that the telegram had been purloined from this box and blamed Bernstorff.[3]

Bernstorff first learned of the telegram's disclosure on March 2 through a *New York World* radiogram requesting a comment from him.[4] He declined to respond, but upon arrival in Christiania (Oslo) on March 10, he told the German ambassador to Norway, Gustav Michahelles, that the telegram had been disclosed through betrayal in Mexico or through a compromised cipher, precisely the two venues through which the British had intercepted and decrypted the telegram.[5] Fully aware of the scapegoating campaign being waged against him in Germany, Bernstorff tried his best to defend himself at his next stop, in Copenhagen, where he stayed one night with his cousin, Ambassador Ulrich von Brockdorff-Rantzau. Bernstorff insisted vis-à-vis Brockdorff-Rantzau that none of his employees at the embassy had disclosed the telegram.[6] During his sojourn in Denmark, he also gave a candid interview to the *National Tidende*, stating with considerable accuracy, "In what way the American Government gained possession of these instructions I do not know: I can only assume that somehow or other the English or American secret police obtained knowledge of the key whereby the message was decoded."[7] This was not what the German foreign office wanted to hear.

On March 7, while Bernstorff was still at sea, Counselor Hans Arthur von Kemnitz prepared an "interview" that Bernstorff would "grant" the correspondent of the *Hamburger Fremdenblatt* in Copenhagen.[8] There can be little doubt that Kemnitz, a minor official, was acting at the behest of his boss, Zimmermann. According to the prepared text, the German ambassador would justify the telegram as an act of self-defense and denounce Americans' outrage as hypocritical. An official from the foreign office, possibly Counselor Adolf von Montgelas, considered Kemnitz's draft a bit extreme and deleted two particularly outrageous statements: a description of the telegram's disclosure as a "monstrous act of betrayal" and a reference to President Woodrow Wilson's "pathetic peace talk." Although these two items did not make it into the released version of the "interview," they reveal how the foreign office sought to maneuver Bernstorff into a corner.

Bernstorff could hardly refuse to sign off on the prearranged piece, but he let the American ambassador to Copenhagen, Maurice F. Egan, know that the "interview was a concoction made by his Government for him." Egan wrote, "The only part intended for American consumption was his denial that he had been involved in any plots. Privately he denies the Carranza note. Bernstorff feels that he would have been candidate for the Vice Chancellorship if the note had not come out. He is very bitter about this. He is accused of disloyalty in not preventing the publication of the note. Until Washington can explain whether the note was obtained in Mexico or in Washington, he thinks that his usefulness in Germany is ended." [9] Unfortunately for Bernstorff, the intended recipients of Egan's message in Washington had no interest in coming to his defense.

By the time Bernstorff arrived in Berlin, on the evening of March 13, the whisper campaign against him had ensured his near-total isolation politically. One of the few officials who extended the returning diplomat a warm welcome was the colonial secretary, Wilhelm von Solf, who had privately condemned unrestricted submarine warfare as "desperado politics." The melancholy Solf wielded little influence with the kaiser or the military. [10] Chancellor Theodor von Bethmann Hollweg cordially received Bernstorff on March 14 and continued to conceal his own doubts about the submarine warfare policy for the sake of presenting a unified leadership to the outside world. Although the United States had not yet entered the war, Bethmann did not solicit detailed information from Bernstorff about the state of American politics or political thinking. Instead, he raised the prospect of sending Bernstorff on an official mission to Sweden, perhaps in an honorable attempt to remove him from Berlin in order to avoid further controversy. [11]

Kaiser Wilhelm II kept Bernstorff at arm's length. Accusing Bernstorff of democratic leanings and holding him responsible for the telegram's disclosure, Wilhelm flatly denied him the Swedish mission and refused to receive him until May 4. By then, American neutrality was of purely historical interest, and the monarch used his brief one-on-one with Bernstorff mostly for non-political small talk. "With his customary skill," Bernstorff recalled, "the Kaiser steered clear of any attempt to enter deeply into the political problems of the hour, and behaved towards me, for the rest, just as affably as he had been wont to do in the past."[12]

Bernstorff's encounter with Germany's strongman, General Erich Ludendorff, took place in a decidedly less friendly atmosphere. Ludendorff received the diplomat with the words, "In America you wanted to make peace. You evidently thought we were at the end of our tether." To this, Bernstorff replied, "No, I did not think that; but I wanted to make peace before we came to the end of our tether." Ludendorff then ended the conversation with a harsh reprimand of the ambassador: "We, however, did not want to. Besides, it would not have been surprising if you had thought that we had come to the end of our resources. The communications you received, which I read from time to time, certainly led to that conclusion."[13] Disillusioned, Bernstorff accepted the ambassadorship to Constantinople later that year. As he told the editor Theodor Wolff, "What else am I to do here?"[14]

Bernstorff served in Constantinople for about a year. In late October 1918 he returned to Berlin, where revolution was in full swing. When the new German president, Friedrich Ebert, offered him the post of foreign secretary, Bernstorff declined, pointing to his negative reputation abroad as Germany's last imperial ambassador to Washington. Instead, Bernstorff chose to end his diplomatic career and enter politics as a member of the left-of-center German Democratic Party (DDP). In 1921 he was elected to the Reichstag as a DDP deputy. A staunch supporter of the republic, he endorsed the government's difficult and unpopular stance of fulfilling the enormous financial demands the Versailles peace treaty had placed on Germany. When right-wing extremists murdered the gifted industrialist and politician Walther Rathenau, a Jew and supporter of the republic, Bernstorff publicly expressed his disgust at the rising tide of anti-Semitism.[15]

His unequivocal pro-republicanism and stance against anti-Semitism and the nationalist challenge won him the lasting odium of the political right. By the mid-1920s, Bernstorff had few illusions about the future of German democracy. He termed Paul von Hindenburg's election as president in 1925 the "death warrant of the Republic." Still, a couple of years later, the two men, who had been political opponents for many years, met in person and reached reconciliation. "I like a man to speak his mind with candor and clearness," Hindenburg told Bernstorff, who, in turn, acknowledged and appreciated the president's human traits. When Bernstorff was appointed German representative to the League of Nations commission on disarmament in 1926, Hindenburg allegedly said, "If I had known that the Americans would get across [the Atlantic], I would not have decided for the U-Boat war. But I relied on the assurances of the Navy."[16]

In 1928 Bernstorff resigned his Reichstag seat and dedicated himself full-time to the League of Nations, whose goals he supported wholeheartedly. Internationalism, however, was not high on Berlin's agenda when the Nazis seized power in 1933. Politically defeated, Bernstorff went into exile in Geneva, thus escaping certain persecution under the Third Reich. On the occasion of the publication of his memoirs in 1936 in Switzerland, the Nazi press disparaged Bernstorff as hopelessly pro-Western and philo-Semitic. On October 6, 1939, a few days after the German invasion of Poland, Bernstorff died largely forgotten and alone in Geneva. The only obituaries for him appeared outside Germany.[17]

In Berlin after Bernstorff's return, Zimmermann worked diligently to freeze the ambassador out of the political process. On March 17, 1917, he established a commission under the counselor Otto Göppert to investigate the telegram's disclosure. Göppert's mandate focused solely on the technical question of communication security, not on the policy rationale behind the telegram. Of particular note, one of the main actors, Bernstorff, would not be called upon to participate in the investigation.[18]

The forty-five-year-old Göppert was a lawyer and a foreign service veteran of nearly two decades. He completed short tours of duty in Russia and Switzerland before the war, but spent most of his time in the legal division of the foreign office. After serving briefly in the army at the outbreak of war, he rejoined the foreign office and worked for two years at the embassy in Constantinople. In early February 1917, he returned to the Wilhelmstrasse, where he was assigned to head the telegram investigation. Göppert's legal background as well as his prolonged absence from Berlin made him a suitable candidate to head an investigation in need of an aura of independence.[19]

Göppert spent less than three weeks reviewing the evidence. He conducted interviews with staff members of the German embassy of Washington (except for the ambassador), all of whom vehemently insisted that the security breach could not have occurred there. The embassy cashier, Josef Schmid, provided this valuable piece of information: "We handed all our telegrams for Mexico to the Western Union Telegraph Company. They collaborated closely with the Mexican Telegraph Company, a line which was almost completely in English hands."[20] Although Schmid's testimony should have alerted Göppert to

the likelihood of British access to the telegram (and all other German correspondence with Mexico), the investigation largely ignored it. Instead, Göppert
quickly zeroed in on the treachery hypothesis.

As the Göppert investigation gathered steam, the foreign office inquired at
the German mission in Mexico about its security measures. Probably based on
information provided by Göppert, the Wilhelmstrasse on March 27 went so
far as to inform Heinrich von Eckardt, the German envoy, that "various indications suggest that treachery was committed in Mexico. The greatest caution
is indicated. Burn all compromising material." An outraged Eckardt denied
any wrongdoing, wiring back on March 30 that his assistant, Arthur Magnus, had immediately burned the original telegram and that "the ashes" had
been "scattered." In a follow-up message on the same day, Eckardt elaborated,
"[g]reater caution than is always exercised here would be impossible. The text
of the telegrams which have arrived is read to me at night in my dwelling house
by Magnus in a low voice. My servant, who does not understand German,
sleeps in an annex. Apart from this, the text is never anywhere but in Magnus'
hand or in the steel safe, the method of opening which is known only to him
and myself." Adding more gist to the mill for those seeking to blame Bernstorff, Eckardt added that according to Richard Kunkel, a staff member who
had recently transferred to Mexico from the defunct Washington embassy, "in
Washington even secret telegrams were known to the whole Chancery. Two
copies were regularly made for the Embassy records. Here there can be no
question of carbon copies or waste paper." Eckardt concluded by demanding
official exculpation or an independent judicial investigation by a German consul. It speaks volumes for the foreign office's prejudice against Bernstorff that
Eckardt's pathetic, denunciatory ultimatum produced the desired result. "After
your telegram it is hardly conceivable that betrayal took place in Mexico,"
cabled the Wilhelmstrasse reassuringly to Eckardt on April 4. "No blame rests
on either you or Magnus."[21]

Göppert submitted his final report on the same day that the foreign office absolved Eckardt.[22] In it, he discussed three possibilities for the telegram's
disclosure: that the Americans were in possession of code 0075 (used for German telegrams between Berlin and Washington), that they were in possession
of code 13040 (used between Washington and Mexico), or that a traitor had
disclosed the telegram. Although Göppert mentioned, and quickly discounted,
the possibility of the British having provided the Americans with German cipher
material, he did not acknowledge the possibility that the British might have
obtained the telegram and given it to the Americans. Moreover, he considered

American knowledge of either code unlikely. Had they been able to break 0075, he argued, the U.S. embassy in Berlin would have been in a position to decrypt the telegram and probably would have refused to convey it. At the least, the U.S. ambassador in Berlin would have informed Washington of its contents. The Germans were routinely intercepting and decrypting the U.S. embassy's diplomatic traffic and thus knew that Ambassador James Gerard remained unaware of the telegram's content.[23]

Göppert conceded the vulnerability of code 13040, but he considered its compromise unlikely. If Germany's opponents had broken this code, surely they would have published other German messages encrypted in 13040 as well. He did not contemplate the possibility that British naval intelligence was even then reading virtually all of Germany's transatlantic traffic—including the back and forth between the Wilhelmstrasse and Eckardt—but managed to keep it secret.

Lending considerable weight to Secretary of State Robert Lansing's deceptive tale about the involvement of a German traitor or an American spy, Göppert concluded that betrayal explained the telegram's disclosure most convincingly. His conclusion thus left the German missions in Mexico and Washington to take the blame. The foreign office, however, had already formally exculpated Eckardt. Göppert, too, had concluded that the leak did not occur in Mexico because Zimmermann's March 5 follow-up message—which did not go through Washington and in which he exhorted Eckardt to immediately contact Carranza—had not been published. For Göppert, that the message was not made public was a "certain" indicator that it had not been intercepted. (The British had, in fact, intercepted the message, but Hall had chosen to withhold it.)

In Washington, on the other hand, sloppy security procedures supposedly prevailed, leaving an inordinate number of mid-level embassy officials with alleged access to cipher material. Without saying so explicitly, Göppert suggested that Bernstorff's failure to put his embassy in order had led to the telegram's betrayal.[24] A couple of months later, the foreign office identified the chief suspect—the former Washington embassy employee Richard Kunkel, who had earlier informed Eckardt about the supposedly lax security situation in Washington. When queried a month later, Bernstorff said he did not believe Kunkel was a traitor.[25]

The conclusion of Göppert's report is particularly astounding in view of the fact that so much evidence collected in the course of the investigation should have pointed Göppert in the *right* direction. Bernstorff had opined as early as

March 10 that cryptanalysis, not betrayal, was at the root of the problem. The former ambassador stuck with his conviction and repeated it in his memoirs and before a postwar investigative committee, several years before the role of British naval intelligence would become public knowledge. Yet Göppert declined to interview Bernstorff in the course of his investigation.[26]

Truly mind-boggling is Zimmermann's private admission to Hugo Phillip von Lerchenfeld, the Bavarian representative in Berlin, that code 13040 was probably compromised and that the foreign office would have preferred to change it but had been unable to do so due to the war.[27] In other words, the foreign office was fully aware how risky it was to send the telegram to Mexico via Washington, where the local embassy was bound to use 13040 for transmission to Eckardt. The director of the foreign office's cipher bureau wrote in a memorandum shortly after the publication of the telegram that he did not possess definitive proof that 13040 was compromised, but in the same breath he warned that Allied intelligence worked feverishly to break German ciphers.[28] Since Göppert himself conceded (and stated in his report) that 13040 was breakable if sufficient encoded messages were amassed, the director's statement that the Allies were working on breaking Germany's codes should have given him further pause.

Other sources also pointed toward compromised communications. The German military and its intelligence agencies had picked up hints early in the war suggesting the vulnerability of Berlin's wireless communication. On September 23, 1914, a military intelligence officer had reported that German radio messages were being intercepted on a daily basis. He cited information from captured enemy records as evidence.[29] Another military intelligence officer reported on November 3, 1914, that papers found on a captured British officer indicated that the British were able to decrypt encoded German wireless messages.[30] A few days later, a German spy reported on November 17, 1914, that the French were capturing German messages by way of an interceptor mounted on the Eiffel Tower and that they were in possession of a German naval code book (*Marinesatzbuch*).[31]

In March 1917, Sektion IIIb (military intelligence) informed the foreign office in two reports that the British were in possession of the German diplomatic code used in the Netherlands, that the Americans could read German encrypts, and that "the German plan regarding Mexico has been discovered by 'the intelligence and enterprising spirit of the English.' The German secret political code is no secret for England."[32] Even the Swedish government warned the Wilhelmstrasse on March 13, 1917, that its codes were not secure.

After the war, Kemnitz claimed that by the time the Wilhelmstrasse had dispatched the telegram, "there was a suspicion that the American government was in possession of our cipher."[33]

Why was Göppert's report so widely off the mark? For one, he apparently fell hook, line, and sinker for Hall's and Lansing's carefully placed red herrings that pointed toward betrayal, as opposed to a broken code. Also, the evidence in support of a compromised code was fragmentary and dispersed. Presumably working mostly by himself and conducting his investigation in rapid time, Göppert may simply have failed, in modern parlance, to "connect the dots." It is remarkable, however, that his settling for betrayal rather than a compromised code dovetailed so well with Zimmermann's domestic agenda. This may not be a mere coincidence. After all, Göppert was Zimmermann's subordinate and would implicate his boss at his own peril. Given his lack of professional independence, it would have been naturally tempting for Göppert to support Zimmermann's well-known opinion, especially since only circumstantial evidence pointed the other way.

The Göppert investigation had no effect on foreign office communications security, even though the compromise of the German codes should have been apparent by then even to a casual observer. Göppert had considered it "unlikely" but not inconceivable that the Americans had broken code 13040. Various German officials, including Bernstorff and Zimmermann, had conceded this possibility as well. Even if codes 13040 and 0075 had been secure in the past, the foreign office ought to have inferred that they were now compromised, regardless of how the Americans had obtained the telegram. Anybody who could get their hands on the encrypted text of the telegram sent from Washington to Mexico would have been able to compare it with the clear text and thus break code 13040. Moreover, the Germans had committed the cryptologist's "capital crime" of sending the same message in two different codes, 13040 and 0075. Since the older code was compromised, the same would be true for the newer code as well, because any foreign cryptanalyst with access to the telegram encoded in 0075 would be able to decrypt it, and thus break the code, by comparing it with the already broken 13040 code. This was exactly what Room 40 had done. The telegram thus provided the British with a Rosetta stone for the decryption of Germany's diplomatic traffic in the future, should the foreign office continue to use their compromised codes.[34]

By and large, the Wilhelmstrasse failed to draw appropriate cryptanalytic lessons from the telegram's disclosure. The foreign office considered code 0075 secure and continued to use it. While the diplomats partially withdrew code

13040, they by no means wholly discarded it. The foreign office informed Eckardt in Mexico on March 23 that "cipher 13040 is compromised and must not be used for secret communications,"[35] but two weeks later, Göppert's report suggested that 13040 was secure. Göppert also correctly described another code, 5950, as compromised, yet in mid-March diplomats began to replace code 13040 with 5950.[36] Evidently, the Wilhelmstrasse had no standing policy on communications security.

The German army and navy, which used foreign office channels to communicate with their overseas agents, were so dismayed by the sloppiness and confusion that they began to intercept and decipher German diplomatic telegrams exchanged by radio between Madrid and Berlin and present them to the foreign office to prove that diplomatic communications security was in dire need of reform.[37] Alas, their efforts were in vain. After reviewing the communications security situation as late as September 1917, Kemnitz feebly concluded, "[o]f course, it would have been warranted to change the ciphers used by the overseas missions after the betrayal of the Mexico dispatch. To this hour this has not been feasible; however, attempts to find a way to do this are continuing."[38] In other words, the foreign office realized that the enemy was eavesdropping on German communications, but the diplomats proved unable or unwilling to do anything about it. With most overseas missions physically out of reach for Berlin, introducing new codes and ciphers may have been a daunting task, but if the Wilhelmstrasse considered this course of action impractical, it should at least have alerted its diplomats abroad that any of their Germany-bound messages were prone to enemy interception and decryption. In the absence of such basic precautions, the next diplomatic disaster was just a question of time.

On September 8, 1917, the British Reuters news agency in Washington released three telegrams sent by Karl von Luxburg, German minister to Argentina, to the German foreign office in May and July of that year.[39] In the messages, Luxburg exhorted Berlin to either spare Argentinean ships bound for Europe, force them to return home, or sink them "without a trace" in order to conceal German responsibility. He also described the Argentinean deputy foreign minister as a "notorious ass and an anglophile." Luxburg had communicated with the Wilhelmstrasse with the help of Sweden's pro-German government, which had agreed to transmit encrypted German messages from Berlin to Buenos Aires and vice versa. Room 40 had broken Sweden's diplomatic code, and since the Wilhelmstrasse and Luxburg used compromised codes for their exchange, British cryptanalysts routinely decrypted German messages embedded in Swedish telegrams. Just as he had done in the case of the Zimmermann telegram, Hall handed the Luxburg telegrams to the State Department for disclosure, with the caveat that Britain's role not be mentioned in public. He also alerted the Americans to the existence of the so-called Swedish roundabout (see chapter 7). This revelation would later fuel speculation about the telegram having taken this route.

Hall showed an excellent sense of timing with the release. Relations between Berlin and Buenos Aires were strained over the sinking of an Argentinean ship by a German submarine, and Sweden was just two weeks away from parliamentary elections that threatened to topple Stockholm's pro-German, conservative government. When the Swedish press published the Luxburg telegrams, the government felt compelled to admit its part in the affair and drew considerable fire from the opposition for its clandestine collaboration with Berlin. The ensuing elections duly swept the conservative party out of office, replacing it with a pro-Allied coalition of liberals and social democrats who quickly closed the Swedish roundabout, thus further limiting Berlin's options for communicating with its overseas missions. Consequently, Germany's transatlantic telegraphy became slow and cumbersome. Although the Germans could rely on a powerful radio in Mexico, it was primarily a receiving station. For transmission of communications to Germany, Eckardt had to go through the German embassy in Madrid, but it could take messages more than a month to reach Berlin.

With regard to Argentina, the Germans dodged a bullet. The Wilhelmstrasse informed the Argentinean government that Luxburg had expressed a personal opinion not shared in Berlin. The foreign office recalled the minister, a brash, swashbuckling career diplomat, and the Argentinean government was sufficiently assuaged to remain neutral for the remainder of the war, contrary to British and American hopes. In his post–World War II memoirs, an unrepentant Luxburg maintained obstinately that the Argentinean ships he referred to "had to disappear so they would do no mischief." The crews—"although they were assorted riff-raff"—should have been spared, he wrote, without explaining how submarines with standing orders to fire without warning would have accomplished this feat. He stubbornly proclaimed to be proud of having served "as a target on behalf of my people" and at the same time accused the foreign office of gross negligence for its continued use of compromised codes. As unqualified as Luxburg may have been for his posting in Buenos Aires, his last statement contained more than a kernel of truth.

In the wake of the Luxburg scandal, the foreign office charged Kemnitz, of all people, with conducting a damage assessment. In his final report of

September 24, the counselor cynically dismissed American outrage at Sweden's telegraphic assistance to Germany as "mere bluster." Washington had acted no different than Stockholm, he argued, when Wilson had agreed to put the State Department's network at Berlin's disposal to convey messages to Bernstorff during 1916–1917. Kemnitz failed to mention that the Americans' offer was made for the express purpose of peace negotiations and that the foreign office had crassly abused it by sending war instructions to Bernstorff and Eckardt. Kemnitz conceded that it "would have been smarter" on Luxburg's part to express himself more cautiously, especially in view of the preceding telegram debacle, but he quickly blunted this mild criticism by asserting that Luxburg had merely voiced a personal opinion, and at any rate, British diplomatic cables certainly contained equally strong language. Once again, the foreign office appeared not so much concerned about *what* its officials had said but rather *how* the information was disclosed.

In Luxburg's case, the Wilhelmstrasse realized that its messages had been compromised through cryptanalysis, not through betrayal or theft. Kemnitz surmised that disclosure of the telegram in January 1917 had provided the Americans with the cryptanalytic tools to attack subsequent encrypts. Although he continued to ignore the possibility of British involvement, and clung to the notion that a traitor had disclosed the telegram, his conclusions were closer to the truth than Göppert's had been. Kemnitz ended his report by conceding that Germany's overseas diplomatic codes were probably compromised, but for technical reasons could not be substituted for the time being.[40]

Given the Wilhelmstrasse's lackadaisical attitude regarding communications security, it comes as no surprise that the foreign office did not completely overhaul its codes until after the war. By this time, London had come to take access to German diplomatic messages virtually for granted, and British code breakers sounded almost piqued at the sudden closure of their chief source of information. Alastair Denniston, director of Britain's postwar cryptanalytic organization, wrote in his memoirs, "Although Germany was a beaten nation, nothing appeared in the terms of Armistice concerning their diplomatic ciphers. Consequently their mission came to [the] Paris [Peace Conference] provided with entirely new books and methods. We obtained all the traffic between Paris and Berlin but failed to produce anything of any value. How could we? Germany knew well we had read her diplomatic traffic for the last three years (e.g. Zimmermann Letter), and no one prevented Germany from replacing her compromised codes by the safest methods she could devise."[41]

Chapter Fifteen

AFTERMATH IN MEXICO

Maintaining secrecy about the alliance proposal outlined in the Zimmermann telegram was a key element of the plan, so its premature disclosure in the American press sank any chance of success the scheme may have had. Despite the telegram's publication, German, Mexican, and Japanese officials still discussed the proposal at some length. In accordance with Zimmermann's instructions of February 5 to begin negotiations immediately, on February 20 Heinrich von Eckardt, Berlin's envoy in Mexico City, communicated the German proposal to Cándido Aguilar, foreign minister for the government of Venustiano Carranza. Aguilar appeared sympathetic but remained non-committal. Four days later, the foreign minister asked a lowly employee of the Japanese embassy, Kinta Arai, how Japan would respond to a U.S. intervention on the Allied side. Arai replied that Japan would probably remain in the Allied camp. Aguilar had asked Arai for his personal opinion, but on February 27, the subject came up again in a conversation between the two men; this time Arai reported officially that Japan would stick with the Allies regardless. Interestingly, Aguilar then told Eckardt that he had talked with the "Japanese chargé d'affaires," not a lowly employee. He did not convey Arai's unpromising reply to Eckardt.[1]

While withholding Japan's lackluster response to Aguilar, Carranza's government asked Eckardt on or shortly after February 20 whether the Germans were in a position to provide them with arms.[2] This question, coupled with Aguilar's lack of commitment to a German alliance, his misleading claim about discussing the subject with the Japanese chargé d'affaires, and his failure to report Arai's negative response to Eckardt, suggests that Aguilar regarded the possibility of an anti-American alliance with Germany chiefly as a bargaining chip, not a realistic option for Mexico. He sought to extract maximum concessions from Germany in return for a minimal, at most, commitment from Mexico.

On March 2, Aguilar told the Japanese chargé d'affaires disingenuously that Mexico had never received Zimmermann's alliance offer. The government's official newspaper, *El Pueblo*, printed an article to the same effect, stymieing discussion of the telegram in the Mexican press. The Japanese foreign minister, Ichiro Motono, replied that Japan had not received such a proposal either. He added that at any rate, driving a wedge between Japan and the United States would be a futile endeavor.[3]

Whether Carranza learned of the telegram through the press in early March or earlier through Aguilar is unclear, but like his foreign minister, the president came to view Germany's ostensible interest in closer cooperation as a bargaining chip for arms and funds, rather than a viable policy option. When he formally declined Zimmermann's offer on April 14, Carranza was careful to leave open a backdoor to future talks: "If Mexico is pulled into the war regardless, we will have to see. The alliance has been frustrated but will become necessary at a later point in time." In the same breath, Carranza affirmed his continued interest in ammunition and money. An eager Zimmermann underlined the first sentence of Carranza's message.[4]

Meanwhile, German officials were busy discussing Mexico's request for material support. On March 3, shortly after the telegram's disclosure in the press, the foreign office conveyed Carranza's request for arms to Captain Ernst von Hülsen, the director of Sektion P, the general staff's sabotage department. Five days later, Hülsen reported the willingness of the supreme army command to provide 30,000 repeating rifles with 9 million rounds of ammunition; 100 machine guns with 6 million rounds of ammunition; six mountain cannons, 7.5 cm caliber with 2,000 shells each; and four howitzers suitable for mountain transport, 10.5 cm caliber with 2,000 shells each.[5]

Several historians have noted that this limited amount of military hardware would have been woefully inadequate to put Carranza's forces in a position of taking on the United States. Therefore, they considered Hülsen's offer variously "symbolic" or "fraudulent" in that it did not correspond with the "generous" support promised in the telegram.[6] At first glance, this assessment may seem accurate, but it is worthwhile bearing in mind that the military had not been involved in the preparation of Zimmermann's alliance scheme and can therefore not be blamed for delivering less than the telegram had promised.

Also, Hülsen's proposal was comparable in scale to German material support provided for similar covert operations during the war. Whenever the Germans clandestinely supported anti-Allied insurgents—be it in India, Ireland, or the Middle East—their material assistance was only limited. In late 1916, for example, Hülsen envisaged the one-time delivery of 30,000 rifles and 10 machine guns to Irish rebels to spark renewed unrest.[7] Presumably, Carranza's arms were to come from the same stock. Sektion P's limited commitment in Ireland, Mexico, and elsewhere was rooted in logistical challenges as well as political calculations. Throughout the war, the OHL remained focused on the European theater. Military intelligence considered covert action overseas a useful supportive measure, but always subordinate to the exigencies on the eastern and western fronts.

Even though limited in scope, Zimmermann found Hülsen's offer politically valuable because it demonstrated the military's support of the Mexican scheme. Should the proposal fall apart, Zimmermann could still point to the fact that Germany's most powerful faction had supported his project. Indeed, on April 4, Hülsen relayed a message from General Erich Ludendorff to Hans Arthur von Kemnitz, who had become the Wilhelmstrasse's point man for covert action in Mexico. In it, the general formally endorsed military support for Mexico against the United States. It was the stamp of approval that Zimmermann had sought.[8]

Hülsen realized that shipping war materiel across the Atlantic posed serious logistical problems, so he advised that Mexico be supplied with funds to purchase arms in Japan or South America instead.[9] Interdepartmental discussions between Sektion P, the foreign office, and the admiralty staff ended with an endorsement of Hülsen's recommendation, and in March the Germans dropped the original plan of shipping arms to Mexico in favor of sending only money.[10] Kemnitz and Hülsen then hammered out the details, and on March 28 presented a proposal, subsequently approved by Ludendorff, to provide Carranza with 30 million marks for arms purchases in Japan and to strengthen German influence in Mexico.[11] It is unclear how much, if any, of this money reached Carranza's coffers. The German treasury had earlier been reluctant to provide money for Sektion P's operations and recommended that the general staff not be given a free hand since earlier covert action schemes had produced dubious results.[12]

Sektion P eventually tasked Vincent Kraft, one of its agents (*Vertrauensmann*) in Mexico, to travel to Japan to purchase arms for Carranza. Kraft, a man apparently of Dutch extraction, was an ill-fated choice for this mission. A former Krupp employee, he was "living the high life" in Mexico, according to one source. In addition to being a big spender, he was also a double agent who provided the British chargé d'affaires, H. Cunard Cummins, with a wealth of information on German intelligence activities. According to Cummins, "Money is [Kraft's] principal object." Some of the intelligence he provided to the British appears to have been exaggerated or far-fetched, for example, that Germany had offered Carranza 300,000 marks (rather than 30,000) and that German agents had orders to burn Seattle, destroy elevators, wood yards, and airplane factories in North America, and spread "sedition amongst negroes in the United States and against recruiting."

Much of Kraft's information proved fairly accurate, however. Inter alia, he gave the British the names or cover names of at least two fellow Sektion P agents, Albert Delmar and Dr. Gehrmann; particulars about German sedition plans for India; information on German communication methods, including types of invisible inks, secret codes, and the local Swedish legation's role in relaying German messages; details about German penetration of the local U.S. embassy and the Mexican telegraph office; and his own instructions for his trip to Japan. When the Germans submitted another proposal for closer coopera-tion with Carranza in the summer of 1917, Kraft informed the British about it as well. In October 1917, Kraft left Mexico, probably headed straight for the Dutch East Indies, rather than Japan. He certainly never purchased any weapons for Mexico.[13] Only in July 1918 did another Sektion P agent record that "apparently Kraft never reached Japan." Thus, Carranza never received his Japanese arms.[14]

British penetration was not the only problem for Germany's secret ser-vices in Mexico. As the United States geared up for war, a number of U.S.-based German secret agents slipped across the border into Mexico. This influx potentially strengthened Berlin's covert capacities south of the border, but the agents took with them many of the problems that had previously plagued Ger-man intelligence in the United States, in particular, the absence of a clear chain of command and, consequently, intense interservice rivalries. The competition between military and naval intelligence was personified in Sektion P's principal agent, Kurt Jahnke, and the admiralty staff's principal agent, Anton Dilger, who went by the alias of Albert Delmar.[15] Both arrived in Mexico in the spring of 1917. Their rivalry appears to have been personal as well as professional in nature. With a doctoral degree in medicine from Heidelberg University, the American-born Dilger was urbane, suave, and darkly handsome, while the poorly educated Jahnke was sallow and pockmarked, sported a memorably vulgar gold front tooth, and spoke "German like a barber." Both men had a long record of covert action in the United States. While operating a germ laboratory in the Chevy Chase neighborhood of Washington, D.C., Dilger had cultured anthrax and glender bacilli designed for Europe-bound cattle and horses. For his part, Jahnke had run a string of daring sabotage operations on the West Coast from his headquarters in San Francisco. As Jahnke and Dilger plotted against one another in Mexico, Eckardt sought authorization from Berlin to have both men subordinated to himself, but Hülsen rebuffed him.[16] Eckardt repeated his request in February 1918, but his plea once again fell on deaf ears.[17] German operations were further complicated by Eckardt's pursuit of his own conspiracies. Fearing that Carranza might buckle under U.S. pressure to join the war against Germany, Eckardt in April 1917 initiated secret talks with several Mexican generals to overthrow Carranza.[18] In the end, the scheme proved unnecessary, as Carranza managed to keep Mexico neutral throughout the war.

Things threatened to get out of hand when a desperate Dilger vowed to make a last-ditch effort to bring Mexico into the war. Under the impression of ever-increasing American troop levels in Europe, Dilger proposed to "sacrifice" Mexico by persuading General Plutarco Elías Calles to attack the United States across the border from the state of Sonora.[19] By this time, however, the foreign office had concluded that Mexico was far more valuable to Germany as a partner in peace than in a futile war and explicitly rejected Dilger's scheme. Undersecretary of State Wilhelm von Stumm explained to Major Hans Maguerre, a sabotage expert of Sektion P, that he doubted Dilger's ability to trigger a U.S.-Mexican war, but the Wilhelmstrasse's chief concern was of a political nature: "In an armed conflict between Mexico and America, the former would sooner or later succumb. The responsibility for this conflict, and its outcome, would be assigned to us. Consequently, not only our friendship with Mexico would be shattered, but we would give America a reason for dominating Mexico, a country important to us as an eventual source for raw materials. From a political and economic perspective, therefore, a war between Mexico and America is *against* our interests."[20]

With Germany on the brink of defeat in Europe, Sektion P endorsed the foreign office's view, and the German intelligence services wound down their operations in Mexico. Jahnke received orders to discontinue his activities,[21] and Dilger returned to Europe, where he died shortly thereafter, in Spain, during an influenza epidemic.[22] Eckardt did not remain in Mexico much longer than Jahnke and Dilger. When the war ended, the U.S. government successfully pressured the Wilhelmstrasse in recalling him on account of his involvement with the telegram and other German conspiracies in Mexico. In early 1919, an anxious Eckardt traveled with his wife and three children across the United States to New York for embarkation to Europe. An agent of the Department of Justice, William Neunhoffer, accompanied the party. To Neunhoffer, Eckardt appeared tense and dispirited due to his professional downfall. "I was once ambitious," the disillusioned former envoy told Neunhoffer, "but now I am a man without ambition."[23] In a formal statement to Neunhoffer after he had reached New York, Eckardt sought to downplay the significance of the Zimmermann telegram and his involvement in German-Mexican alliance talks:

> The Zimmermann note has undoubtedly been an interesting document, but it has never been more than a document, without the slightest practical consequences. With this all is said. . . . I am no more connected with the Zimmermann note than a bootblack. The instructions were addressed to me but they were of no consequences. It is not possible for me or anyone who knows the conditions to suggest such an impracticable thing. If I at that time could have answered Berlin on that suggestion which was contained in the Zimmermann note, I would have said it was impossible or impracticable.[24]

Eckardt had also sought to downplay the telegram and his role in it in conversations with Neunhoffer during the trip from the Mexican border to New York:

> Mr von Eckhardt [sic] thinks he should not be blamed by the United States for the Zimmermann note, because it was simply a note of instructions from the Berlin government addressed to him, and was in no way inspired by him; in fact he claimed if he had been able to communicate with Berlin he would have advised his government that the scheme was impracticable and impossible. He further declared that the inception and exposure of the note terminated the plans enunciated, and that he could have only considered carrying out of instructions if he could have been assured of Japan's friendship. In another conversation he stated to me that if the note had not been exposed he was not prepared to say what he would have done in furtherance of the plan suggested.

Of note, Eckardt appears to have been completely oblivious as to how the telegram had fallen into American hands. Neunhoffer reports that Eckardt was most anxious to learn how the Zimmermann note was secured and several times asked me (with the statement if I could not answer him he would not expect me to do so) how the Zimmermann note was intercepted, being particular[ly] anxious to know if it came into the possession of this government in the course of ordinary investigation (which would include, according to his interpretation "legitimate theft") or whether its exposure was the result of traitorous conduct of a German officer, adding if a German had sold it for money it must have been an officer, and that he suspected a certain German officer. I stated to him I was not in a position to answer his query.[25]

Eckardt returned to the Wilhelmstrasse, where he briefly headed the Mexican section. In the early 1920s, the foreign office sent him on various occasions as a delegate to international conferences. He retired in 1926, having reached the mandatory retirement age of sixty-five for federal employees.[26] Eckardt's wife passed away in the early 1930s, adding to his growing isolation and feelings of loneliness, but he kept in sporadic contact with his former boss, Zimmermann. When David Hazen interviewed Zimmermann in 1933, the former foreign secretary asked the American journalist whether he would like to meet with Eckardt. A delighted Hazen sought out the former German envoy to Mexico and found a small man, enfeebled by years of sorrow. Bitter and lonesome, the former envoy eked out an existence in a one-bedroom flat on the fifth floor of a Berlin apartment building. When Hazen expressed his condolences on the recent death of Eckardt's wife, the latter replied sadly, "Ah, yes, she is gone, money is gone, all is gone." He was happy, however, to have a visitor and eager to chat.

Eckardt still had strong feelings about the telegram. Unlike Zimmermann and Kemnitz, he dismissed the German alliance proposal as foolish, but suggested improbably that a "stronger man in the government than Dr. Zimmermann wanted it sent, and so did the war party—and the note went forth." To Hazen's surprise, Eckardt still had not learned that the British had intercepted and decrypted the telegram, although the third volume of the biography of former American ambassador Walter Hines Page had disclosed this information in 1926. Instead, Eckardt blamed Ambassador Johann Heinrich von Bernstorff for his alleged failure to forward the telegram in a secure manner to Mexico. He vehemently insisted, "He is finished, he is out! Bernstorff is a sick man, he is finished!" As the interview wound down, Eckardt pleaded plaintively with Hazen, "I hope you can come back and chat with me again; it's lonesome here." He died on March 3, 1944.[27]

Eckardt's fall from grace proved to be another man's luck, at least for a short period. Adolf von Montgelas, the foreign office's Mexican division chief until 1917, was one of the few German officials involved in the telegram who received a promotion after the war. During the conflict, conservatives had viewed him with suspicion, due to his comparatively liberal political outlook and his French background. When the United States entered the war, his marriage to an American rendered his position in Berlin untenable, so he asked for a transfer to the German legation in Berne, Switzerland, where he worked as counselor on American affairs throughout the remainder of the war. His personal liabilities metamorphosed into assets with the ascent of the new German republic. When the foreign office recalled Eckardt, Montgelas emerged as Berlin's natural choice as a replacement. His professional competence and familiarity with Mexican as well as American affairs made him the ideal person to be envoy to Mexico, and in spring 1920 the Wilhelmstrasse appointed him Germany's official diplomatic representative there. Unfortunately for Germany, Montgelas was unable to hold the post for long. In the spring of 1924, he suffered a nervous breakdown and returned to Berlin. There, he died on April 23, 1924, barely fifty years of age.[28]

Few of the German players involved in the telegram fared well after the war, and the same was true for several of their Mexican counterparts, including Carranza and his rival, Pancho Villa. As his presidential term drew to a close, Carranza fell out with General Álvaro Obregón and other influential members of his regime. Following an unsuccessful assassination attempt by one of Obregón's aides, Carranza was forced to flee Mexico City. As he made his way to Veracruz, forces of his political rivals killed him on May 21, 1920. Obregón stepped in to claim the presidency for himself. Pancho Villa did not survive much longer than his archrival. Politically sidelined and with his forces decimated, Villa ended his insurgency in 1920, but many a Mexican retained a grudge against the former revolutionary. On the morning of July 20, 1923, seven men gunned down Villa and five of his followers in Parral, in the province of Chihuahua. Villa's assassins were never apprehended, but evidence points firmly in the direction of domestic enemies he had made during his ruthless campaign.[29]

Chapter Sixteen

A GERMAN RECKONING

With Germany's military fortunes in stark decline, Berlin on October 3, 1918, approached President Woodrow Wilson with the intent of exploring possible peace terms. Wilson, however, made it clear that he considered the current German government an autocracy and therefore not a suitable partner for negotiations. Shortly thereafter, the political leadership in Berlin installed a liberal government under a new chancellor, Prince Max of Baden, to transition the nation from war to peace. Prince Max appointed Colonial Secretary Wilhelm von Solf as his foreign secretary. Though not a revolutionary, Solf hailed from a liberal Berlin family and was decidedly less conservative than most of his peers in the imperial leadership. One of the first to congratulate him on his new job was former ambassador Johann Heinrich von Bernstorff.

Solf did not wait long to make his mark. Bent on pursuing negotiations with Wilson, he was not coy about his opinion that General Erich Ludendorff's dismissal would make a positive impression in the United States. Not surprisingly, his suggestion earned him the wrath of the military establishment.[1] Solf followed up his critique of the military with an effort to clean his own house, the Wilhelmstrasse. On October 25, 1918, the *Nürnberger Nachrichten*, a northern Bavarian newspaper, published an anonymous article about the Zimmermann telegram, identifying Hans Arthur von Kemnitz as its author. Kemnitz, the piece stated, had suggested the idea of the alliance proposal to Zimmermann, who, in turn, had dispatched the telegram without prior consultation with Chancellor Theobald von Bethmann Hollweg. The article revealed considerable insider knowledge of the foreign office. Since only a very small circle of officials knew of Kemnitz's role, the author or source of the story was most likely one of the few foreign office officials directly involved in the original decision to draft and send the telegram.[2]

Regardless of whoever authored or inspired the piece, the foreign office quickly took note. Kemnitz had left Berlin in December 1917 to serve as foreign office representative to the German military administration in the Baltic territories. Shortly after the armistice of November 11, 1918, he returned to the Wilhelmstrasse,[3] and a few days later, on November 22, Solf queried him about his part in the telegram affair. Kemnitz sent Solf a written defense of his actions a couple of days later. While not outright denying his authorship, he pointed out that Adolf von Montgelas had been adviser for Mexican affairs at the time. Kemnitz then essentially reiterated Zimmermann's earlier defense by insisting that the alliance offer per se had been a sound idea: If the Mexican leader Venustiano Carranza had accepted the German proposals, Mexico could have tied up significant U.S. forces, with Germany incurring few obligations. If Germany had succeeded in splitting Japan from the enemy alliance, the war "could have been brought to a satisfactory conclusion 2 ½ years ago." If, on the other hand, Carranza had declined the offer, no harm would have been done. Only through its disclosure, Kemnitz averred, did the telegram damage Germany's cause. He placed responsibility in this regard squarely on his former colleague Montgelas, who, Kemnitz claimed, bore responsibility for sending the telegram via Washington and thereby exposing it. He, Kemnitz, would have sent it via Stockholm, "a route that was entirely secure back then. It follows that I bear *no guilt at all* regarding the telegram's disclosure."[4]

The time for subterfuge and scapegoats was, however, over. Solf instructed Edmund Rhomberg, an expert on British affairs, to check the foreign office records for verification of Kemnitz's various claims. On November 29, Rhomberg submitted a devastating report. The telegram's original draft and the instructions to encrypt it in code 13040 were in Kemnitz's handwriting, Rhomberg wrote. Responsibility for using an obsolete code therefore rested with Kemnitz, not with Montgelas. Rhomberg also pointed out that Kemnitz had suggested sending the Mexico dispatch by U-boat to Washington and thence to Mexico, and he concluded that this method would have equally exposed the telegram on its way from Washington to Mexico City. Rhomberg dismissed Kemnitz's claim to the effect that a separate peace or alliance with Japan was a viable option. As the world had learned through the Bolsheviks' publication of secret tsarist documents, Japan had immediately informed the Allies of Germany's overtures. In short, the Rhomberg report exposed Kemnitz as a liar with bad political judgment who sought to blame one of his colleagues for his own mistakes. Solf acted promptly. On December 11, 1918, the foreign office forced Kemnitz into temporary retirement [*einstweiliger Ruhestand*].[5]

Kemnitz spent the following decades seeking reemployment at the foreign office. In April 1919, he spotted a key official, Edmund Schüler, in the corridors of the Wilhelmstrasse, but could not muster the courage to talk to him in person. A few days later, he wrote Schüler a lengthy letter, requesting an interview and explaining that under normal circumstances, his years-long service would have guaranteed him a diplomatic post in Europe, but that he would now "in the changed circumstances" be content to serve in China in order to help rebuild Germany's position in the Far East, although this task would be "twice as painful for someone who had witnessed Germany's earstwhile position of power" there.[6] Schüler did not respond, and Kemnitz reiterated his request a couple of months later. This time, he added his willingness to serve even under the new, "socialist" (that is, Social Democratic Party of Germany, SPD) government, repeated his desire for a post in Beijing, and asserted that he had never been a proponent of an annexationist policy in China—an improbable claim for someone who had come up with the idea of offering pieces of the United States to Mexico.[7]

While expressing sympathy for Kemnitz's situation, Foreign Secretary Hermann Müller responded unequivocally that the Wilhelmstrasse could not afford to assign foreign posts on the basis of seniority alone and that "your stance regarding questions of foreign policy in the past precludes your assignment to a leading position in the foreign service."[8] Three years later, Kemnitz assailed the Wilhelmstrasse again, this time complaining that his early retirement had unduly diminished his pension. In a typed, four-page letter, he detailed his case and asked for a nominal promotion in order to receive a higher pension.[9] By 1923 the brief revolutionary phase of the Weimar Republic had ended, and it was perhaps a sign of the changing times that the foreign office did not dismiss Kemnitz's request out of hand but forwarded it to the treasury, along with the plea to examine it favorably.[10] Still, nothing came of it. Also, for the time being, Kemnitz had dropped the matter, for he had turned his eyes to politics.

As soon as he was dismissed from the Wilhelmstrasse, Kemnitz joined the right-of-center German People's Party (DVP), which was led by wealthy notables but lacked a significant mass following. As a long-standing member of the respected diplomatic service, and with the coveted "von" before his surname, Kemnitz impressed the party leadership, who selected him to run in his hometown, Frankfurt an der Oder, as a candidate for the national assembly in 1919. He did not get a seat, but the party nominated him again for the upcoming Reichstag elections in 1920.[11] Kemnitz's candidacy attracted press scrutiny, and barely four weeks before election day, the liberal *Vossische Zeitung* published "The Envoy v. Kemnitz: A Strange Candidacy," a scathing editorial by Georg Bernhard. In it, Bernhard reminded readers that Kemnitz had recently been identified as the "spiritual father" of the Zimmermann telegram and therefore bore some share of responsibility for the U.S. declaration of war on Germany. He pointed out with gusto that Gustav Stresemann, leader of the DVP, had been one of the fiercest critics of the telegram during the war and expressed his bewilderment at the DVP's decision to nominate Kemnitz.[12]

Clearly jolted and concerned about the political fallout, Kemnitz responded a few days later with a lengthy article in his hometown paper, the *Frankfurter Oder-Zeitung*. He reiterated the arguments he had used vis-à-vis Solf in 1918 virtually verbatim. While omitting his earlier accusations against Montgelas, Kemnitz maintained that the alliance proposal to Mexico and Japan had been based on sound political strategy; only its disclosure had led to international embarrassment. Last but not least, the foreign office could have averted the telegram's disclosure had it only adopted Kemnitz's suggestion to send the message via Stockholm.[13] Quoting Kemnitz's statement at length, Bernhard dismissed it as a "harrowing document of the state of mind of German diplomacy" during the war. He pointed out that any document could potentially fall into the enemy's hands in wartime, and even if the telegram had reached Mexico without being compromised, Carranza's shaky, faction-ridden government might have leaked it anyway. Kemnitz's statement, Bernhard concluded, therefore betrayed naiveté as well as ineptitude, and his candidature "sadly" demonstrated that little had been learned from wartime mistakes.[14]

The *Vossische Zeitung*, an influential newspaper, appealed to the liberal and conservative middle class that Kemnitz needed to sway in order to get elected. In his response to Bernhard, distributed by the DVP, Kemnitz adopted a conciliatory tone, praising Bernhard's editorials on foreign policy and pointing to the many positions he had in common with the *Vossische Zeitung*, particularly their shared goal of collaborating with Russia, rather than the Western powers.[15] Somewhat assuaged, the *Vossische Zeitung* stood by its dismissal of the Mexican-Japanese alliance as absurd but henceforth significantly tempered its attacks against Kemnitz. Since votes were cast for parties, rather than individual candidates, a damage assessment of Bernhard's attack is difficult. On election day, June 6, the DVP tripled the number of its deputies, easily sweeping Kemnitz into the Reichstag.

The exchange did not go unnoticed among Reichstag deputies. When the parliament debated the issue of establishing economic and political relations with Soviet Russia, Kemnitz delivered a bombastic speech in favor of repudiating the Treaty of Versailles and obtaining more favorable terms for Germany. Uttered by any other right-of-center politician, the speech would have been unremarkable since fulminations against Versailles were a common staple of nationalist rhetoric. Kemnitz's involvement in one of imperial German diplomacy's major wartime blunders, however, offered the political Left an opportunity. During a parliamentary debate, Rudolf Breitscheid of the Unabhängige Sozialdemokratische Partei (USPD), the radical left independent social democrats, recalled Kemnitz's authorship of the telegram and claimed that he "even appeared to be proud of" it. Breitscheid's pugnacious concluding remarks to Kemnitz are worthwhile quoting in full as they invoke a larger issue, namely concerns regarding the Weimar Republic's failure to break with the imperial past and the republic's supporters' despair over this troublesome political reality: "It is characteristic that people who played such a calamitous role during the war, now speak up and issue guidelines for the German government's future foreign policy. Yes, because you have money to run for parliament, because you have a nice suit and because you belong to the upper ten thousand who still feel entitled to holding the fate of the German republic in their hands."[16]

As Breitscheid fired his broadside, deputies from the SPD and USPD applauded frenetically. In his pathetic response, Kemnitz vainly sought to turn the tables. After complaining about Breitscheid's ad hominem attack, Kemnitz reiterated his well-worn defense: The Mexican-Japanese project made sense, only disclosure had compromised the scheme. Since he had advised a different route for the telegram, he could not be held responsible for its disclosure. Predictably, this line of argument cut no ice with his opponents. "Exhilaration from the left," as the official transcript puts it, repeatedly interrupted Kemnitz. His fellow party members, on the other hand, remained silent. At some point, a deputy shouted, "A stupid idea, this dispatch." When Deputy Georg Ledebour, who had criticized the telegram in the Reichstag in 1917, interjected, "It was the greatest stupidity ever committed by a German government," Kemnitz lost his cool and yelled back, "The greatest stupidity that was ever committed by a German government was the order for demobilization of the army by the people's representatives"—that is, the political Left. The debate ended in "great turmoil and shouting from different sides."[17]

Kemnitz's star in the DVP firmament soon began to wane. He rarely spoke up in parliament, and when he did, even his political allies expressed astonishment at his lack of nuance and expertise. He annoyed other DVP deputies by needlessly prolonging caucus deliberations with empty rhetoric, and his parliamentary colleague Siegfried von Kardorff bluntly called him an "ass." In 1924 a faction within the DVP unsuccessfully attempted to remove him from the party list for the upcoming elections. As the DVP grew disenchanted with Kemnitz, he gravitated further toward the political Right. In 1923 he joined a militant veterans' association, the Stahlhelm (Steel Helmet). He also began lobbying vigorously for a political alliance between the DVP and the monarchist German National People's Party (DNVP) but ended up being the only member of his party to support a DNVP vote of no confidence for the new government, of which his own party, the DVP, was a part. It was the final straw. Kemnitz officially switched to the nationalists, and although DVP members pleaded with him to resign his seat in parliament, he took his mandate with him. The DNVP received him with some reservations, which turned out to be justified.[18]

Kemnitz spoke up only six times in parliament for his new party, and references to the telegram remained a sure way to derail him. When he attacked the foreign policy of the government in 1927, Hermann Müller, an SPD deputy and former foreign secretary, sarcastically denied "such an exceptional diplomat as the author of the Mexico dispatch, Mr. von Kemnitz" the right to speak about foreign policy. Piqued, Kemnitz responded with a personal attack on Müller and went on to reiterate, again, that the alliance scheme itself had been commendable and that he could not be held responsible for the telegram's disclosure. While his nationalist colleagues kept utterly silent, Social Democrats chuckled and cheered. Kemnitz became more and more agitated, finally bursting out, "Deputy Müller is one of the leaders of the Social Democratic Party. (Hear! Hear! And laughter on the left.) It is responsible for Germany's collapse. (Shouts from the Social Democrats.) It commits treason even on the platform of the Reichstag. (Inquietude among the Social Democrats—bell of the president.) Denigrations from such people will be a high honor for me in the future." At this point, the Reichstag's vice president called Kemnitz to order and gave Müller the opportunity to make a personal comment. A bemused Müller concluded the debate by saying, "I am especially grateful to Mr. Deputy von Kemnitz for giving me the opportunity, through his personal comments, to ascertain before this high house that the charge of diplomatic ineptitude was completely justified. (Very well! And exhilaration among the Social Democrats.)"[19] During Reichstag elections in 1928, the DNVP sustained steep losses, and Kemnitz failed to hold on to his parliamentary seat.

Deprived of his income as a deputy, Kemnitz quickly resumed his quest for reemployment at the foreign office.[20] When the Wilhelmstrasse declined his request once again,[21] Kemnitz embarked on another lengthy campaign to enlist prominent politicians to lobby for his cause.[22] Those he solicited included foreign office officials, like Ernst von Weizsäcker; prominent DNVP politicians, such as Kuno von Westarp, Friedrich von Winterfeld, and Alfred Hugenberg; Kemnitz's former boss, Arthur Zimmermann; the exiled kaiser's brother, Crown Prince Friedrich Wilhelm; and even President Paul von Hindenburg. While the crown prince wholeheartedly supported Kemnitz's request, advising the foreign office to reactivate "such a patriotic and excellent man like Kemnitz," others expressed markedly less enthusiasm. Zimmermann wrote meekly to the Wilhelmstrasse that "the hapless Kemnitz is pursuing me" in his quest for reemployment. Zimmermann recommended a review of Kemnitz's request but was keen to wash his hands of the matter once and for all: "A reply to me [by the foreign office] is completely unnecessary."[23]

In his campaign, Kemnitz put forth a variety of reasons for his reemployment. In a six-page letter to the foreign secretary, dated 1930, Kemnitz mentioned the difficult situation he found himself in financially, having to support his new wife and his only son through university. He also repeatedly justified his participation in the telegram affair and insisted that his reemployment would only be fair because he was allegedly sent into early retirement due to his patriotic leanings. State Secretary Konstantin von Neurath, himself a man of strong national convictions, explicitly rejected this contention: "this is not true," he scribbled in the margins of a letter by a Kemnitz supporter, arguing this point.[24] Time and again, the foreign office rebuffed Kemnitz, who showed up repeatedly in person at the Wilhelmstrasse to plead his case. Foreign office officials found him increasingly difficult to deal with. One of them described him as "extremely bitter" and "not open to any reasoning."[25]

In January 1933, President Hindenburg—following the recommendation of Franz von Papen, his principal adviser and former military attaché to Washington—appointed Adolf Hitler chancellor of Germany. Ludendorff, in one of his more lucid moments, recognized Hindenburg's ominous choice for what it was. "By appointing Hitler Chancellor of the Reich," he wrote his former boss in a prophetic telegram, "you have handed over our sacred German Fatherland to one of the greatest demagogues of all time. I prophesy to you this evil man will plunge our Reich into the abyss and will inflict immeasurable woe on our nation. Future generations will curse you in your grave for this action."[26]

Kemnitz, on the other hand, was delighted at the National Socialists' ascendancy as the new regime appeared to offer him the opportunity of rejoining the foreign service. In 1933 he unleashed another avalanche of missives to the Wilhelmstrasse and assorted politicians, begging for reemployment. He argued that he should be reemployed since he had been let go in 1918 due to his "patriotic beliefs" and in order to "make space for the beneficiaries of the new [republican] system."[27] In a lengthy letter to the foreign office, dated September 22, 1933, Kemnitz went out of his way to highlight his long-standing right-wing credentials, denigrate the "Novemberlings" (a reference to the revolution of November 1918) and "red traitors" and demonstrate his affinity to the Nazis: His son, he pointed out, was a platoon leader in the Sturmabteilung (SA, Storm Troopers or Brownshirts). Kemnitz also stated in unambiguous terms what he thought of Hitler's rise: "Nobody was happier than me about the victory of the national movement [the Nazis], and that they cleaned house and sent the Novemberlings and political appointees [of democratic parties] packing." In the same letter, he wrote that he had already applied for membership in the National Socialist German Workers' Party (NSDAP).[28] These lines are worthwhile bearing in mind in light of statements Kemnitz would utter after World War II about his alleged opposition to the Nazi regime.

As the Wilhelmstrasse continued to rebuff him, Kemnitz solicited the help of the arch-Nazi Wilhelm Kube, governor of Berlin Brandenburg. As a member of the SS (Schutzstaffel), Kube would work briefly at the Dachau concentration camp in 1940. He would also serve as governor (*Generalkommissar*) of Nazi-occupied Belarus during the war, overseeing the large-scale extermination of the local Jewish population. Despite Kube's impeccable Nazi credentials, his pleas on behalf of Kemnitz to Hitler and his deputy, Rudolf Hess, led nowhere.[29] In December 1934, the Wilhelmstrasse advised Kemnitz to "bury his hopes" of ever rejoining the foreign office.[30] Still, Kemnitz did not let go. In July 1939, he asked another high-ranking foreign office official for a meeting to discuss his case. The letter was signed, "Heil Hitler." The official politely declined any assistance.[31]

Germany's invasion of Poland on September 1, 1939, prompted Kemnitz to give it one last shot. On September 2, he showed up in person at the Wilhelmstrasse to volunteer his services, signing his request once again, "Heil Hitler."[32] The foreign office replied that due to the war, they had earmarked him for possible reemployment,[33] but apparently the Wilhelmstrasse never revisited the issue. As Europe descended into the horrors of World War II, even the obstinate Kemnitz had to acknowledge that his quest for reemployment had come to an unsuccessful conclusion.

By the end of World War II, few Germans remembered or showed an interest in the Zimmermann telegram, the more so as most protagonists by

1945 had passed away. Not so for Kemnitz, who was as keen as ever to dispense political advice, even if there was hardly anyone listening. In May 1945, he authored "Are We Liberated?" a lengthy memorandum on Germany's political situation. Written in English and probably intended for an American acquaintance, the piece is stunning testimony to Kemnitz's self-delusion. The pamphlet begins by claiming that he and his "political friends have detested the Nazis from the beginning" and goes on to interpret recent history essentially as a conspiracy against Germany: the rise of the Nazis occurred "because our nation felt to be suddenly attacked in 1914, cheated by Wilson's 14 points in 1918, unjustly robbed by the treaty of Versailles, and economically ruined by the socalled [sic] inflation." The present Allied occupation of Germany meant that "[w]e change the interior servitude against the foreign." Kemnitz then recommends reintroduction of the imperial constitution, rather than a "pure democracy." The military, he argues, stood morally unblemished, and should therefore remain intact as an institution.[34] In several subsequent memoranda, addressed to no one in particular, Kemnitz drives home and refines these points in stilted, grandiloquent prose: the German army was the epitome of heroism; only Hitler introduced a "southern German," criminal spirit into the armed forces; the Allies were responsible for starting World War I and therefore for Hitler's rise and his misdeeds. In a remarkable act of self-deception, he unabashedly portrays himself as an "anti-fascist" who had sought to overthrow the Nazis during the war.[35]

As Kemnitz was never called upon to account for his activities during the Third Reich, and since he wrote most of his memoranda for his own edification, one must conclude that he earnestly believed in the veracity of his various utterances. His political delusion reveals him to be exactly what his political opponents during the Weimar Republic accused him of being: a narrow-minded, spineless, arch-conservative nationalist who was neither able nor willing to learn from past mistakes, be they his own or those of the government he served. He was certainly unaware of the irony inherent in one of the observations he expressed in his 1945 memorandum, when he opined, "Political sense . . . is not the strongest part of our character."[36] It is tempting to read this statement as a characterization of its author. Kemnitz died in Freiburg on August 1, 1955.[37]

Chapter Seventeen

HALL'S INTELLIGENCE LEGACY

World War I transformed the British secret services and their role in the state. For four years, British intelligence recruited and trained thousands of staff members in espionage, counterespionage, and cryptanalysis. Due to personnel reduction after the war, a good number of these spies rejoined civilian life, but many stayed in touch with their former colleagues. Class and education strengthened these informal connections, as British intelligence officers typically shared an elite background, had attended the same boarding schools and universities, frequented the same clubs, and occasionally married the sisters or daughters of their colleagues. After the war, many of these former secret service men (they were always men) found themselves in key positions not only in the world of intelligence but also in the press, in banks, and in key governmental departments. Together, they formed a "para-intelligence" network that was as socially narrow as it was mutually supportive.

Promoted to rear admiral in April 1917 and knighted six months later, William Reginald Hall emerged as a central actor in this twilight world. In May 1917, the Naval Intelligence Division formally incorporated Room 40, giving Hall complete control over the division's naval and diplomatic elements. The Royal Navy's cryptanalytic organization, renamed section 25 (ID 25 for short), was run by Hall's loyal subordinate and later biographer, Commander William "Bubbles" James.[1]

Hall's management of the interception and decryption of the telegram as well as his various promotions served to reinforce his sense of infallibility and self-importance. On October 9, 1917, in a memorandum to the first sea lord, he wrote that he considered his immediate superior, Foreign Secretary Arthur Balfour, "entirely out of touch" with public opinion at home—a cheeky comment that reveals how independent Hall considered himself to be from Foreign Office supervision. In the same spirit, Hall in May 1918 refused to collaborate with the chief secretary for Ireland, who had asked him to make available certain intercepts that would strengthen the government's case against several leading Sinn Fein members awaiting trial. "This was one of the many occasions when Hall's refusal to disclose the purport of intercepted messages led to friction with other Government departments," commented James.[2]

Emboldened by the telegram operation, Hall continued to run naval intelligence as a personal fiefdom, high-handedly choosing when and how to share his intelligence with others. In February 1918, he sent an intercept regarding Austrian peace feelers to the U.S. embassy. In a procedure eerily reminiscent of his handling of the Zimmermann telegram, Hall did so before showing the intercept to the prime minister.[3] There was no reprimand from the Foreign Office. An American cryptanalyst serving as liaison with British naval intelligence in London at the end of the war commented, "[d]iplomatic procedure would require that such sensational information be transmitted by the Foreign Office to Ambassador [Walter Hines] Page, but Admiral Hall did as he pleased. It is no wonder then that he was feared by the Foreign Office."[4]

Meanwhile, Hall displayed a growing interest in domestic politics. Like many of his secret service colleagues, toward the end of the war Hall shifted his attention from the German threat to the rise of the political Left in Britain. Dismissing his colleague Vernon Kell, the director of MI5, as "short-sighted and timorous,"[5] Hall and his assistant, Claud Serocold, devised a plan to earmark £1 million for a peacetime political police force, a job that typically would have belonged to MI5 and Scotland Yard. When the cabinet defanged the project by adopting a watered-down version of the plan, Hall decided to pursue the idea of a private intelligence agency that would stand up to the Left. Early in 1919, Hall and a number of leading industrialists founded an organization to function as a "dirty tricks" department for big business. Called the Economic League, this innocent-sounding organization quickly gained notoriety for blacklisting known communists and agitators to keep such so-called subversives out of employment; providing intelligence on upcoming strikes and providing strikebreakers on a large scale; and sending agitators to communist meetings to heckle and throw stink bombs.[6]

Hall's short-lived involvement with the Economic League portended his political ambitions. Shortly after the war, Hall retired from the navy. The circumstances of his departure from naval intelligence have been the subject of considerable debate. His tenure was certainly not uncontroversial. *The Times* commented upon his retirement, "No doubt Admiral Hall made mistakes."[7] James conceded that Hall had made enemies during the Casement affair and suggested that his boss's insistence on participating in the Paris Peace Conference proved his undoing.[8] Permanent Under-Secretary Charles Hardinge of the Foreign Office in a farewell letter to Hall referred to "differences of opinion."[9] Sir Rosslyn Wemyss, chief of the naval staff, wrote Hall in January 1919 and offered that he didn't "believe the rumours which were put about the other day, and have no recollection of our intercourse during the last 18 months that are not altogether pleasant."[10] Wemyss did not expound on these rumors, but his and Hardinge's comments might be a veiled reference to Hall's criticism of Balfour in 1918.[11]

While recriminations against him abounded, Hall retired chiefly out of a desire to enter politics. He evidently was a political animal, a character streak that he fully developed during the course of the war. As director of naval intelligence, he deliberately maneuvered himself into a position where he would not only provide information to policy makers, but actually influence foreign policy. The Zimmermann telegram was a case in point. As the war came to an end, however, the influence of active military and intelligence officers would inevitably shrink. If Hall wished to stay involved in politics, a switch to civilian life would be the logical next step.

On October 30, 1918, Hall informed his superiors that the Unionist (conservative or Tory) Party had asked him to stand for parliament in the upcoming general elections and requested permission to run while retaining his job as director of naval intelligence (DNI).[12] Navy officials went back and forth on whether he could become a member of parliament (MP) as a sitting DNI. If they granted Hall permission, he could in theory become a conservative MP serving a Liberal or Labour government as DNI. In the end, Whitehall decided that a number of formal objections stood in the way of Hall's request, and the first sea lord informed him accordingly.[13]

On November 11, Germany and the Allies signed an armistice. Shortly thereafter, Hall's retirement was officially announced and scheduled for mid-January 1919. At the same time, Hall publicly declared his intention to run as a Unionist candidate as soon as an opportunity presented itself.[14] He gave some indication as to what platform he would run on in his farewell speech to his colleagues in naval intelligence: "I want to give you a word of warning. Hard and bitter as the battle has been, we now have to face a far, far more ruthless foe. A foe that is hydra-headed and whose evil power will spread over the whole world. That foe is Soviet Russia."[15]

Although Hall had to forgo the opportunity to run for Parliament in December 1918, in his retirement he was presented with another chance when a Tory MP from Liverpool moved up to become lord chancellor, received a peerage, and switched to the House of Lords, necessitating a by-election in March 1919. Hall beat the Labor candidate—albeit by a significantly reduced margin as compared to the general elections four months earlier between the Tory and Labor candidates—and entered Parliament as a Unionist MP.[16] As a conservative backbencher, Hall fought against treasury cuts to the secret services and quickly associated himself with the small but vociferous group of Unionist "diehards," who stood firmly on the extreme right of social, economic, and political issues.[17] In particular, the diehards fervently opposed any accommodation with Moscow (and its supposed Trojan Horse, the Labour Party), which put them at odds with Prime Minister David Lloyd George, who thought some of his ministers had "bolshevism on the brain" and pursued a more pragmatic policy toward Soviet Russia.[18]

Hall's loyalty to the British government was put to the test when Ramsay MacDonald became Britain's first Labour prime minister in January 1924. The Labour government quickly stumbled over a political scandal, and general elections were called for October 29, 1924. The ensuing campaign unfolded in an ideologically charged atmosphere, and the para-intelligence network snapped into action. On October 2, the Riga, Latvia, station of Britain's Secret Intelligence Service (SIS or MI6) dispatched to headquarters in London the copy of a letter allegedly signed by Grigory Zinoviev, president of the Communist International (Comintern), and Arthur MacManus, British representative at the Comintern. Addressed to the British Communist Party (CPGB), the letter called for intensified communist agitation in Britain. If the public learned of the letter before the elections, MacDonald's campaign would face trouble, because his government had normalized diplomatic relations with Moscow and proposed a commercial treaty with the Soviet Union.[19]

The Zinoviev letter was, in all probability, a forgery produced by Russian émigrés in Berlin who were loyal to the czarist regime and sought to drive a wedge between the Soviet Union and Great Britain.[20] For Britain's Labour government, the question of authenticity became purely academic when the conservative *Daily Mail* obtained and published a copy of it. On October 25, four days before the elections, the *Mail's* headline screamed, "Moscow issues order to the British Communists . . . British Communists in turn give orders to the Socialist Government which it tamely and humbly obeys." A day later, the paper declared in bold letters, "THE ONLY THING LEFT TO DO IS VOTE CONSERVATIVE." Just to make sure its readers got the point, the *Mail* exhorted them to "get rid of our shifty Prime Minister."[21] Three days later, Labour suffered a catastrophic defeat at the polls, and the Tories formed a government under Stanley Baldwin. MacDonald expressed his frustration over the letter's premature disclosure in a campaign speech in Cardiff on October 27: "[H]ow can I . . . avoid the suspicion . . . that the whole thing is a political plot?"[22]

If the letter was, indeed, a plot, who had leaked it to the *Daily Mail*? Thomas Marlowe, the staunchly conservative long-time editor of the *Mail*, had first heard of the letter on the morning of October 23, when he found on his writing table a telephone message that had arrived the previous night. It was from "an old and trusted friend" and read, "There is a document in London which you ought to have. It shows the relations between Bolsheviks and the British Labour leaders. The Prime Minister knows all about it, but is trying to avoid publication. It has been circulated today to Foreign Office, Home Office, Admiralty, and War Office."[23]

In 1928 Marlowe stated that "three friends" had offered him copies of the letter. The identities of these three friends have been the subject of considerable speculation, but most historians agree that all three belonged to the para-intelligence network. One person who knew of the letter and eagerly sought to get it published was Donald im Thurn, a former MI5 officer. In his papers, im Thurn identified the "old and trusted friend" who had left the mysterious telephone message for Marlowe that triggered publication of the letter in the *Daily Mail*—it was none other than "R. Hall."[24] Im Thurn's note is the only piece of evidence that identifies Hall by name as the person responsible for leaking the letter to the *Daily Mail,* and his account is not always wholly reliable. As intelligence historian Christopher Andrew points out, however, Hall's action would have been "entirely consistent with his earlier career."[25]

Indeed, as a former director of naval intelligence, and a prominent Tory politician, Hall was ideally placed to obtain and leak a copy of the Zinoviev letter to the press. A study of the Zinoviev letter by a group of British journalists argues that the former DNI "had personal experience of the effect of an intelligence coup on a political situation: his department's brilliant work deciphering the Zimmermann telegram, and Hall's careful timing of its release to the Woodrow Wilson Administration in Washington had been the most significant single episode in the process which brought America into the war in

1917." The journalists concluded that the "Zinoviev letter arrived at exactly the right moment to influence another Governmental decision which seemed crucial to the Conservative Party: whether Britain should forge close links with the Bolshevik revolutionaries or dismiss them as a Red rabble whose existence threatened Conservative democracy in Britain."[26]

Understandably, Hall and his supporters never sought to clarify the former DNI's potentially embarrassing role in the Zinoviev letter disclosure, but the Zimmermann telegram was another matter altogether. According to U.S. diplomat Edward Bell, the British "were always furious that we got the (undeserved) credit."[27] Therefore, the British set out to put the record straight when the war ended. Probably shortly after the armistice, London's wartime naval attaché, Captain Guy Gaunt, informed Lieutenant Colonel Hugh Cabot of the Harvard Surgical Unit (which served with the British army in France) about the role of British intelligence in the telegram affair. Cabot subsequently delivered a lecture at the annual Bunker Hill Monument Association, where he asserted that the telegram "was received by the British Intelligence Department in code and decoded."[28] The revelation did not have a significant impact.

Hall corroborated the role of British naval intelligence in intercepting and decrypting the telegram in 1921, when the American journalist Burton J. Hendrick was compiling material for a biography of the recently deceased American ambassador to London, Walter Hines Page. Hendrick may have first learned about Hall's part in the telegram's disclosure from Irwin Boyle Laughlin, who during the war had been first secretary at the U.S. embassy in London. Laughlin advised Hendrick on the Page biography about the wartime operations of the embassy in London.[29] In the summer of 1921, Hendrick traveled to London and met with Hall, who proved to be exceedingly helpful. "At the direction of the Foreign Office," Hendrick later wrote Bell, "Admiral Hall has given me the complete story of the Zimmermann Mexico telegram. He has supplied me with all the telegrams themselves—about twelve in number—and has given all details about the ways they were sent, decoded. etc. The Foreign Office has given its consent to the publication of all this matter in my forthcoming book."[30] Apparently, Hall had simply taken these documents home with him while he still had access to them as DNI. Back in the United States, Hendrick showed this dossier to a surprised Laughlin and asked him for more information on the U.S. side of the operation. Taken by surprise, Laughlin confirmed and expanded on the intelligence work conducted by the U.S. embassy during the war.[31]

When Hendrick approached Bell to learn more about his part in the story, the latter was not amused. Bell informed Hendrick that "it would be against the public interest that the record of it should become public property for many years to come, if ever." He also told Hendrick that even if he had obtained the British government's permission to proceed, the U.S. government had not granted its approval.[32] To Laughlin, Bell wrote bluntly, "I only wish to Heaven that when this man [Hendrick] approached you had hit him with a sand-bag."[33] Most of all, Bell was furious at Hall: "Whatever Blinker could have been thinking about beats me altogether but at any rate he seems to have spilt the beans," he wrote to William Lee Hurley, the head of the State Department's intelligence section, renamed U-2. In the same letter, Bell accused Hall of a "breach of confidence. The arrangement regarding the Z. telegram was not unilateral: it was entered into between the two Governments."[34] "I hope to Heaven," Bell added a month later, "that you will be able to get this mad man to cut this stuff out."[35] Hurley agreed wholeheartedly. "I am aghast as also are *others* at this method of making public information which we have kept secret," he wrote L. Lanier Winslow at the U.S. embassy in London.[36] In a separate message, Undersecretary of State Henry Fletcher instructed Winslow to "discreetly ascertain whether Hall secured the consent of the Admiralty or of the Foreign Office to make public this information."[37]

According to Hendrick and Laughlin, Hall had previously insinuated that the Foreign Office had given its consent to publishing the telegram and related material, but William Tyrrell of the Foreign Office informed the Americans that the British government had never done so.[38] Tyrrell served as deputy of the permanent undersecretary Eyre Crowe, who was responsible for intelligence. When Hall sensed growing resistance to his initiative from all corners, he quickly backpedaled. Disingenuously, he wrote Hendrick "that approval of British and American governments must be obtained before publication of any of our conversations or documents."[39] On August 13, Hall informed Winslow that he wanted to ensure that everything published had the U.S. government's "consent and approval."[40] This, too, was a somewhat misleading statement as the story was already out and could be expected to leak even if Hendrick did not obtain governmental approval to go ahead. Just how awkward Hall's position had become was further evidenced by his request to Hendrick not to mention his name anywhere in Page's biography since "I have a great horror of appearing in print, and although my relations with Dr. Page were on a most confidential footing, I am not clear in my mind that he would have wished that anything I did should be connected with him."[41] This, of course, was a request that Hall should have made before giving Hendrick material on the telegram. It is also curious for a sitting MP to express "horror" at the idea of having his name appear in print.

When he heard of the controversy, Walter Page's son Arthur wrote to Fletcher, asking for approval to have Hendrick's section on the telegram published,[42] but apparently Fletcher asked Page not to go ahead with the project.[43] In May 1922, Bell made a final effort to prevent publication of Hendrick's book. In a lengthy letter to Leland Harrison, now assistant secretary of state, Bell concluded that Hendrick had received his information on the telegram from Hall and Tyrrell, and cited three reasons for the State Department to withhold consent to publication. First, Hall broke a mutual agreement when handing over the telegram to Hendrick without consulting Bell. Second, publication of the British role in the telegram's disclosures would suggest that the U.S. government had obtained other intercepts, such as the Luxburg telegrams, in the same manner. Bell was particularly worried about the case of Joseph Caillaux, a French socialist politician accused of treason and imprisoned in 1918. In the run-up to his trial, the Americans had provided the French with intercepts implicating Caillaux, but they did not inform Paris that these had originated with the British. This hitherto publicly unknown fact could potentially cast a shadow over U.S.-French relations, not least as Caillaux was still alive. Third, Bell argued, Hendrick's account of the telegram episode was "stiff with inaccuracies." For all of the above, Bell strongly urged Harrison to help thwart publication of Hendrick's book. Harrison concurred and recommended as much to the new secretary of state, Charles Evans Hughes.[44]

As Woodrow Wilson's unsuccessful Republican challenger in the 1916 presidential elections, Hughes apparently took little interest in a subject concerning the bygone Wilson administration. In the end, Hendrick went ahead with the publication of Page's biography, and the U.S. government made no attempt to keep him from doing so. Published in 1926, the third volume of Hendrick's *The Life and Letters of Walter H. Page* for the first time informed a broader audience of the British angle of the telegram's disclosure. Although the biography did not mention Hall by name, it mentioned British naval intelligence, and Hall's affiliation with this agency during the war was no secret. Anybody could therefore easily infer Hall's role. In the same year that the third volume hit the bookshelves, Hall also testified publicly before a German American Mixed Claims Commission regarding German sabotage operations in the United States during the war. In the course of the trial, he acknowledged his role in the famous intelligence operation.[45]

Buoyed by public recognition of his role in the telegram's disclosure, Hall's political career experienced a second spring. In 1925 he was reelected to Parliament for the constituency of Eastbourne. Ill health compelled Hall not to seek reelection in 1929, and his frailty kept him from playing an active role in political or intelligence affairs for the rest of his life. He was confined to the role of an observer during the early years of World War II and died on October 22, 1943.[46]

Hall's legacy in the realm of foreign intelligence was less ambivalent than that in domestic intelligence. Thanks to the diligent wartime work of London's code breakers, and in particular to Hall's telegram scoop, no British politician could henceforth afford to ignore the value of cryptanalysis. Rather than disband the services' cryptanalytic services after the war, the government consolidated and put them on a sure institutional footing. In 1919 Britain's secret service committee fused the nation's naval and military intelligence organizations, creating the Government Code and Cypher School (GC&CS), and in 1939 GC&CS moved to an estate called Bletchley Park, located outside London, roughly between Oxford and Cambridge.

Following Britain's declaration of war on Germany in September 1939, GC&SC expanded rapidly, and the agency rehired several cryptanalysts who had worked for Room 40 during World War I, including Frank Birch, "Dilly" Knox, and Nigel de Grey, who in 1917 had decrypted the Zimmermann telegram. By then, their services were in urgent need. On the eve of World War II, the German military had introduced a sophisticated cipher machine called Enigma. Berlin considered messages generated by Enigma unbreakable, and some leading British cryptanalysts were inclined to agree. Birch, as head of the naval section at Bletchley Park, noted that many of his subordinates believed "*all* German codes were unbreakable." As in World War I, however, methodical cryptanalysis enabled the British to decrypt a large volume of German intercepts. The continual interception and decryption of secret enemy messages opened a window for the Allies into German political decision making and military strategy and may have significantly shortened the war.[47]

Also as in World War I, cooperation with foreign intelligence became a cornerstone of Britain's secret services in World War II. After Hitler's invasion of France in 1940, Britain stood virtually alone against the Axis powers. The United States under President Franklin Delano Roosevelt, Woodrow Wilson's assistant secretary to the navy in World War I, was eager to support London but had to tread carefully in the face of strong isolationist sentiments at home.

Whereas Wilson had always been ambivalent about the work of Allied agents on U.S. soil, Roosevelt privately encouraged British intelligence operations in the United States in order to thwart Nazi fifth columnists as well as isolationists. As he wrestled with domestic discontent over the prospect of intervention, Roosevelt grew eager for any assistance the British might be able to provide. Perhaps in a calculated provocation to replicate the telegram scoop, the president teased Admiral John Henry Godfrey, Hall's successor at GC&CS, "Of course, Hall had a wonderful intelligence service, but I don't suppose it's much good now."[48]

British intelligence set out to prove the president wrong and launched what a historian has aptly called "the search for a second Zimmermann Telegram."[49] The original telegram had been an authentic document, whose disclosure was meant to influence U.S. policy. In modern parlance, the British were practicing "covert action." Had the telegram not been authentic, who is to say that a clever forgery would not have accomplished similar goals? Early in World War II, British intelligence in Buenos Aires had obtained a map of South America with redrawn borders dividing the subcontinent into five Nazi vassal states.[50] The map probably originated with a local Nazi activist who had put his fantasies about Nazi domination of South America to paper. The British touched up the map a bit before presenting it as an authentic German document to William J. "Wild Bill" Donovan, Roosevelt's intelligence coordinator. Donovan, in turn, showed the map to Roosevelt on October 21, 1941, as evidence of Berlin's designs on South America. The president made no attempt to verify the map's authenticity, a question that was of secondary importance to him. Roosevelt had long warned Americans of German designs on the Western Hemisphere, so he gladly availed himself of the map to drive home his point. At the annual Navy Day dinner on October 27, he touted this questionable find as evidence of Hitler's megalomaniac designs:

> I have in my possession a secret map, made in Germany by Hitler's government—by planners of the New World Order. . . . It is a map of South America and a part of Central America as Hitler proposes to reorganize it. . . . The geographical experts of Berlin have ruthlessly obliterated all the existing boundaries; they have divided South America into five vassal states. . . . And they have also so arranged it that the territory of these new puppet states includes the Republic of Panama, and our great lifeline—the Panama Canal. This map, my friends, makes clear the Nazi design not only against South America but against the United States as well.[51]

Nazi spokesmen denounced Roosevelt as a "liar" and a "faker," and Hitler sought to reassure the public by stating that "as far as I'm concerned . . . South America is as far away as the moon."[52] Yet few people outside Germany were inclined to believe the führer. With the Japanese attack on Pearl Harbor in December 1941, the debate over U.S. intervention became moot, but the map had served its purpose by ostensibly corroborating Roosevelt's assertions about the German threat to the United States' security.

World War II formalized and strengthened the ties that a small cadre of intelligence men on both sides of the Atlantic had woven along personal lines in World War I. The British-U.S. Communication Intelligence Agreement of 1943 provided for the large-scale exchange of highly sensitive signals intelligence between American and British cryptanalysts. The United Kingdom–United States of America Agreement of 1947 extended and expanded this exceptionally close cooperation into the Cold War, and it remains in force today.[53] This is the "special relationship" in intelligence that Winston Churchill, the champion of the British secret services in both wars, evoked shortly after World War II when touring the United States.[54] Hall may rightly be regarded as one of this relationship's founding fathers.

CONCLUSION

In 1972 the mathematician Edward Lorenz delivered a paper titled "Predictability: Does the Flap of a Butterfly's Wings in Brazil Set Off a Tornado in Texas?"[1] In his lecture, Lorenz laid out the idea that a butterfly's movement created tiny changes in the atmosphere that could ultimately alter the course of a tornado. His theory gave birth to the popular concept of the butterfly effect—that is, that minor actions might have major consequences. Whatever the scientific merits of Lorenz's theory, the butterfly effect seems an appropriate metaphor for the Zimmermann telegram. The alliance scheme constituted a minor subplot in the war, but due to the telegram's interception, decryption, and eventual publication, it generated significant turbulence from its place of origin, all the way across the Atlantic, and back again in ways completely unforeseen and unintended by its authors. The telegram's inextricable links to several major trends at the time, including the struggle between civilian and military leaders over political control, the rise of public opinion as a factor in decision making, and the emergence of modern intelligence make its study especially instructive.

The idea of a Mexican-Japanese alliance originated with a minor German foreign office official, Hans Arthur von Kemnitz. His proposal would not have gained traction, however, were it not for the convergence of two aspects of imperial German politics. One was the absence of a central decision-making body or an individual decision maker at the highest level of government. The inability of Kaiser Wilhelm II to execute his constitutional role as supreme military commander and head of state left a void that was never adequately filled. The other was the struggle between civilian and military leaders over the course of the nation at war. By early 1917, the supreme army command (Oberste Heeresleitung, OHL) under Field Marshal Paul von Hindenburg and General Erich Ludendorff had succeeded in sidelining Chancellor Theobald von Bethmann Hollweg and the civilian leadership and in subordinating political considerations to military strategy. The military's triumph led directly to Germany's decision to declare unrestricted submarine warfare. With the chancellor outmaneuvered, and the kaiser unable and unwilling to resist the OHL, political concerns about the American reaction were dismissed or over-ruled. The resulting threat of U.S. intervention on behalf of the Allies sparked the telegram.

Zimmermann's search for an insurance policy against U.S. intervention, his management of previous covert operations, his desire to ingratiate himself with the OHL, and previous attempts to conclude a separate peace with Tokyo all played a role in the foreign secretary's decision to sanction the Mexican-Japanese alliance scheme. More remarkable than any specific goal Arthur Zimmermann may have been pursuing as German foreign secretary is that he provided no intellectual input for the telegram bearing his signature and spent only a minimal amount of time considering and authorizing the scheme. The haphazard and precipitous way in which the Wilhelmstrasse conceptualized, reviewed, approved, and dispatched the telegram highlights the fragmented and dysfunctional decision-making process of imperial Germany in early 1917.

While the OHL under Hindenburg and Ludendorff sidelined the chan-cellor and dominated the government's decision-making process, the military did not seek overt control of foreign policy. As a result, no one in the Ger-man leadership assumed responsibility for considering all aspects—military, political, and diplomatic—of the Zimmermann telegram, and at a time when U.S.-German relations were deteriorating rapidly, Zimmermann lacked proper supervision. A careful review of Kemnitz's proposal would probably have bur-ied it. In the absence of a comprehensive evaluation process, his half-baked scheme became official policy.

Organizational deficiencies at the highest levels of the German govern-ment affected the telegram episode in other ways as well. The pursuit of nar-row, departmental interests prevented the foreign office from conducting an effective damage assessment after the telegram's disclosure in the American press. (Of note, the U.S. State Department was equally negligent in drawing conclusions with regard to the security of its diplomatic communications.) A competently conducted and truly independent damage assessment could have found ample evidence to identify cryptanalysis, not espionage or theft, as the cause of the telegram's compromise, including information provided by the German military, references to non-secure codes from foreign office officials, foreign government officials, hints in American newspapers, as well as an explicit reference to Britain's hand in an open debate of the U.S. Senate.

Even if the foreign office could be excused for not identifying cryptanalysis as the source of the telegram's compromise, the Wilhelmstrasse should have realized that German diplomatic codes had been compromised after the plain text of the telegram appeared in American newspapers. In addition, even if British or American cryptanalysts had been unable to decrypt German telegrams prior to March 1, 1917, all they had to do on that day was obtain an encoded copy of the telegram from their own telegraph services, compare it against the published text, and reconstruct the German code. The publication of the telegram provided the Allies with the proverbial Rosetta stone.

Bureaucratic inertia at the Wilhelmstrasse may partially account for the continued use of the compromised code 0075, but so did Zimmermann's personal agenda. The foreign secretary had found it convenient to blame the telegram's disclosure on the ambassador to the United States, Johann Heinrich von Bernstorff, because it checkmated a potential rival and absolved himself from blame. Thus, thanks to the Wilhelmstrasse's cavalier attitude regarding communications security, and Zimmermann's decision to scapegoat Bernstorff, Germany's internal transatlantic communications remained an open book for the British.

Top German officials—with the exception of Bernstorff, who had only a minimal role in the telegram affair—never fully grasped the power of the press and the significance of public opinion as factors in U.S. politics. Throughout the period of American neutrality, U.S. newspapers reported careless remarks by German officials and disclosed secret German documents. Over time, the constant stream of such information created an unfavorable image of imperial Germany in the minds of many Americans. The foreign office intended the telegram as a "secret" offer of alliance, but given previous disclosures of German secret documents, the Wilhelmstrasse should have seriously questioned the likelihood of keeping the gist of the scheme out of the American press and considered the implications of a failure to do so. After the telegram's disclosure, Zimmermann's overriding concern lay in defending his position at home; he made no effort to explain the scheme to an international audience. With this course of action, Zimmermann effectively ceded power to those among Germany's enemies who were intent on bringing the United States into the war.

In hindsight, the telegram lays bare some of the reasons why Germany ultimately lost the war. Insufficient intragovernmental coordination, the subordination of diplomatic considerations to purely military concerns, and a lack of expertise in non-European affairs all conspired to bring about Zimmermann's alliance scheme. Underlying these factors was an attitude of the German leadership bordering on wishful thinking. Key military officers and Wilhelmstrasse officials preferred to see events as they deemed fit because it served their personal or departmental goals. The OHL, for example, belittled U.S. military potential because acknowledging American power would have raised serious questions about the wisdom of unrestricted submarine warfare. After the telegram's disclosure, the Wilhelmstrasse refused to consider the possibility that German diplomatic codes had been compromised, because it would have undermined Zimmermann's position. This type of narrow-mindedness and selective perception pervaded the highest levels of the German government. As a result, Berlin concocted not only the ill-considered Mexican-Japanese alliance proposal, but based many of its policies and strategies during the war on illusions rather than realistic assessments.[2]

During World War I, virtually all the belligerent governments established or expanded their permanent intelligence organizations in order to procure and exploit secret information by means of espionage, cryptanalysis, and covert action. The art of code breaking proved that signals intelligence, in particular, could make a valuable contribution to the war effort. Unfortunately for the Germans, Zimmermann made his secret alliance offer to Mexico at a time when the British were routinely intercepting foreign diplomatic traffic, and the cryptanalysts of Room 40 had honed their skills to near perfection.

The British, however, were not uniquely skilled in the craft of code breaking. Austria-Hungary, France, and Germany also ran first-rate cryptanalytic services. The Germans were reading the easily decryptable messages to and from the U.S. embassy in Berlin as regularly as the British were reading those to and from the U.S. embassy in London. Room 40's cryptanalytic competence was one factor that enabled Captain William Reginald Hall's organization to turn Zimmermann's Mexican alliance scheme into a major coup, but it was not the only one. The British had distinctive advantages over their German rivals in other respects.

One such advantage was geography. The strategic location of the British Isles allowed the Allies control over Germany's access to the Atlantic. As a result, at the outset of war the Royal Navy was able to cut Germany's transatlantic cables, forcing the Germans to send overseas communication by wireless transmission. Since German messages to the embassy in Washington had to cross the isles, British naval intelligence could easily intercept them. The constant stream of German intercepts provided British code breakers with a large volume of material, which in turn aided them in their quest to solve German encryptions.

A unique organizational aspect of British naval intelligence enabled London's code breakers to decrypt the Zimmermann telegram. In the major powers of the World War I era, including Britain, France, Germany, Russia, and the United States, the military oversaw cryptanalysis, so the soldiers (and or sailors) turned into code breakers targeted primarily military or naval communications. In Britain, Hall recognized the importance of capturing diplomatic messages as well and in 1915 set up Room 40's diplomatic section, which would do exactly that. Two years later, it produced its most consequential decryption of the war.

After Room 40 had obtained and decrypted the telegram, the British had to decide how best to exploit it. Here, too, Hall's expertise and vision came into play. Unlike the Germans, with the notable exception of Ambassador Bernstorff, the British were well attuned to the complexities of the American debate over intervention, and Hall had used his access to compromising material repeatedly to "play" the American press, public, and politicians to London's advantage. By 1917, as director of naval intelligence, Hall had become adept at operations to influence opinion in the United States, and he used his expertise to the hilt in the way that he chose to disclose the telegram. At the same time, he did everything in his power to protect his source from the Germans and the Americans in order to ensure continued British access to diplomatic traffic from both countries.

Hall would have been unable to close the deal without the unwavering and enthusiastic support of American diplomats and the State Department's Bureau of Secret Intelligence. Although Hall's charisma was not lost on the Americans, the support he received from U.S. intelligence related first and foremost to political considerations in Washington. After Secretary of State Robert Lansing began pushing for intervention in 1915, the members of the U.S. diplomatic corps and its intelligence organization worked hand in glove with Hall and British intelligence to expose German plots in the effort to bring the United States closer to joining the war. Other nations, notably Germany, could have only dreamed of a similarly cozy relationship with the intelligence service of the most important neutral country.

When Hall approached the U.S. embassy in London with news of the telegram, American officials and politicians on both sides of the Atlantic did their utmost to aid him in disclosing the scheme while simultaneously obscuring the role of British intelligence. The moment Hall showed the telegram to Second Secretary Edward Bell at the U.S. embassy, he ceded exclusive control over it and was rightly concerned about the possible exposure of Britain's invisible hand. Only a determined and disciplined effort by members of the Wilson administration and highly placed interventionists in Washington prevented this from happening. The telegram's successful publication resulted from and reinforced the evolving special relationship between British and American intelligence.

In the long run, British intelligence proved a double-edged sword for the government. By ably combining cryptanalysis with covert action, the British pulled off a major intelligence and propaganda coup. Hall's leadership style, inspiration he provided to others, and political vision contributed greatly to the operation's success. Yet Hall's participation came at a price for British policy makers. During the war, Hall repeatedly leaked secret intelligence without first consulting his superiors, and he had no qualms about using his privileged access to information and his intelligence connections to pursue his own political goals. As a result, he exercised a degree of influence over British foreign policy that far exceeded his position. "This man," recalled an American cryptologist who worked with him, "because of the information he obtained from the messages that his enormous bureau deciphered, stood next to Lloyd George in power."[3]

Hall's imperious handling of secret intelligence points to the larger issue of the secret services' role in the modern state. In order to perform successfully, intelligence agencies require secrecy, but their clandestine modus operandi also means reduced government supervision. In Britain, the intelligence services' wartime autonomy led to a postwar "para-intelligence" network with an agenda of its own. In one instance, the network turned against its government and contributed to its downfall in 1924. By boosting Hall's standing and muting critics of his high-handed approach, the telegram contributed to the emergence of a quasi-secret state in Britain.

The Zimmermann telegram had its biggest impact in the United States. The disclosure of the Mexican alliance scheme in the American press reinforced the interventionist message and handed the pro-war lobby an expedient propaganda tool on the eve of the country's entry into the conflict. Yet the telegram failed to rally non-interventionists, further dividing Americans on the question of belligerency. As a result, the United States entered the war less unified than many contemporaries and historians believed.

Despite the failure to mobilize the majority of the American public for war, the telegram did manage to exert a marked influence over the chief protagonist in the United States' struggle over intervention, the president. Both President Woodrow Wilson's idealism and his touchiness came into play when Lansing informed him of the telegram. In early 1917, the president still retained hope of ending the war through mediation, but the Mexican alliance proposal persuaded him of the futility of his efforts. At the same time, Germany's brazen abuse of U.S. diplomatic cables to send the telegram offended him personally. As a result, Wilson lost any lingering hope and desire for a peaceful settlement with Berlin and instead committed himself to war. This step, however, alienated him from a large segment of the population that continued to favor neutrality. To turn remarks by Lansing on their head, rather than "putting the people solidly behind the government,"[4] the telegram served to reinforce a growing rift between isolationists and the administration. In the debate over American intervention, Zimmermann's scheme proved divisive rather than unifying.

The United States certainly would have entered World War I regardless of the telegram, but by removing Wilson's final doubts about the wisdom of joining the Allies, it accelerated U.S. intervention, though perhaps only by a few weeks. A slightly later date of the U.S. declaration of war on Germany would not have affected the conflict's outcome, but it may well have had serious implications for London. By early 1917, the British treasury was rapidly running out of funds, and only the U.S. entry into the war allowed London to conceal its dire financial situation from Washington. Though it is impossible to say whether and how Wilson would have reacted to the news of Britain's utter economic dependence on the United States, the information might have elevated the United States to primus inter pares status among the Allies. Ultimately, U.S. preeminence would have strengthened Wilson's hand during the remainder of the war and at the ensuing peace conference. While this train of thought is speculative, it goes to show how even a small change in the United States' trajectory toward intervention may well have caused significant ripples. For the United States, the telegram certainly had a butterfly effect.

In the various ways described in this book, the Zimmermann telegram made history, but its significance transcends its historical impact. The telegram has provided later generations an instrument with which to bring into sharp focus some of the key political dynamics of modern times. By examining the circumstances of the telegram's inception, interception, and disclosure, one can understand more broadly the consequences of a national policy guided by military strategy, opportunities and challenges created by having a powerful intelligence organization, and the process of a nation's descent into war. The events surrounding the telegram affair unfolded a century ago, but complex decisions and events involving secrecy, diplomacy, and propaganda have played out time and again in societies across the globe. In this respect, the Zimmermann telegram remains as relevant for understanding the present as it is for considering the past.

Names and Terms

The Language of Cryptology

A code is a system for replacing words, phrases, letters, or numbers by other words or groups of letters or numbers for concealment or brevity. A cipher, on the other hand, replaces each individual letter or figure with another letter or figure. The Wilhelmstrasse did not use a cipher but a code, 0075, to send the Zimmermann telegram from Berlin to Washington, and the German embassy in Washington used another code, 13040, to forward it to Mexico. On occasion, the Germans enciphered an already encoded message in an effort to make it more difficult for the enemy to decrypt it. This process came to be known as "superencipherment." The Germans did not use it in the case of the Zimmermann telegram between Berlin and Washington or Washington to Mexico City.

Encryption or encrypting refers to the encoding as well as to the enciphering of a message. Decryption or decrypting typically refers to the process of cryptanalysis, that is, the conversion of an encoded or enciphered message into plain (readable) text without having initial knowledge of the original code or cipher. German diplomats used codebooks to encode and decode their telegrams, but the British needed to reconstruct the relevant German code before they could read an intercepted and encrypted message. Therefore, as long as the British were not in possession of a full, reconstructed codebook, they decrypted, rather than decoded, the intercepted messages. Once they had reconstructed the relevant codebook, the cryptanalysts could use their reconstructed codebook to decode the message in the same manner as the "legitimate"

German recipient. An encoded message is called an encrypt or cryptogram, and a decrypted message, a decrypt. An intercepted message is an intercept, regardless of whether it is encrypted.

The Zimmermann Telegram

The alliance proposal signed by German foreign secretary Arthur Zimmermann has been known by a plethora of names over the years. Zimmermann himself used multiple terms for the plan. In two closed sessions of the German budget committee in early March 1917, he referred to it variably as the *Telegramm, Instruktionen* (instructions), *Depesche* (dispatch), and *Mexiko-Note*. A month later in the same forum, he again used *Note* but also *Brief* (letter), though he implied he was referring to a description used by others.[1] An official foreign office investigation into the compromising of Zimmermann's alliance proposal referred to it alternatively as the *Instruktion, Telegramm, Ziffern-text* (cipher text), *Depesche, Note,* and *Schriftstück* (typescript or document).[2] Contemporary German newspapers similarly used a range of terms, including *Weisung* (directive), *Brief,* and *Note*.[3] Germany's ambassador to Washington, Johann Heinrich von Bernstorff, called it the "Mexico telegram," and the German envoy in Mexico, Heinrich von Eckardt, referred to it as "the Zimmermann note."[4] In foreign office parlance, Zimmermann's alliance proposal was a *Depesche*—an expeditiously delivered, brief instruction. The term *Mexiko-Depesche* came to be a widely used German term after the war, although other descriptors persisted. In 1931 Zimmermann wrote about his diplomatic initiative as an *Instruktion,* and two years later, he referred to it as a "message" while talking to a visiting American journalist.[5]

The director of British naval intelligence, Captain William Reginald Hall, seems to have thought of Zimmermann's proposal chiefly in terms of its transmission mode. According to his autobiography, he called it a "cablegram" when one of his cryptanalysts first showed it to him in January 1917.[6] Several weeks later, he used the word *cable*,[7] and he continued to use these terms long after the war.[8] In February 1917, British Foreign Office officials simply referred to the proposal as "this information" and "this news,"[9] indicating that Whitehall had not yet agreed on a universally accepted term. After the American press revealed the scheme to the public, the London *Times* referred to it as a "document."[10] When the British handed a copy of Zimmermann's intercept to the U.S. embassy in London, they may have used the term *cipher telegram*, because the American ambassador, Walter Hines Page, called it that when communicating the news to Secretary of State Robert Lansing.[11]

On March 1, American newspapers used mostly pejorative terms to describe Zimmermann's alliance proposal. Some of the more colorful descriptors included "conspiracy," "dark plot," "machination," "intrigue," and "villainous treachery."[12] By far the most common term employed that day was *plot*. On the following day, cooler editorial heads prevailed, and journalists began to use neutral expressions, such as "note" or "letter,"[13] though many continued to use disparaging descriptors, such as "plot" or "scheme."[14] Meanwhile, American officials internally quickly settled on the term *telegram*, first employed by Ambassador Page, on February 24, 1917. Secretary of State Lansing called it that in a message to the American envoy in Mexico, and other U.S. officials involved in the operation also adopted it.[15] In the interwar period, the term *Zimmermann telegram* gained traction on both sides of the Atlantic, as evidenced by popular works such as Walter Millis' bestseller, *Road to War*.[16] Hall, too, titled the relevant chapter in his autobiography "The Zimmermann Telegram."

After World War II, the Germanized *Zimmermann Telegramm* began to appear in German-language-publications,[17] although the older term *Depesche* continued to be in use throughout the Cold War.[18] Of note, the German translation of Tuchman's *Zimmermann Telegram* became *Zimmermann Depesche*.[19] Only after the end of the Cold War did the term *Telegramm* marginalize *Depesche*, making the former the universally accepted descriptor in German and English for the Mexican-Japanese alliance proposal.

This book adopts the shorthand "telegram." The term is used both in a literal and in a figurative sense. It refers narrowly to the text of Zimmermann's alliance proposal to Mexico as well as to larger aspects of the plan, such as German motivations, British interception and decryption, and American perceptions.

Chronology

1916

November 25

Arthur Zimmermann becomes Germany's foreign secretary.

December 12

In a speech at the Reichstag, German chancellor Theobald von Bethmann Hollweg extends an offer of peace to the Allies.

December 18

In an effort to reach a negotiated peace, President Woodrow Wilson sends a note asking the Allies and the Central Powers to state their war aims.

1917

January 9

At a meeting in Pless, German leaders decide to launch unrestricted submarine warfare beginning February 1.

January 13

German foreign office official Hans Arthur von Kemnitz completes the initial draft of what will become known as the Zimmermann telegram, in which Germany proposes the idea of an alliance with Mexico should the United States enter World War I on behalf of the Allies.

January 16

The Wilhelmstrasse dispatches the telegram via the U.S. embassy in Berlin, telling the Americans that the message only contains instructions to the German embassy in Washington, D.C.

January 17

Room 40, a cryptanalysis unit established by British naval intelligence, receives an encoded copy of the telegram. Within a few hours, the cryptanalyst Nigel de Grey produces a partial decrypt.

January 19

The telegram reaches the German embassy in Washington, where it is forwarded to Mexico. It reaches the German legation later in the day.

January 22

President Wilson delivers his "peace without victory" speech.

January 31

In Washington, German ambassador Johann Heinrich von Bernstorff informs Secretary of State Robert Lansing of Berlin's decision to wage unrestricted submarine warfare.

February 1

Germany launches unrestricted submarine warfare.

February 2

President Wilson informs his cabinet that the United States will not enter the war without an "overt act" committed by Germany.

February 3

The United States severs diplomatic relations with Germany.

February 5

Captain William Reginald Hall, director of British naval intelligence, informs Permanent Under-Secretary Charles Hardinge of the Foreign Office about the Zimmermann telegram.

Hall asks Edward Thurstan, a diplomat at the British legation in Mexico, to procure a copy of the telegram sent to Mexico from Washington. Hall suspects that that telegram will be more easily decryptable than the one intercepted earlier between Berlin and Washington.

Zimmermann sends a telegram to Mexico with instructions for the German envoy, Heinrich von Eckardt, to begin "negotiations even now" with the Mexican leader Venustiano Carranza.

February 8

Room 40 receives an intercepted copy of Zimmermann's encoded telegram of February 5.

February 10

Room 40 completes decryption of Zimmermann's telegram of February 5.

February 14

Ambassador Bernstorff leaves New York on board the *Frederik VIII.*

February 17

Zimmermann instructs the German envoy in Sweden to sound out his Japanese colleague there on a separate peace.

February 19

Room 40 receives a copy of the telegram sent to Mexico by Ambassador Bernstorff and procured there by Thurstan of the British legation.

Cryptanalyst de Grey produces a complete decrypt of the telegram sent from Washington to Mexico.

Hall shows the telegram decrypt to Second Secretary Edward Bell of the U.S. embassy in London.

February 20

Hall, Hardinge, and Ronald Campbell, his secretary, and Foreign Secretary Arthur Balfour discuss the most effective way of officially submitting the telegram to the Americans.

Eckardt, the German envoy to Mexico, discusses the telegram with Mexican foreign minister Cándido Aguilar.

February 23

Balfour hands a copy of the decrypted Zimmermann telegram to U.S. ambassador Walter Hines Page in London.

February 24

Ambassador Page sends the telegram to Washington.

State Department counselor Frank Polk receives the telegram at 8:30 p.m.

Foreign Minister Aguilar asks a Japanese legation official in Mexico about Tokyo's intentions in case of U.S. intervention.

February 25

State counselor Polk shows the telegram to President Wilson.

February 26

President Wilson asks Congress for emergency powers to arm merchant ships.

State counselor Polk informs the American ambassador in Mexico about the telegram and discusses it with the Japanese ambassador in Washington.

Foreign Minister Aguilar denies knowledge of the telegram to the American ambassador.

Polk mentions the telegram to Edward M. House, adviser to President Wilson.

February 27

State Department official William Phillips shows the telegram to Secretary of State Lansing.

President Wilson meets with Lansing to discuss the telegram.

A Japanese official informs Foreign Minister Aguilar that Japan has no intention of defecting from the Allies.

State counselor Polk obtains a copy of the encoded telegram from Western Union in Washington.

February 28

Secretary of State Lansing discloses the Zimmermann telegram to Associated Press correspondent Edwin Milton Hood.

March 1

American newspapers publish the telegram.

The U.S. House of Representatives debates and approves the arming of merchant ships (but the Senate subsequently filibusters the resolution).

The Senate debates the telegram's authenticity and possible British involvement in procuring it.

At 9 p.m., Secretary of State Lansing sends the encoded text of the telegram obtained from Western Union to the U.S. embassy in London with instructions to decrypt it with British assistance.

March 2

Bell and de Grey decrypt the Western Union copy of the telegram in London.

Ambassador Page sends the Western Union decrypt to Secretary of State Lansing.

Zimmermann issues an official statement to Wolff's Telegraph Bureau acknowledging his authorship of the telegram.

March 3

Zimmermann reiterates his authorship of the telegram to the German Overseas News Agency.

March 5

Zimmermann defends his authorship of the telegram in a closed session of the Reichstag budget committee.

March 10

Ambassador Bernstorff arrives in Christiania, Norway.

March 11

President Wilson announces the arming of American merchant ships by executive order.

March 13

Ambassador Bernstorff arrives in Berlin.

March 14

Chancellor Bethmann meets with Ambassador Bernstorff.

March 17

German foreign office official Otto Göppert is instructed to investigate the telegram's disclosure.

March 20

U.S. cabinet members unanimously advise President Wilson to declare war.

March 21

President Wilson requests that Congress meet for a special session on April 2.

April 2

President Wilson asks Congress for a declaration that a state of war exists with Germany.

April 4

The U.S. Senate votes in favor of war.

In Berlin, foreign office official Göppert submits his final report on the telegram's disclosure, implying theft at the German embassy in Washington, rather than cryptanalysis, as the source of its disclosure.

April 6

The House of Representatives votes in favor of war.

August 5

Zimmermann resigns as foreign secretary.

Abbreviations

AA	Auswärtiges Amt (German Foreign Office)
ADM	Records of the Admiralty (Royal Navy)
BA-MA	Bundesarchiv-Militärarchiv (German Military Archives), Freiburg
CAB	British Cabinet Minutes and Memoranda, 1916–1939, Library of Congress, Washington, D.C.
FO	British Foreign Office
FRUS	U.S. Department of State, *Papers Relating to the Foreign Relations of the United States, 1914–1918: Supplement— The World War.* 9 vols. Washington, D.C.: Government Printing Office, 1928–1933
GFM	German Foreign Ministry, 1867–1920, captured records (microfilm copies held at the National Archives and Records Administration)
HALL	Admiral Sir William Reginald Hall, "Draft Autobiography," chapter 25, Churchill College Cambridge Archive Center, Hall Papers, HALL 3/6
HW	Records of the Codes and Cypher School, United Kingdom
INF	Records of the Ministry of Information, United Kingdom
LC	Library of Congress, Washington, D.C.
M	Microcopy
NA	National Archives, London
NARA	National Archives and Records Administration, College Park, Maryland

OHL	Oberste Heeresleitung (German supreme army command)
PA-AA	Politisches Archiv des Auswärtigen Amtes (German foreign office political archives), Berlin
R	Akten des Deutschen Reiches (German foreign office records, 1867–1945)
RG	Record Group
RM	Reichsmarine (imperial Germany naval records)
T	Microfilm publication number, National Archives and Records Administration

Notes

Introduction

1. Cooper, *Woodrow Wilson*, 163.
2. Lansing, *War Memoirs*, 232.
3. HALL, 31.
4. Leonard, *War Addresses*, 42.
5. Henry F. Schorreck, "The Telegram That Changed History," NARA, RG 457, entry 9002, box 87, folder SRH-234, "The Zimmermann Telegram and Related Papers" (declassified 15 March 1983).
6. Nassua, *Gemeinsame Kriegführung*, 2.
7. Peterson, *Propaganda*, 315.
8. Warner, "Wanted," 21.

Chapter 1. The Zimmermann Telegram in History

1. Memo, Lansing, March 4, 1917, cited in Lansing, *War Memoirs*, 229.
2. Jones and Hollister, *German Secret Service*, 298–300.
3. Lansing, *War Memoirs*, 225.
4. Tumulty, *Woodrow Wilson*, 159.
5. Seymour, *American Diplomacy*, 204.
6. For an overview of American revisionism, see Cohen, *American Revisionists*.
7. Bernstorff, *My Three Years*, 380–81.
8. Turner, *Shall It Be Again?*, 14.
9. Grattan, *Why We Fought*, 403–405.
10. Millis, *Road to War*, 405–408.
11. Transill, *America Goes to War*, 653–54; and Morrissey, *American Defense*, 183–84.
12. Peterson, *Propaganda for War*, 313–15.
13. "Dr. Zimmermann Dies in Germany," *New York Times*, June 8, 1940.
14. Grattan, *Why We Fought*, 405; Transill, *America Goes to War*, 654; Millis, *Road to War*, 408; Peterson, *Propaganda for War*, 314.
15. Spencer, *Decision for War*, 64–65, 77, 79, 108.
16. Tuchman, *Zimmermann Telegram*, 8, 25, 70, 185, 199.
17. Katz, *Secret War*, 350.
18. Katz, *Secret War*, 361.
19. Link, *Wilson: Campaigns*, 354.
20. Cooper, *Vanity*, 177.

21. Möckelmann, "Deutschlandbild," 133.
22. Devlin, *Too Proud*, 648, 653.
23. Witcover, *Sabotage*, 215, 219, 225.
24. Mead, *Doughboys*, 64.
25. Koopmann, *Diplomatie*, 295, 297.
26. Nassua, *Gemeinsame Kriegführung*, 46, 48, 147.
27. Nickles, *Under the Wire*, 143–45.
28. Hodgson, *Right Hand*, xi.
29. Ross, *Propaganda*, 3, 22.
30. Fleming, *Illusion of Victory*, 2, 27, 78, 307, 490.
31. For details, see chapter 7.
32. Friedman and Mendelsohn, *Zimmermann Telegram*, 14, 17, 19, 26, 28.
33. Kahn, *Codebreakers*, 286–88, 1025, note to page 284; Kahn, "Zimmermann Telegram," 69.
34. Nickles, *Under the Wire*, 240, note 25.
35. Ramsay, *"Blinker" Hall*, 188.

Chapter 2. Arthur Zimmermann

1. For biographical details, see Auswärtiges Amt, *Biographisches Handbuch*, vol. 5, s.v. "Zimmermann, Arthur." On Zimmermann's family background, see also Jagow, memoirs, 179, PA-AA, Nachlass Jagow.
2. Hürter, "Die Staatssekretäre," 225; Fischer, *Germany's Aims*, 122.
3. Auswärtiges Amt, *Biographisches Handbuch*, vol. 5, s.v. "Zimmermann, Arthur."
4. Gerard, *My Four Years*, 423.
5. Auswärtiges Amt, *Biographisches Handbuch*, vol. 5, s.v. "Zimmermann, Arthur," and Jagow, memoirs, 179, PA-AA, Nachlass Jagow.
6. Letter, Grew to William Phillips, February 22, 1916, Grew, *Turbulent Era*, vol. 1, 220.
7. Wolff, *Tagebücher*, vol. 1, no. 170, entry, June 12, 1915.
8. Bülow, *Denkwürdigkeiten*, vol. 3, 159.
9. Gilbert Hirsch in the *Evening Post*, November 25, 1916. For a physical description of Zimmermann, see also Fischart, "Neue Politikerköpfe," 173.
10. Grew, *Turbulent Era*, vol. 1, 220.
11. Wolff, *Tagebücher*, vol. 1, no. 31, entry, September 28, 1914.
12. Jagow, memoirs, 180, PA-AA, Nachlass Jagow.
13. Grew, *Turbulent Era*, vol. 1, 287.
14. Jagow, memoirs, 180, PA-AA, Nachlass Jagow.
15. Bülow, *Denkwürdigkeiten*, vol. 3, 159, 271.
16. For Zimmermann's arguments, see Vierhaus, *Tagebuch*, entry, January 9, 1913; see also Lerchenfeld to Hertling, December 31, 1912, in Deuerlein, *Briefwechsel*, vol. 1, no. 44; Lerchenfeld to Hertling, January 5, 1913, ibid., no. 45; and Hanssen, *Diary*, entry, September 14, 1914. For Jagow's arguments, see Jagow, memoirs, 174–75, 177, PA-AA, Nachlass Jagow. Jagow suggests that Zimmermann secretly coveted the appointment, but his contention is not supported by any evidence.
17. Gerard, *My Four Years*, 391; *Evening Post*, November 25, 1916.
18. Wolff, *Tagebücher*, vol. 1, no. 287, entry, January 15, 1916; and no. 461, entry, November 3, 1916.
19. Jagow to Bernstorff, September 2, 1919, cited in Bernstorff, *Memoirs*, 165.
20. Fischer, *Germany's Aims*, 43.
21. Fischer, *Germany's Aims*, 52.
22. Wolff, *Tagebücher*, vol. 1, no. 12, entry, August 18, 1914. In fact, Japan had submitted an ultimatum to this effect the previous day.
23. Wolff, *Tagebücher*, vol. 1, no. 26, entry, September 1, 1914.
24. Ritter, *Sword and Scepter*, vol. 3, 23; Fischer, *Germany's Aims*, 102.
25. Hürter, "Die Staatssekretäre," 236.

26. The author expresses his gratitude to Cord Eberspächer for providing information on the German consular intelligence network in China. On German naval intelligence and the foreign office, see generally Koopmann, *Diplomatie,* 69–70, and Boghardt, *Spies of the Kaiser,* 19–20.
27. Cited in Fischer, *Germany's Aims,* 120.
28. Fischer, *Germany's Aims,* 122, 128, 143, 147; for the Middle East, see especially Lüdke, *Jihad Made in Germany.*
29. Gerard, *My Four Years,* 237. In his telegram to Secretary of State William J. Bryan, Gerard apparently made no mention of his witty response, see Doerries, *Imperial Challenge,* 144.
30. Doerries, *Imperial Challenge,* 64, 66, 144, 151, 157, 171, 179.
31. Lerchenfeld to Hertling, November 24, 1916, in Deuerlein, *Briefwechsel,* vol. 2, no. 328; see generally Ritter, *Sword and Scepter,* vol. 3, 213–14; and Birnbaum, *Peace Moves,* 216–17.
32. Wolff, *Tagebücher,* vol. 1, no. 152, entry, May 10, 1915.
33. Jagow to Bernstorff, September 2, 1919, cited in Bernstorff, *Memoirs,* 165; Jagow, memoirs, 181, PA-AA, Nachlass Jagow.
34. Auswärtiges Amt, *Biographisches Handbuch,* vol. 5, s.v. "Zimmermann, Arthur."
35. Lerchenfeld to Hertling, November 28, 1916, in Deuerlein, *Briefwechsel,* vol. 2, no. 332.
36. Grew, *Turbulent Era,* vol. 1, 264–65; *Evening Post,* November 25, 1916.

Chapter 3. The Mexican Imbroglio

1. Kunimoto, "Japan and Mexico," 249.
2. Hayashima, *Illusion des Sonderfriedens,* 55.
3. Hürter, "Die Staatssekretäre," 230. Hintze moved on to become minister in China and, eventually, foreign secretary, for two months, in 1918. For Magnus, see Hohler, *Diplomatic Petrel,* 222.
4. Memorandum, Eckardt to AA, January 24, 1916, cited in Nassua, *Gemeinsame Kriegführung,* 31.
5. Commander of SMS *Nürnberg,* Captain Mörsberger, Mazatlán, to kaiser, December 3, 1913, BA-MA, RM 5/5823.
6. Magnus to AA, via Stockholm, May 24, 1915, GFM, Mexiko 1, vol. 53, NARA, T 141, roll 20.
7. See *Washington Post,* February 19, 1917; *New York Times,* April 24, 1924; for details on Montgelas' career, see Ministerium des Innern, *Handbuch,* volumes for the years 1901 through 1922. It was in Japan that Montgelas met his future wife, Fanny Dickinson Hazeltine, the daughter of Charles S. Hazeltine, who had served as U.S. consul to Milan under President Grover Cleveland. The couple married in 1908, and the countess joined her husband when he was recalled to Berlin in late 1911 and was appointed counselor for North American and Mexican affairs.
8. Montgelas, Tokyo, to Bethmann, March 23, 1911, GFM, Mexiko 10, NARA, T 149, roll 378.
9. Grew, *Turbulent Era,* vol. 1, 221; Gerard, *My Four Years,* 376, 386.
10. Wolff, *Tagebücher,* vol. 1, entry, October 31, 1916.
11. *New York Times,* April 24, 1924.
12. Gerard, *My Four Years,* 382.
13. Memoranda, Montgelas, August 25, 1915, and June 19, 1916, cited in Birnbaum, *Peace Moves,* 345 and 115, note 2.
14. Bernstorff to AA, June 2, 1915, GFM, Mexiko 1, vol. 53, NARA, T 141, roll 20. The report reached Berlin on June 19, and Montgelas signed and commented on it on June 21. For Wilson's note, see Katz, *Secret War,* 299.
15. Bernstorff to Bethmann, March 29, 1916, GFM, Mexiko 1, vol. 53, NARA, T 141, roll 20.

16. Top secret, Lieutenant Commander Walther Freyer to chief of admiralty staff, March 17, 1916, GFM, Mexiko 1, vol. 56, NARA, T 141, roll 20. Prieger forwarded the message to the Wilhelmstrasse, where Montgelas initialed it on March 23.

17. Memorandum, Montgelas, March 23, 1916, GFM, Mexiko 1, vol. 56, NARA, T 141, roll 20.

18. Lansing desk diary, October 10, 1915, LC, Lansing Papers.

19. Nassua, *Gemeinsame Kriegführung*, 32.

20. Ratibor to AA, December 7, 1914, GFM, Mexiko 1, vol. 52, NARA, T 141, roll 19.

21. Eckardt to Bethmann Hollweg, May 5, 1916, GFM, Mexiko 1, vol. 56, NARA, T 141, roll 20.

22. Thomson, *Scene Changes,* entries, May 31 and June 2, 3, 1916.

23. Page to State Department, July 5, 1916, NARA, RG 59, decimal file 862.20212, M 336, roll 55; handwritten note, Montgelas, June 14, 1916, GFM, Mexiko 1, vol. 56, NARA, T 141, roll 20.

24. Einsiedel, Berne, to Jagow, September 5, 1916, GFM, Mexiko 1, vol. 57, NARA, T 141, roll 20; Jagow to Einsiedel, September 9, 1916, ibid.

25. Einsiedel to Bethmann, September 15, 1916, GFM, Mexiko 1, vol. 57, NARA, T 141, roll 20; Memorandum by [ill.], September 11, 1916, ibid.

26. Krumm Heller, Berlin, to Jagow, October 21, 1916, GFM, Mexiko 1, vol. 57, NARA, T 141, roll 20; Jagow to Krumm Heller, October 28, 1916, ibid.; memorandum, Montgelas, October 30, 1916, ibid.

27. War ministry to AA, December 18, 1916, GFM, Mexiko 1, vol. 57, NARA, T 141, roll 20; Friedrich, war ministry, to Bethmann, January 24, 1917, with attached report by first lieutenant (reserve) Commerell of January 22, 1917, ibid.

28. Memorandum, admiralty staff, February 7, 1917, BA/MA, RM 5/5822.

29. Commerell to war ministry, January 22, 1917, GFM, Mexiko 1, vol. 57, NARA, T 141, roll 20; Krumm Heller, Charlottenburg, to Zimmermann, July 23, 1917, GFM, Mexiko 16, vol. 1, NARA, T 149, roll 378; Zimmermann to Krumm Heller, July 28, 1917, ibid.

30. Bell, London, to Harrison, State Department, January 9, 1918, NARA, RG 59, Office of the Counselor, entry 543, box 2, confidential file no. 7.

31. Bell to Harrison, April 16, 1918, NARA, RG 59, Office of the Counselor, entry 543, box 2, confidential file no. 7.

32. Bell to Harrison, April 17, 1918, NARA, RG 59, Office of the Counselor, entry 543, box 2, confidential file no. 7.

33. Bell to Harrison, November 5, 1918, NARA, RG 59, Office of the Counselor, entry 543, box 2, confidential file no. 7.

34. Hurley, London, to Winslow, State Department, December 18, 1918, NARA, RG 59, Office of the Counselor, entry 543, box 2, confidential file no. 7.

35. Ratibor to AA, February 17, 1916, GFM, Mexiko 1, vol. 56, NARA, T 141, roll 20.

36. Ratibor to AA, February 17, 1916, GFM, Mexiko 1, vol. 56, NARA, T 141, roll 20; Zimmermann's comments and reply, February 23, 1916, ibid. For the report of the Mexican consul in Havana, see Katz, *Secret War,* 331. For a U.S. report on Enrile, see W. E. D. Stokes, New York, to Lansing, June 28, 1916, NARA, RG 59, decimal file 862.20212, M 336, roll 55.

37. Deputy general command intelligence division, Karlsruhe, to AA, April 29, 1916, with Zimmermann's response scribbled at bottom, GFM, Mexiko 1, vol. 56, NARA, T 141, roll 20; General Manteuffel, Karlsruhe, to AA, May 5, 1916, with enclosure of Islas' papers, ibid.

38. Note by intelligence officer Berlin, OHL, April 28, 1916, GFM, Mexiko 1, vol. 56, NARA, T 141, roll 20.

39. Memorandum, Enrile, April 19, 1916, GFM, Mexiko 1, vol. 56, NARA, T 141, roll 20.

40. Memorandum, Enrile, April 19, 1916, GFM, Mexiko 1, vol. 56, NARA, T 141, roll 20.

41. Memorandum, Enrile, to AA, June 14, 1916, GFM, Mexiko 1, vol. 56, NARA, T 141, roll 20.
42. Memorandum, Montgelas, June 27, 1916, GFM, Mexiko 1, vol. 56, NARA, T 141, roll 20.
43. Berlin police president to AA, June 21, 1916, GFM, Mexiko 1, vol. 56, NARA, T 141, roll 20.
44. Ratibor to AA, July 24, 1916, GFM, Mexiko 1, vol. 57, NARA, T 141, roll 20; Kemnitz's handwritten note, on behalf of Zimmermann, ibid.
45. Ratibor to AA, August 16, 1916, GFM, Mexiko 1, vol. 57, NARA, T 141, roll 20; Zimmermann to war minister, August 23, 1916, ibid.; war ministry to AA, September 3, 1916, ibid.; Jagow to Ratibor, September 4, 1916, ibid.; Ratibor to AA, February 7, 1917, ibid.; Zimmermann to Ratibor, February 10, 1917, ibid.; Ratibor to AA, August 21, 1917, GFM, Mexiko 1, vol. 58, NARA, T 141, roll 20.
46. Katz, *Secret War,* 348.
47. Memorandum, Mexican minister [Rafael Zubáran Capmany], Berlin, November 3, 1916, GFM, Mexiko 1, vol. 57, NARA, T 141, roll 20.
48. Memorandum, Zimmermann, November 3, 1916, GFM, Mexiko 1, vol. 57, NARA, T 141, roll 20; see also Nassua, *Gemeinsame Kriegführung,* 24.

Chapter 4. The German Quest for Japan

1. Iklé, "Japanese-German Peace Negotiations," 62.
2. Hayashima, *Illusion des Sonderfriedens,* 31.
3. Ibid., 44.
4. Ibid., 50–51, 125.
5. Ibid., 125.
6. Ibid., 50.
7. Iklé, "Japanese-German Peace Negotiations," 63–65.
8. Hayashima, *Illusion des Sonderfriedens,* 64, 70.
9. Iklé, "Japanese-German Peace Negotiations," 64.
10. Hayashima, *Illusion des Sonderfriedens,* 71–72.
11. Gerard, *Face to Face,* 88.
12. Iklé, "Japanese-German Peace Negotiations," 70.
13. Mehnert, "Deutsche Weltpolitik," 1469.
14. The official biographical reference book of the German foreign office gives Kemnitz's first name as "Arthur." See Auswärtiges Amt, *Biographisches Handbuch,* vol. 3, s.v. "Kemnitz, Arthur von." Kemnitz, however, referred to himself as "Hans Arthur." See his various memoranda in the Kemnitz Papers at the Hoover Institution.
15. Memorandum, Kemnitz, May 1945, Hoover Institution, Kemnitz Papers.
16. Hayashima, *Illusion des Sonderfriedens,* 45, 116.
17. Hayashima, *Illusion des Sonderfriedens,* 129.
18. Kemnitz to foreign secretary, December 4, 1930, PA-AA, Personalakte Kemnitz, vol. 7170.
19. For Kemnitz's career details, see Auswärtiges Amt, *Biographisches Handbuch,* vol. 3, s.v. "Kemnitz, Arthur von"; Ministerium des Innern, *Handbuch für das Deutsche Reich,* volumes for years 1904–1918.
20. Fischart, "Neue Politikerköpfe," 172–73.
21. Memorandum, Kemnitz, summer 1927, PA-AA, Personalakte Kemnitz, vol. 7170; Auswärtiges Amt, *Biographisches Handbuch,* vol. 3, s.v. "Kemnitz, Arthur von."
22. Hayashima, *Illusion des Sonderfriedens,* 94.
23. Erdmann, *Riezler: Tagebücher,* entry, May 7, 1916.
24. Hayashima, *Illusion des Sonderfriedens,* 95.
25. Fischer, *Germany's Aims,* 228–32.
26. Hayashima, *Illusion des Sonderfriedens,* 106.

27. Jagow to Lucius, May 4, 1916, cited in Mehnert, "Japanese Peril," 1470.
28. Iklé, "Japanese-German Peace Negotiations," 73.
29. Handwritten comment, Kemnitz, on report, Lucius to AA, May 17, 1916, cited in Hayashima, *Illusion des Sonderfriedens*, 116.
30. Kemnitz to Solf, November 24, 1918, GFM, Mexiko 16, vol. 2, NARA, T 141, roll 378.
31. Mehnert, "Japanese Peril," 1471.
32. Kemnitz to Solf, November 24, 1918, GFM, Mexiko 16, vol. 2, NARA, T 141, roll 378.
33. Memorandum, Kemnitz, July 2, 1916, cited in Hayashima, *Illusion des Sonderfriedens*, 122.
34. Hayashima, *Illusion des Sonderfriedens*, 127.
35. Kemnitz to Solf, November 24, 1918, GFM, Mexiko 16, vol. 2, NARA, T 141, roll 378.
36. Herwarth, Washington, D.C., to war ministry, December 14, 1910, BA-MA, RM 5/5807; Montgelas, Tokyo, to AA, March 3, 1911, GFM, Mexiko 10, NARA, T 49, roll 378; Boy-Ed, Washington, D.C., to imperial navy office, May 7, 1914, BA-MA, RM 5/5826.
37. Kunimoto, "Japan and Mexico," 197.
38. Ibid., 210.
39. Ibid., 216–21.
40. Ratibor, Madrid, to AA, July 24, 1916, GFM, Mexiko 1, vol. 57, NARA, T 141, roll 20.
41. Katz, *Secret War*, 353.

Chapter 5. Drafting the Telegram

1. Chickering, *Imperial Germany*, 88–94; Stevenson, *First World War*, 74–75.
2. Ritter, *Sword and Scepter*, vol. 3, 214.
3. Asprey, *German High Command*, 64.
4. Birnbaum, *Peace Moves*, 207.
5. Ludendorff to Zimmermann, December 20, 1916, and Zimmermann to Lersner, December 21, 1916, both cited in Ludendorff, *General Staff*, vol. 1, 289.
6. Hanssen, *Diary*, March 31, 1916.
7. Grew, *Turbulent Era*, vol. 1, 255.
8. For the Pless council, see Ritter, *Sword and Scepter*, vol. 3, 313–15; and Birnbaum, *Peace Moves*, 222–23.
9. Schwertfeger, *Valentini*, 145–46.
10. Görlitz, *Regierte der Kaiser?* entry, February 17, 1917.
11. Wolff, *Tagebücher*, vol. 1, no. 503, entry, January 23, 1917.
12. Erdmann, *Riezler: Tagebücher*, no. 694, entry, January 31, 1917.
13. Schwertfeger, *Valentini*, 149.
14. Jagow, memoirs, 185, PA-AA, Nachlass Jagow.
15. For firsthand accounts of the dinner, see Wolff, *Tagebücher*, vol. 1, no. 494, entry, January 6, 1917; Gerard, *My Four Years*, 361–62; and *Frankfurter Zeitung*, January 8, 1917.
16. Jagow, memoirs, 184–85, PA-AA, Nachlass Jagow.
17. Gerard, *Face to Face*, illustration facing page 304.
18. Birnbaum, *Peace Moves*, 314.
19. Nassua, *Gemeinsame Kriegführung*, 16.
20. Memorandum, Kemnitz, summer 1927, PA-AA, Personalakte Kemnitz, vol. 7170.
21. Erdmann, *Riezler: Tagebücher*, no. 701, entry, March 4, 1917
22. Jordan to Lersner, March 5, 1917, PA-AA, R 22222.
23. Memorandum, Rhomberg to undersecretary of state, November 29, 1918, GFM, Mexiko 16, vol. 2, NARA, T 149, roll 378.

24. Kemnitz to Solf, November 24, 1918, GFM, Mexiko 16, vol. 2, NARA, T 149, roll 378; *New York Times*, May 15, 1920; and *Vossische Zeitung*, May 8, 1920.
25. Kemnitz's handwritten draft with comments can be found in PA-AA, R 16919; German foreign office historian Peter Grupp identified the signatories of the document. Personal communication, Grupp to author, July 14, 2004. For a complete transcription of the handwritten draft, including all marginal comments, see von zur Gathen, "Zimmermann Telegram," 5–10.
26. Memorandum, Enrile, April 19, 1916, GFM, Mexiko 1, vol. 56, NARA, T 141, roll 20.
27. Von zur Gathen, "Zimmermann Telegram," 3.
28. Auswärtiges Amt, *Biographisches Handbuch*, vol. 3, s.v. "Langwerth von Simmern, Ernst."
29. Jordan to Lersner, March 5, 1917, PA-AA, R 22222. Comment by Reichstag deputy Eduard David in Carnegie, *Official German Documents*, vol. 2, 715. Gottfried zu Hohenlohe-Schillingfürst to Czernin, April 2, 1917, cited in Katz, *Secret War*, 353.
30. Memorandum, Rhomberg, November 29, 1918, GFM, Mexiko 16, vol. 2, NARA, T 149, roll 378.
31. Grew, *Turbulent Era*, vol. 1, 220.
32. Wolff, *Tagebücher*, vol. 1, no. 14, entry, August 20, 1914.
33. Wolff, *Tagebücher*, vol. 1, no. 37, entry, October 16, 1914.
34. Jagow, memoirs, 183, PA-AA, Nachlass Jagow.
35. Erdmann, *Riezler: Tagebücher*, no. 701, entry, March 4, 1917.
36. Katz, *Secret War*, 353.
37. Schiffers and Koch, *Hauptausschuss*, vol. 3, session 122, March 3, 1917, and session 123, March 5, 1917.
38. Thurstan to FO, February 14, 1917, NA, FO 204/488.
39. *New York Times*, March 1, 1917.
40. Tuchman, *Zimmermann Telegram*, 146.
41. German foreign office official Otto Göppert was the first to remark on the mistranslation. Report, Göppert, April 4, 1917, PA-AA, R 16919.
42. Schiffers and Koch, *Hauptausschuss*, vol. 3, session 123, March 5, 1917.
43. Hanssen, *Diary*, February 22, 1917.
44. Schiffers and Koch, *Hauptausschuss*, vol. 3, session 123, March 5, 1917.
45. Schiffers and Koch, *Hauptausschuss*, vol. 3, session 123, March 5, 1917. For the thesis that Zimmermann used the telegram principally to cater to the military, see Nassua, *Gemeinsame Kriegführung*, 45.
46. Erdmann, *Riezler: Tagebücher*, no. 701, entry, March 4, 1917.
47. *Nürnberger Nachrichten*, October 25, 1918, referenced by Katz in Link, *Wilson: Campaigns*, 434.
48. Jagow, memoirs, 180, PA-AA, Nachlass Jagow.
49. Von Papen to Boy-Ed, August 25, 1919, cited in Reiling, *Deutschland*, 294.
50. Katz, *Secret War*, 354.
51. Draft, Kemnitz, January 11, 1917, PA-AA, R 16919.
52. Heitmann, *Unter Wasser*, 284–87.
53. Memorandum, Montgelas, January 16, 1917, GFM, Mexiko 16, secret, NARA, T 149, roll 378; see also Rhomberg to undersecretary of state, November 29, 1918, subheading 4, GFM, Mexiko 16, vol. 2, NARA, T 149, roll 378.
54. Von zur Gathen, "Zimmermann Telegram," 13.
55. Report, Göppert, April 4, 1917, PA-AA, R 16919; memorandum, Montgelas, January 17, 1917, GFM, Mexiko 16, secret, NARA, T 149, roll 378.
56. Freeman, "Zimmermann Telegram Revisited," 117; Nickles, *Under the Wire*, 160.
57. Bavarian military plenipotentiary at GHQ to Bavarian war ministry, January 12, 1917, cited in Nassua, *Gemeinsame Kriegführung*, 37.

58. Carnegie, *German Official Documentsv* vol. 2, 462–63.
59. Wolfgang Heyne, a Social Democrat, to Wolff, see Wolff, *Tagebücher,* vol. 1, no. 507, entry, January 30, 1917
60. H. Rumbold, Berne, to FO, February 13, 1917, NA, FO 371/3109. Also testifying to Zimmermann's genuine surprise, see Grew, *Turbulent Era,* vol. 1, 308.
61. Zimmermann to Lucius, February 5, 1917, initialed by Kemnitz, February 4, Montgelas and Zimmermann, February 5, GFM, Mexiko 16, secret, NARA, T 149, roll 378. Since American diplomatic cables were not available after the rupture of diplomatic relations with Washington, Kemnitz used the so-called Swedish roundabout for transmission of this message to Mexico.
62. Iklé, "Japanese-German Negotiations," 75.

Chapter 6. "Blinker" Hall

1. Beesly, *Room 40,* 8–20; Ewing, "Special War Work, Part 2," 33–34.
2. Beesly, *Room 40,* 16–17.
3. Ibid., 20.
4. For biographical data and Hall's early naval career, see O'Halpin, "Hall," 646, and the obituary of Admiral Sir William Reginald Hall, *The Times,* October 23, 1943.
5. Andrew, *Secret Service,* 91–92.
6. Kahn, *Codebreakers,* 276. For another physical description of Hall, see Andrew, *Secret Service,* 91.
7. Quotes are from James, *Eyes of the Navy,* xvii, 202.
8. Kahn, *Codebreakers,* 285.
9. Beesly, *Room 40,* 123–24; Andrew, *Secret Service,* 94.
10. Porter, *Plots and Paranoia,* 169.
11. Memorandum, de Grey, October 31, 1945, NA, HW 3/177; memorandum, Knox, 1927, NA, HW 3/182.
12. O'Halpin, "British Intelligence in Ireland," 58.
13. Beesly, *Room 40,* 190.
14. James, *Eyes of the Navy,* 38–41.
15. Andrew, *Secret Service,* 106; James, *Eyes of the Navy,* 131; email, Peter Freeman to author, March 8, 2006.
16. James, *Eyes of the Navy,* 206.
17. House diary, November 28, 1915, Yale University Library, House papers.
18. Cooper, *Wilson,* 317 (emphasis in the original).
19. May, *World War,* 355–56.
20. Hall to Roger Keyes, May 15, 1915, cited in Larsen, "British Intelligence," 687.
21. Freeman, "MI1(b)," 216–17: "Either Room 40 (which then had no access to American telegrams, and never attacked them) was somehow acquiring and reading those sent by Colonel House: or—more likely—Hall showed Hankey decrypts produced by MI1(b)."
22. Larsen, "British Intelligence," 702, argues that it was Hall's lobbying that turned the British government against House's mediation project.
23. Roskill, *Hankey,* vol. 1, 247.
24. Yardley, *American Black Chamber,* 140.
25. James, *Eyes of the Navy,* 206.
26. Roskill, *Hankey,* vol. 1, 160–61.
27. Quoted in Andrew, *Secret Service,* 307. Like the Gallipoli operation itself, Hall's plot came to naught.
28. Beesly, *Room 40,* 37–38.
29. HALL, 2; Beesly, *Room 40,* 205, 207.
30. James, *Eyes of the Navy,* 71.
31. Memorandum, Bell, May 1, 1919, NARA, RG 59, Office of the Counselor, entry 543, box 5, confidential file no. 121, "secret service."

Chapter 7. Interception and Decryption

1. See chapter 5.
2. Bernstorff, *My Three Years*, 53, 65–66.
3. "Chapter entitled Intelligence, written by Frank Birch in 1919 for the joint Birch/ Clarke history of First World War," 11–12, NA, HW 3/8. One can only speculate why Room 40 did not begin attacking these intercepts earlier. Peter Freeman suggested that Swedish intercepts simply fell through the cracks. With Room 40 responsible for attacking German encrypts, and army intelligence MI1b responsible for all others, the German-Swedish messages did not fall clearly into either agency's purview and might have ranked low in priority—as long as no one guessed their explosive content: "It would have been nice to have been a fly on the wall at a meeting between Hall and DMI [director of military intelligence] which I imagine would have taken place around July/August 1916 at which the question of who was supposed to be doing what about 'Swedish' telegrams was discussed." Email, Freeman to author, October 13, 2005.
4. For details, see chapter 5.
5. For a technical discussion of the various channels, see Friedman and Mendelsohn, *Zimmermann Telegram*, 6–8. For the U.S. route, see memorandum, Kemnitz, September 24, 1917, PA-AA, R 16463, and Cooper, *Walter Hines Page*, 329.
6. Report, Göppert, April 4, 1917, PA-AA, 16919.
7. Hall, "Affidavit."
8. HALL, 11.
9. Hendrick, *Life and Letters*, vol. 3, 335, 339–40; Carnegie, *Official German Documents*, vol. 2, 1337.
10. Hendrick to Bell, June 17, 1921, NARA, RG 59, Office of the Counselor, entry 539, box 7, folder 1.
11. Friedman and Mendelsohn, *Zimmermann Telegram*, 6, 14.
12. Kahn, *Codebreakers*, 1025, note to page 284.
13. Nickles, *Under the Wire*, 240, note 25.
14. Freeman, "Zimmermann Telegram Revisited," 130; and von zur Gathen, "Zimmermann Telegram," 12, 18, 24.
15. Tuchman, *Zimmermann Telegram*, 146.
16. Katz, *Secret War*, 354–55; and Nassua, *Gemeinsame Kriegführung*, 54–55.
17. Singh, *Code Book*, 110.
18. Yardley, *American Black Chamber*, 4. Yardley decided not to inform his superiors about the vulnerability of the State Department's codes, probably because he feared retribution for his unauthorized attack of a State Department code and for reading a highly confidential message to the president.
19. Yardley, *American Black Chamber*, 10.
20. See intercepted American messages from August 1917 in NA, HW 7/22. I am grateful to Peter Freeman for sharing this material with me.
21. Yardley, *American Black Chamber*, 136.
22. Bamford, *Puzzle Palace*, 30, 540.
23. Yardley, *American Black Chamber*, 241–45.
24. Hall and Peaslee, *Three Wars*, 8. The relevant paragraph suggests that the British obtained the telegram by eavesdropping on German wireless communications: "What happened was this: Hall picked up and decoded those cables just as he did all other cables and radios which the Germans were sending and receiving."
25. Aldrich, *Hidden Hand*, 247; Bamford, *Puzzle Palace*, 30.
26. Email, Freeman to author, March 8, 2006.
27. I am grateful to Peter Freeman for clarifying the British procedure of sorting through intercepted messages; email, Freeman to author, March 8, 2006.
28. Kahn, *Codebreakers*, 282; Freeman, "Zimmermann Telegram Revisited," 114; and report, Göppert, April 4, 1917, PA-AA, R 16919.

29. Memorandum, de Grey, October 31, 1945, NA, HW 3/177; Freeman, "Zimmermann Telegram Revisited," 118, note 46, argues persuasively that it was indeed Knox who first received the telegram.
30. Memorandum, de Grey, October 31, 1945, NA, HW 3/177.
31. HALL, 10.
32. Telegram decrypt, NA, HW 3/187, with Hall's handwritten note on top left: "Main line—not exposed." See Freeman, "Zimmermann Telegram Revisited," 114, 117–18. For an overview of the decryption process, see Kahn, Codebreakers, 286.
33. HALL, 11–12.
34. Hall and Peaslee, Three Wars, 9–10.
35. HALL, 11–12.
36. Freeman, "MI1(b)," 217.
37. Cited in Friedman and Mendelsohn, Zimmermann Telegram, 24.
38. Freeman, "Zimmermann Telegram Revisited," 121.
39. HALL, 13.
40. Ibid., 12, 14.
41. See chapter 8. He obscured the fact that the British had plucked the telegram from American cables.
42. Freeman, "Zimmermann Telegram Revisited," 121–22.
43. Freeman, "Zimmermann Telegram Revisited," 121–22.
44. HALL, 12.
45. Ibid.,13.
46. Freeman, "Zimmermann Telegram Revisited," 123; email, Freeman to author, April 10, 2006: "there is no evidence that the Admiralty ever sent this [i.e., Zimmermann's telegram to Eckardt of February 5, 1917] to the FO."
47. Gaunt, Yield of the Years, 256; HALL, 16; Cooper, Walter Hines Page, 364.
48. DID to naval attaché New York, February 5, 1917, "sent 1000," NA, HW 3/178.
49. Hohler, Diplomatic Petrel, 223–24. HALL, 7–10, recounts a variation of the same story, probably relying on information provided by Hohler. The tale sounds somewhat improbable but cannot be disproved. That Hohler planted a spy in the Mexican telegraph office seems certain.
50. Cummins, Mexico, to FO, September 22, 1917, NA, FO 371/3068.
51. HALL, 17. Hall mistakenly gives the date for his telegram to Gaunt as February 6. For a different interpretation of the sequence of events, see Freeman, "Zimmermann Telegram Revisited," 123, note 66.
52. HALL, 18.
53. Kahn, Codebreakers, 289.
54. See Edmonds, "Persian Gulf Prelude."
55. Freeman, "Zimmermann Telegram Revisited," 141.
56. Andrew, Secret Service, 107.
57. For a British reconstruction of the German 13040 codebook, see NA, HW 3/176.
58. Freeman, "Zimmermann Telegram Revisited," 138–41, persuasively dismisses the notion that Room 40 used a captured German codebook.
59. For de Grey's handwritten decrypt, dated February 19, 1917, and a typewritten version thereof, see NA, HW 3/187.

Chapter 8. A Special Relationship

1. Gaunt, Yield of the Years, 135.
2. Beesly, Room 40, 228–29.
3. Gaunt, Yield of the Years, 137–38.
4. Seymour, Intimate Papers, vol. 2, 426.
5. House to Balfour, November 23, 1916, cited in Sanders and Taylor, British Propaganda, 180.
6. Herbert Yardley, cited in Beesly, Room 40, 233.

7. On American intelligence during World War I, see Jeffreys-Jones, *American Espionage*, 46–47. For Polk, see Srodes, *Allen Dulles*, 48; and Jeffreys-Jones, *American Espionage*, 44–45. For Harrison and the establishment and operations of BSI, see Lansing, *War Memoirs*, 318–25.
8. Srodes, *Allen Dulles*, 50–52.
9. Kahn, "Edward Bell," 144–47.
10. Lansing, *War Memoirs*, 318–19.
11. Cooper, *Walter Hines Page*, 355.
12. Handwritten note, Balfour, January 12, 1917, and response, Drummond, NA, FO 800/383.
13. Rintelen, *Dark Invader*, xiv–xxii.
14. Beesly, *Room 40*, 229–30. After the U.S. entry into the war, Rintelen was extradited to the United States and sentenced to four years in prison. He was released in 1920.
15. Beesly, *Room 40*, 228; Bernstorff, *My Three Years*, 197–99.
16. Thomson, *The Scene Changes*, entry, September 4, 1915.
17. Doerries, *Imperial Challenge*, 115.
18. Beesly, *Room 40*, 232; for operational consequences of the Papen papers, see Boghardt, *Spies of the Kaiser*, 125.
19. Tóibín, "Tragedy of Roger Casement," 53, 56.
20. O'Halpin, "British Intelligence in Ireland," 60.
21. William Dean Howells, letter to the editor, *New York Evening Post*, May 8, 1916, cited in Link, *Wilson: Campaigns*, 13.
22. Tóibín, "Tragedy of Roger Casement," 54.
23. Porter, *Plots and Paranoia*, 134, 144.
24. Thomson, *The Scene Changes*, 296, entry, April 23, 1916.
25. Sanders and Taylor, *British Propaganda*, 175.
26. James, *Eyes of the Navy*, 112–15.
27. HALL, 12.
28. Ibid., 17.
29. Ibid., 17. On Hardinge's interactions with Hall generally, see Hardinge, *Old Diplomacy*, 205; Tomes, *Balfour and Foreign Policy*, 17; Zebel, *Balfour*, 232; and Beesly, *Room 40*, 199, 235.
30. HALL, 20.
31. Balfour to Spring Rice, February 20, 1917, NA, FO 115/2266.
32. Spring Rice to Balfour, February 23, 1917, NA, FO 115/2266.
33. Balfour to Greene, Admiralty, February 17, 1917, NA, FO 800/204.
34. Thurstan to Balfour and Spring Rice, February 26, 1917, NA, FO 204/488.
35. Memorandum, Spring Rice, March 12, 1917, NA, FO 115/2266.
36. See chapter 7.
37. HALL, 19.
38. Bell, Tokyo, to Hurley, Washington, July 13, 1921, NARA, RG 59, Office of the Counselor, entry 539, box 7, folder 1.
39. HALL, 20.
40. Ibid., 17.
41. Campbell to Hardinge, February 20, 1917, HALL, 21.
42. Memorandum, Hardinge, no date, HALL, 21–22.
43. Note, Balfour, no date, HALL, 22.
44. Cooper, *Walter Hines Page*, 367.
45. Memorandum, Laughlin, "Interception of the Zimmermann Note in 1917," no date, Herbert Hoover Library, Irwin Boyle Laughlin papers. Laughlin wrote some time after the war from memory, and his account is somewhat confused. It confirms, however, that Hall called on him and that he did not know of the telegram at this point in time.

46. Quotes are from Cooper, *Walter Hines Page*, 368.
47. Memorandum, de Grey, October 31, 1945, NA, HW 3/177; Bell to Hurley, July 13, 1921, NARA, RG 59, entry 539, box 7, folder 1.
48. Page to Lansing, February 24, 1917, *FRUS*, 1917, supplement 1; a copy of the telegram handed to Page can be found in NA, HW 3/187, with Hall's handwritten comment, "Inland cable on American soil—this was the one handed to Dr Page and exposed [published] by the President."
49. For the Foreign Office's reminder to Page about secrecy, see Drummond to Page, February 23, 1917, NARA, RG 59, Office of the Counselor, entry 543, box 5, file 123.
50. Dugdale, *Balfour*, vol. 2, 138.
51. Cooper, *Walter Hines Page*, 368.
52. Page to Lansing, February 24, 1917, 2 a.m., cited in Hendrick, *Life and Letters*, vol. 3, 332.
53. Bell to Hurley, July 13, 1921, NARA, RG 59, Office of the Counselor, entry 539, box 7, folder 1.
54. Page to Lansing, February 24, 1917, 1 p.m., cited in Hendrick, *Life and Letters*, vol. 3, 333–34.
55. HALL, 25–26.
56. Page to Lansing, February 24, 1917, *FRUS*, 1917, supplement 1.
57. "Effort will be made," Lansing wrote Page, "to secure copies of all German cipher messages as far back as possible." Lansing to Page, February 28, 1917, *FRUS*, 1917, supplement 1.
58. Memorandum, Lansing, March 4, 1917, cited in Lansing, *War Memoirs*, 228. Polk obtained the Western Union telegrams on February 27.
59. Winkler, *Nexus*, 121–22.
60. Lansing to Page, February 28, 1917, *FRUS*, 1917, supplement 1.
61. Page to Lansing, March 1, 1917, cited in Hendrick, *Life and Letters*, vol. 3, 344.
62. Freeman, "Zimmermann Telegram Revisited," 126–27.
63. HALL, 26–27.
64. Lansing to Page, March 1, 1917, *FRUS*, 1917, supplement 1.
65. Bell to Hurley, July 13, 1921, NARA, RG 59, Office of the Counselor, entry 539, box 7, folder 1.
66. HALL, 28.
67. Memorandum, de Grey, October 31, 1945, NA, HW 3/177.
68. Bell's and de Grey's telegram decrypt is in NARA, RG 59, decimal file 862.20212, M 336, roll 55.
69. Kahn, *Codebreakers*, 294.
70. HALL, 28
71. Page to Lansing, March 2, 1917, cited in Hendrick, *Life and Letters*, vol. 3, 345.
72. Diary, Chandler Anderson, entry, March 11, 1917, LC, Chandler Anderson papers.
73. Balfour to Thurstan, February 27, 1917, NA, FO 115/2266.
74. Thurstan to Balfour, February 27, 1917, NA, FO 115/2266.
75. Page to Lansing, March 1, 1917, NARA, RG 59, decimal file 862.20212, M 336, roll 55.
76. Balfour to Spring Rice and Thurstan, March 14, 1917, NA, FO 115/2266.
77. Spring Rice to Balfour, March 12, 1917, NA, FO 115/2266.
78. Hohler, Washington, to Hardinge, London, March 23, 1917, Hardinge papers, vol. 31, referring to a conversation with House on March 9, 1917.
79. Memorandum, Thurstan, June 23, 1917, cited in Katz, *Secret War*, 466.
80. Gaunt to Hall, February 26, 1917, NA, HW 3/178.
81. Hall to Gaunt, February 27, 1917, NA, HW 3/178.
82. Hall to Gaunt, March 1, 1917, NA, HW 3/178.

Chapter 9. The Smoking Gun

1. Memorandum, Montgelas, January 17, 1917, GFM, Mexiko 16, secret, NARA, T 149, roll 378; for details, see chapter 5.
2. Report, Göppert, April 4, 1917, PA-AA, R 16919; von zur Gathen, "Zimmermann Telegram," 20–22.
3. Bernstorff, *My Three Years*, 380.
4. Bernstorff to AA, January 19, 1917, cited in Bernstorff, *My Three Years*, 359.
5. Bernstorff to AA, January 27, 1917, and AA to Bernstorff, January 29, 1917, both cited in Doerries, *Imperial Challenge*, 216–17.
6. Memorandum, Lansing, February 4, 1917, cited in Lansing, *War Memoirs*, 210–12; Bernstorff, *My Three Years*, 379.
7. Elkus, Constantinople, to Lansing, January 8, 1917, *FRUS*, 1917, supplement 1.
8. Gerard, Berlin, to Lansing, January 10, 1917, *FRUS*, 1917, supplement 1.
9. Lansing, "Note on the Probable Renewal of Submarine Warfare," January 24, 1917, cited in Lansing, *War Memoirs*, 206–7.
10. Memorandum, Lansing, February 4, 1917, cited in Lansing, *War Memoirs*, 210.
11. MacMillan, *Paris 1919*, 5.
12. On Wilson's life and presidency, see Cooper, *Woodrow Wilson*.
13. House had never served in the military but found it useful to sport the honorary title "colonel," which an appreciative benefactor had conferred upon him. See Ross, *Propaganda for War*, 148.
14. Seymour, *Intimate Papers*, vol. 1, 114.
15. Cooper, *Woodrow Wilson*, 318.
16. Ibid., 367.
17. Link, *Wilson: Campaigns*, 291–96.
18. Memorandum, Lansing, February 4, 1917, cited in Lansing, *War Memoirs*, 210–12.
19. Link, *Wilson: Campaigns*, 296–97.
20. Houston, *Eight Years*, vol. 1, 229.
21. Franklin Lane to George Lane, February 9, 1917, in Lane, *Letters*, 233–34.
22. Spring Rice to FO, February 17, 1917, NA, FO 371/3109.
23. "Convoys for Shipping," *Washington Post*, February 14, 1917.
24. Franklin Lane to George Lane, February 9, 1917, in Lane, *Letters*, 234.
25. Franklin Lane to George Lane, February 16, 1917, in Lane, *Letters*, 237; Cronon, *Cabinet Diaries*, 105–106.
26. Houston, *Eight Years*, vol. 1, 232, 235.
27. Mirow, *Seekrieg*, 140.
28. Spring Rice to FO, February 10, 1917, NA, FO 371/3108.
29. Houston, *Eight Years*, vol. 1, 235–36.
30. Franklin Lane to George Lane, February 25, 1917, in Lane, *Letters*, 240.
31. Nickles, *Under the Wire*, 149.
32. Memorandum, Lansing, March 4, 1917, cited in Lansing, *War Memoirs*, 229.
33. House diary, February 26, 1917, Yale University Library, House papers.
34. Lansing did not return to Washington until February 27, by which time "I found Polk had [already] obtained the original cipher message filed [with Western Union] by Bernstorff." See memorandum, Lansing, March 4, 1917, cited in Lansing, *War Memoirs*, 228.
35. Polk to Fletcher, February 26, 1917, *FRUS*, 1917, supplement 1.
36. Fletcher to State Department, February 26, 1917, *FRUS*, 1917, supplement 1.
37. Lansing to Page, February 27, 1917, *FRUS*, 1917, supplement 1.
38. Fletcher to State Department, March 10, 1917, *FRUS*, 1917, supplement 1. Only after Washington's declaration of war did Carranza declare Mexico's strict neutrality, thereby openly rejecting an alliance with Germany.
39. Memorandum, Polk, February 23, 1917, Yale University Library, Polk papers, confidential diary, vol. 1.

40. Memorandum, Polk, February 28, 1917, Yale University Library, Polk papers, confidential diary, vol. 2.
41. Guthrie, Tokyo, to State Department, March 3, 1917, *FRUS*, 1917, supplement 1.
42. House diary, February 26, 1917, Yale University Library, House papers.
43. Wilson to House, February 26, 1917, in Link, *Papers of Woodrow Wilson*, vol. 41.
44. House to Wilson, February 27, 1917, in Seymour, *Intimate Papers*, vol. 2. For House's tip to Gaunt, see chapter 7.
45. *Proceedings of the 64th Congress*, March 1, 1917, 4599; Link, *Wilson: Campaigns*, 346, denies this claim. Katz, *Secret War*, 359, suggests the telegram reached Wilson "at an opportune moment." Tuchman, *Zimmermann Telegram*, 170, contends the president sought to use the telegram to preempt a looming Senate filibuster against his armed ships bill. Nassua, *Gemeinsame Kriegführung*, 62, argues that Wilson sought to sway Congress in favor of the bill by publishing the telegram on the day of the House vote.
46. May, *World War*, 422.
47. Cooper, *Vanity of Power*, 176: "Two simultaneous events [the telegram and the sinking of the *Laconia*] insured that armed neutrality would be considered entirely in light of the prospect of intervention."
48. Seymour, *Intimate Papers*, 452.
49. *Congressional Record*, 64th Cong., 2nd Sess., March 1, 1917, 54:4595.
50. Lansing desk diary, Tuesday, February 27, 1917, LC, Lansing papers.
51. Phillips, *Ventures in Diplomacy*, 80.
52. Lansing desk diary, Tuesday, February 27, 1917, LC, Lansing papers.
53. Memorandum, Lansing, March 4, 1917, cited in Lansing, *War Memoirs*, 228.
54. Cabinet diaries, Josephus Daniels, Tuesday, February 27, 1917, LC, Daniels papers.
55. "A News Report," no date, in Link, *Papers of Woodrow Wilson*, vol. 41, 302–4.
56. Link, *Wilson: Campaigns*, 345.
57. Memorandum, Lansing, March 4, 1917, cited in Lansing, *War Memoirs*, 228.
58. Tuchman, *Zimmermann Telegram*, 174.
59. Memorandum, Lansing, March 4, 1917, cited in Lansing, *War Memoirs*, 228; Lansing desk diary, Wednesday, February 28, 1917, LC, Lansing papers.
60. On Hitchcock, see Cooper, *Vanity of Power*, 28; and Fleming, *Illusion of Victory*, 31.
61. Memorandum, Lansing March 4, 1917, cited in Lansing, *War Memoirs*, 229.
62. Lansing desk diary, Wednesday, February 28, 1917, LC, Lansing papers.
63. Memorandum, Lansing, March 4, 1917, cited in Lansing, *War Memoirs*, 229.
64. House diary, February 28, 1917, Yale University Library, House papers.
65. Memorandum, Lansing, March 4, 1917, cited in Lansing, *War Memoirs*, 230.
66. Lansing desk diary, Wednesday, February 28, 1917, LC, Lansing papers.
67. For the published text and accompanying AP explanatory note, see *New York Times*, March 1, 1917; for a linguistic critique of the "generous Anglo-Saxon translation practice," see Koopmann, *Diplomatie*, 292.
68. Chalkley, *Zach Lamar Cobb*, 58, 84, 86.
69. Letter, Lansing to Edward N. Smith, March 3, 1917, LC, Lansing papers, vol. 35. Smith was a personal friend of Lansing's.
70. *Congressional Record*, 64th Cong., 2nd Sess., March 1, 1917, 54:4600; Lansing memorandum, March 4, 1917, cited in Lansing, *War Memoirs*, 230–31.
71. HALL, 33.
72. Lansing desk diary, March 1, 1917, LC, Lansing papers.
73. House diary, March 1, 1917, Yale University Library, House papers; only the United Press correspondent was unhappy because Lansing had given the telegram to the rival AP. Ever keen on maintaining excellent relations with all press organs, House asked Wilson "to see that the U.P. get the next sensation."
74. Lansing, *War Memoirs*, 232.

Chapter 10. Congress Debates the Telegram

1. Cooper, *Woodrow Wilson*, 358.
2. Cooper, *Vanity of Power*, 178.
3. Memoir, Lansing, March 4, 1917, cited in Lansing, *War Memoirs*, 229.
4. Cooper, *Vanity of Power*, 179–80.
5. *Congressional Record*, 64th Cong., 2nd Sess., March 1, 1917, 54:4603.
6. Cooper, *Vanity of Power*, 182–83.
7. Ibid., 181.
8. "Text of the President's Statement to the Public," *New York Times*, March 5, 1917.
9. Cooper, *Vanity of Power*, 174–89; Millis, *Road to War*, 410.
10. Lodge to Roosevelt, March 2, 1917, Roosevelt, *Correspondence*, vol. 2, 499.
11. *Congressional Record*, 64th Cong., 2nd Sess., March 1, 1917, 54:4569–70.
12. Tuchman, *Zimmermann Telegram*, 177.
13. *Congressional Record*, 64th Cong., 2nd Sess., March 1, 1917, 54:4598, 4603–5.
14. Lodge to Roosevelt, March 2, 1917, in Roosevelt, *Correspondence*, vol. 2, 500.
15. *Congressional Record*, 64th Cong., 2nd Sess., March 1, 1917, 54:4571.
16. *Congressional Record*, 64th Cong., 2nd Sess., March 1, 1917, 54:4570–71.
17. *Congressional Record*, 64th Cong., 2nd Sess., March 1, 1917, 54:4571.
18. *Congressional Record*, 64th Cong., 2nd Sess., March 1, 1917, 54:4572.
19. *Congressional Record*, 64th Cong., 2nd Sess., March 1, 1917, 54:4604.
20. See the AP note, as reprinted in the *New York Times*, March 1, 1917: "This document has been in the hands of the Government since President Wilson broke off diplomatic relations with Germany. It has been kept secret while the President has been asking Congress for full authority to deal with Germany, and while Congress has been hesitating. It was in the President's hands while Chancellor [Theobald] von Bethmann Hollweg was declaring that the United States had placed an interpretation on the submarine declaration 'never intended by Germany' and that Germany had promoted and honored friendly relations with the United States 'as an heirloom from Frederick the Great.'" Lansing certainly did not deliberately provide AP correspondent Hood with a false date when informing him of the telegram on February 28, therefore a simple misunderstanding between the two men is the most likely explanation for the AP's misstatement.
21. *Congressional Record*, 64th Cong., 2nd Sess., March 1, 1917, 54:4569, 4571–72, 4596, 4599, 4604.
22. Lodge to Roosevelt, March 2, 1917, in Roosevelt, *Correspondence*, vol. 2, 499.
23. For Stone, see Towne, *Senator William J. Stone*.
24. *Congressional Record*, 64th Cong., 2nd Sess., March 1, 1917, 54:4593.
25. *Congressional Record*, 64th Cong., 2nd Sess., March 1, 1917, 54:4593.
26. *Congressional Record*, 64th Cong., 2nd Sess., March 1, 1917, 54:4593
27. *Congressional Record*, 64th Cong., 2nd Sess., March 1, 1917, 54:4593.
28. *Congressional Record*, 64th Cong., 2nd Sess., March 1, 1917, 54:4593.
29. *Congressional Record*, 64th Cong., 2nd Sess., March 1, 1917, 54:4594.
30. *Congressional Record*, 64th Cong., 2nd Sess., March 1, 1917, 54:4594.
31. *Congressional Record*, 64th Cong., 2nd Sess., March 1, 1917, 54:4594.
32. *Congressional Record*, 64th Cong., 2nd Sess., March 1, 1917, 54:4594.
33. *Congressional Record*, 64th Cong., 2nd Sess., March 1, 1917, 54:4594–95.
34. *Congressional Record*, 64th Cong., 2nd Sess., March 1, 1917, 54:4595.
35. *Congressional Record*, 64th Cong., 2nd Sess., March 1, 1917, 54:4595.
36. *Congressional Record*, 64th Cong., 2nd Sess., March 1, 1917, 54:4596.
37. *Congressional Record*, 64th Cong., 2nd Sess., March 1, 1917, 54:4596.
38. *Congressional Record*, 64th Cong., 2nd Sess., March 1, 1917, 54:4597.
39. *Congressional Record*, 64th Cong., 2nd Sess., March 1, 1917, 54:4597.
40. *Congressional Record*, 64th Cong., 2nd Sess., March 1, 1917, 54:4597.
41. *Congressional Record*, 64th Cong., 2nd Sess., March 1, 1917, 54:4601.

42. *Congressional Record,* 64th Cong., 2nd Sess., March 1, 1917, 54:4603.
43. *Congressional Record,* 64th Cong., 2nd Sess., March 1, 1917, 54:4618.

Chapter 11. The American Public

1. Memorandum, Lansing, March 4, 1917, cited in Lansing, *War Memoirs,* 229.
2. Lansing, *War Memoirs,* 232.
3. Wellington House, "American Press Resumé," March 7, 1917, cited in Peterson, *Propaganda for War,* 314.
4. HALL, 27.
5. Tuchman, *Zimmermann Telegram,* 199.
6. Link, *Wilson: Campaigns,* 354.
7. Nassua, *Gemeinsame Kriegführung,* 65.
8. Cooper, *Woodrow Wilson,* 378.
9. The sample includes the *Albuquerque Morning Journal, Arizona Republican, Atlanta Journal, Boston Globe, Chicago Daily Tribune, Dallas Morning News, Florida Times-Union, Houston Post, Los Angeles Times, Milwaukee Journal, Milwaukee Sentinel, New York American, New York Times, New Yorker Staats-Zeitung, News and Courier* (Charleston, S.C.), *San Antonio Express, San Francisco Chronicle, Santa Fe New Mexican, Savannah Tribune, Tucson Citizen, Washington Post, Wisconsin State Journal.* The *New Yorker Staats-Zeitung* had the largest circulation (120,000) among German American newspapers. Due to its size and editorial weight, it is included in this sample as well as in the analysis of German American papers below.
10. Memorandum, Spring Rice, December 29, 1916, NA, FO 800/242.
11. *New York World,* February 1, 1917, and *New York Times,* February 1, 1917.
12. See editorials in the *Chicago Daily Tribune, Milwaukee Journal, New Yorker Staats-Zeitung,* and *San Francisco Chronicle,* February 1, 1917; *New York American,* quoted in Millis, *Road to War,* 387; *Dallas Morning News* and *Houston Post,* February 2, 1917. The *Staats-Zeitung*'s "wait and see" stance was not dissimilar to Wilson's subsequently adopted "overt act" policy.
13. See editorials in the *Milwaukee Sentinel,* February 1, 1917, and *Florida Times-Union,* February 2, 1917.
14. *Arizona Republican, Albuquerque Morning Journal,* both February 1, 1917; *Tucson Citizen, Santa Fe New Mexican, San Antonio Express,* all February 2, 1917.
15. Peterson, *Propaganda for War,* 8.
16. See editorials in the *Washington Post,* February 20 and February 28, 1917; *Florida Times-Union,* February 25 and February 28, 1917; *San Francisco Chronicle,* February 27, 1917; and *Arizona Republican,* February 28, 1917.
17. Spring Rice to FO, February 2, 1917, NA, FO 800/242.
18. Spring Rice to Balfour, February 9, 1917, NA, FO 371/3109.
19. Letter, Spring Rice, February 23, 1917, NA, FO 800/242.
20. Spring Rice to FO, February 20, 1917, NA, FO 371/3109; Spring Rice to FO, February 24, 1917, ibid.; and Spring Rice to FO, February 23, 1917, NA, FO 800/211.
21. House diary, February 24, 1917, Yale University Library, House papers.
22. Letter, Spring Rice, February 23, 1917, NA, FO 800/242.
23. Lansing to Edward N. Smith, February 27, 1917, LC, Lansing papers, vol. 24.
24. Cooper, *Vanity of Power,* 167.
25. Tuchman, *Zimmermann Telegram,* 185.
26. See editorials in the *Boston Globe, Los Angeles Times, Milwaukee Journal, News and Courier, Santa Fe New Mexican,* March 1, 1917; in *Albuquerque Morning Journal, Atlanta Journal, Chicago Tribune,* and *New York World,* March 2, 1917; and in *Tucson Citizen,* March 3, 1917.
27. *Arizona Republican* and *New York Times,* March 2, 1917.

28. *Houston Post, New Yorker Staats-Zeitung,* and *Washington Post,* March 2, 1917.
29. *Florida Times-Union* and *San Francisco Chronicle,* March 2, 1917. See below, note 33, for the *Milwaukee Sentinel.* The remaining papers variably uttered caution, surprise, and disgust. None of them regarded the telegram as a casus belli. The Missouri press portrayed the telegram as either insidious or ridiculous. See Crighton, *Missouri,* 177–78.
30. Katz, *Secret War,* 361.
31. Lansing, *War Memoirs,* 231–32.
32. Memorandum, Lansing, March 4, 1917, cited in Lansing, *War Memoirs,* 231. Following in Lansing's footsteps, Tuchman, *Zimmermann Telegram,* 183. Zimmermann's motives for admitting his authorship are explored in the following chapter.
33. *Dallas Morning News, Houston Post, New York Times,* and *San Francisco Chronicle,* March 2, 1917. It is true that the hitherto pro-German *Milwaukee Sentinel* called the telegram "serious if authentic" and counseled postponement of a final judgment until the German foreign secretary had had a chance to comment. Even the *Sentinel,* however, voiced no serious doubt about the telegram's authenticity, as the editorial went on to play it down as "a move on the diplomatic chessboard," quite common in European diplomacy, and conceded that "adequate measures" must be "taken by the government for the full protection of the honor and interests and possessions of this republic." *Milwaukee Sentinel,* March 2, 1917.
34. Gaunt to Hall, March 6, 1917, HALL, 30.
35. Tuchman, *Zimmermann Telegram,* 181, argues that the Round Table dinner represented an example of genuine doubt about the telegram's authenticity.
36. For example, see Link, *Wilson: Campaigns,* 356.
37. Doerries, "Promoting *Kaiser* and *Reich,*" 149.
38. Telegram, Viereck to Burleson, March 1, 1917, LC, Burleson papers, 2886–88.
39. Viereck, *Strangest Friendship,* 190.
40. Mugridge, *View from Xanadu,* 114.
41. *New York American,* March 2, 1917.
42. Viereck, *Germs of Hate,* 114.
43. Tuchman, *Zimmermann Telegram,* 185, portrays Viereck as a "leader of pro-German sentiment" at the time of the telegram's disclosure.
44. Devlin, *Too Proud to Fight,* 651–52.
45. *New York Times,* March 2, 1917, comments by Herman Metz and Ludwig Nissen, respectively.
46. The following review of ten German American newspapers is based on Nassua, *Gemeinsame Kriegführung,* 93–106. Unless otherwise noted, all quotes were translated from German into English by the author here.

Chapter 12. War

1. Hall to Gaunt, March 1, 1917, NA, HW 3/178.
2. Gaunt to Hall, March 1, 1917, NA, HW 3/178.
3. British propaganda report to Norman Thwaites, April 20, 1917, NA, FO 115/2185.
4. Lansing to Wilson, March 19, 1917, in *FRUS, Lansing Papers,* vol. 1.
5. Link, "That Cobb Interview"; Fleming, *Illusion of Victory,* 6.
6. Roosevelt to Lodge, March 18, 1917, Roosevelt, *Correspondence,* vol. 2, 504.
7. Hohler to Hardinge, March 23, 1917, Cambridge University Library, Hardinge papers, vol. 31.
8. Cronon, *Cabinet Diaries of Josephus Daniels,* March 20, 1917.
9. Link, *Papers of Woodrow Wilson,* 401–8.
10. Hodgson, *Woodrow Wilson's Right Hand,* 139.
11. Franklin K. Lane to George W. Lane, April 1, 1917, in Lane, *Letters,* 242.
12. Tumulty, *Woodrow Wilson,* 256. Fleming, *Illusion of Victory,* 21, doubts the accuracy of the presidential crying scene.

13. Cooper, *Woodrow Wilson*, 387, calls it "the greatest presidential speech since Lincoln's second inaugural address."
14. Leonard, *War Addresses*, 41–42.
15. For a description of reactions to Wilson's speech, see Link, *Wilson: Campaigns*, 430.
16. "Is La Follette Mad?" *Madison Democrat*, April 6, 1917.
17. Fleming, *Illusion of Victory*, 31–32.
18. Link, *Wilson: Campaigns*, 430.
19. For accounts of La Follette's speech and reactions thereto, see Cooper, *Vanity of Power*, 198; Millis, *Road to War*, 440, 453; and Fleming, *Illusion of Victory*, 30–37.
20. Fleming, *Illusion of Victory*, 36.
21. Ibid., 37–42.
22. "Debate Lasted 16 1/2 Hours," *New York Times*, April 6, 1917.
23. Foreign intelligence post (*Auslandsnachrichtenstelle*) of the AA to Kemnitz and Montgelas, April 10, 1917, GFM, Mexiko 16, vol. 1, NARA, T 149, roll 378. Zimmermann initialed the report on the same day.
24. Fleming, *Illusion of Victory*, 37–42.
25. Cooper, "United States," 437, 441.
26. Roosevelt to Lodge, April 6, 1917, in Roosevelt, *Correspondence*, vol. 2, 507.
27. "Toasts Kaiser, Is Hanged. Man in Wyoming Is Cut Down and Driven from Town," *New York Times*, April 3, 1917.
28. Lansing to Senator Claude A. Swanson, March 29, 1917, LC, Lansing papers, vol. 25; Franklin K. Lane to George W. Lane, April 1, 1917, Lane, *Letters*, 243. For U.S. war sentiment in March, see generally Cooper, *Vanity of Power*, 191.
29. Memorandum, Spring Rice, March 9, 1917, NA, FO 800/242.
30. Fleming, *Illusion of Victory*, 82.
31. Ibid., 14.
32. Millis, *Road to War*, 433–34. The injured man, Alexander Bannwart, was of Swiss German descent.
33. Cooper, *Vanity of Power*, 206; Unger, *La Follette*, 343, note 26.
34. Spring Rice to Hardinge, April 13, 1917, Cambridge University Library, Hardinge papers, vol. 31.
35. Keith, "Southern Draft Resistance," 1338.
36. Link, *Wilson: Campaigns*, 391, 429, note 103.
37. As Cooper, "United States," 437, points out, "Contrary to the fulminations of war hawks like Roosevelt, an outraged public was not forcing a reluctant Wilson into war."
38. "German Plotting in Mexico," *Washington Post*, March 16, 1917.
39. Burk, *Sinews of War*, 81.
40. Minutes, war cabinet meeting, December 9, 1916, CAB 23/1, LC.
41. "The Duty of Americans," *Florida Times-Union*, April 6, 1917.

Chapter 13. Fallout in Berlin

1. *Berliner Lokalanzeiger* telephone service from Holland, March 2, 1917, GFM, Mexiko 16, secret, NARA, T 149, roll 378.
2. As cited in "Defending 'Plot,' Zimmermann Accuses U.S.," *Washington Post*, March 4, 1917.
3. Lansing, *War Memoirs*, 228; Tuchman, *Zimmermann Telegram*, 183; Katz, *Secret War*, 372, contends that a flat-out denial would "undoubtedly have been the most clever maneuver."
4. HALL, 31.
5. The notion that Zimmermann first admitted his role to Hale appears to originate with Hale himself. See Ross, *Propaganda for War*, 141, quoting from Hale's papers at Yale University. See also Viereck, *Strangest Friendship*, 190, and Tuchman, *Zimmermann Telegram*, 183. For Zimmermann's statement to the anonymous

Overseas News Agency correspondent, see "Defending 'Plot,' Zimmermann Accuses U.S.," *Washington Post*, March 4, 1917.

6. Peter Freeman explained Hall's decision to pass up on releasing the February 5 message thus: "The ZT stands alone as demonstrating German perfidy; if we add the 5 Feb message, which is frankly a bit of a detail, there is a danger of diluting the impact. What will German security authorities think? The ZT went via Washington and there are plenty of potential suspects, but the 5 Feb message went only to Mexico City and there are only two people there (Eckardt and Magnus) who read it. And the Germans (unlike the Americans) will know about the Swedes' part in transmitting the 5 Feb message; we do not plan to give the Germans any idea that the British were involved at all in the acquisition of the ZT, but every new revelation (especially when the technical details of transmission are different—the only common factors between the ZT and the 5 Feb message are that they were transmitted via London, arrived in Mexico, and were encoded in 13040) is going to make that a bit more difficult to conceal from them." Email, Freeman to author, April 18, 2006.

7. Zimmermann to Lucius, February 17, 1917, cited in Iklé, "Japanese-German Peace Negotiations," 75; memorandum, Ludendorff to Bethmann, February 26, 1917, ibid.

8. Bethmann to Ludendorff, March 3, 1917, cited in Iklé, "Japanese-German Peace Negotiations," 75.

9. Hayashima, *Illusion des Sonderfriedens*, 151.

10. *Leipziger Zeitung*, March 5, 1917, cited in Katz, *Secret War*, 370.

11. *Vorwärts*, March 4, 1917.

12. Wolff, *Tagebücher*, vol. 1, entry no. 525, March 2, 1917; *Berliner Tageblatt*, March 5, 1917, cited in Katz, *Secret War*, 371.

13. *Frankfurter Zeitung*, March 5, 1917, evening edition.

14. Erdmann, *Riezler: Tagebücher*, entry, March 4, 1917.

15. Lerchenfeld to Hertling, March 20, 1917, in Deuerlein, *Briefwechsel*, entry no. 357.

16. *Deutsche Tageszeitung*, March 3, 1917.

17. Wolff, *Tagebücher*, vol. 1, no. 526, entry, March 5, 1917, and no. 547, entry, April 3, 1917; Lerchenfeld, Berlin, to Hertling, Munich, March 20, 1917, in Deuerlein, *Briefwechsel*, doc. no. 357.

18. Wolff, *Tagebücher*, vol. 1, no. 590, entry, August 15, 1917.

19. Egan, Constantinople, to secretary of state, March 16, 1917, NARA, RG 59, decimal file 862.20212, M 336, roll 55.

20. *National-Zeitung*, March 6, 1917; *Kölnische Zeitung*, March 3, 1917, both cited in Katz, *Secret War*, 369.

21. *Deutsche Tageszeitung*, March 6, 1917, cited in Katz, *Secret War*, 371.

22. *Vossische Zeitung*, March 5, 1917.

23. During the last two years of the war, while parliament was adjourned, the Reichstag's budget committee met on a regular basis, taking on the character of an executive agency for the broader body. See Chickering, *Imperial Germany*, 165.

24. Schiffers and Koch, *Hauptausschuss*, sessions of March 3 and 5, 1917, 1149–55; translation of Zimmermann's quote implicating Bernstorff adopted from Nickles, *Under the Wire*, 153.

25. Deutscher Reichstag, *Stenographische Berichte*, vol. 309, 95th session, March 29, 1917, 2836, 2863, 2874.

26. Hohenlohe to Austrian foreign ministry, March 3, 1917, cited in Katz, *Secret War*, 372.

27. "Kaiser calls Zimmermann for a Long Conference," *Washington Post*, March 4, 1917.

28. Nassua, *Gemeinsame Kriegführung*, 35–37.

29. Ludendorff, *Own Story*, vol. 2, 15.

30. Lerchenfeld to Hertling, May 31, 1917, in Deuerlein, *Briefwechsel*, doc. no. 369.

31. House to Hall, September 22, 1917, in Seymour, *Intimate Papers*, 454.

32. Chickering, *Imperial Germany,* 163–64; Hürter, "Die Staatssekretäre," 238.
33. Erdmann, *Riezler: Tagebücher,* entry, May 8, 1917.
34. Müller, in Görlitz, *Regierte der Kaiser?,* entry, July 12, 1917.
35. Boghardt, *Spies of the Kaiser,* 129–31; Zimmermann to Kühlmann, Constantinople, July 16, 1917, GFM, Unterstaatssekretär Zimmermann, NARA, T 137, roll 88.
36. Hayashima, *Illusion des Sonderfriedens,* 151.
37. For the history of the commission, see Fischer-Baling, "Der Untersuchungsausschuss," 117–19, 123–25; and Schnauber, "Die parlamentarische Untersuchung," 2, 7.
38. Link, *Wilson: Campaigns,* 344; and letter, Katz to Link, ibid., 433.
39. Transcript of commission's 11th session, November 14, 1919, Carnegie, *Official German Documents,* vol. 2, 715.
40. Vietsch, *Solf,* 197–98, 384.
41. Transcript of commission's 11th session, November 14, 1919, Carnegie, *Official German Documents,* vol. 2, 715.
42. Viereck, *Strangest Friendship,* 190.
43. Zimmermann, "Fürst Bülows Kritik," 234.
44. Hazen, *Giants and Ghosts,* 37–38.
45. Ibid., 4, 34, 37–38, 42–44.
46. "Dr. Zimmermann Dies in Germany," *New York Times,* June 8, 1940.

Chapter 14. Scapegoat

1. Doerries, *Imperial Challenge,* 228.
2. HALL, 34
3. Bernstorff, *My Three Years,* 406. Bernstorff suggests that "someone had laid the matter before the Kaiser in a distorted light." Given Zimmermann's efforts to deflect blame from himself, it is entirely possible that the "someone" could have been the foreign secretary or one of his supporters.
4. Nickles, *Under the Wire,* 153.
5. Michahelles, Christiania, to AA, March 10, 1917, GFM, Mexiko 16, vol. 1, NARA, T 149, roll 378.
6. Brockdorff-Rantzau to AA, March 11, 1917, cited in Katz, *Secret War,* 375.
7. *National Tidende* interview cited in von zur Gathen, "Zimmermann Telegram," 34.
8. Kemnitz set up the interview with the *Hamburger Fremdenblatt* editor in chief, Felix von Eckardt, March 7, 1917, GFM, Mexiko 16, vol. 1, NARA, T 149, roll 378.
9. "Strictly confidential for Col. House," Egan, Copenhagen, to secretary of state, March 16, 1917, NARA, RG 59, decimal file 862.20212, M 336, roll 55.
10. Vietsch, *Solf,* 197, 371.
11. Bernstorff, *My Three Years,* 404.
12. Ibid., 409.
13. Ibid., 413–14.
14. Wolff, *Tagebücher,* vol. 1, doc. no. 590, entry, August 15, 1917.
15. Bernstorff to Viereck, October 29, 1929, Hoover Institution, Viereck papers, box 2, folder XX237–10.V.
16. Bernstorff, *Memoirs,* 242, 266, 273–74, 285–87, 290–92.
17. Doerries, *Imperial Challenge,* 10–13.
18. Zimmermann's appointment of Göppert, March 17, 1917, GFM, Mexiko 16, secret, NARA, T 149, roll 378.
19. For Göppert, see Auswärtiges Amt, *Biographisches Handbuch,* vol. 2, s.v. "Göppert, Otto."
20. Statement, Schmid to Göppert, March 1917, cited in von zur Gathen, "Zimmermann Telegram," 22.
21. The telegram exchange between the foreign office and Eckardt is translated and reprinted in Hendrick, *Life and Letters,* vol. 3, 357–60.

22. Report, Göppert, April 4, 1917, PA-AA, R 16919. An English translation of Göppert's report can be found in "The Zimmermann Telegram," *Cryptologic Quarterly* 20, no. 1–2 (Summer/Spring 2001): 46–52. The journal is published by the National Security Agency. The author's name has been redacted.
23. Nickles, *Under the Wire*, 171–72. According to Nickles, the State Department used simplistic codes designed to save money rather than provide communications security.
24. Report, Göppert, April 4, 1917, PA-AA, R 16919.
25. AA notice, May 28, 1917, GFM, Mexiko 16, secret, NARA, T 149, roll 378.
26. Bernstorff, *Memoirs*, 402; Carnegie, *Official German Documents*, vol. 2, 480–81.
27. Lerchenfeld to Hertling, March 20, 1917, in Deuerlein, *Briefwechsel*, doc. no. 357.
28. Memorandum, director of cipher bureau, March 12, 1917, GFM, Mexiko 16, secret, NARA, T 149, roll 378.
29. Report, intelligence officer no. 2, Captain Schlenther, September 23, 1914, Collection Markus Pöhlmann, "Material über die Kompromittierung deutscher Chiffrierverfahren."
30. Report, intelligence officer no. 4, Captain Witte, November 3, 1914, Collection Markus Pöhlmann, "Material über die Kompromittierung deutscher Chiffrierverfahren."
31. Report, collection post Lörrach, November 17, 1914, Collection Markus Pöhlmann, "Material über die Kompromittierung deutscher Chiffrierverfahren."
32. Sektion IIIb to AA, March 13, 1917, GFM, Mexiko 16, secret, NARA, T 149, roll 378; and general staff to AA, March 27, 1917, cited in Katz, *Secret War*, 377.
33. Lucius, Stockholm, to foreign office, March 13, 1917, GFM, Mexiko, vol. 1, NARA, microcopy no. T 149, roll 378; memorandum, Kemnitz, summer 1927, "strictly confidential" attachment, PA-AA, Personalakte Kemnitz, vol. 7170.
34. Nickles, *Under the Wire*, 156.
35. Wedel, AA, to Eckardt, March 24, 1917, LC, Wilson papers, series 2, reel 92.
36. Freeman, "Zimmermann Telegram Revisited," 130, 133.
37. Ibid., 107.
38. Memorandum, Kemnitz, September 24, 1917, PA-AA, R 16463.
39. Different aspects of the Luxburg telegrams are covered by Doss, *Amt*, 46–79; Beesly, *Room 40*, 237–40; Katz, *Secret War*, 420; and Luxburg, *Erinnerungen*, 109–13.
40. Memorandum, Kemnitz, September 24, 1917, PA-AA, R 16463.
41. Denniston, *Thirty Secret Years*, 100.

Chapter 15. Aftermath in Mexico

1. Kunimoto, "Japan and Mexico," 240–42.
2. Eckardt to AA, February 26, 1917, GFM, Mexiko 16, vol. 1, NARA, T 149, roll 378.
3. Hayashima, *Illusion des Sonderfriedens*, 139.
4. Eckardt to AA, March 2, 1917, GFM, Mexiko 16, secret, NARA, T 149, roll 378.
5. Secret, Hülsen to AA, March 8, 1917, GFM, Mexiko 16, vol. 1, NARA, T 149, roll 378.
6. Nassua, *Gemeinsame Kriegführung*, 141, considers the military's offer "symbolic." Katz, *Secret War*, 379, describes it as "fraudulent."
7. Doerries, *Imperial Challenge*, 163.
8. Hülsen to Kemnitz, April 4, 1917, GFM, Mexiko 16, vol. 1, NARA, T 149, roll 378.
9. Top secret, admiralty staff to AA, March 8, 1917, GFM, Mexiko 16, vol. 1, NARA, T 149, roll 378.
10. Zimmermann to Lucius, for relay to Mexico, March 17, 1917, GFM, Mexiko 16, vol. 1, NARA, T 149, roll 378.
11. Memorandum, Kemnitz to Sektion P, March 28, 1917, GFM, Mexiko 16, vol. 1, NARA, T 149, roll 378.

12. Montgelas to Zimmermann, February 23, 1917, GFM, Mexiko 16, vol. 1, NARA, T 149, roll 378.
13. I am grateful to Phil Tomaselli for pointing out to me Kraft's status as a double agent and sharing documentary evidence to this effect. See Cummins, Mexico City, to FO and Spring Rice, September 22, 1917, NA, FO 371/3068. Without revealing their source, the British subsequently shared much of Kraft's information with the Americans. See R. Sperling, FO, to Bell, December 18, 1917, NARA, RG 59, Office of the Counselor, entry 543, box 5, confidential file 113.
14. Sektion P to AA, August 2, 1917, GFM, Mexiko 16, vol. 2, NARA, T 149, roll 378.
15. On the Jahnke-Dilger rivalry, see Koenig, *Fourth Horseman*, 228–30
16. Hülsen to AA, April 29, 1917, GFM, Mexiko 16, vol. 1, NARA, T 149, roll 378, designating Jahnke as Sektion P's principal agent and "Delmar" as the navy's man and refusing their subordination to Eckardt.
17. Eckardt to AA, February 21, 1918, GFM, Mexiko 16, vol. 2, NARA, T 149, roll 378, asking for subordination of Jahnke and Dilger to Eckardt.
18. Katz, *Secret War*, 382–83.
19. Sektion P to AA, August 2, 1918, GFM, Mexiko 16, vol. 2, NARA, T 149, roll 378.
20. Stumm to Maguerre, Sektion P, August 15, 1918, GFM, Mexiko 16, vol. 2, NARA, T 149, roll 378 (emphasis in the original).
21. Admiral Ebert to Eckardt, May 19, 1919, GFM, Mexiko 16, vol. 2, NARA, T 149, roll 378.
22. Koenig, *Fourth Horseman*, 263–67.
23. Report, Neunhoffer, March 29, 1919, NARA, RG 59, Office of the Counselor, entry 539, box 3, folder, "Dr. Heinrich von Eckardt's trip through U.S. to Mexico March 1919."
24. "Statement dictated by Heinrich von Eckhardt [*sic*], at New York City, on March 25th, 1919, to Wm. Neunhoffer, of the Department of Justice," NARA, RG 59, Office of the Counselor, entry 539, box 3, folder, "Dr. Heinrich von Eckardt's trip through U.S. to Mexico March 1919."
25. Report, Neunhoffer, March 29, 1919, NARA, RG 59, Office of the Counselor, entry 539, box 3, folder, "Dr. Heinrich von Eckardt's trip through U.S. to Mexico March 1919."
26. Auswärtiges Amt, *Biographisches Handbuch*, vol. 2, s.v. "Eckardt, Heinrich von."
27. Hazen, *Giants and Ghosts*, 45–52; Auswärtiges Amt, *Biographisches Handbuch*, vol. 2, s.v. "Eckardt, Heinrich von."
28. "May Take Post: Count Montgelas Being Considered as German Minister," *New York Times*, March 7, 1920; "Count Montgelas Is Dead in Berlin," *New York Times*, April 24, 1924; and Wolff, *Tagebücher*, vol. 1, 431, note 5.
29. Katz, *Pancho Villa*, 764–66.

Chapter 16. A German Reckoning

1. Chickering, *Imperial Germany*, 188; Vietsch, *Solf*, 197, 206, 216.
2. All original issues of that edition of the *Nürnberger Nachrichten* appear to have been lost. The article is referred to in a letter by Friedrich Katz to Arthur Link, quoted in Link, *Wilson: Campaigns*, 434. Katz informed this author that he did not have a copy of the article. Email, Katz to Boghardt, June 6, 2005. It is tempting to see the hand of Adolf von Montgelas behind the article, given Kemnitz's subsequent attempt to shift responsibility to Montgelas, the two men's natural rivalry as regional experts, and Montgelas' Bavarian background. Definitive proof, however, remains lacking.
3. Auswärtiges Amt, *Biographisches Handbuch*, vol. 2, s.v. "Kemnitz, Arthur von."
4. Kemnitz to Solf, November 24, 1918, GFM, Mexiko 16, vol. 2, NARA, T 149,

roll 378 (emphasis in the original, probably by Solf or his subordinate, Edmund Rhomberg).

5. Rhomberg to undersecretary of state, November 29, 1918, GFM, Mexiko 16, vol. 2, NARA, T 149, roll 378; and Rat der Volksbeauftragten (Council of the People's Representatives), signed by Wilhelm von Solf, Friedrich Ebert, and Hugo Haase, Berlin, December 11, 1918, PA-AA, Personalakte Kemnitz, vol. 7170.

6. Kemnitz to Schüler, April 11, 1919, PA-AA, Personalakte Kemnitz, vol. 7170.

7. Kemnitz to Schüler, June 29, 1919, PA-AA, Personalakte Kemnitz, vol. 7170.

8. Müller to Kemnitz, July 24, 1919, PA-AA, Personalakte Kemnitz, vol. 7170.

9. Kemnitz to AA, January 19, 1923, PA-AA, Personalakte Kemnitz, vol. 7172.

10. AA to treasury, January 31, 1923, PA-AA, Personalakte Kemnitz, vol. 7172.

11. Fischart, "Neue Politikerköpfe," 173–74.

12. *Vossische Zeitung,* May 8, 1920, evening edition.

13. "Admits Authorship of Note to Mexico; Kemnitz Explains Aim of German Plot," *New York Times,* May 15, 1920. The *Times* picked up the *Frankfurter* article, thus introducing Americans to Kemnitz and his part in the telegram affair.

14. *Vossische Zeitung,* May 14, 1920, morning edition.

15. *Vossische Zeitung,* May 21, 1920, morning edition.

16. Deutscher Reichstag, *Stenographische Berichte,* vol. 347, 1st legislative period, 55th session, Monday, January 24, 1921, 2070.

17. Deutscher Reichstag, *Stenographische Berichte,* vol. 347, 1st legislative period, 55th session, Monday, January 24, 1921, 2048–51, 2070–75.

18. Fischart, "Neue Politikerköpfe," 173–74.

19. Deutscher Reichstag, *Stenographische Berichte,* vol. 391, 3rd legislative period, 262nd session, Thursday, February 3, 1927, 8800, 8825.

20. Kemnitz to foreign secretary, December 4, 1930, PA-AA, Personalakte Kemnitz, vol. 7170; memorandum, Kemnitz, summer 1927, ibid.

21. Daniel to Kemnitz, July 30, 1929, PA-AA, Personalakte Kemnitz, vol. 7170; memorandum, AA, December 16, 1930, ibid.; Kemnitz to foreign secretary, December 4, 1930, ibid.; memorandum, Kemnitz, summer 1927, ibid.

22. Crown Prince Friedrich Wilhelm to Neurath, September 14, 1932, PA-AA, Personalakte Kemnitz, vol. 7170; Neurath to "His Imperial Highness" (i.e., Friedrich Wilhelm), September 17, 1932, ibid.; Kemnitz to Weizsäcker, June 21, 1933, ibid.; Lammers to Neurath, July 21, 1933, ibid.; Crown Prince Friedrich Wilhelm to Neurath, April 30, 1933, ibid.; Alfred Hugenberg to Neurath, April 10, 1933, ibid.; Winterfeld to Neurath, April 3, 1933, ibid.

23. Kemnitz to AA, September 22, 1933, PA-AA, Personalakte Kemnitz, vol. 7170; Zimmermann to AA, January 30, 1934, ibid.

24. Friedrich von Winterfeld to Neurath, April 3, 1933, PA-AA, Personalakte Kemnitz, vol. 7170. Winterfeld was deputy chairman of the DNVP.

25. Memorandum, Grünau, August 26, 1933, PA-AA, Personalakte Kemnitz, vol. 7172.

26. Cited in Kershaw, *Hitler,* vol. 1, 377.

27. Kemnitz to Neurath, March 17, 1933, PA-AA, Personalakte Kemnitz, vol. 7170.

28. Kemnitz to AA, September 22, 1933, PA-AA, Personalakte Kemnitz, vol. 7170. It is unclear whether Kemnitz ever joined the NSDAP. According to the NSDAP central archives in Berlin, Kemnitz's name is not listed in their records. However, only 80 percent of all NSDAP members are included in the surviving records. Email, Franz Goettlicher to author, August 19, 2004.

29. Kube to Hitler, December 15, 1933, PA-AA, Personalakte Kemnitz, vol. 7170; Kube to Hess, December 15, 1933, ibid.

30. AA to Kemnitz, December 14, 1934, PA-AA, Personalakte Kemnitz, vol. 7170.

31. Kemnitz to Kriebel, July 20, 1939, PA-AA, Personalakte Kemnitz, vol. 7170; Kriebel to Kemnitz, July 29, 1939, ibid.

32. Kemnitz to AA, September 3, 1939, PA-AA, Personalakte Kemnitz, vol. 7170.

33. AA to Kemnitz, September 9, 1939, PA-AA, Personalakte Kemnitz, vol. 7170.
34. Memorandum, Kemnitz, "Are We Liberated?" May 1945, Hoover Institution, Kemnitz papers.
35. Essay, Kemnitz, "Befreiung oer Deklassierung?" January 27, 1947, Hoover Institution, Kemnitz papers; memorandum, Kemnitz, "Deutschland als Leidtragender," n.d. (1947–1948), ibid.; memorandum, Kemnitz, "Preussischer und Deutscher Militarismus," n.d., ibid.; memorandum, Kemnitz, 1947, ibid.; memorandum, Kemnitz, Berlin, November 6, 1946. Kemnitz's various memoranda found their way to Stanford University through Ferdinand Stibi, who had met Kemnitz in Berlin in 1948, was given the papers, and then donated them to the Hoover Institution. See letter, Stibi, Washington, D.C., to Hoover Library, November 30, 1950, ibid.
36. Memorandum, Kemnitz, "Are We Liberated?" May 1945, Hoover Institution, Kemnitz papers.
37. Auswärtiges Amt, *Biographisches Handbuch*, vol. 2, s.v. "Kemnitz, Arthur von."

Chapter 17. Hall's Intelligence Legacy

1. Andrew, *Secret Service*, 120; and Beesly, *Room 40*, 169, 236. Hall's promotion to rear admiral had probably already been decided upon before the interception of the Zimmermann telegram.
2. James, *Eyes of the Navy*, 167, 169.
3. Beesly, *Room 40*, 291–92.
4. Yardley, *American Black Chamber*, 140.
5. Memorandum, Bell, London, May 1, 1919, NARA, RG 59, Office of the Counselor, entry 543, box 5, confidential file 121, "secret service."
6. Hughes, *Spies at Work*, 8, 13–15 (online edition pagination); McIvor, "Economic League," 634, 640–48, 651.
7. "Retirement of Admiral Hall: To Stand for Parliament," *The Times*, December 21, 1918.
8. James, *Eyes of the Navy*, 175–77.
9. Beesly, *Room 40*, 236.
10. Wemyss to Hall, January 20, 1919, Churchill College Cambridge, Archive Centre, Hall papers, HALL 1/5.
11. O'Halpin, "Hall," 647, refers to "Hall's independence of mind" as having antagonized Whitehall officials, precipitating his retirement.
12. Hall to secretary of the navy, October 30, 1918, NA, ADM 1/8541/279.
13. Memorandum, October 30, 1918, NA, ADM 1/8541/279; memorandum, November 4, 1918, ibid.; and board minutes, November 7, 1918, ibid.
14. *The Times*, December 21, 1918.
15. Knightley, *Second Oldest Profession*, 55.
16. "Sir Reginald Hall Adopted for Liverpool Constituency," *The Times*, January 20, 1919; "Lloyd George to Hall: 'Wish You Success in Your Candidature,'" *The Times*, February 25, 1919; and "Coalition Win at West Derby," *The Times*, March 12, 1919.
17. Hughes, *Spies at Work*, 39.
18. Knightley, *Second Oldest Profession*, 57.
19. Bennett, *Mysterious Business*, 34–35; Chester, Fay, and Young, *Zinoviev Letter*, 66.
20. West and Tsarev, *Crown Jewels*, 33, 40–43. Gill Bennett, who analyzed the Zinoviev letter on the basis of British records, concedes that West and Tsarev's account "is plausible in many respects." See Bennett, *Mysterious Business*, 90. For a comprehensive selection of White Russian forgery activities, see *Anti-Soviet Forgeries*.
21. Bennett, *Mysterious Business*, 50; Chester, Fay, and Young, *Zinoviev Letter*, 125–26.
22. Marquand, *Ramsay MacDonald*, 386.
23. Chester, Fay, and Young, *Zinoviev Letter*, 95.

24. Chester, Fay, and Young, *Zinoviev Letter*, 98.
25. Andrew, *Secret Service*, 306–307. See also Andrew, *Defend the Realm*, 150.
26. Chester, Fay, and Young, *Zinoviev Letter*, 109.
27. Bell to Hurley, July 13, 1921, NARA, RG 59, Office of the Counselor, entry 539, box 7, folder 1.
28. Press cutting from "*Bos[ton Globe?]*," not dated, NARA, RG 59, Office of the Counselor, entry 543, box 5, confidential file, Bell 123, "Zimmermann's Intercepted Telegram and Subsequent Correspondence, Feb.–Apr. 1917"; Cabot gives Gaunt's age as forty-five, which would date the speech to 1915. This is obviously impossible. The speech's content suggests it was delivered during the association's annual meeting, typically June 17. Since the unit returned from France in January 1919, the speech may have been delivered in June 1919.
29. Laughlin to Bell, July 28, 1921, NARA, RG 59, Office of the Counselor, entry 539, box 7, folder 1.
30. Hendrick to Bell, June 17, 1921, NARA, RG 59, Office of the Counselor, entry 539, box 7, folder 1.
31. Laughlin to Hurley, July 23, 1921, NARA, RG 59, Office of the Counselor, entry 539, box 7, folder 1.
32. Bell to Hendrick, July 13, 1921, NARA, RG 59, Office of the Counselor, entry 539, box 7, folder 1
33. Bell to Laughlin, August 24, 1921, NARA, RG 59, Office of the Counselor, entry 539, box 7, folder 1.
34. Bell to Hurley, July 13, 1921, NARA, RG 59, Office of the Counselor, entry 539, box 7, folder 1.
35. Bell to Hurley, August 24, 1921, NARA, RG 59, Office of the Counselor, entry 539, box 7, folder 2.
36. Hurley to Winslow, July 29, 1921, NARA, RG 59, Office of the Counselor, entry 539, box 7, folder 1.
37. Secret, undersecretary [Henry Fletcher] to Winslow, no date [August 1921], NARA, RG 59, Office of the Counselor, entry 539, box 7, folder 2.
38. Telegram, Hall to Hendrick, no date, written on Office of the Under Secretary stationery, with sentence added: "Tyrrell says Brit. Gov't. (never?) gave (?) consent for publication," NARA, RG 59, Office of the Counselor, entry 539, box 7, folder 1.
39. Cablegram, Hall to Hendrick, no date [July/August 1921], NARA, RG 59, Office of the Counselor, entry 539, box 7, folder 1.
40. Letter, Hall to Winslow, August 13, 1921, NARA, RG 59, Office of the Counselor, entry 539, box 7, folder 1.
41. Hall to Hendrick, July 23, 1921, NARA, RG 59, Office of the Counselor, entry 539, box 7, folder 1.
42. Page to Fletcher, August 22, 1921, NARA, RG 59, Office of the Counselor, entry 539, box 7, folder 2.
43. Page to Fletcher, August 25, 1921, NARA, RG 59, Office of the Counselor, entry 539, box 7, folder 2.
44. Bell to Harrison, May 1, 1922, NARA, RG 59, Office of the Counselor, entry 539, box 7, folder 3. Tyrrell's role appears ambivalent. On the one hand, the Americans suspected him of having provided Hendrick with information about the telegram; on the other hand, he later denied that the British government had ever given its consent to publication. Possibly, Tyrrell meant to provide Hendrick with background information that would not be published, or like Hall, he backpedaled after he sensed strong resistance from his American colleagues. A colleague described Tyrrell as "a little man as quick as a lizard with scintillating eyes and wit and a great aversion to any work not transacted orally." His reluctance to commit his thoughts to paper renders tracing his thoughts difficult. See Harrison to Hughes, 22 May 1922, ibid., and Goldstein, "Tyrrell."
45. Millman, *The Detonators*, 135–36.

46. James, *Eyes of the Navy*, 183–84.
47. Andrew, *Secret Service*, 450.
48. Ibid., 466.
49. MacDonnell, "Second Zimmermann Telegram."
50. For Roosevelt and the map story, see generally, Persico, *Roosevelt's Secret War*, 78, 125–27, 173–75.
51. Mahl, *Desperate Deception*, 55.
52. MacDonnell, "Second Zimmermann Telegram," 498.
53. Bamford, *Puzzle Palace*, 397, 399.
54. Churchill, *Never Give In*, 413–23.

Conclusion

1. Lorenz, "Predictability."
2. This is the central theme of Fischer, *War of Illusions*.
3. Yardley, *American Black Chamber*, 139–40.
4. Lansing, *War Memoirs*, 232.

Names and Terms

1. Statement, Zimmermann, budget committee, 122rd session, March 3, 1917, Schiffers and Koch, *Hauptausschuss*, 1149; statement, Zimmermann, budget committee, 123rd session, March 5, 1917, Schiffers and Koch, *Hauptausschuss*, 1152; statement, Zimmermann, budget committee, 148th session, April 28, 1917, GFM, Mexiko 16, vol. 1, NARA, T 149, roll 378.
2. Report, Göppert, April 4, 1917, PA-AA, R 16919.
3. *Frankfurter Zeitung*, March 3, 1917; *Vorwärts*, March 4, 1917; *Vossische Zeitung*, March 5, 1917.
4. Bernstorff, *My Three Years*, 380; "Statement Dictated by Heinrich von Eckhardt [*sic*], at New York City, on March 25th, 1919, to Wm. Neunhoffer, of the Department of Justice," NARA, RG 59, Office of the Counselor, entry 539, box 3, folder, "Dr. Heinrich von Eckardt's Trip Through U.S. to Mexico March 1919."
5. Zimmermann, "Fürst Bülows Kritik," 234; Hazen, *Giants and Ghosts*, 38.
6. HALL, 11.
7. Hall's handwritten comment on the fully decrypted and translated copy of Zimmermann's message, no date [shortly after 1 March 1917], NA, HW 3/187.
8. Hall, "Affidavit," 31; Hall and Peaslee, *Three Wars*, 7.
9. Campbell to Hardinge, February 20, 1917, HALL, 21; Hardinge to Campbell, no date, HALL, 21–22.
10. *The Times*, March 2, 1917.
11. Page to Lansing, February 24, 1917, *FRUS*, 1917, supplement 1.
12. *News and Courier, Arizona Republican, Washington Post, New York Times, Santa Fe New Mexican*, March 1, 1917.
13. *Houston Post, Milwaukee Sentinel*, March 2, 1917.
14. *Dallas Morning News*, March 2, 1917.
15. Lansing to Fletcher, March 2, 1917, NARA, RG 59, decimal file 862.20212, M 336, roll 55. Hall's liaison at the U.S. embassy in London, Edward Bell, referred to it as "Z. telegram." Bell to Hurley, July 13, 1921, NARA, RG 59, Office of the Counselor, entry 539, box 7, folder 1.
16. Millis, *Road to War*, 466.
17. For example, Ritter, *Staatskunst und Kriegshandwerk*, vol. 3, 564; and Möckelmann, "Deutschlandbild," 133
18. Koopmann, *Diplomatie*, 289.
19. Tuchman, *Zimmermann Depesche*.

Bibliography

Archival and Manuscript Sources

Bundesarchiv-Militärarchiv (German Military Archives), Freiburg
RM 3 Acta betreffend Mobilmachung (Records on Military Mobilization)
RM 5 Admiralstab der Marine (Admiralty Staff of the Navy)
RM 8 Reichsmarineamt (Imperial Navy Office)

Cambridge University Library
Papers of Charles Hardinge

Churchill College, Cambridge, Archive Centre
Admiral Sir William Reginald Hall, "Draft Autobiography," Hall Papers, HALL 3/6

Collection Markus Pöhlmann, Potsdam
"Material über die Kompromittierung deutscher Chiffrierverfahren" (Material
    Regarding Compromising of German Ciphering Methods)

Herbert Hoover Library, West Branch, Iowa
Papers of Irwin Boyle Laughlin

Hoover Institution, Stanford, California
Great Britain, Foreign Office, Wellington House
Papers of Hans Arthur von Kemnitz
Selected Papers of George Sylvester Viereck

Library of Congress, Washington, D.C.
Papers of Chandler P. Anderson
Papers of Newton D. Baker
Papers of Albert S. Burleson
Papers of Josephus Daniels
Papers of Robert Lansing
Papers of William G. McAdoo
Papers of Theodore Roosevelt
Papers of Woodrow Wilson
Records of the (British) Cabinet Office

National Archives, London
Records of the Admiralty (ADM)
Records of the Cabinet Office (CAB)
Records of the Code and Cypher School (HW)
Records of the Foreign Office (FO)
Records of the Information Ministry (INF)

National Archives and Records Administration, College Park, Maryland
RG 15 RECORDS OF THE DEPARTMENT OF VETERANS AFFAIRS
Papers of the Mixed Claims Commission, United States and Germany

RG 59 RECORDS OF THE DEPARTMENT OF STATE
German Military Activities in Mexico, 1910–1929
Internal Affairs of Germany, 1910–1929
Internal Affairs of Mexico, 1910–1929
Records of the Office of the Counselor

RG 242 COLLECTION OF FOREIGN RECORDS SEIZED
Generalmajor a.D. Fritz Gempp, "Der Geheime Nachrichtendienst und die Spionage des Heeres von 1866 bis 1918" (The Secret Intelligence Service and Espionage of the Army from 1866 to 1918)
German Foreign Ministry (GFM, Auswärtiges Amt)

RG 457 RECORDS OF THE NATIONAL SECURITY AGENCY
Entry 9002, box 87, folder SRH-234, "The Zimmermann Telegram and Related Papers (declassified 15 March 1983)"

Politisches Archiv des Auswärtigen Amtes (Political Archives of the Foreign Office, PA-AA), Berlin
Akten des Deutschen Reiches (R series) (Records of the German Empire)
Nachlass Gottlieb von Jagow (Papers of Gottlieb von Jagow)
Personalakte Arthur Zimmermann (Personnel File of Arthur Zimmermann)
Personalakte Hans Arthur von Kemnitz (Personnel File of Hans Arthur von Kemnitz)

Yale University Library
Papers of Edward M. House
Papers of Frank L. Polk

Government Documents and Publications

Anti-Soviet Forgeries: A Record of Some of the Forged Documents Used at Various Times against the Soviet Government. London: Workers' Publications, 1927.
Auswärtiges Amt. *Biographisches Handbuch des deutschen Auswärtigen Dienstes, 1871–1945.* 5 vols. Paderborn: Schöningh, 2000–2012.
Bureau des Reichstags. *Reichstags-Handbuch III: Wahlperiode 1924.* Berlin: Norddeutsche Buchdruckerei, 1925.
Carnegie Endowment for International Peace, ed. *Official German Documents Relating to the World War: Translated under the Supervision of the Carnegie Endowment for International Peace, Division of International Law.* 2 vols. New York: Oxford University Press, 1923.
Deutsche Nationalversammlung. *Beilagen zu den Stenographischen Berichten über die öffentlichen Verhandlungen des Untersuchungsausschusses: Bericht des zweiten Untersuchungsausschusses über die Friedensaktion Wilsons, 1916/17.* Berlin: Norddeutsche Buchdruckerei, 1920.
———. *Stenographische Berichte über die öffentlichen Verhandlungen des Untersuchungsausschusses. 15. Ausschuss.* Berlin: Norddeutsche Buchdruckerei, 1919.

Deutscher Reichstag. *Stenographische Berichte über die Verhandlungen des Deutschen Reichstags, 1871–1939.* 458 vols. Berlin: Norddeutsche Buchdruckerei, 1871–1939.

Reichsamt/Reichsministerium des Innern. *Handbuch für das Deutsche Reich.* 65 vols. Berlin: Heymanns, 1871–1936. (The Reichsamt became the Reichsministerium after 1918.)

Schiffers, Reinhard, and Manfred Koch, eds. *Der Hauptausschuss des Deutschen Reichstages, 1915–1918.* 4 vols. Düsseldorf: Droste, 1981.

U.S. Congress. *Congressional Record.* 64th Congress, 2nd Sess., 1917. Vol. 54, pt. 5.

U.S. Department of State. *Papers Relating to the Foreign Relations of the United States, 1914–1918: Supplement—The World War.* 9 vols. Washington, D.C.: Government Printing Office, 1928–1933.

———. *Papers Relating to the Foreign Relations of the United States: The Lansing Papers, 1914–1920.* 2 vols. Washington, D.C.: Government Printing Office, 1939–1940.

Correspondence, Memoirs, Contemporary Works

Addams, Jane. *Peace and Bread in Time of War.* New York: Macmillan, 1922.

Baker, Newton Diehl. *Why We Went to War.* New York: Harper, 1936.

Baker, Ray Stannard. *Woodrow Wilson: Life and Letters.* 8 vols. Garden City: Doubleday, 1927–1939.

Batey, Mavis, and Edward Wakeling, eds. *Alice in I.D. 25: A Code-Breaking Parody of Alice's Adventures in Wonderland.* 1918. Reprint, with an introduction by Mavis Batey and Edward Wakeling. London: Aznet, 2007.

Bauer, Max. *Der Große Krieg in Feld und Heimat: Erinnerungen und Betrachtungen.* Tübingen: Ostandersche Buchandlung, 1921.

Bernstorff, Johann Heinrich von. *My Three Years in America.* New York: Scribner, 1920.

———. *Memoirs of Count Bernstorff.* New York: Random House, 1936.

Bethmann Hollweg, Theobald von. *Betrachtungen zum Weltkriege.* 2 vols. Berlin: Ullstein, 1919.

Boy-Ed, Karl, *Verschwörer? Die ersten siebzehn Kriegsmonate in den Vereinigten Staaten von Nord-Amerika.* Berlin: Scherl, 1920.

Bülow, Bernhard von. *Denkwürdigkeiten.* 4 vols. Berlin: Ullstein, 1930–1931.

Cambon, Henri, ed. *Paul Cambon: Correspondence, 1870–1924.* 3 vols. Paris: Editions Bernard Grasset, 1940–1946.

Churchill, Winston. *Never Give In! The Best of Winston Churchill's Speeches.* New York: Hyperion, 2004.

———. *The World Crisis.* 6 vols. New York: Charles Scribner's Sons, 1923.

Cronon, E. David, ed. *The Cabinet Diaries of Josephus Daniels, 1913–1921.* Lincoln: University of Nebraska Press, 1963.

Czernin, Count Ottokar von. *In the World War.* New York: Harper, 1920.

Daniels, Josephus. *The Wilson Era: Years of War and After.* 2 vols. Chapel Hill: University of North Carolina Press, 1944.

Deuerlein, Ernst, ed. *Briefwechsel Hertling-Lerchenfeld, 1912–1917: Dienstliche Privatkorrespondenz zwischen dem bayerischen Ministerpräsidenten Georg Graf von Hertling und dem bayerischen Gesandten in Berlin Hugo Graf von und zu Lerchenfeld.* 2 vols. Boppard am Rhein: Boldt, 1973.

Dobson, Miles C. E. *At the Edge of the Pit.* Pasadena, Calif.: New Publishing Company, 1914.

Dugdale, Blanche E. C. *Baffy: The Diaries of Blanche Dugdale, 1936–1947.* Edited by N. A. Rose. London: Valentine, Mitchell, 1973.

Dumba, Constantin. *Memoirs of a Diplomat.* Boston: Little, Brown, 1932.

Erdmann, Karl D., ed. *Kurt Riezler: Tagebücher, Aufsätze, Dokumente.* Göttingen: Vandenhoeck & Ruprecht, 1972.

Ewing, Alfred Washington. *The Man of Room 40: The Life of Sir Alfred Ewing*. London: Hutchinson, 1939.

———. "Some Special War Work, Part 1. With an Introduction by David Kahn." *Cryptologia* 4, no. 4 (October 1980): 193–203.

———. "Some Special War Work, Part 2." *Cryptologia* 5, no. 1 (January 1981): 33–39.

Flicke, Wilhelm F. *War Secrets in the Ether*. Parts I and II. Translated by Ray W. Pettengill. Washington, D.C.: National Security Agency, 1953.

Gaertringen, Friedrich Freiherr von, ed. *Wilhelm Groener: Lebenserinnerungen. Jugend, Generalstab, Weltkrieg*. Göttingen: Vandenhoeck & Ruprecht, 1957.

Gaunt, Guy. *The Yield of the Years: A Story of Adventure Afloat and Ashore by Admiral Sir Guy Gaunt, Naval Attaché and Chief of the British Intelligence Service in the United States, 1914–1918*. London: Hutchinson, 1940.

Gerard, James. *Face to Face with Kaiserism*. New York: Doran, 1918.

———. *My First Eighty-three Years in America: The Memoirs of James W. Gerard*. New York: Doubleday, 1951.

———. *My Four Years in Germany*. New York: Doran, 1917.

Görlitz, Walter, ed. *Regierte der Kaiser? Kriegstagebücher, Aufzeichnungen und Briefe des Chefs des Marine-Kabinetts Admiral Georg von Müller, 1914–1918*. Göttingen: Musterschmidt, 1959.

Grew, Joseph C. *Turbulent Era*. 2 vols. Boston and New York: Houghton Mifflin, 1952.

Grey, Edward. *Twenty-Five Years, 1892–1916*. 2 vols. New York: Frederick A. Stokes, 1925.

Gwynn, Stephen, ed. *The Letters and Friendships of Sir Cecil Spring Rice*. 2 vols. London: Constable, 1929.

Hall, William Reginald. "Admiral Hall on the Zimmermann Telegram." *World's Work* 51, no. 6 (April 1926): 578.

Hall, William Reginald. "Affidavit of Admiral Sir W. Reginald Hall, K. C. M. G., C. B., D. C. L., L. L. D., Formerly Chief of the Intelligence Department of the British Admiralty, Verified December 28, 1926, with Annexed Copies of German Cablegrams, Wireless and Other Messages Intercepted by the British Government during the War." In *The Zimmermann Telegram of January 16, 1917, and Its Cryptographic Background*, edited by William F. Friedman and Charles J. Mendelsohn, 30–32. 1938. Reprint, Laguna Hills: Aegean Park Press, 1976.

Hall, William Reginald, and Amos J. Peaslee. *Three Wars with Germany*. New York: Putnam, 1944.

Hankey, Lord Maurice. *The Supreme Command, 1914–1918*. 2 vols. London: Allen and Unwin, 1961.

Hanssen, Hans Peter, *Diary of a Dying Empire*. Bloomington: Indiana University Press, 1955.

Hazen, David W. *Giants and Ghosts of Central Europe*. Portland: Metropolitan Press, 1933.

Helfferich, Karl. *Der Weltkrieg*. 2 vols. Berlin: Ullstein, 1919.

Hendrick, Burton J. *The Life and Letters of Walter H. Page*. 3 vols. Garden City, N.Y.: Doubleday, Page, 1924–26.

Hindenburg, Paul von. *Aus meinem Leben*. Leipzig: Hirzel, 1933.

Hohler, Thomas B. *Diplomatic Petrel*. London: J. Murray, 1942.

Houston, David F. *Eight Years with Wilson's Cabinet, 1913 to 1920*. 2 vols. Garden City, N.Y.: Doubleday, Page, 1926.

Hoy, Hugh Cleland. *40 O.B. Or, How the War was Won*. London: Hutchinson, 1932.

Jones, Thomas. *Whitehall Diary*. Edited by Keith Middlemas. 3 vols. Oxford and New York: Oxford University Press, 1969–1971.

Jusserand, Jean Jules, *Le sentiment américain pendant la guerre*. Paris: Payot, 1931.

Kemnitz, Hans Arthur von. "Nationalitätenprinzip und Selbstbestimmungsrecht." *Österreich-Deutschland "Heim ins Reich!"* 4 (1931).

Lane, Anne W., and Louise W. Wall, eds. *The Letters of Franklin K. Lane.* Boston: Houghton Mifflin, 1922.

Lansing, Robert. *War Memoirs of Robert Lansing.* Indianapolis: Bobbs-Merrill, 1935.

Lea, Homer. *The Valor of Ignorance.* New York: Harper, 1909.

Lennox, Lady Algernon G., ed. *The Diary of Lord Bertie of Thames, 1914–1918.* 2 vols. London: Hodder and Stoughton, 1924.

Leonard, Arthur R., ed. *War Addresses of Woodrow Wilson.* Boston: Ginn, 1918.

Link, Arthur, ed. *The Papers of Woodrow Wilson.* 69 vols. Princeton: Princeton University Press, 1966–1994.

Ludendorff, Erich. "The American Effort." *Atlantic Monthly* 129 (May 1929): 676–87.

———. *The General Staff and Its Problems: The History of the Relations between the High Command and the German Imperial Government as Revealed by Official Documents.* Translated by F. A. Holt. 2 vols. New York: Dutton, 1920.

———. *Meine Kriegserinnerungen.* Berlin: Mittler, 1919.

Luxburg, Karl Graf von. *Nachdenkliche Erinnerung.* Schloss Aschach, 1953.

Marshall, Thomas R. *Recollections of Thomas R. Marshall, Vice-President and Hoosier Philosopher: A Hoosier Salad.* Indianapolis: Bobbs-Merrill, 1925.

Matthias, Erich, and Susanne Miller, eds. *Das Kriegstagebuch des Reichstagsabgeordneten Eduard David, 1914–1918.* Düsseldorf: Droste, 1966.

McAdoo, William G. *Crowded Years.* Boston: Houghton Mifflin, 1931.

Papen, Franz von. *Der Wahrheit eine Gasse.* Munich: List, 1952.

Phillips, William. *Ventures in Diplomacy.* Boston: Beacon Press, 1953.

Redfield, William C. *With Congress and Cabinet.* New York: Doubleday, Page, 1924.

Riddell, George Allardice, ed. *Lord Riddell's War Diary, 1914–1918.* London: Ivor Nicholson & Watson, 1918.

Rintelen von Kleist, Captain Franz. *The Dark Invader: Wartime Reminiscences of a German Naval Intelligence Officer.* 1939. Reprint, with an introduction by Reinhard R. Doerries. London, Portland: Frank Cass, 1998.

Roosevelt, Theodore. *Letters.* Edited by Elting E. Morison. 8 vols. Cambridge, Mass.: Harvard University Press, 1951–1954.

———. *Selections from the Correspondence of Theodore Roosevelt and Henry Cabot Lodge.* Edited by Henry Cabot Lodge and Charles Redmond. 2 vols. New York: Scribner, 1925.

Scheidemann, Philip. *Memoirs of a Social Democrat.* Translated by J. E. Michell. 2 vols. London: Hodder and Stoughton, 1929.

Schwertfeger, Bernard, ed. *Rudolf von Valentini: Kaiser und Kabinettschef.* Oldenburg: Gerhard Stalling, 1931.

Seymour, Charles, ed. *The Intimate Papers of Colonel House.* 4 vols. Boston: Houghton Mifflin, 1926–1928.

Stopford, Francis, ed. *Raemaekers' Cartoons: With Accompanying Notes by Well-Known English Writers, with an Appreciation from H. H. Asquith, Prime Minister of England.* Garden City, N.Y.: Doubleday, Page, 1916.

Taylor, A. J. P., ed. *Lloyd George: A Diary by Frances Stevenson.* London: Hutchinson, 1971.

Thomson, Basil. *The Scene Changes.* Garden City, N.Y.: Doubleday, 1937.

Thwaites, Norman. *Velvet and Vinegar.* London: Grayson & Grayson, 1932.

Tirpitz, Alfred von. *Politische Dokumente von A. von Tirpitz.* 2 vols. Stuttgart and Berlin: Cotta, 1924–1926.

Tumulty, Joseph P. *Woodrow Wilson As I Know Him.* Garden City, N.Y.: Doubleday, Page, 1921.

Valentini, Rudolf. *Kaiser und Kabinettschef: Nach eigenen Aufzeichnungen und dem Briefwechsel des wirklichen Geheimen Rats Rudolf von Valentini dargestellt von Bernhard Schwertfeger.* Edited by Bernhard Schwertfeger. Oldenburg: Gerhard Stalling, 1931.

Viereck, George Sylvester. *Spreading Germs of Hate.* With a foreword by Colonel Edward M. House. New York: Horace Liveright, 1930.

———. *The Strangest Friendship in History: Woodrow Wilson and Colonel House.* 1932. Reprint, Westport: Greenwood Press, 1976.

Vierhaus, Rudolf, ed. *Das Tagebuch der Baronin Spitzemberg geb. Freiin v. Varnbüler: Aufzeichnungen aus der Hofgesellschaft des Hohenzollernreiches.* 5th ed. Göttingen: Vandenhoeck & Ruprecht, 1989.

Voska, Emanuel Victor, and Will Irwin. *Spy and Counter Spy.* Garden City, N.Y.: Doubleday, 1941.

Willert, Sir Arthur. *Washington and Other Memories.* Boston: Houghton Mifflin, 1972.

Wilson, Edith Bolling. *My Memoir.* Indianapolis: Bobbs-Merrill, 1939.

Wolff, Theodor. *Tagebücher, 1914–1919: Der erste Weltkrieg und die Entstehung der Weimarer Republik in Tagebüchern, Leitartikeln und Briefen des Chefredakteurs am "Berliner Tageblatt" und Mitbegründer der "Deutschen Demokratischen Partei."* Edited by Bernd Sösemann. 2 vols. Boppard am Rhein: Boldt, 1984.

Yardley, Herbert. *The American Black Chamber.* 1931. Reprint, Laguna Hills: Aegean Press, 1990.

Zimmermann, Arthur. "Bülow und Holstein–Die Daily Telegraph-Affäre–Bülow und Bethmann Hollweg." *Süddeutsche Monatshefte* 28, no. 6 (March 1931): 391–92.

———. "Fürst Bülows Kritik am Auswärtigen Amt." In *Front wider Bülow: Staatsmänner, Diplomaten und Forscher zu seinen Denkwürdigkeiten,* edited by Friedrich Thimme, 221–34. Munich: F. Bruckmann, 1931.

Books, Articles, Papers, and Theses

Adams, Henry H., and Robin K. *Rebel Patriot: A Biography of Franz von Papen.* Santa Barbara, Calif.: MacNally & Loftin, 1987.

Adams, John Coldwell. *Seated with the Mighty: A Biography of Sir Gilbert Parker.* London: Borealis Press, 1979.

Adler, Selig. *The Isolationist Impulse: Its Twentieth-Century Reaction.* New York: Abelard-Schuman, 1957.

Aldrich, Richard J. "British Intelligence and the Anglo-American 'Special Relationship' during the Cold War." *Review of International Studies* 24, no. 3 (July 1998): 331–51.

———. *The Hidden Hand: Britain, America, and Cold War Secret Intelligence.* New York: Overlook Press, 2001.

Altenhöner, Florian. "Total War–Total Control? German Military Intelligence on the Home Front, 1914–1918." *Journal of Intelligence History* 5, no. 2 (Winter 2005): 55–72.

Ambrosious, Lloyd E. *Wilsonian Statecraft: Theory and Practice of Liberal Internationalism during World War I.* Wilmington, Del.: Scholarly Resources, 1991.

———. *Wilsonianism: Woodrow Wilson and His Legacy in American Foreign Relations.* New York: Palgrave Macmillan, 2002.

Andrew, Christopher. *Her Majesty's Secret Service: The Making of the British Intelligence Community.* New York: Viking, 1985.

———. *Defend the Realm: The Authorized History of MI5.* New York: Viking, 2010.

Angermann, Erich. "Ein Wendepunkt in der Geschichte der Monroe-Doktrin und der deutsch-amerikanischen Beziehungen." *Jahrbuch für Amerikastudien* 3 (1958): 22–58.

Asprey, Robert B. *The German High Command at War: Hindenburg and Ludendorff Conduct World War I.* New York: Morrow, 1991.

Auerbach, Jerold S. "Woodrow Wilson's 'Prediction' to Frank Cobb: Words Historians Should Doubt Ever Got Spoken." *Journal of American History* 54 (December 1967): 608–17.

Avery, Laurence G. "Maxwell Anderson's Report on Frank Cobb's Interview with Woodrow Wilson: The Documentary Source." *North Dakota Quarterly* 45, no. 3 (1977): 5–14.

Baecker, Thomas. "The Arms of the Ypiranga: The German Side." *Americas* 30 (July 1973): 347–62.

———. *Die deutsche Mexikopolitik, 1913/14.* Berlin: Colloquium, 1971.

Bailey, Thomas Andrew. *The Policy of the United States toward the Neutrals, 1917–1918.* Baltimore: Johns Hopkins University Press, 1942.

———. "The United States and the Blacklist during the Great War." *Journal of Modern History* 6 (March 1934): 14–35.

———. *A Diplomatic History of the American People.* 10th ed. Englewood Cliffs, N.J.: Prentice-Hall, 1980.

Bamford, James. *The Puzzle Palace: A Report on America's Most Secret Agency.* Boston: Houghton Mifflin, 1982.

Barie, Ottavio. *L'opinione interventistica negli Stati Uniti, 1914–1917.* Milan: Istituto Editoriale Cisalpino, 1960.

Barnes, Trevor. "Special Branch and the First Labour Government." *Historical Journal* 22, no. 4 (December 1979): 941–51.

Bass, Herbert J., ed. *America's Entry into World War I: Submarines, Sentiment, or Security?* New York: Holt, Rinehart and Winston, 1964.

Batey, Mavis. *Dilly: The Man Who Broke Enigmas.* London: Dialogue, 2009.

Beckett, Ian F. W. *The First World War: The Essential Guide to Sources in the National Archives.* Kew: PRO Publications, 2002.

Beckman, Bengt, and C.G. McKay. *Swedish Signal Intelligence, 1900–1945.* London: Frank Cass, 2003.

Beesly, Patrick. *Room 40: British Naval Intelligence, 1914–1918.* London: Harcourt Brace Jovanovich, 1982.

Bemis, Samuel Flagg. *The United States as World Power: A Diplomatic History, 1950–1950.* New York: Holt, 1950.

———. *The United States as a World Power, 1900–1955.* New York: Holt, 1955.

Benbow, Mark E. "'All the Brains I Can Borrow': Woodrow Wilson and Intelligence Gathering in Mexico, 1913–15." *Studies in Intelligence* 51, no. 4 (December 2007).

Bennett, Gill. *'A Most Extraordinary and Mysterious Business': The Zinoviev Letter of 1924.* London: Foreign and Commonwealth Office, 1999.

———. *The Records of the Permanent Under-Secretary's Department.* London: Foreign & Commonwealth Office, 2005.

———. *Churchill's Man of Mystery: Desmond Morton and the World of Intelligence.* London: Routledge, 2006.

Billington, Monroe L. "The Gore Resolution of 1916." *Mid-America* 47 (1965): 89–98.

———. "The Sunrise Conference: Myth or Fact?" *Southwestern Social Science Quarterly* 37 (March 1957): 330–40.

Birdsall, Paul M. "Neutrality and Economic Pressure, 1914–1917." *Science and Society* 3 (1939): 217–28.

Birnbaum, Karl E. *Peace Moves and U-Boat Warfare.* Stockholm: Almqvist & Wiksell, 1958.

Blum, John M. *Joe Tumulty and the Wilson Era.* Boston: Houghton Mifflin, 1951.

Bodnar, John, ed. *Bonds of Affection: Americans Define Their Patriotism.* Princeton: Princeton University Press, 1996.

Boghardt, Thomas. *Spies of the Kaiser: German Covert Operations in Great Britain during the First World War Era.* Basingstoke: Palgrave Macmillan, 2004.

Brands, Henry W. *Woodrow Wilson.* New York: Times Books, 2003.

Brandes, Stuart. *Warhogs: A History of War Profits in America.* New York: Times Books, 2003.

Bruce, Robert B. *A Fraternity of Arms: America and France in the Great War.* Lawrence: University Press of Kansas, 2003.

Brückner, Hilmar-Detlef. "Die Deutsche Heeres-Fernmeldeaufklärung im Ersten Weltkrieg an der Westfront." In *Geheimdienst, Militär und Politik in Deutschland*, edited by Jürgen W. Schmidt, 199–246. Ludwigsfelde: Ludwigsfelder Verlagshaus, 2008.

Buchanan, Albert Russell. "European Propaganda and American Public Opinion, 1914–1917." PhD diss., Stanford University, 1935.

Buehrig, Edward Henry. "Wilson's Neutrality Re-Examined." *World Politics* 3 (October 1950): 1–19.

———. *Woodrow Wilson and the Balance of Power.* Bloomington: Indiana University Press, 1955.

Burdick, Charles B. "A House on Navidad Street: The Celebrated Zimmermann Note on the Mexican Border?" *Arizona and the West* 8, no. 1 (Spring 1966): 19–34.

Burk, Kathleen. *Britain, America and the Sinews of War, 1914–1918.* Boston: Allen & Unwin, 1985.

Burton, David H. *Cecil Spring Rice: A Diplomat's Life.* Rutherford, N.J.: Fairleigh Dickinson University Press, 1990.

Carroll, John M., and George C. Herring, eds. *Modern American Diplomacy.* Wilmington, Del.: Scholarly Resources, 1986.

Cecil, Lamar. *The German Diplomatic Service, 1871–1914.* Princeton: Princeton University Press, 1976.

Chalkley, John F. *Zach Lamar Cobb: El Paso Collector of Customs and Intelligence during the Mexican Revolution, 1913–1918.* El Paso: Texas Western Press, 1998.

Chester, Lewis, Stephen Fay, and Hugo Young. *The Zinoviev Letter: A Political Intrigue.* London: Heinemann, 1967.

Chickering, Roger. *Imperial Germany and the Great War, 1914–1918.* Cambridge: Cambridge University Press, 1998.

Child, Clifton J. "German-American Attempts to Prevent the Exportation of Munitions of War, 1914–1915." *Mississippi Valley Historical Review* 25, no. 3 (December 1938): 351–68.

———. *The German-Americans in Politics, 1914–1917.* Madison: University of Wisconsin Press, 1939.

Clements, Kendrick. "Woodrow Wilson's Mexican Policy, 1913–15." *Diplomatic History* 4 (Spring 1980): 113–36.

———. *The Presidency of Woodrow Wilson.* Lawrence: University Press of Kansas, 1992.

———. *Woodrow Wilson, World Statesman.* Chicago: I. R. Dee, 1999.

Coerver, Don M., and Linda B. Hall. *Texas and the Mexican Revolution: A Study in State and National Border Policy.* San Antonio: Trinity University Press, 1984.

Cohen, Warren I. *The American Revisionists: The Lessons of Intervention into World War I.* Chicago: University of Chicago Press, 1967.

Coletta, Paolo E. "A Question of Alternatives: Wilson, Bryan, Lansing, and America's Intervention in World War I." *Nebraska History* 63, no. 1 (1982): 33–57.

Cook, Andrew. *Ace of Spies: The True Story of Sidney Reilly.* Stroud: Tempus, 2002.

Cooper, John Milton, Jr. "The Great War and American Memory." *Virginia Quarterly Review* 79, no. 1 (Winter 2003): 70–84.

———. "The United States." In *The Origins of World War I*, edited by Richard F. Hamilton and Holger H. Herwig, 415–42. New York: Cambridge University Press, 2003.

———. *The Vanity of Power: American Isolationism and the First World War, 1914–1917.* Westport, Conn.: Greenwood, 1969.

———. *Walter Hines Page: The Southerner as American, 1855–1918.* Chapel Hill: University of North Carolina Press, 1977.

———. *Woodrow Wilson: A Biography.* New York: Knopf, 2003.

———. "World War I: European Origins and American Intervention." *Virginia Quarterly Review* 56 (Winter 1980): 1–18.

Costrell, Edwin. *How Maine Viewed the War, 1914–1917.* Orono, Me.: University Press, 1940.

Cowling, Maurice. *The Impact of Labour.* Cambridge: Cambridge University Press, 1971.

Crighton, John Clark. *Missouri and the World War, 1914–1917: A Study in Public Opinion.* Columbia: University of Missouri Press, 1947.

Cummins, Cedric. *Indiana Public Opinion and the World War, 1914–1917.* Indianapolis: Indiana Historical Bureau, 1947.

Dalton, Brian J. "Wilson's Prediction to Cobb: Notes on the Auerbach-Link Debate." *Historian* 32 (August 1970): 545–63.

De Grey, Nigel. *The Dartington Hall Experiment.* Totnes: Dartington Hall, 1934.

Deist, Wilhelm. *Militär und Innenpolitik im Weltkrieg, 1914–1918.* 2 vols. Düsseldorf: Droste, 1970.

Denniston, Robin. *Thirty Secret Years: A. G. Denniston's Work in Signals Intelligence, 1914–1944.* Clifton-upon-Teme: Polperro Heritage Press, 2007.

Devlin, Patrick. *Too Proud To Fight: Woodrow Wilson's Neutrality.* Oxford: Oxford University Press, 1974.

DeWeerd, Harvey A. *President Wilson Fights His War: World War I and American Intervention.* New York: Macmillan, 1968.

Dickinson, Frederick R. *War and National Reinvention: Japan in the Great War, 1914–1919.* Cambridge, Mass.: Harvard University Press, 1999.

Dietl, Ralph. "Friedensvermittlung oder Siegfrieden? William Jennings Bryan und der Erste Weltkrieg, 1914–1917." In *Zwei Wege in die Moderne: Aspekte der deutsch-amerikanischen Beziehungen, 1900–1918,* edited by Ragnhild Fiebig-von Hase and Jürgen Heideking, 211–27. Trier: Wissenschaftlicher Verlag Trier, 1998.

Doerries, Reinhard R. *Imperial Challenge: Ambassador Count Bernstorff and German American-Relations, 1908–1917.* Chapel Hill: University of North Carolina Press, 1989.

———. "Promoting *Kaiser* and *Reich*: Imperial German Propaganda in the United States during World War I." In *Confrontation and Cooperation: Germany and the United States in the Era of World War I, 1900–1924,* edited by Hans-Jürgen Schröder, 135–66. Providence, R.I.: Berg, 1993.

———. "Die Tätigkeit deutscher Agenten in den USA während des Ersten Weltkrieges und ihr Einfluss auf die diplomatischen Beziehungen zwischen Washington und Berlin." In *Diplomaten und Agenten: Nachrichtendienste in der Geschichte der deutsch-amerikanischen Beziehungen,* edited by Reinhard Doerries, 11–52. Heidelberg: C. Winter, 2001.

Doss, Kurt. *Das deutsche Auswärtige Amt im Übergang vom Kaiserreich zur Weimarer Republik: Die Schülersche Reform.* Düsseldorf: Droste, 1977.

Dugdale, Blanche E. C. *Arthur James Balfour.* 2 vols. London: Hutchinson, 1936–1937.

Durán, Esperanza. "Revolution and International Pressures: The Mexican Experience, 1910–1920." *Journal of Interamerican Studies and World Affairs* 24, no. 4 (November 1982): 483–95.

Edmonds, Cecil J. "The Persian Gulf Prelude to the Zimmermann Telegram." *Journal of the Royal Central Asian Society* 47 (1960): 58–67.

Egremont, Max. *Balfour: A Life of Arthur James Balfour.* London: Collins, 1980.

Esposito, David M. *The Legacy of Woodrow Wilson: American War Aims in World War I.* London and Westport, Conn.: Praeger, 1996.

Farr, Barbara. *The Development and Impact of Right Wing Politics in Britain, 1902–1932.* London, New York: Garland, 1987.

Fay, Sidney Bradshaw. *The Origins of the World War.* 2 vols. New York: Macmillan, 1928.

————. "Wilson and Neutrality." *Nation*, January 22, 1936, 109–10.

Fearon, Peter. "Manufacturing Industry in the United States during the First World War." In *The First World War and International Economy*, edited by Chris Wrigley, 52–75. Cheltenham and Northampton: Edward Elgar, 2000.

Ferguson, Niall. *The Pity of War*. New York: Basic Books, 1999.

Fiebig-von Hase, Ragnhild. *Lateinamerika als Konfliktherd der deutsch-amerikanischen Beziehungen, 1890–1903: Vom Beginn der Panamapolitik bis zur Venezuelakrise von 1902/03*. 2 vols. Göttingen: Vandenhoeck & Ruprecht, 1986.

————. "The United States and Germany in the World Arena, 1900–1917." In *Confrontation and Cooperation: Germany and the United States in the Era of World War I, 1900–1924*, edited by Hans-Jürgen Schröder, 33–68. Providence, R.I.: Berg, 1993.

Fiebig-von Hase, Ragnhild, and Jürgen Heideking, eds. *Zwei Wege in die Moderne: Aspekte der deutsch-amerikanischen Beziehungen, 1900–1918*. Trier: Wissenschaftlicher Verlag Trier, 1998.

Fischart, Johannes. "Hans Arthur von Kemnitz (Neue Politikerköpfe, XV. Teil)." *Die Weltbühne: Wochenschrift für Politik, Kunst Wirtschaft* 31 (1924).

Fischer, Fritz. *Germany's Aims in the First World War*. Translated by C. A. Macartney with an introduction by James Joll. New York: Norton, 1967.

————. *War of Illusions: German Policies from 1911 to 1914*. Translated by Marian Jackson with a foreword by Sir Alan Bullock. New York: Norton, 1975.

Fischer-Baling, Eugen. "Der Untersuchungsausschuss für die Schuldfrage des ersten Weltkrieges." In *Aus Geschichte und Politik: Festschrift für Ludwig Bersträsser*, edited by Alfred Herrmann, 117–37. Düsseldorf: Droste, 1954.

Fitzgerald, Michael, and Richard Ned Lebow. "Iraq: The Mother of all Intelligence Failures." *Intelligence and National Security* 21, no. 5 (October 2006): 884–909.

Fitzgerald, Penelope. *The Knox Brothers*. London: Macmillan, 1977.

Fleming, Thomas James. "Woodrow Wilson's Fight for Peace." *Reader's Digest* 99 (September 1971): 87–91.

————. *The Illusion of Victory: America in World War I*. New York: Basic Books, 2003.

Foley, Robert T. "Easy Target or Invincible Enemy? German Intelligence Assessments of France before the Great War." *Journal of Intelligence History* 5, no. 2 (Winter 2005): 1–24.

Forsbach, Ralf. *Alfred von Kiderlen-Wächter (1852–1912): Ein Diplomatenleben im Kaiserreich*. 2 vols. Göttingen: Vandenhoeck & Ruprecht, 1997.

Freeman, Peter. "The Zimmermann Telegram Revisited: A Reconciliation of the Primary Sources." *Cryptologia* 30, no. 2 (April 2006): 98–150.

————. "MI1(b) and the Origins of British Diplomatic Cryptanalysis." *Intelligence and National Security* 22, no. 2 (April 2007): 206–28.

Freud, Sigmund, and William C. Bullitt. *Thomas Woodrow Wilson: A Psychological Study*. Boston: Houghton Mifflin, 1967.

Friedman, William F., and Charles J. Mendelsohn. *The Zimmermann Telegram of January 16, 1917, and Its Cryptographic Background*. 1938. Reprint, Laguna Hills: Aegean Park Press, 1976.

Garcés, Laura. "The German Challenge to the Monroe Doctrine in Mexico, 1917." In *Confrontation and Cooperation: Germany and the United States in the Era of World War I, 1900–1924*, edited by Hans-Jürgen Schröder, 281–314. Providence, R.I.: Berg, 1993.

von zur Gathen, Joachim. "Zimmermann Telegram: The Original Draft." *Cryptologia* 31, no. 1 (January 2007): 2–37.

Gatzke, Hans W. *Germany and the United States: A "Special Relationship?"* London, Cambridge, Mass.: Harvard University Press, 1980.

Gilderhus, Mark T. *Pan American Visions: Woodrow Wilson in the Western Hemisphere, 1913–1921*. Tucson: University of Arizona Press, 1986.

———. *Diplomacy and Revolution: U.S.-Mexican Relations under Wilson and Carranza.* Tucson: University of Arizona Press, 1977.

Goldstein, Erik. "Tyrrell, William George, Baron Tyrrell." In *Oxford Dictionary of National Biography: From the Earliest Times to the Year 2000,* edited by H. C. J. Matthew and Brian Harrison. 61 vols. New York: Oxford University Press, 2004.

Grattan, C. Hartley. *Why We Fought.* Indianapolis: Bobbs-Merrill, 1929.

Gregory, Ross. *The Origins of American Intervention in the First World War.* New York: Norton, 1971.

———. *Walter Hines Page: Ambassador to the Court of St. James.* Lexington: University Press of Kentucky, 1970.

Grenville, John Ashley Soames. "The United States Decision for War, 1917: Excerpts from the Manuscript Diary of Robert Lansing." *Renaissance and Modern Studies* 4 (1960): 59–81.

Griffiths, Richard. *Fellow Travellers of the Right.* Oxford: Oxford University Press, 1983.

Grigg, John. *Lloyd George: War Leader, 1916–1918.* London: Allen Lane, 2002.

Hall, Linda B., and Don M. Coerver. *Revolution on the Border: The United States and Mexico, 1910–1920.* Albuquerque: University of New Mexico Press, 1988.

———. "Woodrow Wilson, Public Opinion, and the Punitive Expedition: A Re-Assessment." *New Mexico Historical Review* 72 (April 1997): 171–94.

Handlin, Oscar. "A Liner, a U-boat . . . and History." *American Heritage* 6 (1955): 40–45.

Hardinge, Charles. *Old Diplomacy: The Reminiscences of Lord Hardinge of Penshurst.* London: J. Murray, 1947.

Harris, Charles H., III, and Louis R. Sadler. *The Archaeologist Was a Spy: Sylvanus G. Morley and the Office of Naval Intelligence.* Albuquerque: University of New Mexico Press, 2003.

———. "Pancho Villa and the Columbus Raid: The Missing Documents." In *The Border and the Revolution: Clandestine Activities of the Mexican Revolution, 1910–1920,* edited by Charles H. Harris III and Louis R. Sadler, 101–112. Las Cruces: New Mexico State University Press, 1990.

———. "The Plan of San Diego and the Mexican-U.S. War Crisis of 1916: A Reexamination." In *The Border and the Revolution: Clandestine Activities of the Mexican Revolution, 1910–1920,* edited by Charles H. Harris III and Louis R. Sadler, 71–98. Las Cruces: New Mexico State University Press, 1990.

———. *The Texas Rangers and the Mexican Revolution: The Bloodiest Decade, 1910–1920.* Albuquerque: University of New Mexico Press, 2004.

———. "The Witzke Affair: German Intrigue on the Mexican Border, 1917–18." *Military Review* (February 1979): 36–50.

Hayashima, Akira. *Die Illusion des Sonderfriedens: Deutsche Verständigungspolitik mit Japan im ersten Weltkrieg.* Munich: Oldenburg, 1982.

Heaton, John Langdon, ed. *Cobb of "The World": A Leader in Liberalism.* New York: Dutton, 1924.

Heitmann, Jan. *Unter Wasser in die Neue Welt: Handelsunterseeboote und kaiserliche Unterseekreuzer im Spannungsfeld von Politik und Kriegführung.* Berlin: Berliner Wissenschafts-Verlag, 1999.

Hieber, Hanne. "'Mademoiselle Docteur': The Life and Service of Imperial Germany's Only Female Intelligence Officer." *Journal of Intelligence History* 5, no. 2 (Winter 2005): 91–108.

Hodgson, Geoffrey. *Woodrow Wilson's Right Hand: The Life of Colonel Edward M. House.* New Haven, Conn.: Yale University Press, 2006.

Hope, John. "Fascism, the Security Service and the Curious Careers of Maxwell Knight and James McGuirk Hughes." *Lobster* 22 (November 1991): 1–5.

Horn, Martin. *Britain, France, and the Financing of the First World War.* Montreal: McGill-Queens University Press, 2002.

Hornbeck, Stanley Kuhl. "Cause and Occasion of Our Entry into the World War, 1917." *Annals of the American Academy of Political and Social Science* 192 (July 1932): 56–66.

Hughes, Mike. *Spies at Work.* London: 1 in 12 Publications, 1994.

Hulnick, Arthur S. "What's Wrong with the Intelligence Cycle." *Intelligence and National Security* 21, no. 6 (December 2006): 959–79.

Hürter, Johannes. "Die Staatssekretäre des Auswärtigen Amtes im Ersten Weltkrieg." In *Der Erste Weltkrieg: Wirkung, Wahrnehmung, Analyse,* edited by Wolfgang Michalka, 216–51. Munich: Piper, 1994.

Iklé, Frank. "Japanese-German Peace Negotiations during World War I." *American Historical Review* 71 (October 1965): 62–76.

Jähnicke, Burkhard. *Washington und Berlin zwischen den Kriegen: Die Mixed Claims Commission in den transatlantischen Beziehungen.* Baden-Baden: Nomos, 2003.

James, William M. *The Eyes of the Navy: A Biographical Study of Admiral Sir Reginald Hall.* London: Methuen, 1955.

Jarausch, Konrad Hugo. *The Enigmatic Chancellor: Bethmann Hollweg and the Hubris of Imperial Germany.* New Haven, Conn.: Yale University Press, 1973.

Jeffreys-Jones, Rhodri. *American Espionage: From Secret Service to CIA.* New York: Free Press, 1977.

Jervis, Robert. "Intelligence and Foreign Policy: A Review Essay." *International Security* 11, no. 3 (Winter 1986/1987), 141–61.

Johnson, Charles T. *Culture at Twilight: The National German-American Alliance, 1901–1918.* New York: Peter Lang, 1999.

Johnson, Niel M. *George Sylvester Viereck: German-American Propagandist.* Urbana: University of Illinois Press, 1972.

Jonas, Manfred. *The United States and Germany: A Diplomatic History.* Ithaca and London: Cornell University Press, 1984.

Jones, John Price, and Paul Merrick Hollister. *The German Secret Service in America.* Boston: Small, Maynard & Co., 1918.

Jordan, William G. *Black Newspapers and America's War for Democracy, 1914–1920.* Chapel Hill: University of North Carolina Press, 2001.

Jore, Jeff. "Pershing's Mission in Mexico: Logistics and Preparation for the War in Europe." *Military Affairs* 52, no. 3 (July 1988): 117–21.

Kahn, David. *The Codebreakers: The Story of Secret Writing.* London: Weidenfeld and Nicolson, 1967.

———. "Edward Bell and His Zimmermann Telegram Memoranda." *Intelligence and National Security* 14, no. 3 (Autumn 1999): 143–59.

———. "The Rise of Intelligence." *Foreign Affairs* 85, no. 5 (Sept.–Oct. 2006): 125–34.

———. "The Zimmermann Telegram: The Original Plaintext of What Became the Most Important Cryptogram Solution in History." *Cryptogram* 38, no. 2 (March–April 1972): 49, 53, 61, 71.

Katz, Friedrich. *Deutschland, Diaz und die mexikanische Revolution: Die deutsche Mexikopolitik, 1870–1920.* Berlin: VEB Deutscher Verlag der Wissenschaften, 1964.

———. *The Life and Times of Pancho Villa.* Stanford: Stanford University Press, 1998.

———. "Pancho Villa and the Attack on Columbus, New Mexico." *American Historical Review* 83, no. 1, suppl. (1978): 101–30.

———. *The Secret War in Mexico: Europe, the United States and the Mexican Revolution.* London and Chicago: University of Chicago Press, 1981.

Kawamura, Noriko. *Turbulence in the Pacific: Japanese-U.S. Relations during World War I.* Westport, Conn.: Praeger, 2000.

Keene, Jennifer D. *The United States and the First World War.* New York: Longman, 2000.

Keith, Jeannette. "The Politics of Southern Draft Resistance, 1917–1918: Class, Race, and Conscription in the Rural South." *Journal of American History* 87, no. 4 (March 2001): 1335–61.

Kennedy, David. *Over Here: The First World War and American Society.* Oxford and New York: Oxford University Press, 1980.

Kershaw, Ian. *Hitler.* 2 vols. New York: Norton, 1999–2000.

Kestler, Stefan, *Die deutsche Auslandsaufklärung und das Bild der Ententemächte im Spiegel zeitgenössischer Veröffentlichungen während des Ersten Weltkrieges.* Frankfurt am Main: Peter Lang, 1994.

Kitchen, Martin. *The Silent Dictatorship: The Politics of the German High Command under Hindenburg and Ludendorff, 1916–1918.* London: Croom Helm, 1976.

Knight, Alan. *The Mexican Revolution.* 2 vols. Cambridge: Cambridge University Press, 1986–1990.

Knightley, Philip. *The First Casualty: The War Correspondent as Hero, Propagandist and Myth Maker from the Crimea to Vietnam.* New York: Harcourt Brace Jovanovich, 1975.

———. *The Second Oldest Profession: The Spy as Bureaucrat, Patriot, Fantasist and Whore.* London: Deutsch, 1986.

Knock Thomas J. *To End All Wars: Woodrow Wilson and the Quest for a New World Order.* Oxford and New York: Oxford University Press, 1992.

Koenig, Robert. *The Fourth Horseman: One Man's Mission to Wage the Great War in America.* New York: Public Affairs, 2006.

Koistinen, Paul A. C. "The 'Industrial-Military Complex' in Historical Perspective: World War I." *Business History Review* 41 (1967): 378–403.

Koopmann, Friedhelm. *Diplomatie und Reichsinteresse: Das Geheimdienstkalkül in der deutschen Amerikapolitik, 1914–1917.* Frankfurt am Main: Peter Lang, 1990.

Kunimoto, Iyo. "Japan and Mexico, 1888–1917." PhD diss., University of Texas at Austin, 1975.

La Follette, Belle C., and Fola La Follette. *Robert M. La Follette.* 2 vols. New York: Macmillan, 1953.

Larsen, Daniel. "British Intelligence and the 1916 Mediation Mission of Colonel Edward M. House." *Intelligence and National Security* 25, no. 5 (October 2010): 682–704.

Leberke, Botho. *Die wirtschaftlichen Ursachen des amerikanischen Kriegseintritts, 1917.* Berlin: Junker und Dünnhaupt, 1940.

Leuchtenburg, William E. *The Perils of Prosperity, 1914–1932.* Chicago: University of Chicago Press, 1993.

Levin, Norman Gordon, Jr. *Woodrow Wilson and World Politics: America's Response to War and Revolution.* Oxford and New York: Oxford University Press, 1968.

Link, Arthur. *Wilson: Campaigns for Progressivism and Peace, 1916–1917.* Princeton: Princeton University Press, 1965.

———. "That Cobb Interview." *Journal of American History* 72, no. 1 (June 1985): 7–17.

Livermore, Seward W. *Politics Is Adjourned: Woodrow Wilson and the War Congress, 1916–18.* Middletown, Conn.: Wesleyan University Press, 1966.

Lorenz, Edward N. "Predictability: Does the Flap of a Butterfly's Wings in Brazil Set Off a Tornado in Texas?" Paper presented at the 139th meeting of the American Association for the Advancement of Sciences, 1972.

Ludendorff, Erich von. *Ludendorff's Own Story.* 2 vols. New York and London: Harper & Brothers, 1920.

Luebke, Frederick C. *Bonds of Loyalty: German Americans and World War One.* DeKalb: Northern Illinois University Press, 1974.

Lüdke, Tilman. *Jihad Made in Germany: Ottoman and German Propaganda and Intelligence Operations in the First World War.* Münster: Lit Verlag, 2005.

MacDonnell, Francis. "The Search for a Second Zimmermann Telegram: FDR, BSC, and the Latin American Front." *International Journal of Intelligence and Counterintelligence* 4, no. 4 (Winter 1990): 487–505.

MacMillan, Margaret. *Paris 1919: Six Months that Changed the World.* New York: Random House, 2002.

Madeira, Victor. "'No Wishful Thinking Allowed': Secret Service Committee and Intelligence Reform in Great Britain, 1919–23." *Intelligence and National Security* 18, no. 1 (Spring 2003): 1–20.

Mahl, Thomas E. *Desperate Deception: British Covert Operations in the United States, 1939–44.* Washington, D.C.: Brassey's, 1998.

Marquand, David. *Ramsay MacDonald.* London: J. Cape, 1977.

Masterman, Lucy. *C.F.C. Masterman: A Biography.* London: Cassell, 1968.

Matthew, H. C. J., and Brian Harrison, eds. *Oxford Dictionary of National Biography: From the Earliest Times to the Year 2000.* 61 vols. New York: Oxford University Press, 2004.

May, Ernest R. *The World War and American Isolation, 1914–1917.* Cambridge, Mass.: Harvard University Press, 1959.

May, Henry F. *The End of American Innocence: A Study of the First Years of Our Own Time, 1912–1917.* New York: Knopf, 1959.

McDonald, Timothy G. "The Gore-McLemore Resolutions: Democratic Revolt against Wilson's Submarine Policy." *Historian* 26, no. 1 (1963): 50–74.

McIvor, Arthur. "'A Crusade for Capitalism': The Economic League, 1919–1939." *Journal of Contemporary History* 23, no. 4 (October 1988): 631–55.

McMahon, Paul. *British Spies and Irish Rebels: British Intelligence and Ireland, 1916–1945.* Woodbridge: Boydell Press, 2008.

Mead, Gary. *The Doughboys: America and the First World War.* New York: Overlook Press, 2000.

Mehnert, Ute. "Deutsche Weltpolitik und amerikanisches Zweifronten-Dilemma: Die 'Japanische Gefahr' in den deutsch-amerikanischen Beziehungen, 1904–1917." *Historische Zeitschrift* 257, no. 3 (December 1993): 647–92.

———. "German Weltpolitik and the American Two-Front Dilemma: The 'Japanese Peril' in German-American Relations, 1904–1917." *Journal of American History* 82, no. 4 (March 1996): 1452–1477.

Meine, Arnold. *Wilsons Diplomatie in der Friedensfrage, 1914–1917.* Stuttgart: Kohlhammer, 1938.

Meyer, Michael C. "The Mexican-German Conspiracy of 1915." *Americas* 23 (July 1966): 76–89.

Millis, Walter. *Road to War.* London: Faber & Faber, 1935.

Millman, Chad. *The Detonators: The Secret Plot to Destroy America and an Epic Hunt for Justice.* New York: Little Brown, 2006.

Mirow, Jürgen. *Der Seekrieg 1914–1918 in Umrissen.* Göttingen: Musterschmidt, 1976.

Möckelmann, Jürgen. "Das Deutschlandbild in den USA 1914–1918 und die Kriegszielpolitik Wilsons." PhD diss., University of Hamburg, 1965.

Mooney, Christopher F. "Moral Consensus and Law." *Thoughts* 51, no. 202 (September 1976): 231–54. °

Morrissey, Alice M. *The American Defense of Neutral Rights, 1914–1917.* Cambridge, Mass.: Harvard University Press, 1939.

Mugridge, Ian. *The View from Xanadu: William Randolph Hearst and United States Foreign Policy.* Montreal and London: McGill-Queen's University Press, 1995.

Mulder, John M., Ernest M. White, and Ethel S. White, eds. *Woodrow Wilson: A Bibliography.* Westport, Conn., and London: Greenwood Press, 1997.

Müller, Klaus-Jürgen. "On the Difficulties of Writing Intelligence History." *Studies in Intelligence* 30, no. 3 (Fall 1986): 57–62.

Nassua, Martin. *"Gemeinsame Kriegführung. Gemeinsamer Friedensschluß." Das Zimmermann-Telegramm vom 13. Januar 1917 und der Eintritt der USA in den 1. Weltkrieg.* Frankfurt am Main: Peter Lang, 1992.

Nickles, David Paull. *Under the Wire: How the Telegraph Changed Diplomacy.* Cambridge, Mass.: Harvard University Press, 2003.

Ninkovich, Frank. *The Wilsonian Century: U.S. Foreign Policy since 1900.* Chicago and London: University of Chicago Press, 1999.

O'Halpin, Eunan. "British Intelligence in Ireland, 1914–1921." In *The Missing Dimension: Governments and Intelligence Communities in the Twentieth Century,* edited by Christopher Andrew and David Dilks, 54–77. Chicago: University of Illinois Press, 1984.

———. "Hall, Sir (William) Reginald." In *Oxford Dictionary of National Biography: From the Earliest Times to the Year 2000,* edited by H. C. J. Matthew and Brian Harrison, 646–48. 61 vols. New York: Oxford University Press, 2004.

O'Keefe, Kevin. *A Thousand Deadlines: The New York City Press and American Neutrality, 1914–1917.* The Hague: Martinus Nijhoff, 1972.

Orde, Anne. *The Eclipse of Great Britain: The United States and British Imperial Decline, 1895–1956.* Basingstoke: Palgrave Macmillan, 1996.

Parker, Gilbert. "The United States and the War." *Harper's Monthly Magazine,* March 1918, 521–31.

Parkinson, Roger. *Tormented Warrior: Ludendorff and the Supreme Command.* London: Hodder & Stoughton, 1978.

Persico, Joseph E. *Roosevelt's Secret War: FDR and World War II Espionage.* New York: Random House, 2001.

Peterson, Horace C. *Propaganda for War: The Campaign against American Neutrality, 1914–17.* Norman: University of Oklahoma Press, 1939.

Piehler, P. Kurt. *Remembering War the American Way.* Washington, D.C.: Smithsonian Institution Press, 1995.

Pöhlmann, Markus. "Towards a New History of German Military Intelligence in the Era of the Great War: Approaches and Sources." *Journal of Intelligence History* 5, no. 2 (Winter 2005): 1–9.

———. "German Intelligence at War, 1914–1918." *Journal of Intelligence History* 5, no. 2 (Winter 2005): 25–54.

Porter, Bernard. *Plots and Paranoia: A History of Political Espionage in Britain, 1790–1988.* Boston: Unwin Hyman, 1989.

Raat, W. Dirk. "U.S. Intelligence Operations and Covert Actions in Mexico, 1900–1947." *Journal of Contemporary History* 22 (1987): 615–38.

Rafalko, Frank J., ed. *A Counterintelligence Reader.* Washington, D.C.: National Counterintelligence Center, 2004.

Ramsay, David. *"Blinker" Hall, Spymaster: The Man Who Brought America into World War I.* Stroud, Gloucestershire: Spellmount, 2008.

Reiling, Johannes. *Deutschland: Safe for Democracy?* Stuttgart: Franz Steiner Verlag, 1997.

Rielage, Dale C. *Russian Supply Efforts in America during the First World War.* Jefferson, N.C.: McFarland, 2002.

Ritter, Gerhard. *Staatskunst und Kriegshandwerk: Das Problem des "Militarismus" in Deutschland.* 4 vols. Munich: Oldenburg, 1954–1968.

———. *The Sword and the Scepter: The Problem of Militarism in Germany.* Translated from the German by Heinz Norden. 4 vols. Coral Gables: University of Miami Press, 1972.

Rochester, Stuart. *American Liberal Disillusionment in the Wake of World War I.* University Park and London: Pennsylvania State University Press, 1977.

Roskill, Stephen W. *Hankey: Man of Secrets.* 3 vols. London: Collins, 1970–1974.

Ross, Stewart H. *Propaganda for War: How the United States Was Conditioned to Fight the Great War of 1914–1918.* Jefferson, N.C., and London: McFarland, 1996.

Sanders, Michael L., and Philip M. Taylor. *British Propaganda during the First World War, 1914–1918.* London and Basingstoke: Macmillan, 1982.

Sandos, James A. "German Involvement in Northern Mexico: A New Look at the Columbus Raid." *Hispanic American Historical Review* 50 (February 1970): 70–88.

Scheiber, Harry Noel. "What Woodrow Wilson Said to Cobb in 1917: Another View of Plausibility." *Wisconsin Magazine of History* 52, no. 4 (1969): 344–47.

Schiff, Warren. "German Military Penetration into Mexico during the Late Diaz Period." *Hispanic American Historical Review* 39 (August 1959), 568–79.

Schnauber, Jens. "Die parlamentarische Untersuchung der 'Ursachen des deutschen Zusammenbruches im Jahre 1918.'" University seminar paper, Universität der Bundeswehr, Munich, 1998.

Schöllgen, Gregor. "Die Großmacht als Weltmacht: Idee, Wirklichkeit und Perzeption deutscher 'Weltpolitik' im Zeitalter des Imperialismus." *Historische Zeitschrift* 248, no. 1 (February 1989): 79–100.

Schorreck, Henry F. "The Telegram That Changed History." *Cryptologic Spectrum* (Summer 1970): 22–32.

Schröder, Hans-Jürgen, ed. *Confrontation and Cooperation: Germany and the United States in the Era of World War I, 1900–1924.* Providence, R.I.: Berg, 1993.

Schwabe, Klaus. *Das diplomatische Korps, 1871–1945.* Boppard/Rhein: Boldt, 1985.

Schwartz, E. A. "The Lynching of Robert Prager, the United Mine Workers, and the Problems of Patriotism in 1918." *Journal of the Illinois State Historical Society* 95, no. 4 (Winter 2002/2003): 414–37.

Seaburg, Paul. *The Wilhelmstraße: A Study of German Diplomats under the Nazi Regime.* Berkeley: University of California Press, 1954.

Seymour, Charles. *American Diplomacy during the World War.* Baltimore: Johns Hopkins University Press, 1934.

———. *American Neutrality, 1914–1917: Essays on the Causes of American Intervention in the World War.* New Haven: Yale University Press, 1935.

Simpson, Colin. *The Lusitania.* Boston: Little, Brown, 1973.

Singh, Simon. *The Code Book: The Evolution of Secrecy from Mary, Queen of Scots to Quantum Cryptography.* New York: Doubleday, 1999.

Sloan, Geoff. "Dartmouth, Sir Mansfield Cumming and the Origins of the British Intelligence Community." *Intelligence and National Security* 22, no. 2 (April 2007): 298–305.

Smith, Daniel M. *The Great Departure: The United States and World War I, 1914–1920.* New York: J. Wiley, 1965.

———. "National Interest and American Intervention, 1917: An Historical Appraisal." *Journal of American History* 52, no. 1 (June 1965): 5–24.

———. "President Wilson and the German 'Overt Act' of 1917: A Reappraisal." *University of Colorado Studies Series in History* 2 (1961): 129–39.

———. *Robert Lansing and American Neutrality, 1914–1917.* Berkeley: University of California Press, 1958.

Smith, Dean. "The Zimmermann Telegram, 1917." *American History Illustrated* 13, no. 3 (1978): 28–37.

Smith, Michael M. "The Mexican Secret Service in the United States, 1910–1920." *Americas* 59, no. 1 (July 2002): 65–85.

Spence, Richard B. "Englishmen in New York: The SIS American Station, 1915–21." *Intelligence and National Security* 19, no. 5 (Autumn 2004): 511–37.

———. "K. A. Jahnke and the German Sabotage Campaign in the United States and Mexico, 1914–1918." *Historian* 59, no. 1 (1996): 89–112.

———. "Sidney Reilly in America, 1914–1917." *Intelligence and National Security* 10, no. 1 (January 1995): 92–121.

Spencer, Samuel R., Jr. *Decision for War, 1917: The Laconia Sinking and the Zimmermann Telegram.* Rindge, N.H.: R. R. Smith, 1953.

Squires, James D. *British Propaganda at Home and in the United States from 1914 to 1917.* Cambridge, Mass.: Harvard University Press, 1935.

Srodes, James. *Allen Dulles: Master of Spies.* Washington, D.C.: Regnery, 2000.

Stafford, David. *Churchill and Secret Service.* Woodstock, N.Y.: Overlook Press, 1998.

Stegman, Dirk. "Die deutsche Inlandspropaganda 1917/18: Zum innenpolitischen Machtkampf zwischen OHL und ziviler Reichsleitung in der Endphase des Kaiserreiches." *Militärgeschichtliche Mitteilungen* 2 (1972): 75–116.

Sterba, Christopher M. *Good Americans: Italian and Jewish Immigrants during the First World War.* New York: Oxford University Press, 2003.

Stevenson, David. *The First World War and International Politics.* Oxford: Clarendon Press, 1988.

Swain, Joseph Ward. "Woodrow Wilson's Fight for Peace." *Current History* 35, no. 6 (March 1932): 805–12.

Syrett, Harold C. "The Business Press and American Neutrality, 1914–1917." *Mississippi Valley Historical Review* 32 (1945): 215–30.

Taylor, A. J. P. *English History, 1914–1945.* Oxford: Oxford University Press, 1965.

Taylor, Philip M. "The Foreign Office and British Propaganda during the First World War." *Historical Journal* 15 (1980): 113–59.

———. *British Propaganda in the 20th Century: Selling Democracy.* Edinburgh: Edinburgh University Press, 1999.

Thimme, Friedrich, ed. *Front wider Bülow: Staatsmänner, Diplomaten und Forscher zu seinen Denkwürdigkeiten.* Munich: Bruckmann, 1931.

Thompson, J. Lee. *Politicians, the Press and Propaganda: Lord Northcliffe and the Great War, 1914–1919.* Kent, Ohio: Kent State University Press, 1999.

Thompson, John A. "Woodrow Wilson and World War I: A Reappraisal." *Journal of American Studies* 19, no. 3 (December 1985): 325–48.

Tóibín, Colm. "The Tragedy of Roger Casement." *New York Review of Books*, May 27, 2004, 53–57.

Tomes, Jason. *Balfour and Foreign Policy: The International Thought of a Conservative Statesman.* Cambridge: Cambridge University Press, 1997.

Towne, Ruth Warner. *Senator William J. Stone and the Politics of Compromise.* Port Washington, N.Y., and London: Kennikat Press, 1979.

Transill, Charles C. *America Goes to War.* Boston: Little, Brown, 1938.

Trask, David F. "Woodrow Wilson and International Statecraft: A Modern Assessment." *Naval War College Review* 27, no. 4 (1975): 23–31.

Tuchman, Barbara W. *Die Zimmermann Depesche.* Bergisch Gladbach: Lübbe, 1986.

———. *The Zimmermann Telegram.* 4th ed. New York: Ballantine Books, 1985.

Tucker, Robert W. "An Inner Circle of One: Woodrow Wilson and His Advisers." *National Interest* 51 (Spring 1998), 3–26.

Turner, Jason. *British Politics and the Great War: Coalition and Conflict, 1915–1918.* New Haven, Conn.: Yale University Press, 1992.

Turner, John Kenneth. *Shall It Be Again?* New York: Huebsch, 1922.

Unger, Nancy C. *Fighting Bob La Follette: The Righteous Reformer.* Chapel Hill: University of North Carolina, 2000.

Unnewehr, Lewis E. *Silent Night, Unholy Night: The Story of German-Americans during World War I.* New York: Vantage Press, 2000.

Vietsch, Eberhard. *Wilhelm Solf: Botschafter zwischen den Zeiten.* Tübingen: Reiner Wunderlich Verlag, 1961.

West, Nigel, and Oleg Tsarev. *The Crown Jewels: The British Secrets at the Heart of the KGB Archives.* New Haven, Conn.: Yale University Press, 1999.

Yockelson, Mitchell. "The War Department: Keeper of Our Nation's Enemy Aliens during World War I." Paper presented to the Society for Military History Annual Meeting, April 1998.

Young, Robert J. *Marketing Marianne: French Propaganda in America, 1900–1940.* New Brunswick, N.J.: Rutgers University Press, 2004.

Warner, Michael. "The Kaiser Sows Destruction." *Studies in Intelligence* 46, no. 1 (2002): 3–9.

———. "Wanted: A Definition of Intelligence." *Studies in Intelligence* 46, no. 2 (2002): 15–22.

Williams, William J. *The Wilson Administration and the Shipbuilding Crisis of 1917: Steel Ships and Wooden Steamers.* Lewiston, N.Y.: Mellen, 1992.

Winkler, Jonathan Reed. *Nexus: Strategic Communications and American Security in World War I.* Cambridge, Mass.: Harvard University Press, 2008.

Winkler, John K. *William Randolph Hearst: A New Appraisal.* New York: Hastings House, 1955.

Witcover, Jules. *Sabotage at Black Tom: Imperial Germany's Secret War in America, 1914–1917.* Chapel Hill, N.C.: Algonquin, 1989.

Wright, Esmond. "Foreign Policy of Woodrow Wilson: A Re-Assessment." *History Today* 10, Nos. 3–4 (March and April 1960): 149–57, 223–31.

Zebel, Sidney H. *Balfour: A Political Biography.* Cambridge: Cambridge University Press, 1973.

"The Zimmermann Telegram." *Cryptologic Quarterly* 20, no. 1–2 (Spring/Summer 2001): 43–52.

Index

Allied powers: arms sales to, 2; covert programs to cause problems for, 4, 29; enemy territories, apportionment of, 18; explosives in Allied ships, German scheme to plant, 200–201; German-Japanese negotiations, leaking terms of to, 51–52, 55, 226; Japanese allegiance to, 48, 52, 97, 116; peace conference promotion by Wilson and House, 131–32; State Department diplomats and intelligence operations in, 110

Archibald, James F. J., 112–13

Arizona, 1, 15, 44, 67, 71, 73–74, 117, 142, 162, 165–66

Austria, 12, 27, 112–13

Balfour, Arthur J.: Foreign Secretary appointment, 89; Gaunt, House commendation about, 109; German activity in Mexico, confirmation of, 125, 128; Hall, relationship with, 89, 235, 236; intelligence sharing with, 88; telegram delivery, thanks for, 120, 121; telegram delivery to U.S. embassy, 115–17, 118–120

Belgium, 15, 16, 28, 160, 184

Bell, Edward "Ned": appearance and character of, 110; Bernstorff telegram decryption, 123–25, 126–27; family and early life of, 110; foreign service career and promotions, 110; Hall, relationship with, 110, 240; intelligence operations role of, 110–11; Page support for, 111; Rintelen covert operations, information about, 112; telegram delivery to, 116–17, 118, 119, 250; telegram interception and decryption, credit for, 239, 240, 241

Bernstorff, Johann Heinrich von: attitudes toward and, 205; Canadian Pacific Railway and plans to destroy, 30; Constantinople ambassadorship, 208; death of, 209; diplomacy and keeping U.S. out of war, 17, 202, 208; diplomatic message that included telegram to, 95; diplomatic messages from, obtaining copies of, 122, 276n57; Eckardt, decryption of telegram to, 123–25, 126–27; Eckardt, telegram to, 100, 104–5, 116–17, 121–22, 136, 274n49; election of, 208; encrypted messages as part of State Department diplomatic cables, 77–78; Hindenburg, opinion of, 208–9; League of Nations representative, 208–9; memoir of, 11, 19; Mexican revolution, threat of U.S. intervention in, 37; Solf, congratulations to, 225; as source of telegram and a traitor, 194, 197–98, 206–8, 211–12, 223, 247, 284n3; submarine warfare, diplomacy in preparation for, 71; submarine warfare, opinion about, 59–60, 129–130; U.S.-German diplomatic relations break and return to home, 102, 133, 158, 205–6; Zimmermann telegram delivery, 76–78, 129; Zimmermann telegram, disclosure of source of, 11; Zimmermann telegram, interview about, 206–7; Zimmermann telegram, names for, 254

Bethmann Hollweg, Theobald von: attitudes toward and opinions of, 24; authority of, 65; broken spirit of, 62; character of, 60–61; German-Japanese negotiations, 49, 51, 52, 193–94; leadership of, 60–61, 62; military and

attitude, 111; Bell, support for, 111; Bernstorff telegram, copy to send to State Department, 122, 136; biography of, 11, 19, 92, 239–241; Casement activities, opinion about, 115; disclosure of information to by Hall, 235; German activity in Mexico, information about, 128; Hall, opinion of, 83, 119; Papen papers on covert operations, 113; recall or resignation of, 111; telegram delivery, thanks to Balfour for, 120, 121; telegram delivery to, 119–120, 276n48; telegram source, disclosure of, 223; Zimmermann telegram delivery to State Department, 120, 135; Zimmermann telegram, names for, 254, 255

Papen, Franz von, 42–43, 45–46, 75–76, 112, 113, 160, 167, 197, 231

Polk, Frank K., 109, 110, 111, 122, 135–36, 137, 158, 277n34

public and public opinion, American: annexation of Southwest, attitudes toward, 15; anti-German attitudes, 10, 18; anti-war protests, 188, 282n32; Archibald courier activity, outrage about, 113; authenticity of telegram, questions about, 172, 175–79, 281n33, 281n35; German Americans, response to telegram by, 176–79, 281n43; intervention in war, opinions about, 187–190, 282n37; interventionist opinions, 6, 11, 13, 187–89; isolationist/noninterventionist opinions, 6, 13, 163, 187–89; opinions about telegram, 4, 6, 15–16, 22, 163–172, 281n29; opinions about telegram, measurement of, 160, 280n9; postwar revisionist attitudes about war and telegram, 10, 11–13; pro-war rallies, 185, 187–88; rally for war opinions, 9; submarine warfare, opinions about, 160–63, 280n12; telegram disclosure and mobilization for war, 6, 22, 159–160, 179–180, 189–190, 249–251; telegram interception, information about, 7; war hysteria, 13; WWII entrance, attitudes toward, 13, 190

Rhomberg, Edmund, 49, 50, 226–27
Rintelen von Kleist, Franz, 30, 111–12, 113, 275n14

Roosevelt, Franklin D., 83, 109, 110, 181, 242–44
Roosevelt, Theodore, 109, 145, 147, 150, 182–83, 187, 282n37
Russia, 1, 29–30, 52, 54–55, 56, 237–39, 288n20

Solf, Wilhelm von, 196, 202, 207, 225–27, 228
State Department, U.S.: anti-German/pro-Allied attitudes in, 110; Bernstorff telegram, obtaining copy of, 121–22, 136; Bureau of Secret Intelligence operations, 109–10; diplomacy and keeping U.S. out of war, 17; diplomatic codes used by, 101, 211, 285n23; diplomatic messages, interception and decryption of, 20, 86, 91, 93–95, 101, 104, 118, 121, 248–49, 273n18, 273n24; encrypted messages as part of State Department diplomatic cables, 77–78, 91, 216; files and records about telegram, 3, 4; interception of telegram, role in, 19; Luxburg messages, disclosure of, 215, 241; telegram delivery to, 120–22, 135; telegram relay and interception via cable, 19, 20, 21, 91–95, 118, 139, 140, 226, 248–49, 273n24
Stumm, Wilhelm von, 29, 67, 71–72, 78, 221
submarines, German: anti-German attitudes in US because of, 10; Argentinean ships, sinking of, 214–16; armed merchant ships to defend against, 134–35, 137–38, 141, 146–47, 158, 182, 278n45; attacks on merchant ships/neutral and Allied ships, 2, 25, 30–31, 36–37, 59, 62, 138, 182; diplomatic preparations for unrestricted warfare, 64–65, 71, 73; *Lusitania*, sinking of, 15, 16, 31, 36, 38, 77, 111, 160, 163, 171, 184; mail and codebook delivery to Washington by, 76, 95; Mexican support for, 46; submarine warfare, Hindenburg regret in use of, 209; unrestricted submarine warfare and U.S. intervention, 56, 59–60, 63, 65, 101–3, 115, 117–18, 130, 132–35, 182, 201–2, 246; unrestricted submarine warfare and U.S.-German diplomatic relations, 78–79, 132–33; unrestricted submarine warfare, con-

About the Author

Thomas Boghardt is Senior Historian at the U.S. Army Center of Military History in Washington, D.C. He has published widely on the history of intelligence and World War I and is the author of *Spies of the Kaiser: German Covert Operations in Great Britain during the First World Era*. He received his PhD in modern history from the University of Oxford. He lives with his wife and two children in Bethesda, MD.

The **Naval Institute Press** is the book-publishing arm of the U.S. Naval Institute, a private, nonprofit, membership society for sea service professionals and others who share an interest in naval and maritime affairs. Established in 1873 at the U.S. Naval Academy in Annapolis, Maryland, where its offices remain today, the Naval Institute has members worldwide.

Members of the Naval Institute support the education programs of the society and receive the influential monthly magazine *Proceedings* or the colorful bimonthly magazine *Naval History* and discounts on fine nautical prints and on ship and aircraft photos. They also have access to the transcripts of the Institute's Oral History Program and get discounted admission to any of the Institute-sponsored seminars offered around the country.

The Naval Institute's book-publishing program, begun in 1898 with basic guides to naval practices, has broadened its scope to include books of more general interest. Now the Naval Institute Press publishes about seventy titles each year, ranging from how-to books on boating and navigation to battle histories, biographies, ship and aircraft guides, and novels. Institute members receive significant discounts on the more than eight hundred Press books in print.

Full-time students are eligible for special half-price membership rates. Life memberships are also available.

For a free catalog describing Naval Institute Press books currently available, and for further information about joining the U.S. Naval Institute, please write to:

Member Services
U.S. NAVAL INSTITUTE
291 Wood Road
Annapolis, MD 21402-5034
Telephone: (800) 233-8764
Fax: (410) 571-1703
Web address: www.usni.org